Convict Workers
Reinterpreting Australia's past

Studies in Australian History

Series editors: Alan Gilbert and Peter Spearritt

Convict Workers

Reinterpreting Australia's past

Edited by

Stephen Nicholas

School of Economics
University of New South Wales

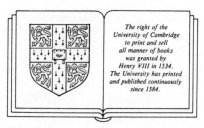

The right of the
University of Cambridge
to print and sell
all manner of books
was granted by
Henry VIII in 1534.
The University has printed
and published continuously
since 1584.

CAMBRIDGE UNIVERSITY PRESS

Cambridge
New York   New Rochelle   Melbourne   Sydney

For Jennifer Nicholas and Amy Shergold

Published by the Press Syndicate of the University of Cambridge
The Pitt Building, Trumpington Street, Cambridge CB2 1RP, England.
32 East 57th Street, New York, NY 10022, USA
10 Stamford Road, Oakleigh, Melbourne 3166, Australia.

© Cambridge University Press 1988

First published in 1988
Reprinted 1989

Typeset in Ballardvale by Love Computer Typesetting Pty Ltd, Sydney.
Printed by Macarthur Press, Parramatta, Australia.

National Library of Australia cataloguing in publication data
Convict workers: reinterpreting Australia's past.
    Bibliography.
    Includes index.
    ISBN 0 521 36126 5.
    [1]. Convicts — Australia — History. 2. Convict labor — Australia — History. 3. Penal colonies —
    Australia — History. 4. Australia — History — 1788-1900. I. Nicholas, Stephen. (Series: Studies in
    Australian history (Cambridge, England)).
364.3'0994

British Library cataloguing in publication data
Convict workers: reinterpreting Australia's past
    1. Australia. British criminals. Social conditions, 1788-1890
    I. Nicholas, Stephen
364.3'08921094

Library of Congress cataloguing in publication data
Convict workers: reinterpreting Australia's past/edited by Stephen Nicholas.
        p. ca. — (Studies in Australian history series)
    Bibliography: p.
    Includes index.
    ISBN 0 521 36126 5
    1. Convict labor — Australia — History — 19th century. 2. Penal colonies — Australia — History —
    19th century. 3. Penal colonies — Great Britain — History — 19th century. I. Nicholas, Stephen,
    1946–   . II. Series.
HV8931.A86C86 1988
365'.65'0994—dc19

ISBN 0 521 36126 5

CONTENTS

LIST OF TABLES AND FIGURES

FOREWORD

Convict Workers forces us to re-assess the foundations of those values which we recognise as distinctively Australian. In two hundred years we have developed from a British open prison to an independent nation enmeshed in the economies of Asia and the Pacific Rim. That remarkable development has coloured the way in which we have viewed our past.

In 1888 convictism was viewed as a stain on our history, a deep embarrassment to an affluent society in which workers were building one of the world's first Labor parties. In 1938, the transported criminals had been retrospectively pardoned. Australian school children were taught that those who were really guilty remained back in Britain: the convicts were victims, pushed into poaching or theft by poverty, and often sent to Australia for their political persuasions. In my generation a new historical vision emerged, expounded most brilliantly by Manning Clark. I was taught that we had to be more honest about our past — and that honesty meant coming to terms with our unsavoury beginnings, and recognising that those transported were unskilled hardened criminals. But, as Manning Clark himself emphasised recently, each generation has the task of re-interpreting its history, of viewing the past from a new present. *Convict Workers* is just such a radical challenge to prevailing orthodoxy.

At a time when our immigration policy has become a matter of debate, *Convict Workers* examines transported criminals as migrants. Our contemporary concern with improving education and training opportunities for Australian workers has found expression in a book which assesses our convict forbears, both women and men, in terms of their human capital — not as thieves but as youthful workers possessing high levels of literacy, work skills and physical fitness; not prisoners undergoing punishment but as a well-organised, efficient labour force. *Convict Workers* achieves a sophisticated re-examination of our beginning as a convict society, and the impact of that experience on our values today.

No doubt many of the conclusions — that convict diet was nutritionally sound, that working conditions were good, that the lash was used in moderation — will arouse considerable controversy. But more fundamentally this book, by presenting transported convicts as migrants and workers, allows Australia's history as a penal settlement to become an integral part of the economic history of an immigrant society, rather than an unsavoury aberration that preceded free settlement.

The Hon R. J. L. Hawke, A.C. M.P.
Prime Minister of Australia

PREFACE

Each generation rewrites its history. A reaction against familiar ways of understanding our past is a common historiographic phenomenon. It reflects the task of historians to pursue the 'truth' through the continuous critical reassessment of established interpretations. The result is revisionist history. By overturning traditional views, revisionist history offers new and radically different ways of understanding the past. The success of revisionist history depends on the new and different questions asked, and the methodology and new data sources employed to answer those questions. By asking new questions, collecting new data and relying on a different methodology, this book offers a radical reinterpretation of our convict past.

The book is a collaborative work. Although individual chapters carry attributions to specific authors, we all read each other's chapters and during early 1987 held weekly seminars to discuss the general interpretations in our drafts. While each author remains responsible for her or his own chapter, each chapter emerged stronger after the criticisms of other members of the group. The result is a single book, with each chapter contributing to a consistent story about different aspects of the convict system.

At the beginning of 1987 Peter Shergold was seconded to the Department of Prime Minister and Cabinet as Director of Multicultural Affairs and was not available for the seminar discussions. He was to have been co-editor of the book and I missed his insights, energy and enthusiasm on a day-to-day basis. In spite of his other commitments, he actively supported the book and is co-author of Chapters 3, 4, 5 and 7; he also co-authored the introductory chapter. I would like to acknowledge his help as colleague and friend over nearly seven years' work on this project. I would also like to acknowledge the help of my other co-workers, particularly Barrie Dyster, and their criticisms and comments.

Between 1980 and 1982 David Alexander, Mariane Chaffe, Martin Woodhams and Christine Regan were employed part-time to transcribe the details of nearly twenty thousand convicts onto coding sheets. We were fortunate to find such diligent and careful workers. Kris Corcoran joined the team as a research assistant in 1983 and remained as a co-author, responsible for the statistical appendix. During mid-1987 Mariane Chaffe returned to the project to help with the final stages of the book, and I express my particular thanks to her. The project was funded by Special Research Grants from the Faculty of Commerce at the University of New South Wales and I appreciate Dean John Nevile's long term financial support for the project.

Over the past seven years the project has accumulated numerous debts of gratitude. Mr John Cross, chief archivist at the New South Wales Archives Office made available to our research assistants the printed indents which greatly facilitated transcription of the data onto coding sheets. The staff of the New South Wales State Archives, Mitchell Library, State Library and University of New South Wales Library have been especially helpful, answering numerous enquiries. The Academic Computing Service at the University of New South Wales made special concession to one of their larger users.

During 1985–87 while I was a visitor at the University of Reading, Mark Casson, Peter Hart, Colin Ash and Tim Worral discussed several chapters with me and read some early drafts. Ann Walker, from the Food Sciences Department at Reading, provided me with the computer program to calculate the calories and nutritional content of the convict ration. Roderick Floud and Ann Gregory, from Birkbeck College, University of London gave us access to their pre-published results of the height of male recruits into the British army in the early nineteenth century. Stephen Foster, from the Research School of the Social Sciences at the Australian National University, kindly sent us his working notes on convict assignment in the 1830s. John Perkins would like to thank Ms Penny Pemberton, Australian National University Archives of Business and Labour, and Kris Corcoran is grateful for the research assistance of Mrs M. Little.

Robin Derricourt at Cambridge University Press was a tolerant and helpful editor, giving the book his full support. My thanks also to M. Metz for the proof-reading and to A. Walker for the index. Kathy Cheeseman typed the early drafts of Chapters 9 and 11. Charleen Borlase typed numerous drafts of the bulk of the book, then the final manuscript, subject to a very tight schedule. Her efficiency, carefulness and goodwill meant that we met our final deadline. I greatly appreciate her help. Most of all, I thank my wife and daughter for their help and encouragement.

Stephen Nicholas

PART ONE

REVISING THE PAST

Chapter One

Unshackling the Past

Stephen Nicholas and Peter R. Shergold

Introduction

During the first quarter of a century of white settlement in Australia, the economy and society was the creation of convict workers transported from Britain and Ireland. No other period of Australian history evokes such strong images in the popular mind than the convict years. Collectively, Australians perceive their past in terms of a fatal shore, the convict stain and the shame of Botany Bay: the sombre shadows of Australia's history reveal the silhouettes of the gallows and the triangle. To a remarkable extent these images have been created from the detailed academic work on the convict period by Australian historians. For more than a generation, the received interpretation of our past has emphasised male convicts as hardened and professional criminals, females as prostitutes and convictism as a brutal and inefficient system of forced labour. This book offers a new and dramatic reinterpretation of the convict system.

As economic historians, trained in economics and quantitative techniques, we ask new and different questions about the early economic and social development of New South Wales. Our methodology is empirical and comparative. Data on 19,711 convicts transported to New South Wales between 1817 and 1840 form the quantitative basis for our analysis of the convict system. Our sample represents about one-third of the post-1817 convict inflow into New South Wales and nearly one-quarter of the total convict arrivals. From Britain, the English comprised roughly 60 per cent of the sample, the Scots 5 per cent and the Welsh less than one per cent. The Irish accounted for most of the remaining arrivals (34 per cent), leaving about one per cent of the transportees from outside the United Kingdom.[1] In Australia, the British and Irish convicts and ex-convicts made up the overwhelming proportion of the total labour force (71 per cent in 1840) compared with the free immigrants (24 per cent) and the colonial born (5 per cent).[2]

Like much contemporary social history, we seek to interpret the past from the 'bottom up'. Unfortunately, the convicts, who had a high level of literacy, have been made inarticulate by the passage of time. First-hand written records of their experiences in Australia are rare. But the statistical record of their servitude based on our sample provides a wealth of personal information on their occupation, age, sex, education, height, birthplace and crimes. This extant data allows us to reinterpret our convict past. The result is a quantitative history of forced labour in New South Wales which combines the insights of the historian with the formal theory and quantitative technique of the economist. We have not sought to write narrow economic history, but a sweeping analysis of convictism which challenges the traditional interpretations of social and labour history. This broad approach leads us to reject the curious insularity of much Australian history which treats transportation and convictism as peculiarly Australian. Convictism in New South Wales is compared both with the experience of free workers in Britain and with other forms of coerced labour, including Indian and Melanesian bonded workers, American slaves, and other convicts.

A mythology created: the historiography of Australian convictism

It is now 30 years since Manning Clark suggested that the nationalist interpretation of the convict settlers as 'innocent and manly' unfortunates fighting for freedom and social justice grossly distorted Australia's past.[3] Clark argued that those transported to New South Wales could not be typified as poor rural workers pushed into poaching by enclosure and economic exigency; still less were they Chartists or Whiteboys, Captain Swings or Tolpuddle Martyrs, imprisoned for their political convictions. They were not helpless victims of a repressive and cruel British society, but persistent thieves engaged in a life of crime.

This revisionist characterisation of the convicts which has come to dominate Australian history has gained support from statistical analyses of the convict indents. This quantification has presented what appears to be an objective group portrait of the some 160,000 transported convicts. From the work of Lloyd Robson and A.G.L. Shaw we know that some 80 per cent of the transportees were men; their mean age was 26; 51 per cent were sentenced to seven years' imprisonment; 81 per cent of the men and 83 per cent of the women were convicted of offences against property, overwhelmingly theft; most were single; two-thirds were Protestants, and one-third Roman Catholic.[4]

However, the 'new' revisionism is not merely a collection of statistics. It offers an interpretation, not just enumeration. And the basis of that interpretation is that those transported as convict labour were, not to put too fine a point on it, hardened criminals. They came from a unique subgroup in Britain, the professional criminal class. This interpretation has become the accepted paradigm for Australian historians. For example, in 1983 John Hirst wrote that Shaw's work 'finally established the large professional criminal element among the convicts' and, more recently, Robert Hughes argued that the innocence of convicts as a class was 'first exposed to criticism by Manning Clark in the 1950s and finally demolished with statistical analysis by L.L. Robson in 1965'.[5] On taking up his appointment to Australia's first chair in Australian history, Brian Fletcher declared in mid-1987 that 'The convicts sent to Australia really were criminals . . . [not] basically decent people forced into a life of crime by adverse economic conditions'.[6]

What, then, underpins these assertions? Clark distinguished the criminal classes from the urban working class, from which they largely came, by a 'certain character and upbringing', by a 'psychological aberration' which made them 'permanent outcasts of society'.[7] Shaw thought that those transported had 'sprung from the dregs of society, and had been trained to crime from the cradle'.[8] Lloyd Robson sought the criminal class in 'indifferent or non-existent parental control' and the 'professional class of thieves who taught children, not always their own but waifs and strays, how to pick pockets'.[9] B. and M. Schedvin identified a criminal subculture which emphasised easy money, idleness and self-indulgences — values traced to 'parental neglect and indifference accompanied by lack of discipline'.[10] There was a subculture of crime in Britain, and in

London most of all, according to Hughes, from which 'many Britons made their living, wholly or in part'.[11] Following Clark, Shaw, and Robson, other Australian historians — including M. Weidenhofer, L. Evans, P. Nicholls, D. Horne and H. McQueen — have described the convicts as 'outcast people', habitual criminals, ne'er-do-wells and part of the criminal branch.[12]

Since the bulk of the convicts were professional criminals quite distinct from the urban working class from which they came, Humphrey McQueen argued that what Australia gained from the convicts was a 'deformed stratification which had itself been vomited up by the maelstrom which was delineating class in Britain'.[13] For McQueen, the value system of the convicts was essentially lumpenproletariat, combining hatred of authority with individual acquisitiveness. According to Hughes, 'mateship, fatalism, contempt for do-gooders and God-botherers, harsh humour, opportunism, survivors' disdain for introspection, and an attitude to authority in which private resentment mingled with ostensible recognition were the meagre baggage of values the convicts brought with them to Australia'.[14]

Little of this interpretation stems from quantitative examination of the convict indents. Rather, the careful elaboration of the nineteenth century notion that there existed a criminal class actually determined Clark, Shaw, and Robson's statistical analyses rather than evolved from it. Criminal offences are painstakingly categorised and counted; indications of working class background, particularly recorded occupational skills, are virtually ignored. Where the statistics do not fit the 'criminal class' hypothesis they are given short shrift. For example, even though Clark found that the transported criminals had surprisingly high levels of literacy, he argued that the criminal class was characterised by mental imbecility, low cunning and ignorance.[15] The fact that the percentage of town workers, by which Clark appears to mean skilled urban tradespeople, was higher than the percentage of labourers and agricultural labourers combined, is ignored.[16]

In his 37–page analysis of 'Who are the Convicts?', A.G.L. Shaw barely mentions their occupational backgrounds.[17] And the most thorough and careful quantitative study by Lloyd Robson displays a near total disregard for the statistical evidence on occupations. The subject is mentioned only in passing in the text, and of 64 tables located in the Appendix, a mere two purport to examine occupations, although half the categories presented could be defined more accurately as industries. There can be little doubt that Robson dismissed the occupational statistics he collected as of little worth. He quotes with approval the surgeon-superintendent on the transport *Recovery* in 1819, Peter Cunningham, who claimed that 'labourer' was entered in the indents under trade to disguise the convicts' true calling, that of thief.[18] Having discounted the occupational data and searched inconclusively for professional criminals among the detailed listing of offences in the indents, historians have based their case for a criminal class on the fragmentary evidence in the court records in London and, far more importantly, upon the colourful descriptions of middle class English 'moral entrepreneurs', such as Henry Mayhew and Charles Dickens. Robson thought '*Oliver Twist* is only partly a work of fiction, and the illegitimate and orphaned child, as well as the Noah Claypoles, fell a ready prey to the Fagins of the metropolis'. Hughes quotes Mayhew extensively (although with more caution than Robson showed towards Dickens) as evidence of London's criminal underworld.[19]

If this perception of the nature of transported convicts has now become accepted, so too has that of the labour system in which they were forced to work. Much of the analysis of the convict system in Australia rests on two assumptions by historians: that the organisation of forced convict labour differed significantly from free labour, and that convictism was inefficient. Both assumptions have received unanimous assent; neither assumption has been explicitly tested.

For historians, the road gang has typified both the work organisation of public labour and its inefficiency. The gangs have been depicted as instruments of punishment, rather than as a way of organising useful work. Because the convicts were shirkers doing the 'government stroke', they performed just enough work to keep the flogger at bay. Without monetary incentives, Hughes believed that only the whip could motivate convicts to work.[20] According to Clark, the convicts had an innate aversion to labour. The result was that convicts had to be terrorised at work.[21] R.W. Connell and T.H. Irving agreed, equating the convict system with brute force.[22] John Hirst has suggested that the urban convicts, hardened, desperate and profligate professional thieves, unused to regular hours, regular employment or hard manual labour, were difficult to motivate without physical punishment.[23] The lash, and the careful counting of beatings — 332,810 in 1835 or a quarter of a million in 1837 — still dominates much of the current historiography.[24] Hughes reminds us that even 25 strokes was a draconic torture, able to skin a man's back; worse still was the psychological damage of the whip which effectively demoralised the workforce.[25] It is true that during the last few years Australian historians have begun a major re-evaluation of the convict system. However, while John Hirst, Alan Atkinson, Portia Robinson, and Norma Townsend have shown that the convict system was less arbitrary and unjust than popularly believed, convictism is still portrayed as a brutal and inefficient system, reliant on the whip.[26]

The allegation that assignment of convicts was a 'giant lottery' has been presented as further confirmation of the inefficiency of forced convict labour. The persistent complaints by private masters that few skilled mechanics were assigned to rural employment, and that those convict workers who were assigned to rural jobs were indifferently trained in their trades, gave rise to the lottery thesis in the *Bigge Report*.[27] Without any empirical test of the lottery hypothesis, the claim that assignment was largely a matter of chance has been repeated by Driscoll, Hughes, Evans and Nicholls, Weidenhofer, and Hirst.[28] A recent study of assignment in the 1830s by S.G. Foster found 'certain elements remained much the same during the 50 or so years of the system's operation, most notably the arbitrary allocation of individual convicts which is often described, from the convicts' point of view, as a "giant lottery"'.[29] Historians have also taken up the complaints by the private masters that convict labour was not much good. Hughes has argued that poor quality convicts were dumped on the settlers, saddling the average settler with an unskilled urban convict 'who could not tell a hoe from a shovel'. The skilled mechanics were no better; they were always in short supply and rarely of high quality.[30] According to Manning Clark, what few skills the convicts brought with them to Australia were neither recognised nor useful.[31] Assignment was inefficient, and the state, which worked in the interests of a favoured individual, group or class, shared much of the blame.

A mythology destroyed: new hypotheses on Australian convictism

Australian historians, reacting to the early nationalistic romanticisation of convicts as founding fathers, have created a world of Artful Dodgers and Fagins, of Sawney-Hunters and Dead Lurkers, and then identified them as members of a distinct class. In Benjamin Franklin's evocative phrase applied to British criminals transported to America, Australia's convicts have been dismissed by historians as 'human serpents'. In contrast, this book analyses the convicts as 'human capital', assessing the quality of the workers' occupational skills, education and physical fitness. The picture which emerges shares little in common with the traditional interpretation.

Our extensive analysis of the convict data, and our empirical and comparative methodology, lead us to the following new hypotheses and major revisions of the current historiography.

The convicts transported to Australia were part of a global system of forced migration

Australian historians generally have viewed transportation of convicts as an exceptional feature of their history. Historians of immigration have analysed the international movement of labour during the nineteenth century in terms of free choice. Both are wrong. The British and Irish convicts sent to Australia were part of a larger international and intercontinental flow of forced migration including Indian, French, Spanish and Russian convicts, and 'bonded' Indian and Melanesian contract labour. After 1820 a quarter of a million convicts were shipped across the world's oceans to colonise Australia, New Caledonia, Singapore and French Guiana, and to meet labour demand in Gibraltar, Bermuda, Penang, Malacca and Mauritius. If the forced migration of Russians to Siberia is included, the figure swells to 2 1/4 million, and the addition of the bonded Indians and Pacific Islanders doubles the number to 5 million. Transportation, like the recruiting of slaves and the contracting of bonded workers, was complementary to the international migration of free European peoples before 1914. Convictism was a labour system existing in many countries of the world in the nineteenth century.

The convicts transported to Australia were ordinary British and Irish working class men and women. They were not professional and habitual criminals, recruited from a distinct class and trained to crime from the cradle

Our analysis of the character of the male convicts transported to New South Wales, and Deborah Oxley's assessment of their female counterparts, does not indicate that they were habitual or professional criminals. Most were first offenders found guilty of petty theft. Most had been employed as free workers in the British or Irish labour markets prior to their conviction. For many, their crimes were work related: they had stolen tools or material from their employers, or possessions from their masters. Most were young working men and women who had been found guilty of larceny or receiving stolen goods.

That Australian historians have clung so tenaciously to the Victorian notion of a distinct and separate criminal class is surprising. Historians of Victorian crime in England — such as David Philips, David Jones and George Rude — have rejected the idea of a dangerous class, born and bred to a life of crime and operating as organised gangs.[32] What was noticeable about crime was its casualness and lack of planning. Not only were those transported to New South Wales not part of a criminal class, the fact is that there existed no such class in Victorian Britain from which to select the transportees.

The convict settlers were Australia's first immigrants

Today the Department of Immigration awards points on the basis of age in order to select the most productive immigrants to Australia. While the department prefers 16 to 35 year olds, only 47 per cent of immigrants fit into that category. In contrast more than 80 per cent of convict arrivals in New South Wales were aged 16 to 25 years. The convicts also displayed a better age distribution than the colony's first free migrants. At most, 60 per cent of the assisted and 70 per cent of the unassisted immigrants to the eastern colonies between 1829 and 1851 arrived in the 16 to 35 years age group while over 80 per cent of the convicts fell into that age category. Australia's alternative labour supply, the free transatlantic migrants who arrived in American ports between 1820 and 1840, had 30 per cent of their inflow under 15 years or over 40 years while the equivalent figure for convicts was only 10 per cent.

Unlike free settlers, the convict immigrants arrived without the young and the old, avoiding the burden of dependent service provisions, such as schools, trade training and old-age care, for two generations. Most convict migrants were men. Free migration before 1850 was 'folk migration', with most migrants to North America travelling as family units. Australia's inflow of overwhelmingly single male convicts created an exceptionally high labour participation rate in which over 65 per cent of the total population were members of the male workforce. The age-sex structure of the convicts provided a unique workforce upon which to build economic growth.

The convicts' pre-transportation experience of migration allowed them to adjust more easily to Australia

Many of those transported to New South Wales were experienced migrants. At least 38 per cent of the British and Irish convicts had moved county within the British Isles prior to finding themselves shipped to the other side of the world; 12 per cent of the Irish had moved to Britain. Our statistical analysis shows that those who had moved within the United Kingdom were the best educated and skilled. The traditional historical stereotype of convicts as a wandering criminal class, a species of travelling thief in search of criminal opportunity is rejected. For many of those uprooted and enchained, imprisonment and transportation may have been a trauma; migration was not.

Immigration of convicts was 'effective'

Today's immigration policy tries to ensure 'migration effectiveness', displaying concern over migrants who, by returning to their homeland, reduce the level of net immigration. The lower the level of net immigration the greater the cost of maintaining

Australia's immigrant workforce. Between 1982 and 1987 net immigration was only 67 per cent of immigrant arrivals; in contrast, over 95 per cent of the convicts never saw Britain or Ireland again.

The convicts brought useful skills to Australia

The proportion of convicts in the skilled, semi-skilled and unskilled occupational categories was roughly the same as the percentages of each skill class for the English workforce in 1841. Our statistical tests confirmed that the convicts came from the same occupational population as the free workers in England. The convicts were the English working classes transported, bringing a cross-section of useful skills. There was an urban skill bias in the convict inflow. But the wide range of skills possessed by transported convicts was well suited to building a new colony. Early New South Wales should not be too readily treated as rural-orientated. The standard of living, tastes of the settlers and the isolation of the colony created a strong demand for consumer and producer goods requiring non-rural occupational skills which the convict workers were able to provide. The building skills which the convicts brought with them were particularly valuable. Even in the crucial area of rural job requirements, the proportion of skilled convict farm workers was almost identical to that in the 1841 English census. While some job restructuring was required to adapt convict skills to rural employment needs, retraining generally involved unskilled urban convicts learning unskilled rural jobs. Free unskilled migrants would have to have made the same adjustments to Australian colonial society as the unskilled convicts.

The English convicts were better educated than the working population left at home

Three-quarters of the English convicts who arrived in New South Wales could read and/or write, a significantly higher percentage than the average for all English workers (58 per cent) who could sign the marriage register. Economists who have viewed education as a process of human capital formation found that a 40 per cent literacy rate seemed the threshold level for economic development. Australia's convicts easily attained the threshold education level needed for sustained economic growth. Their literacy level was higher than that found in many parts of the underdeveloped world today.

The convicts were physically fit and productive

Only healthy convicts were selected for embarkation on the long, four-month voyage to Australia. Low mortality on the transports meant that most convicts arrived fit and well. The convicts were productive workers, as measured indirectly by their height. Contrary to prevailing historiography, those transported to New South Wales were not of very short stature as compared with their British contemporaries. Rather they were as tall as those workers left at home. It is recognised today that height reflects accurately the accumulated past nutritional experience of each individual over all their growing years. Nutrition is a direct input into guaranteeing a high level of labour productivity. Since the convicts were as physically robust as other members of the British working class, they were potentially as productive as workers in Great Britain.

Most transported females were not prostitutes, but ordinary working class women possessing immediately useful skills

While male convicts have been assessed for the significance (or insignificance) of their crimes, the female convicts have been stereotyped as useless whores. Prostitution was not a crime. What fragmentary evidence there is on prostitution among the women convicts suggests that no more than 20 per cent of the females practised prostitution prior to transportation. To be condemned by A.G.L. Shaw as 'singularly unattractive' or dismissed by Lloyd Robson as having 'little to recommend them', shows scant regard for the statistical data on the female convicts' occupations and literacy.[33] Deborah Oxley shows that the female convicts brought to Australia immediately useful skills, especially as general servants, laundresses, kitchenhands, needleworkers and housemaids, which (unlike many of the skills of male transportees) required no adapting to the Australian environment. According to the current evidence, the female convicts were undervalued and underemployed in New South Wales. We suggest that the skills of the female convicts were squandered, denying the young colony the full potential of a valuable productive resource. The detrimental impact on economic development was lessened by the fact that only 11 per cent of the transported workers were women.

An English labour aristocracy with a unique system of values was transported to Australia

An elite hierarchy of skilled workers accounting for between 6 per cent and 14 per cent of all transported convicts was transported. These English labour aristocrats retained their jobs, values and self-perceptions as elite workers in New South Wales. We know they became members of the Trade Union Benefit Society, the printer's union and the Sydney Mechanics School of Arts. Not only was a labour elite transported, but they retained their values and identity in New South Wales, both at work and through the traditional institutions of their class.

The labour market was efficient, and the allocation of convict labour was not a lottery

The efficiency of the labour market is judged by how well it matches the 'right' workers to the 'right' jobs. Comparing the occupation of each convict in the United Kingdom with that in the 1828 muster, Nicholas found that skilled urban, rural and construction workers were largely matched to the same types of jobs in New South Wales as they had held at home. This was true of assignment by the state as well as allocation through the labour market. There was no lottery in the allocation of convict labour.

Domestic workers and unskilled urban workers brought skills less well suited to the needs of the colony. These workers bore the brunt of job restructuring, assigned to unfamiliar employment in agriculture or the public service. Significantly, as these convicts gained their freedom, they chose to utilise their old skills learned at home. However, Australia was fortunate in being able to assign men to jobs such as building roads and clearing land during their period of forced labour, which they rejected once they gained their freedom. Of equal importance, the state chose for these jobs the men whose United Kingdom skills were least useful to Australian job requirements. The state was an efficient agent for the allocation of convict labour.

The organisation of public labour was efficient, corresponding to the way similar work was organised in the free labour system

Skilled convict tradesmen (tailors, shoemakers, carpenters, wheelwrights and blacksmiths) were organised into workshop-factories in the lumber and dockyards while the workers engaged in building, land clearing, ploughing and thrashing were organised into gangs. These forms of work organisation corresponded to those found in free labour Britain. Using an economic theory of gangs, Nicholas shows that the assignment, supervision and incentive attributes attached to particular work structures were maximised in the way convict labour was organised in New South Wales.

Incentives and rewards were an integral part of the extraction of work from public labour

Care-intensive work, especially that requiring skill, was motivated largely by rewards, while effort-intensive work, such as clearing scrub and road building was susceptible to being driven through fear of pain. Work which was difficult to measure tended to be tasked, and relied on a system of rewards including extra rations and clothing, indulgences (such as tea, tobacco and rum), preferred work, apprenticeship training and time to work on one's own account. A structure of rewards and tasks rather than the whip was the standard device for extracting work from convicts in government service.

The lash was used judiciously in colonial Australia, and there is little evidence of a society terrorised by corporal punishment

Selecting 1835, the peak year for floggings, the probability of being beaten every year during a five-year sentence was 0.001, and roughly two-thirds of all convicts received one or no floggings during their period of servitude. The official statistics on corporal punishment disprove the popular picture of convictism as a society where workers were demoralised physically and psychologically by the whip. Physical violence in Australia was no greater than that in the British army or navy, and less than that for American slaves. Physical violence against child workers and apprentices was a daily occurrence in early nineteenth century Britain.

The standard ration provided convicts with a higher level of energy and nutrition than currently recommended Australian levels

The standard ration delivered an average 4005 calories per day, which was greater than that recommended today by the Australian National Health and Medical Research Council for 18 to 35 year-old men. It was also greater than the British Department of Health's recommended levels for very active 18 to 34 year-old men. The convict diet was sufficient to sustain a worker performing continuous moderate grade work for the entire work week or some combination of heavy and light work. In nutritional content, the ration meets current Australian and United Kingdom recommended daily levels. Overall, the convict's standard ration was substantial, with a high nutritional content.

The convicts' hours of work were less than that of most free British workers

The convicts worked an average of 56 hours per week which was considerably less than other coerced labour elsewhere in the world and less than most free workers in Britain. The shorter hours worked in New South Wales and the experience of the regularity and discipline in the household and factory gained in Britain, meant that transported workers would have been able to adjust readily to the fixed work days and work week under convictism.

The barracks provided healthy and spacious accommodation relative to the urban housing of the poorer sections of the working class in Britain

The physical conditions of barrack accommodation in New South Wales was superior to the back-to-backs, tenements and cellars inhabited by the poorer workers in Britain's great towns. In terms of cubic feet of sleeping space per person, the barracks provided more space than the typical houses of poor British workers and American slaves and more room than the barracks and ships allowed British soldiers and sailors.

The convicts were provided with a high standard of medical care and were generally healthy

Convicts had free access to medical care in the colony's hospitals before 1831, and access after 1831 on payment by private masters for the medical costs of their assigned men. The mortality in colonial hospitals was no more than that in the general voluntary hospitals in Britain which strictly controlled admission by requiring patients to pay a deposit before entry. The quality of care in the colony's hospital was superior to that provided at the infirmaries where most poor Englishmen sought medical care after 1834. Australia was a healthy country. Morbidity was relatively low and child mortality was less than one-eighth of that in the great industrial cities of England.

NOTES

1. Throughout the book Britain or Great Britain include England, Wales and Scotland. The United Kingdom refers to Britain and Ireland.
2. N. Butlin, 'White Human Capital in Australia 1780–1800', *Australian National University Papers in Economic History* 32 (1985), 18–9.
3. M. Clark, 'The Origins of the Convicts Transported to Eastern Australia, 1787–1852', *Historical Studies: Australia and New Zealand* 7 (1956).
4. L.L. Robson, *The Convict Settlers of Australia*; A.G.L. Shaw, *Convicts and the Colonies*.
5. J. Hirst, *Convict Society and Its Enemies*, p.33; R. Hughes, *The Fatal Shore*, p.159.
6. *The Australian*, 2 September 1987, p.12.
7. Clark, 'Origins of the Convicts', 125, 133.
8. Shaw, *Convicts and the Colonies*, p.12.
9. Robson, *Convict Settlers*, p.150.
10. M.B. and C.B. Schedvin, 'The Nomadic Tribes of Urban Britain: A Prelude to Botany Bay', *Historical Studies: Australia and New Zealand* 18 (1978), 255–7.

11. Hughes, *Fatal Shore*, pp.170–1.
12. M. Weidenhofer, *The Convict Years: Transportation and the Penal System 1788–1868*; L. Evans and P. Nicholls, *Convicts and Colonial Society 1788–1853*; D. Horne, *The Australian People*; H. McQueen, 'Convicts and Rebels', *Labour History* 15 (1968).
13. McQueen, 'Convicts and Rebels', 25.
14. Hughes, *Fatal Shore*, p.175.
15. Clark, 'Origins of the Convicts', 314.
16. Clark, 'Origins of the Convicts', 130.
17. Shaw, *Convicts and the Colonies*, pp.146–83.
18. Robson, *Convict Settlers*, pp.181–2.
19. Robson, *Convict Settlers*, p.150; Hughes, *Fatal Shore*, pp.170–2.
20. Hughes, *Fatal Shore*, p.285.
21. Clark, 'Origins of the Convicts', 314, 317; M. Clark, *A History of Australia* I, pp.243–4.
22. R.W. Connell and T.H. Irving, *Class Structure in Australian History: Documents, Narrative and Argument*, p.45.
23. Hirst, *Convict Society*, p.32, 75.
24. A. Atkinson and M. Aveling, *Australians 1838*, p.287.
25. Hughes, *Fatal Shore*, p.428.
26. Hirst, *Convict Society*; A. Atkinson, 'Four Patterns of Convict Protest', *Labour History* 37 (1979), 28–51; P. Robinson, *The Hatch and Brood of Time*; N. Townsend, 'A "Mere Lottery": The Convict System in New South Wales Through the Eyes of the Molesworth Committee', *Push From the Bush* 21 (1985), 58–86.
27. *Report from the Commissioner of Inquiry into the State of the Colony of New South Wales (Bigge Report)*, Parliamentary Papers, 1822, XX, C448, 18–19.
28. F. Driscoll, 'Macquarie's Administration of the Convict System', *Journal of the Royal Australian Historical Society* 27 (1941); 394; Hughes, *Fatal Shore*, p.201; Evans and Nicholls, *Convicts and Colonial Society*, pp.8–9; Weidenhofer, *Convict Years*; Hirst, *Convict Society*, p.61.
29. S.G. Foster, 'Convict Assignment in New South Wales in the 1830s', *Push From the Bush* 15 (1983), 35.
30. Hughes, *Fatal Shore*, pp.298–304.
31. Clark, 'Origins of the Convicts', 131.
32. D. Philips, *Crime and Authority in Victorian Britain*; D. Jones, *Crime, Protest, Community and Police in Nineteenth-Century Britain*; G. Rude, *Criminal and Victim: Crime and Society in Early Nineteenth Century Britain*.
33. Shaw, *Convicts and the Colonies*, p.164; Robson, *Convict Settlers*, p.145.

Chapter Two

Full Circle?
Contemporary Views on Transportation

David Meredith

Introduction

Transportation to New South Wales was the subject of numerous British official enquiries from the 1790s onwards. This chapter explores some of the themes examined by these investigations and the conflict of views which emerged. Such conflicts reflected the ambivalence of the arguments put forward about the efficacy — economically and penally — of transportation and the way in which enquiries of this sort could be 'stacked' by the selection of witnesses whose views were well known and whose first-hand knowledge of Australia might be small or even non-existent.

Transportation of convicts involved both penal and economic objectives. The penal objectives were to rid Britain of criminals, to deter others from committing crime and to reform the convicts. The economic functions were referred to in the first Transportation Act of 1717: 'in many of His Majesty's colonies and plantations in America, there was a great want of servants, who by their labour and industry might be the means of improving and making the said colonies and plantations more useful to this nation'.[1] Australian colonies were eventually substituted for the American ones, but the economic role of transportation remained that of labour supply.

The purpose of this chapter is to bring into perspective the working of the convict system by examining the views of certain contemporaries who gave evidence to parliamentary inquiries on the economic and penal elements in transportation, the relationship between these elements and the question of whether by the end of the 1830s the system was failing to fulfil either set of objectives adequately.

Economic objectives

Not all of the convicts sentenced to transportation were actually sent to the Australian penal colonies. The criteria for selection were age (males 15 to 50 years, females under 45 years), health (they had to be fit enough to withstand the voyage) and sentence: all those sentenced to life and fourteen year terms were transported as long as they met the age and health requirements.[2] Of those sentenced to seven year terms, selection was from the fit and healthy who had committed the most serious crimes, or who had been in the hulks before or who were badly behaved in prison or in the hulks.

Convicts were assigned — to private masters or to the government — according to their abilities and not with reference to their sentence, crime or general 'character'.[3]

Governor Hunter stated that convicts were 'employed in such works as required men of particular professions; blacksmiths were employed in making-up iron work, and tools of agriculture, and carpenters and bricklayers in buildings; and we had them all classed into their different gangs . . .'[4]

Similarly, Governor Bligh described the system he used: 'They were arranged in our book for the purpose of distinguishing their ages, trades and qualifications and whether sickly, or not, in order to enable me to distribute them according'.[5] The Select Committee on Transportation, 1837–38 (the 'Molesworth Committee') concluded, 'The previous occupation of the convict in this country mainly determines his condition in the penal colonies'.[6]

While attempting to satisfy the settlers' and the government's need for labour, the assignment system also had penal attributes. It was intended that a period of hard and regular work would lead towards reformation. The 1812 Select Committee on Transportation noted: 'Nor is it to be lost sight of, that in the service of settlers they are likely to acquire some knowledge of farming; and that if from convicts, they become well-behaved and industrious servants, a farther possibility is opened to them of becoming prosperous and respectable settlers'.[7] Commissioner Bigge, reporting on New South Wales 10 years later, agreed: in the service of the 'more opulent' settlers, the convict 'everyday becomes more skilful in that species of labour, by which he may hereafter seek to establish himself in the possession of property, and make it available for his support'.[8]

The costs of supervising and disciplining convict labour were high. Punishment was both ineffective and expensive: in order for a private settler to administer corporal punishment the convict had to be taken before a magistrate, often at some distance, and this took time and money as well as losing the labour of the accused while the process went on.[9] Other punishments could be resorted to, such as reducing the food ration to the government minimum, and task work was used where practicable.[10] More effective were humane treatment and material rewards. James Macarthur stated in 1837:

> Of course it is in the interests of the assignee to make his convict servant as comfortable as possible. The principle on which we have conducted our establishment is, where a man behaves well, to make him forget, if possible, that he is a convict . . . You never could have obtained profitable labour from them on any other system? — The system of forcing labour on a private establishment I conceive would not be a very profitable one; at all events, it would be an exceedingly disagreeable one . . . [11]

Material rewards included extra rations and luxuries such as tobacco, sugar and tea. Wages were also paid in kind and money, despite government opposition to the practice after 1823.[12]

Whether the stick or the carrot was the favoured instrument for extracting labour, the costs of extraction increased as the economy of New South Wales expanded and the labour shortage intensified, involving settlers 'in daily trouble, expense and disappointment'.[13] James Macarthur explained in 1837: 'In the former years the number of convicts assigned to each individual was much greater than at present, out of every ship we might receive ten, where we only receive five now . . . we are obliged to employ men as shepherds now, whom we should not have thought of so employing formerly'.[14] These costs, he continued, limited the size of his flocks to 25,000.

> We have found, from the disorderly habits of the shepherds, and the difficulty of keeping up a large establishment of servants, that it is not so profitable to extend beyond that number.

When you get beyond 25,000 there is a loss, from the difficulty of management, or rather a diminished profit.

Such experience pointed to convict labour not being 'cheap' labour at all, at least by the 1830s. Macarthur argued in 1838: 'From my own experience, and also looking at it upon general principles, I am of the opinion that free labour must be cheaper in the end than slave or forced labour'.[15] Another large employer of convict labour, Sir Edward Parry of the Australian Agricultural Company, stated in 1838:

> A convict, unless he is well watched, will not perform the same amount of labour [as a free worker], except in the case of what is called task work . . . that is the only case in which convict labour is really valuable labour at all; if you cannot watch them, that is, if you cannot establish a competent superintendence, which is often a very expensive thing to do, their labour is by no means valuable.[16]

The advantage of free wage labour lay in its alleged propensity to work harder than coerced labour. The perceived disadvantages of free labourers were firstly that they could not be compelled to remain on the estate and that they could not be disciplined like convicts;[17] secondly, it was not practicable to work convict and free alongside;[18] thirdly, that free immigrants were often no more skilled than the average convict at the beginning of his assignment;[19] fourthly, that it was difficult to see how public works, especially road building, could be carried on with free wage labour except at inordinate cost;[20] and finally, that the small, mainly subsistence, settlers would not be able to compete effectively with the large estates for free labour especially if the free worker's wages were to be paid mainly in money.[21] All of these disadvantages could be eliminated only if the inflow of free labour was substantially increased. The 'tyranny of distance' meant that emigration from Britain to Australia was unlikely without subsidisation: the time and cost involved in a passage to New South Wales or Van Diemen's Land deterred free immigrants, especially given the opportunities available across the Atlantic in the United States or British North America. Would the settlers be willing to pay for assisted passages for migrants? There was considerable resistance from the settlers to making direct payments to the government towards transportation costs for convicts, but through the Land Fund, established in 1831, free immigration could be paid for indirectly.[22] The number of free assisted migrants increased during the 1830s and the Land Fund was described as 'one of the greatest benefits ever bestowed on New South Wales'[23] but the number of immigrants was still regarded as grossly inadequate by the largest private employers by 1838.[24]

Macarthur (and others) predicted that a sudden end to the transportation of convicts to New South Wales 'would be productive almost of ruin to individuals' but it was also acknowledged that transportation itself was an obstacle to increasing free immigration.[25] Tradesmen and upper class migrants were put off by the reputation Australia had for lawlessness while Macarthur argued there was a great aversion in the minds of the British labourer to emigrate to New South Wales or Van Diemen's Land because they were penal colonies.[26] Heath made the argument — repeated by Molesworth — that the main fear caused by transportation was that of expatriation; and encouraging fear of expatriation among the British working class as a deterrent to crime also had the effect of discouraging free emigration, especially among agricultural labourers.[27]

Whatever the influence of transportation on emigration from Britain to New South

Wales at this time — and it may have discouraged it — there was no doubt in the minds of many commentators that transportation stunted the colony's population growth because the sex-ratio was heavily biased towards males from the earliest times of white settlement. If free immigration took place, it was argued, the sex imbalance would be reduced and the birth rate would rise. However, in the absence of large-scale free immigration — and attracting large numbers appeared to be a daunting task — population growth would be circumscribed. For this reason a special role was often assigned to female convicts as the 1812 Select Committee commented:

> . . . such women as these were the mothers of a great part of the inhabitants now existing in the colony, and from this stock only can a reasonable hope be held out of rapid increase to the population; upon which increase, here as in all infant colonies, its growing prosperity in great measure depends.[28]

And in the 1830s some argued that abolition of transportation should be for men only — women would be required to be forcibly supplied to the colony.[29] Others called for more family emigration, including convict families.

Thus from an economic perspective the transportation of convicts to Australia had, in the minds of some commentators, turned a full circle by 1838: from being a method of supplying labour to the settlers in New South Wales it was now seen as an obstacle to the immediate and longer-term labour supply.

Penal objectives

For Britain, the economic benefits of transportation lay in disposing of convicts more cheaply than maintaining them in prison at home, and in the fact that they did not return to Britain upon the expiration of their sentence.

The British government attempted to keep the expense of transportation to a minimum. There were numerous complaints about the conditions of convicts during the voyage and a reluctance to make significant improvements, on the grounds of economy. Allegations of overcrowding on the transports were numerous, yet to give each convict his own hammock would have reduced the number of convicts per ship by about half.[30] Convicts were not closely supervised, especially at night, beyond the minimum necessary to avoid mutiny. It was claimed they received poor rations — two-thirds of the military ration — and were in general in worse health when landed in Australia than when they left the United Kingdom.[31] Conditions in the female transports were reported to be just as bad.[32]

Although the cost per head of sending convicts fell during the 1830s — mainly because more were sent — the costs of administration and the military appeared to be rising.[33] By 1837, calculated Heath, the cost to the British government of transportation and maintenance of New South Wales and Van Diemen's Land would be about £439,000 per annum, while the cost of keeping all the convicts in Britain would be about £435,000. These figures did not take into account whether Britain would still have to pay something towards the colonial administrations even after transportation was abolished, or the capital cost of building a penitentiary large enough to accommodate the convicts if they could not be transported (estimated at £1.3 million). Nevertheless, it raised the question whether, as the penal colonies expanded, the costs to Britain of ridding itself of large numbers of convicts might not be as economical as before: the Molesworth Committee's Report increased Heath's estimate of £439,000 per annum to £488,000 and concluded it might be cheaper to keep them in Britain.[34] The cost of transportation is shown in Table 2.1. As the number of convicts per ship increased (together with the decline in the number of tons of shipping per convict) the cost per convict clearly fell. It was the indirect costs of military supervision and government administration of the convict system, however, which alarmed the British authorities, even though many of these costs might also have been incurred under a system of free settlement.

Since the settlers appeared to be major beneficiaries of the labour of British convicts, it was suggested in the 1830s that they should pay something towards the cost of transportation and administration. The Select Committee on Secondary Punishments in 1832 recommended payment by the settlers to the government for convicts but this recommendation was not implemented. To do so would have required widespread support from the settlers and by the time the Report was published the Land Fund in New South Wales had been established and the wealthiest graziers were looking to the fund to pay assisted passages for free wage labour.

The central penal function of transportation was deterrence. The punishment of transportation was intended to be so dreadful as to deter potential criminals from becoming actual ones, or once-convicted persons from committing further criminal acts. Until the end of the Napoleonic Wars the efficacy of transportation in producing 'dread' among the working class was not often questioned. As the actual conditions of convicts in New South Wales became better known, however, it gradually became more commonly stated that transportation was losing its ability to terrify. Considerable opinion was placed before the 1831 Select Committee on Secondary Punishments to the effect that transportation was no longer feared, but rather, welcomed. John Henry Capper, from his long experience as superintendent of the hulks, said in 1831 that prisoners on the hulks preferred to be sent to Australia than remain in England, particularly artisans.[35] Similarly, the governor of Newgate gaol stated that prisoners did not fear transportation and expected to obtain a good situation in the colonies.[36] Edward Gibbon Wakefield observed Newgate prisoners over a three year period and could not recall 'a single instance in which a prisoner appeared to me to be deeply affected by the prospect of being transported to the colonies'; a convict expected to obtain 'a degree of

Table 2.1: *Costs of Transportation*

Annual average of years	Average no. of convicts transported per year	Cost per convict £	Average no. of convicts per ship	No. of tons of shipping per convict
1816–18	1806	45.00	139	3.5
1819–21	2390	48.93	126	3.9
1822–24	1739	45.92	109	4.4
1825–27	1822	65.22	94	5.0
1828–30	3809	33.22	134	3.3
1831–33	4250	17.90	154	2.9
1834–36	4531	15.95	203	2.2

Source: *Report from the Select Committee on Transportation, 1837–38*, Parliamentary Paper, XXII, C669, Appendix (I), No. 58, 320.

wealth and happiness, such as he had no prospect of attaining in this country'.[37] The more educated the convict, the more he looked forward to transportation. Although there were some witnesses who were prepared to say that transportation was dreaded, the conclusion which the 1832 Select Committee reached was that transportation had lost its terror and that it should now be considered 'a most valuable ingredient in the system of secondary punishment' but not its sole or main element.[38] Transportation, the Report stated, could no longer deter criminals: 'In the event of a conviction, they know that the worst that can befall them, will be a change to a condition often scarcely inferior to that in which they were before'.[39]

Similar views were put forward to a House of Lords Select Committee on Prisons in 1835. W. Cope, governor of Newgate gaol, testified that 'nineteen out of twenty are glad to go';[40] Owen, overseer of the convict hulk, *Fortitude*, at Chatham, put it higher: 'ninety-nine out of a hundred are very desirous of going'.[41] Once again, the correlation between ignorance and dread was frequently mentioned: to the extent that transportation was dreaded by prisoners, it was fear of the unknown and of exile on which the dread was predicated, rather than terror induced by a knowledge of what awaited them in the colonies.[42] By the time the Molesworth Committee collected evidence on transportation in 1837, it was already widely accepted that transportation had lost its deterrent effect. The views put before Molesworth confirmed this conclusion. One of the Poor Law Commissioners, the Rev. Henry Bishop, stated that among the general public most did not fear transportation, 'in fact, they rather looked to it as a reward' and he did not find the general public to be ignorant about conditions in New South Wales; many saw transportation simply as emigration ' . . . the transport would consider he was going out to emigrate; in fact, that there would be very little difference between those who went out as emigrants, and those who went out under sentence of transport'.[43] John Ward, who visited some 14 prisons and interviewed prisoners extensively on the subject of transportation, found that it was not dreaded, though he thought the prisoners were ignorant — 'scarcely one of them had any idea of the place to which they were going, or of the punishment that awaited them', but whatever the conditions in the colonies, the prisoners told Ward, they could not be worse than those inside an English gaol.[44] The Molesworth Committee came to the same conclusions as its predecessors: transportation was not dreaded and it was not acting as a deterrent to crime in Britain.[45]

On the question of why transportation was not dreaded, various opinions were held. In 1798 it was argued its efficacy was prejudiced by its inequality: 'To some the emigration remains a punishment, to others it may become an adventure; but a punishment should be the same thing to all persons, and at all times'.[46] Achieving this aim was impossible since the treatment of the convict in Australia bore no relation to his crime, general character and behaviour or the length of his sentence, except as regards when he would be eligible for a ticket-of-leave or be freed. This aspect was highlighted by numerous commentators as a basic fault in the penal function of transportation. Governor Bligh reported in 1812: 'If one person convicted of a great offence, and another of an inferior one, come out together, the Governor, having no such information, is not enabled to distribute them in reference to that circumstance; upon their arrival in the settlement they are all treated alike'.[47] Bigge pointed out that a convict's previous crime and character 'are points that are altogether overlooked' — selection was entirely on the basis of capacity for labour 'and not upon any retrospect of their former lives, or characters, or the length of their sentences'.[48] Busby and Scott in 1831 and Sir Francis Forbes, Dr John Dunmore Lang, and Sir Richard Bourke in 1837 provided evidence of the absence of any discrimination in the treatment of convicts on the basis of their past.[49] Molesworth concluded: 'Therefore on the whole, it must be a mere lottery with regard to the condition of the convict'.[50]

Secondly, the material conditions of most convicts in New South Wales were such that it appeared to many in Britain to be quite rational not to fear a sentence of transportation. Convicts received wages in kind and money. Although convict wages were not as high as those free labour received — for 'a convict would gladly do that for a shilling, which a free man would not do for five',[51] — the payment of wages in a society usually very short of labour guaranteed a convict's economic security compared to that of many of the labouring class in England. The payment of wages in kind or money was condemned by the government, but widespread in both private and public employment, as Sir Richard Bourke himself admitted.[52] Convicts were well fed, both on the hulks and in the colonies.[53]

The image of convicts as paid employees who were extremely well-fed, who were generally under-worked and who could look forward to substantially superior job prospects at the end of their sentence (or upon gaining a ticket-of-leave) was one which was persistent in England even though the individual experience undoubtedly varied enormously.

Sir Edward Parry, who ran the Australian Agricultural Company in New South Wales from 1829 to 1834, and was also a Poor Law Commissioner for Norfolk, compared convict conditions with those of agricultural labourers in that county and concluded that in terms of diet, clothes and accommodation the convicts' conditions were ' . . . very superior to the condition of many of the lower classes of the agricultural population in this country . . . '.[54] The Molesworth Committee concurred.[55]

The alleged material comforts of the convict population were partly disseminated in Britain by letters sent home by the convicts themselves. Capper claimed in 1831 to have seen letters sent to prisoners on the hulk from convicts in Australia describing 'living luxuriously after a very short period';[56] the governor of Newgate gaol reported letters sent to prisoners there suggesting their authors 'were going on very comfortably'.[57] James Macarthur recounted meeting a group of potential free emigrants in 1837 who thought highly of conditions in New South Wales on the basis of letters sent to various families in the district by convicts.[58] Others were sceptical: James Walker, a settler, and Thomas de la Condamine (Governor Darling's private secretary) were doubtful if most convicts sent any letters at all; while a number of witnesses thought convicts tended to exaggerate the 'good life' they were leading.[59] Governor Arthur developed a subtle argument — accepted and repeated by the Molesworth Committee — that some convicts' favourable accounts were accurate except that they omitted to mention the array of severe punishments which would be inflicted if misdemeanours were committed; some favourable accounts were exaggerated in order to induce a wife or relations to emigrate (with the expectation that the convict would be given a ticket-of-leave in order to support them); and some favourable accounts were written by convicts whose actual situation was extremely miserable but who wished to obtain revenge on the authorities in Britain by denying the pains of the punishment. Thus, whether by telling the partial truth, exaggerating, or simply lying, most letters written by convicts tended to give a favourable account. This was reinforced by the possibility of a letter written by a convict being read by his master and by the difficulty in sending letters from the more remote — and therefore probably less comfortable — parts of the colony.[60]

The inequality of the transportation experience, the undoubted higher material standard of living of many convicts and the impression conveyed by convicts' letters home, combined to render it almost impossible to convince the general public in Britain, or prisoners in gaols or the hulks, that transportation should be feared. The chaplain of Millbank penitentiary, the Rev. W. Russell, in 1835 referred to the difficulty experienced in convincing prisoners of the terrors of transportation:

> ... we endeavour to represent to them the conditions in which they will be, but they cannot be persuaded to believe the statement; they think they will be placed in the circumstances in which they hear that others have been — that they get into good places, get good masters, get liberty tickets after a short time, and we cannot reason the prisoners out of that conviction ... [we have] spent hours in endeavouring to convince the prisoners what would be their condition ... [but] they cannot be convinced of the severity of the punishment now inflicted in the colonies.[61]

Two lines of approach to remedy this situation were explored: to improve propaganda among the British working class and to intensify the element of punishment in transportation. It was suggested in 1835 that a statement setting out the condition of convicts in the colonies and the severe punishments to which they were liable should be put up in every cell and exercise yard in British gaols and be read out by every magistrate when passing sentence of transportation.[62] To some extent this was put into practice, but, it was reported in 1838, it was generally ineffective: most prisoners could not read the statement, the general public did not see the statements, and many regarded the descriptions read out by judges with scepticism.[63] Even if newspapers carried articles emphasising the punishment of transportation, they too would be regarded with suspicion by the working class.[64]

The most frequently proposed method of intensifying the punishment of transport-ation was to make each convict undergo a period on the road gangs, in chains, for a period to vary with his sentence, crime, character and behaviour, before being assigned to a private settler or the government.[65] Such proposals were objected to on the grounds of cost, reducing the supply of labour to the settlers and the detrimental effects on the convicts themselves. Edward Macarthur, for example, argued that this reform would be expensive to the government which would have to pay the supervision costs of vastly increased road gangs, would treat all convicts in a way which the majority among them who were good workers did not deserve and lead to employers receiving men from the road gangs who had been turned into hardened criminals by the brutalising experience.[66]

The conclusion which was drawn from these surveys of opinion in the 1830s was that transportation did not deter people from committing crime. Archdeacon Scott stated in 1831 that transportation 'has most decidedly failed in producing the effects originally proposed, both as a punishment for, and a prevention of crime.'[67] Heath found 'for the purpose of deterring crime, this system is very inefficient'.[68] Ullathorne put forward the view in 1838 which was accepted by the Molesworth Committee:

> We remove crime from the sight of the people as soon as it is committed, and they never perceive the punishment; the very distance to which it is removed, and the uncertainty and vagueness in which all punishment is veiled, from the remote distance, I conceive will prevent its ever being very efficient as a means of intimidating others.[69]

The 1832 Select Committee Report went further in attributing crime in Britain to poverty:

> It cannot then be deemed surprising that, in an over-peopled country, where a great portion of the community must necessarily be exposed to considerable privation, and where consequently the inducement to the commission of crime, under any circumstances, must be great, that those who have been brought up with little attention to their moral improvement, should, when urged by the pressure of want, yield to temptation.[70]

Samuel Hoare in 1832 commented that it was no wonder that when convicts were released in Britain they committed further crimes since 'under the circumstances of the times an honest man procures employment with difficulty, and a rogue has very little chance'.[71] Governor Arthur observed in 1837

> If you were in any part of England at a time when the poor are suffering very much indeed, if you were to place before their eyes a class of men, even if they were working in irons, and those men had plenty of food and clothing, and were otherwise taken care of, it would not be productive of terror to that class of persons upon whom you want to operate as an example. They see one man getting food and clothing while they are destitute of it, and therefore the situation in which they would be placed has no terror for them.[72]

Transportation did not act as a deterrent. Indeed it encouraged crime since the poor and destitute in Britain saw committing a crime and being transported to New South Wales as a way out. At least, this was the opinion of a number of observers, though difficult to prove and impossible to measure. James Busby stated in 1831: 'I have known individuals who have committed crimes to get to New South Wales, and I think I have known of people who have endeavoured to induce their relatives or connections to commit crimes in order to get them sent out'.[73] No hard evidence was put forward to substantiate the claims of witnesses such as Busby, yet their assertions appeared to reflect widely held opinion. Myth or not, the effect of transportation in encouraging crime in Britain was seen by many to be further evidence of the system's failure.

If transportation did not deter people from committing crime in Britain, could it be said in its favour that it reformed the convicts in Australia? To a large extent this came down to a matter of interpretation of the term 'reform'. To Bigge, writing in 1822, and to a number of the witnesses who appeared before the 1831 and 1837 Select Committees, convicts would be reformed through being assigned to settlers from whom they would learn useful skills, regular habits and responsible attitudes.[74] In the service of a private landowner, the convicts entered 'their period of probation'.[75] Upon acquiring a ticket-of-leave or upon expiration of their sentence, the emancipists would have a chance of obtaining good employment at high wages and thus 'with the opportunity of gaining an honest livelihood, they would not have recourse to crime ... '.[76] Parry described emancipists generally as 'fair-dealing, active, honest people' whom one could trust.[77] Thus, as far as outward appearance and behaviour were concerned, many convicts became 'reformed'. Some, however, could not accept this interpretation: what mattered was whether transportation produced moral reformation — a 'change of heart', and not just better behaviour.[78] Parry stated in 1838: 'The cases in which I should feel inclined to apply the word reformation, which is a very strong word, were very few indeed ... I cannot recollect above 12 instances in which I could say that the moral condition and moral feeling of the convicts had undergone an improvement'.[79] And if moral improvement was uncommon under private assignment, it was even less likely in those working for the government or in road gangs, while after a period in a penal settlement such as Norfolk Island convicts 'became useless, and sink . . . their physical force is gone by starvation . . . their moral force is gone by the discipline . . . they become mere useless machines, in nine cases out of ten'.[80] Molesworth seized upon these views to condemn transportation as a reforming experience: whether treated well or badly by a private master, or whether in government service or the road gangs, the convicts were not morally reformed. Moreover, an unreformed convict population tended to pull everyone down to a lowest common level and to lead to excessively bad behaviour by emancipists.[81] Governor Bourke retorted that this view was based upon 'manifestly great exaggerations'. There was no evidence that the crime rate among emancipists in New South Wales was higher than in Britain or any higher than in other new settlements where there were no convicts, such as South Australia or Upper Canada.[82] Much of the 'crime' Molesworth complained of was nothing worse than drunkenness and Molesworth himself had praised the ticket-of-leave convicts who were well behaved and obtained employment at high wages.[83] Bourke argued that outward behaviour was the only relevant kind of evidence:

> Real reformation of heart and disposition can be known to Him only who is the Searcher of Hearts. It may be stated, however, of the convicts in general, that a large proportion of those who have served their sentences, or obtained pardons, or tickets-of-leave, scattered over all parts of this immense colony, conduct themselves in such a manner as to keep out of the hands of the police and the clutches of the law.[84]

If emancipists did well in New South Wales it was 'by a course of industry and frugality, pursued steadily for many years'.[85] Such gubernatorial pragmatism was not, however, favourably received by the 1837 Select Committee, who could find no reason for regarding transportation as anything but a penal failure.[86]

To the extent that penal efficiency depended upon severity of treatment of the convicts — to deter, punish, and reform — there was a contradiction between the penal and economic functions of transportation. As early as 1798, an enquiry noted: 'It may also be worth enquiry, whether the advantage looked for from this establishment [a penal settlement in New South Wales] may not be dependent upon its weakness? and whether, as it grows less disadvantageous in point of finance, it will not be apt to grow less advantageous in the character of an instrument of police?'[87] Bigge saw no such conflict: as long as convicts were assigned to 'respectable and opulent settlers', transportation would meet 'the colonial as well as the penal objects of the establishment of New South Wales'.[88] However, as the colony became more prosperous, transportation, as we have seen, became less of a punishment altogether. It served New South Wales well economically, Busby (and others) argued in 1831 'by supporting at a cheap rate its demands for labour (to it the most valuable of all commodities)' but was not efficient penally.[89] By 1837, however, the alleged cheapness of convict labour was being seriously doubted. As we saw above, James Macarthur alluded to the limits to expansion imposed by the nature of convict labour and Lang regarded the economic advantages of convict labour as 'rather imaginary than real'.[90] Transportation in some ways was an obstacle to further economic development: it tended to restrict free emigration and resulted in stagnant population growth. The taint of 'convict work' even put off the native born from taking employment alongside convicts, claimed Macarthur.[91] However, if the element of punishment in transportation was increased, the convicts 'would be useless as assigned servants'.[92] Road gangs and other punishment gangs in particular might increase the dread of transportation and its severity as a punishment, but they were not an efficient way to build roads according to the surveyor-general, Thomas Mitchell.[93] In the view of many observers by the late 1830s, transportation was no longer fulfilling a useful role either economically or penally.

Conclusion

Governor Bourke pointed out that in the early stages of development unfree labour was highly valuable:

> The great demand for labour ... has seldom, if ever, been adequately supplied by free people. In New South Wales, by the aid of convict labour, the industrious and skillful settlers have, within a period of fifty years, converted a wilderness into a fine and flourishing colony ... [but] when a colony has attained that degree of internal strength, which removes all doubt of its progressive advancement in numbers and wealth, it will be well gradually to put an end to transportation.[94]

By 1837 the governor and the largest of the landowners, at least, had come to the conclusion that the point had been reached. Transportation had turned a full circle: from an economic perspective it had turned from being an essential element in the development and expansion of the colonies to being an obstacle to further growth of their labour force and population: 'If, therefore, the penal colonies are to continue to depend on our gaols for their supply of labour, their prosperity has reached its climax, and must decline, without such an extension of crime in this country as it must be hoped is altogether unlikely'.[95] Penally, it had turned from being a dreaded punishment sufficiently terrifying to deter crime, to being held out as a reward for prisoners in Britain who behaved well: the 1837 Select Committee recommended that convicts should be given assisted passages to Australia after serving a period of confinement in Britain, this privilege to be 'limited to convicts who should have conducted themselves uniformly well during their confinement ... '[96] Thus throughout the history of transportation to New South Wales, the penal and economic elements interacted. Essentially the aims of penal and economic efficency were in conflict. After 50 years of white settlement in New South Wales, the contradiction inherent in the system of transportation could no longer be fully contained, at least in that colony: assignment to private masters was abolished in New South Wales in 1838 and transportation itself to New South Wales in 1840.[97]

List of witnesses referred to in the text and footnotes:

Arthur, Colonel George, Lieutenant-Governor of Van Diemen's Land.
Bedwell, R., Ship's Surgeon.
Bishop, Rev. Henry, Commissioner of the Poor Law Inquiry.
Breton, Lieutenant-Colonel Henry, in charge of convict gangs, Sydney, 1832–36.
Bromley, Dr. E.F., Ship's Surgeon.
Busby, James, Collector of Inland Revenue, Member of the Land Board, New South Wales.
Capper, John Henry, Superintendent of Convict Hulks.
Condamine, Thomas de la, Private Secretary and Aide-de-Camp to Governor Darling.
Cope, W.W., Governor of Newgate Gaol.
Crawford, William, Expert sent to the United States to inspect prisons there.
Dexter, Thomas, Prisoner at Newgate Gaol.

Forbes, Sir Francis, Chief Justice of New South Wales.

Fry, Elizabeth, British Society for the Reformation of Female Prisoners.

Galloway, Thomas, Ship's Surgeon and Agent for recruiting free emigrants to New South Wales from Britain.

Heath, D.D., British Home Office bureaucrat.

Hoare, Samuel, Chairman of the Prison Discipline Society, Britain.

Lang, Rev. Dr John Dunmore, Minister, Presbyterian Church in New South Wales.

Macarthur, Edward, large landowner and sheepfarmer, New South Wales absentee landlord).

Macarthur, James, large landowner and sheepfarmer, New South Wales.

Macqueen, T. Potter, absentee landowner in New South Wales, British M.P., Magistrate in Bedfordshire, England.

Mitchell, Major T.L., Surveyor-General of New South Wales.

Mudie, James, large landowner, New South Wales.

Murdock, P., landowner, New South Wales; dairy farmer, Van Diemen's Land.

Owen, S., Overseer, convict hulk, *Fortitude*, Chatham Dockyard.

Parry, Sir Edward, Commissioner of the Australian Agricultural Company.

Price, Dr M., Ship's Surgeon.

Riley, Alexander, Merchant and Magistrate, New South Wales.

Rutherford, Dr George, Ship's Surgeon.

Russell, John, Commandant Port Arthur.

Scott, Rev. T.H., Anglican Archdeacon in New South Wales.

Stephen, John, Magistrate, New South Wales.

Ullathorne, Very Rev. William, Catholic Vicar-general of New Holland and Van Diemen's Land.

Wakefield, Edward Gibbon, Prison Reformer, promotor of emigration schemes.

Walker, James, landowner and sheepfarmer, New South Wales.

Walker, William, Sydney merchant and shipowner.

Ward, John, Home Office investigator of English prisons.

Wentworth, W.C., lawyer, politician, large landowner and sheepfarmer, New South Wales.

Wontner, James, Keeper at Newgate Gaol.

NOTES

1. Paper on secondary punishment by D.D. Heath, *Report from the Select Committee on Transportation*, British Parliamentary Papers (hereafter P.P.) 1837, XIX, C518 (Appendix 10), 258.
2. *Report from the Select Committee on Convict Establishments*, P.P. 1810, IV, C348, 16 [originally published in 1798 and reprinted in 1810]; *Report from the Select Committee on Transportation*, P.P. 1812, II, C306, 48; *Report from the Select Committee on Secondary Punishments*, P.P., 1831, VII, C276; *Report from the Select Committee on Gaols and Houses of Correction*, P.P., 1835, XI, C438, 277.
3. Evidence of Alexander Riley, *Report from the Select Committee on the State of Gaols*, P.P. 1819, VII, C579, 12; Evidence of William Walker, *S.C. on Secondary Punishments*, 1831, 63.
4. Evidence of Admiral Hunter, *S.C. on Transportation*, 1812, 19.
5. Evidence of William Bligh, *S.C. on Transportation*, 1812, 29.
6. *Report from the Select Committee on Transportation*, P.P., 1837–38, XXII, C669, vi.
7. *S.C. on Transportation*, 1812, p.12.
8. *Report from the Commissioner of Inquiry into the State of the Colony of New South Wales (Bigge Report)*, P.P., 1822, XX, C448, 76.

9.Evidence of James Busby, *S.C. on Secondary Punishments*, 1831, 76.
10.Busby 1831, 84; Evidence of James Macarthur, *S.C. on Transportation*, 1837, 164; Evidence of Sir Edward Parry, *S.C. on Transportation*, 1837–38, 63.
11.J. Macarthur 1837, 164.
12.Sir Richard Bourke to Lord Glenelg, 4 December 1837, *S.C. on Transportation*, 1837–38 (Appendix (C) No. 41), 231.
13.*S.C. on Transportation*, 1837, 305.
14.J. Macarthur 1837, 164–5.
15.Evidence of James Macarthur, *S.C. on Transportation*, 1837–38, 7.
16.Parry 1838, 63, 65.
17.J. Macarthur 1838, 9. Evidence of Henry Breton, *S.C. on Transportation*, 1837, 156.
18.J. Macarthur 1837, 166; J. Macarthur 1838, 12; Parry 1838, 70.
19.Riley 1819, 11; Evidence of Rev. Henry Bishop, *S.C. on Transportation*, 1837, 157; J. Macarthur 1837, 207; Evidence of John Russell, *S.C. on Transportation Committee on Transportation*, 1837–38, 61.
20.Evidence of Major T.L. Mitchell, *S.C. on Transportation*, 1837–38, 79–80.
21.Evidence of James Mudie, *S.C. on Transportation, 1837*, 36; Breton 1837, 156; J. Macarthur 1837, 269.
22.E. Macarthur, 1831, 114; Evidence of John Stephen, *Report from the Select Committee on Secondary Punishments*, P.P., 1831–32, VII, C547, 29. The Land Fund channelled money raised from the sale of Crown Land to subsidies for immigration.
23.*S.C. on Transportation*, 1837–38, XXXV.
24.'Paper Respecting Immigration. (Indian and European) into New South Wales', Appendix (B) of *S.C. on Transportation*, 1837–38.
25.J. Macarthur 1838, 7; Parry 1838, 68; Evidence of John Dunmore Lang, *S.C. on Transportation*, 1837, 265–6.
26.J. Macarthur 1837, 208; Evidence of J. Macqueen, *S.C. on Secondary Punishments*, 1831, 94–5
27.Heath 1837, 265–66; *S.C. on Transportation*, 1837–38, xx.
28.*S.C. on Transportation*, 1812, 12.
29.Heath 1837, 279.
30.Evidence of E.E. Bromley M.D., *Report from the Select Committee on the State of Gaols*, P.P., 1819, VII, C579, 104; Evidence of R. Bedwell, *S.C. on State of Gaols*, 1819, 109; Evidence of Rev. William Ullathorne, *S.C. on Transportation*, 1837–38, 15.
31.Evidence of Dr George Rutherford, *S.C. on Secondary Punishments*, 1831, 67–9; Galloway 1837, 186.
32.Fry 1831, 125–26.
33.Heath 1837, 277.
34.*S.C. on Transportation*, 1837–38, xxxvi.
35.Capper 1831, 54.
36.Evidence of James Wontner, *S.C. on Secondary Punishments*, 1831, 31.
37.Wakefield 1831, 99.
38.*S.C. on Secondary Punishments*, 1831–32, 16.
39.*S.C. on Secondary Punishments*, 20.
40.Evidence of W.W. Cope, *S.C. on Gaols*, 1835, 304.
41.Owen 1835, 255.
42.Hoare 1835, 27; Evidence of William Crawford, *S.C. on Gaols*, 1835, 14.
43.Evidence of Rev. Henry Bishop, *S.C. on Transportation*, 1837, 156–57; Evidence of Dr M. Price, *S.C. on Transportation*, 1837, 268; Galloway 1837, 183.
44.Evidence of John Ward, *S.C. on Transportation*, 1837–38, 1.
45.*S.C. on Transportation*, 1837–38, xix.
46.*S.C. on Convict Establishments*, 1810, 27.
47.Bligh 1812, 33.
48.*Bigge Report*, 1822, 17, 103.
49.Busby 1831, 81; Busby 1831 (Appendix) 127; Scott 1831, 146; Forbes 1837, 3; Lang 1837, 247; Bourke to Glenelg 1837, 231.
50.*S.C. on Transportation*, 1837, 4.
51.Breton 1837, 151.
52.Bourke to Glenelg 1837, 232.
53.Capper 1831, 52; Busby 1831, 126; Mudie 1837, 32; Heath 1877, 267.
54.Parry 1838, 63.
55.*S.C. on Transportation*, 1831–32, xx; see also: Ullathorne 1838, 33.
56.Capper 1831, 54.
57.Cope 1835, 305.
58.J. Macarthur 1838, 6.
59.J. Walker 1831, 59; Condamine 1831, 73; see also Ward 1838, 3.

60. *S.C. on Transportation*, 1837–38, xix.
61. Russell 1835, 61.
62. Hoare 1835, 27.
63. Ward 1838, 3–4.
64. *S.C. on Transportation*, 1837–38, xx.
65. Wakefield 1831, 100–01; J. Walker 1831, 60; W. Walker 1831, 64–65; Busby 1831 (Appendix), 130–31.
66. E. Macarthur 1831, 114; Stephen 1832, 28.
67. Scott 1831, 145.
68. Heath 1837, 264; see also Ward 1838, 5.
69. Ullathorne 1838, 33; *S.C. on Transportation*, 1837–38, xxi.
70. *S.C. on Secondary Punishments*, 1831–32, 20.
71. Hoare 1832, 98.
72. *S.C. on Transportation*, 1837, 289.
73. Busby 1831, 79.
74. *Bigge Report*, 1822, 76; E. Macarthur 1831, 116; Scott 1831, 147; J. Macarthur 1837, 198; Arthur 1837, 286.
75. Stephen 1832, 116.
76. Hoare 1832, 99; see also Walker 1831, 65; Parry 1838, 67.
77. Parry 1838, 71.
78. Ullathorne 1838, 19; Busby 1831, 127; Galloway 1837, 184; Lang 1837, 247; Ward 1838, 5.
79. Parry 1838, 67.
80. Busby 1831, 127; Mitchell 1838, 79.
81. *S.C. on Transportation*, 1837–38, xxi-xxix.
82. Memorandum by Sir Richard Bourke, 26 Dec. 1838, *Papers Relating to Transportation and Assignment of Convicts*, P.P., 1838, XXXVIII, C582, 12–13.
83. *S.C. on Transportation*, 1837–38, xvii.
84. Bourke to Glenelg, 1837, 235.
85. Bourke to Glenelg, 1837, 235.
86. *S.C. on Transportation*, 1837–38, xxix-xxx.
87. *S.C. on Convict Establishments*, 1810, 27.
88. *Bigge Report*, 1822, 76.
89. Busby 1831, 127.
90. Lang 1837, 263.
91. J. Macarthur 1838, 9.
92. Parry 1838, 68.
93. Mitchell 1838, 77.
94. Memorandum by Bourke 1838, 12–13.
95. *S.C. on Transportation*, 1837–38, xxxiv.
96. *S.C. on Transportation*, 1837–38, xvii.
97. J. Ritchie, 'Towards Ending an Unclean Thing: The Molesworth Committee and the Abolition of Transportation to N.S.W. 1837–40', *Historical Studies: Australia and New Zealand* 17 (1976), 144–64.

Chapter Three

Transportation as Global Migration

Stephen Nicholas and Peter R. Shergold

Introduction

Analyses of immigration in the nineteenth century, at least after the end of Britain's slave trade in 1807, have been written within the context of freedom. European migration has been presented in terms of individual response to push and pull forces, and to free choice. The movement of millions from Europe to lands of recent white settlement may have been accompanied by the traumas of uprooting but the pain suffered was born of free will. Charlotte Erickson has emphasised the atomistic character of the movement. European emigrants, Erickson emphasises,

> were free people, in a legal sense, free to depart and return at will and free of any obligations to work for a particular employer in a particular place in return for assistance in travelling ... obstacles to freedom of movement were being removed ... migrants had freedom of choice. . . [1]

Erickson, it must be recognised, qualified her arguments. She noted that Brazilian coffee plantations came to rely on contract labour towards the end of the century, and that convicts were sent to Australia. Those qualifications are clearly correct. They are, also, understated. European countries remain far more attached to forced or indentured labour than has generally been recognised. The emigration of whites from Europe, and the immigration of settlers into European colonies, were not nearly so free as standard interpretations have indicated.

This traditional emphasis of historians has been questioned in recent years. David Eltis, for example, has stressed the need for historians to overcome their tendency to write of the two immigrant flows, free and coerced, in isolation from one another.[2] He has argued that the first significant reduction in forced migration from Africa occurred only when the Brazilian slave trade was suppressed at the end of the 1850s, and that not until the second wave of mass migration began in the 1880s did the sum of net European immigration start to match the cumulative influx from Africa. 'In terms of immigration alone' Eltis writes, 'America was an extension of Africa rather than Europe until late in the nineteenth century'.[3] Stanley Engerman, too, has drawn attention to the growing importance of contract labour migration in the nineteenth century, particularly in sugar production. The gross number of contract labourers moving between continents was similar to the size of the flow of slaves from Africa to the Americas in the last half-century of the slave trade.[4] Yet both these valuable studies have continued to ignore the forced migration of Europeans.

In large measure this reflects the fact that the transportation of criminal convicts or political deportees has not yet been analysed within a global framework. Misinterpretations are frequent. Erickson, for example, notes that convicts were sent to Australia during the first third of the nineteenth century. In fact more convicts arrived in the Australian colonies after 1833 than before. Coerced migration played a significant role in the development of Australia right up to Federation. New South Wales, Van Diemen's Land and Western Australia remained dependent on the labour of transported convicts for more than a generation after the end of transportation, while the Queensland sugar industry was developed in the 1860s with the imported labour of indentured Pacific islanders known as kanakas.[5] Engerman asserts that there was only 'one instance of nonfree white migration' (the United Kingdom to Australia).[6] This is simply not true as shown in Table 3.1. The number of nonfree British whites sent to Gibraltar and Bermuda was greater than the number of Chinese contract labourers who migrated to British Guiana and the British Caribbean islands (17,800); the forced migration of French whites to New Caledonia was larger than the flow of African contract labourers to the French Caribbean islands (1850); and the removal of European Russians to Asian Siberia between 1800 and 1918 was greater than the total intercontinental flow of Indian contract labourers (1.3 million).[7]

Such mistakes are not surprising. Australian historians themselves have viewed the transportation of convicts as an exceptional feature of their history. While it is common to note that some 50,000 British convicts had been forcibly removed to North America before the United States won its independence, and while it is recognised that Botany Bay was only selected after abortive attempts to send British criminals to the coast of West Africa, the Australian experience is generally treated as an aberration. The transportation of British convicts to Gibraltar or Bermuda is only usually mentioned in passing; and the comparative experience of France in Guiana and New Caledonia is rarely examined. Asian historians, it is true, have often taken Australia as a reference point. Thus, surveys of the Straits Settlements routinely refer to Singapore, Penang and Malacca as 'the Botany Bays of India', and a history of Russia's east has argued that the 'convict element in the broad history of settlement in Siberia has probably been no more important than it was in Australia'.[8]

British and Indian penal transportation

Effective organisation of punishment by removal overseas was first achieved in 1718 with the passage of the Transportation Act. During the eighteenth century there were introduced an increasing number of offences for which felons could be sentenced to (or reprieved from) terms of banishment. By 1770 the number transported amounted to about 1000 a year most of whom were sent to the colonies of Virginia and Maryland. Private enterprise ruled. The prisoners were committed under bond to ships masters, who were responsible for their safe transportation and who could dispose of their services in the colonies as they saw fit. Those convicts who possessed capital were able to buy freedom on the other side of the Atlantic: those who did not were sold as indentured servants, for between £10 and £25, according both to the length of their unexpired sentence and on the basis of their age, health and skill.[9]

The outbreak of the American revolution brought the traffic in convicts across the Atlantic to a standstill. Thus, as Eris O'Brien emphasised half a century ago, the

American War of Independence 'stands out as the real beginning of Australian history'.[10] The British government sought an alternative location to send residents of her increasingly crowded prison hulks. There was no shortage of suggestions. Canada, Nova Scotia, the Floridas and the Falklands were all considered; so too, were both the West and East Indies. Already, between 1755 and 1776, 746 convicts had been transported to Cape Coast Castle in West Africa. Although mortality had been horrendously high, many in the House of Commons still believed Yanimarew (on the River Gambia),

Table 3.1: *Forced Migration of Convict Labour, 1787–1920*

Period of transportation	Origin	Destination	Flow	Stock
1787–1825	India	Sumatra (Bencoolen)[a]	4000–6000	500(1818), 800–900(1823)
1788–1840	Britain[b]	New South Wales	80,000	12,200(1821) 21,825(1831) 26,977(1841)
1790–1860	India[cd]	Straits Settlements[e]	15,000	4000(max.) 3000(1857) 2275 (Singapore 1860) 1255 (Penang) 532 (Malacca) 1100–1200 (av. in Singapore)
1801–1852	Britain[b]	Van Diemen's Land (Tasmania)	67–69,000	3827(1821) 12,018(1831) 20,062(1841) 24,188(1847)
1815–1837	India	Mauritius		800(mid-1830s)
1820–1920[f]	European Russia	Siberia	916,000(1823–98) 1,000,000(1870–1920)	
1824–1863	Britain	Bermuda	9000	1600(max.)
1842–1875	Britain	Gibraltar	9000	1000(max.)
1846–1850	Britain	New South Wales, Victoria	3000	
1847–1856	Hong Kong	Straits Settlements		94(1864)
1849–1873	Ceylon[c]	Malacca[g]	1000–1500	659(1868)
1850–1868	Britain	Western Australia	9700	3,060(1854) 3305(1866)
1854–1920	France[h]	French Guiana (Cayenne)		3,780(1855) 6465(1911)
1858–1920	India[d]	Andaman Islands	11,373(1906–18)	14,000(max.), 12,000(1901)
1865–1897	France	New Caledonia	24,000 18,078(1852–67) 3656(1867–79)	9,000(1891) 12,000(1894)

a. Bencoolen passed into Dutch hands when it was exchanged for Malacca in 1825.
b. Small numbers of convicts were sent from Canada, the West Indies, St. Helena, Cape Colony, Mauritius, India and Ceylon.
c. Until 1854 small numbers of Europeans resident in Asia were also transported to the Straits Settlements.
d. Also includes convicts from Burma.
e. Comprised Singapore, Penang, Malacca.
f. European Russians had been exiled to Siberia as early as the 1590s.
g. Small numbers were sent to the other Straits Settlements.
h. Small numbers of political prisoners had been condemned to French Guiana during the Revolution: 193 in 1794, and 530 in 1797.

Podore (on the River Senegal), or Das Voltas Bay (between Angola and the Cape) were the best alternative overseas locations in which to establish penal colonies. However, the argument of Edmund Burke and others that such African sites offered little but 'plague, pestilence and famine' made the Pitt government think again. Finally, persuaded by the optimistic recommendations of Sir Joseph Banks and James Matra — both of whom had sailed with Captain Cook to 'New Holland' — Botany Bay on the eastern seaboard of Australia was chosen. The 'First Fleet' of 778 convicts sailed from Portsmouth in May 1787.

Although the Australian convict colonies were by far the most important, they were not the only areas to receive British criminals. The 'temporary expedient' of housing prisoners in ship's hulks in England's naval ports, turned to during the American Revolution, continued for almost a century. The convicts were employed to dredge harbours and rivers, build breakwaters and clean rust from chains and shot. As many contemporaries suggested, their living conditions were crowded, unhealthy and a temptation to 'immorality'. It is equally clear that their employment was deemed efficient, providing a source of cheap dockyard labour available for any exigency. Certainly the hulk system of Chatham, Portland and Plymouth set an example for the employment of British criminals in Bermuda and Gibraltar.

If the transportation of convicts to New South Wales can be attributed to the War of American Independence, the transportation of convicts to Bermuda can be attributed — albeit more indirectly — to the War of 1812. That war emphasised the island's strategic importance for the Imperial government, and prompted the creation of a fortified naval depot on Ireland Island. Initially the labour employed was that of reluctant slaves. But from 1824 — when convicts arrived on the *Antelope* — construction work was undertaken by British convicts under the supervision of imported artificers and the watchful eye of a 400-strong detachment of Royal Marines. Working with pick and shovel, wheelbarrow and crowbar, the transported convicts hacked out of the wilderness a dockyard capable of maintaining a squadron of sailing frigates.

From then until the abolition of penal exile in 1863 the *Antelope*, together with three other hulks and eventually an on-shore barracks, provided the crowded accommodation for between 1200 and 1400 convict labourers. Although historians have condemned the brutality of life between the dark, stinking decks of the hulks, contemporaries generally extolled the convicts' lot: convict warden Stephen Norton suggested that, compared with hulk or prison life in Britain, conditions were good. Convicts enjoyed 0.75 lb of fresh beef four times a week; pork three times; and 1.25 lbs of soft bread, a church service and (until 1847) a gill of rum each day.[11] Principally engaged in quarrying and cutting stone, the convicts were paid threepence a day for their efforts, one penny of which they were 'at liberty to expend in the purchase of the cheap luxuries of the colony', the other twopence being held until their liberation. More qualified men were employed on board the hulks as clerks, cooks, servants, carpenters and shoemakers. All, it was suggested, were 'having the best diet of their lives, and many were labouring less than before their conviction'. Indeed it was rumoured that many old soldiers, weary of the army, purposely deserted to try and gain a place on one of Bermuda's hulks.[12]

The monumental fortress of Gibraltar also owed its might to the sweat and skill of transported British criminals. Desperate for labour the British government turned to the 'Botany Bay' principle. In 1842 a first convoy of 200 convicts was sent from Britain to build a breakwater, and from then until 1875 some 9000 workers were transported to Gibraltar. On average there were about 1000 transportees labouring at any time, representing more than 10 per cent of the workforce. They built the massive underground fort that symbolised both the strength of 'the Rock' and, in measure, the might of the empire itself — a mid-nineteenth century monument to a system of forced migration which one historian of Gibraltar has described, quite incorrectly, as 'an outmoded relic of eighteenth century thinking'.[13]

It was not only English and Irish convicts who found themselves forcibly shipped to British colonies. Among those transported to the Australian colonies one finds criminals sent from the loneliest outposts of the empire: from Cape Colony, India, Ceylon and the Straits Settlements; from St Helena and Mauritius; from Corfu, Gibraltar, Malta and the Ionian Islands; and, after the failed rebellions of 1838–39, English and French Canadian 'exiles'.[14] In general, however, Indian and Chinese residents of Britain's far-flung empire were transported within the perimeters of the Indian ocean. Within this area there existed a demand for labour that could not be met. The British government saw, in the long term inhabitants of its colonial prisons, a ready source of labour to construct public works — roads, harbours, offices and churches. The first overseas penal settlement for Indians was established in Bencoolen, a small British enclave in south-east Sumatra. From 1787 until 1825, when it was transferred to Dutch rule, a stock of between 500 and 900 Indian convicts was maintained. Unlike the white felons who were sent to Bermuda and Gibraltar and later repatriated to Britain, many Indian convicts remained in Bencoolen after their sentence had expired. According to Lady Raffles, the wife of the Governor, writing in 1818, it 'rarely happens that any of those transported have any desire to leave the country . . . they form connections in the place and find so many inducements to remain that to be sent away is considered by most a severe punishment'.[15]

It is usual for historians of Mauritius to argue that immigration of Indian labour 'began on an organised scale in 1834'.[16] This is untrue. From 1815 Mauritius received thousands of Indian convicts banished to the island for life. When Charles Darwin visited Port Louis in 1836 there were about 800 convicts employed constructing buildings and roads. Darwin was impressed with the gangs he observed, unlike the contemporary resident James Holman who argued that the convict parties were idle when employed on public works.[17] Certainly the convicts laboured for the state under conditions which were more generous than those experienced by many of their compatriots who were soon to arrive as indentured labour for the sugar planters. Indeed the major limit on the freedom of the Indians related to the need to keep them apart from the plantation slaves. It is not unreasonable to hypothesise that when the black slaves were emancipated in 1834 the Mauritians' two decades of experience with Indian convict labour helped to persuade them of the value of importing Indians under terms of indenture to grow and cut the sugar cane.

The most important destination for Indian convicts was the Straits Settlements (now Malaysia and Singapore).[18] Over a hundred Indian convicts had been sent to Malacca between 1805 and 1808, before the colony reverted to the Dutch. However its full development as a penal colony did not begin until it was again in British hands in 1822. More continuous was the enforced flow of Indians to Penang. With the exception of 1811–13, during which brief interregnum the punishment of transportation was suspended in India, convicts arrived in every year between 1796 and 1860. But the most important destination was Singapore: from 1830 until the final removal of Indian convicts in 1873 the island held more than half of those transported.

In all some 15,000 Indian convicts, and smaller numbers from Burma and Ceylon, were sent to the Straits Settlements between 1790 and 1860. A significant minority were women. Some 10 per cent had their terms expire each year. Until the early 1830s the Indian government paid the return passage for these emancipists, and perhaps 90 per cent returned home. When that benefit was stopped the number of returning convict migrants was significantly reduced. By 1838 only about 60 per cent of Indians returned and many of these were sufficiently disillusioned at their homecoming to go back to the land of their imprisonment. After 1860 very few returned to India.

According to K.S. Sandhu, most of the Indian convicts were sent for crimes of violence such as thuggee and dacoity (gang robbery and murder); in consequence three-quarters were lifers.[19] Nevertheless their treatment after transportation was liberal and their employment and rehabilitation in the Straits Settlements was carefully managed. The 'first class' of trustworthy convict was allowed out of gaol on ticket-of-leave, only having to attend a muster once a month; the 'second class' of convict was employed in hospitals and public offices and had to return to prison to sleep; the 'third class' of convict — the majority — employed on roads and public works, had to return to their gaols by 6 p.m.; while the 'fourth class' (newly arrived) and 'fifth' (punishment), were confined to prison. Many of the ticket-of-leave men and women were, as in the Australian colonies, assigned to private masters, often working as gardeners or domestic servants for white planters. Other skilled workers — tailors, iron founders, potters, carpenters — took on private work while convicts gained sufficient business so that, after emancipation, they were able to establish their own workshops, forges, kilns and furniture workshops. They, like the emancipist merchants of New South Wales, exhibited entrepreneurial initiative. It was Indian convicts, for instance, who realised the suitability of the *pelas tukus* palm for making walking sticks: by mid-century the sticks, known as 'Penang lawyers', were much sought after in Europe and America.

Most of the convicts were employed directly by the state. A few of their jobs, such as tiger hunting and snake killing, were as exotic as they were dangerous. But many of the tasks to which the Indians were set would have been familiar to British convicts in Australia — they dug wells, drained marshes, excavated canals, built roads and bridges, made and laid bricks and tiles, felled timber and erected massive fortifications. The convicts were, in effect, the public works department of the Straits governments. The monuments that made Singapore grand — St. Andrew's Cathedral, Government House, Canning Fort, the Horsburgh Lighthouse and a score of elegant mansions — were the product of the labour of transported convicts. So too were the roads throughout the island, and every bridge and all the existing canals, sea walls, jetties, and piers. The infrastructure of Singapore, Penang and Malacca was created by the concentrated scourings of the Indian gaols.

In the 1850s there emerged a vocal opposition to convicts as a source of cheap migrant labour which was made more urgent by the panic engendered with the news of the Indian Mutiny in 1857. 'As in Australia', L.A. Mills has noted, 'what was once hailed as a blessing was in the end regarded as a burning grievance'.[20] As a result the Indian government began looking for another suitably distant penitentiary in which to detain the political prisoners of the uprising. They found just such a site 800 miles across the

Bay of Bengal in the Andaman Islands — islands which had briefly served this purpose in the late eighteenth century. Beginning in 1858 when Port Blair was established as a penal colony, and continuing well into the twentieth century, thousands of Indian convicts, most serving long sentences, were transported to the Andamans. The exact numbers are not known, but it was sufficient to sustain a workforce of some 12,000 (of whom about 800 were women) in spite of appallingly high rates of malarial death. Some of the convicts came from Burma; during 1861–62, for example, all the convicts at Moulmein were transferred to the Andamans.[21]

The society created was, argued that island's Chief Commissioner, Lieutenant-Colonel R.C. Temple, a monument to the 'capacity of the [British] race for colonial enterprise and the maintenance of empire'.[22] Writing as the twentieth century dawned, he noted how Indian and Burmese convicts had, under British officers, managed 'to create in little more than 40 years, upon primeval forest and swamp, situated in an enervating, and . . . a deadly climate, a community supporting itself'. It supplied itself with animal food and vegetables, tea and coffee, tapioca and arrowroot. It constructed its own buildings and boats. And, most important, some 600 convicts were employed in the interior, felling and sawing timber for export to India and Europe.

Initially the dacoits and thuggees of India, Ceylon and Burma had feared transportation, but as word filtered back to the subcontinent of the conditions under which convicts laboured, the threat became less horrifying. Govindarajalu, who had come to the Andamans' Forest Co-operative Society as a free man in 1919, remembered the convicts as contented:

> They wore ordinary clothes and were paid a monthly wage of twelve rupees which was not bad at that time. All that marked them as prisoners were their number discs. In their free time they could play games, or go out for walks, or go to the pictures . . . A prisoner who showed good conduct could bring out his family at government expense. For that he received an extra allowance of five rupees for the wife, and two rupees for each child . . . [23]

In the following year the Indian Gaol Committee concluded that the deterrent effect had 'long since ceased to operate'.[24]

European penal transportation

Britain was not the only European government to subject its criminal population to forced overseas migration. Both France and Spain had traditionally sentenced criminals to work as galley slaves. After the abolition of the galleys in 1748, Spain's *presidios* in North Africa became virtual penal colonies where convicts worked for individuals as well as for the state. After the Seven Years War (1756–63) *presidiarios* from North America, together with growing numbers of prisoners from Spain and Mexico, were sent to San Juan (Puerto Rico) and Havana (Cuba) to repair and strengthen the defences.[25] In France the galleys were replaced by committal to a *bagne* in one of France's naval ports. These penitentiaries provided cheap labour for improving harbours and arsenals in much the same way as did the hulks in Britain. Inspired by Botany Bay the French considered, but rejected, plans to establish convict stations in the Malouines and the Marquesas Islands. Nevertheless, following the 1848 revolution, 13,500 unemployed French workers were sent to the colony of Algeria. Some 450 *insurgés* were genuine *transportés* who found themselves interned at Bône and

Lambése: most of the rest were selected from the 'élements indésirables' of Paris who, with some persuasion, chose to migrate to Algeria as rural workers.[26]

Even before then, the Revolutionary government in the 1790s had deported 5000 political prisoners to Cayenne in French Guiana.[27] This set an unfortunate precedent. When Guiana's slaves were freed in 1848 many plantations fell into decay and the areas of land under cultivation declined. Neither the bush negroes (*négres marrons*) who had escaped from slavery in the eighteenth century, nor those slaves liberated in the nineteenth century, were keen to labour on another's land. Few Indians were attracted, unlike elsewhere in the Guianas and the Caribbean and a promise of land in hot, malarial Guiana held no attraction to free French migrants. Gold discoveries in 1853 saw a further diminution of labour supply for the plantations. Against this background French convicts were transported to Guiana.

From the 1850s the French closed their metropolitan *bagnes* — at Rochefort, Brest and Toulon — and turned instead to *transportation* (for convicted criminals) and *deportation* (for political prisoners). Then, from 1884, a third form of forced migration was introduced — *relegation* — by which persistent petty thieves could be sent abroad as a form of preventive detention. Under the *Recidiviste* (Habitual Criminals) Act those repeatedly convicted of larceny could be compulsorily shipped overseas to a destination of the government's choosing.

Cayenne became, in 1854, France's first penal colony. From then until well into the twentieth century the deportation of criminals was to provide the major solution to the labour problem in Guiana. Convicts were employed upon public works and contributed to agricultural and forest development. They could also be hired to work for private employers. By 1911 there were 6465 transported convicts in Guiana representing 13.2 per cent of the population. In addition there were those who had been freed from detention, including a number of Algerian Arabs who had become plantation owners. In 1915 the penal settlement of 8568 was comprised of *transportés* (50 per cent), *relégués* (34 per cent) and *libérés* (16 per cent) able to enjoy freedom so long as they remained within the colony. The numbers included female convicts who had made the voyage in order to marry a male transportee.

Guiana probably represents France's best known attempt to provide a source of forced labour for colonial enterprise. However it was not the only, nor perhaps the most important, example. In 1864, at the other side of the world, and two decades after the first missionaries landed, an initial convoy of French prisoners was disembarked in New Caledonia. Between then and the cessation of transportation in 1897 some 20,000 convicts — *forcats* and *relégués* — were transported. By 1877, on the eve of the desperate uprising by the indigenous Kanaks, there were about 16 thousand whites in New Caledonia — 4000 deported *Communards* and their families, 6000 transported criminals, 2700 military and guards and only 3000 free civilian settlers.[28] New Caledonia then, even more than Guiana, was a colony whose development was dependent upon the forced migration and bonded labour of French and Algerian workers.

Historians of New Caledonia, like those of New South Wales, have generally presented convict agricultural enterprise as inefficient. It is noted that attempts to grow silkworms and cultivate sugar cane proved costly failures, although it remains unclear whether this was attributable to dependence on convict labour. Moreover, paroled *libérés*, allotted small agricultural concessions and given five years to make their farms pay or be hired out to free settlers, sought self-sufficiency through production of corn and beans rather than growing crops for export. This interpretation underestimates the remarkable success of the small-scale cultivation undertaken. Even G. Griffith, implacably hostile to convictism, could not help being impressed by the vineyards, orchards and maize farms established by *libérés* at Bourail. 'I could well have imagined myself driving through a thriving little colony of freemen in some pleasant tropical islands' he recorded. Every 'turn of the road brought us to fresh proofs of the present success of the system'.[29]

Moreover, as in Singapore and Sydney, convicts were employed to build the social infrastructure necessary for economic development. Under the control of military officers, the convicts reclaimed land on which to build the capital, Noumea. They built roads, strung telegraph wires, and worked in forestry and mining enterprises. Most valuable were the *Communards*. Generally skilled workers, they were allowed to hire out their services for pay and 'were responsible for the remarkable development of the Isle of Pines'.[30]

Many other European countries were attracted by the possibility of forcing their criminals overseas. By the mid-1880s, London was worried that both Austria and Italy were keen to use New Guinea as an open gaol. The Netherlands was also interested. In 1864 the Resident of Rhio was appointed by the Dutch government to study and report upon the convict system in force in Singapore. Both the Siamese and Japanese governments sent special missions to study the effectiveness of transportation to the Straits Settlements.[31]

Germany, too, was suspected of wanting to send criminals to the Pacific islands.[32] The appeal of transportation was not new in that country. Most German states had toyed with the idea of transportation at various times, and occasional instances had occurred. At the turn of the nineteenth century Prussia had entered into an agreement with Russia to send convicts to Siberia, and in the mid-1820s Mecklenburg-Schwerin sent consignments of criminals to Brazil. As early as 1835–36 an agreement was actually worked out between the Australian Agricultural Company and the State of Hamburg by which German convicts would be shipped annually to New South Wales. Only at the last moment, when 40 men had been mustered and taken to the waiting ship, did the British Secretary of State, Lord Glenelg, veto the scheme.[33]

The forced migration of criminals and political offenders from Britain, France and Spain pales into insignificance compared with the coerced movement of European Russians thousands of miles to the east.[34] Deportation to Siberia began in the late sixteenth century, and from the mid-seventeenth century 'exile' across the Urals became an integral part of the criminal system. In 1763 capital punishment was abolished in Russia, and perpetual banishment to Siberia with hard labour substituted. By 1820 the flow of forced labour to Siberia was reaching new proportions. Between then and the end of the century it is estimated that some 187,000 criminals, 513,000 political exiles and 216,000 followers were sent to the east, most after 1850. At first the majority were confined to western Siberia, but after the construction of the trans-Siberian railway, the eastern provinces of Irkutsk and Transbaikal gained more. A few unfortunate groups were isolated in the bitterly cold Yakutsl territory in the far north. Most were marched overland via Tomsk and Mariiusk, but those destined for Sakhalin were transported each spring, in the 'Volunteer Fleet', from Odessa via the Suez Canal, Hong Kong and Nagasaki. In 1894, a typical year, some 2200 convicts were shipped around the world on this two month voyage. For the majority who were marched across the Urals, one's homeland was even more remote; those confined to the lower Kolyma in the early twentieth century, were two years' march — or 7000 kms — away from Moscow.

The extent of freedom enjoyed in Siberia by these involuntary settlers varied considerably. Some exiles (*poselentzi*) were able to live and work freely, the only limitation being that they could not return to the west. Others, condemned to forced labour (*katorjniki*), usually in the southern provinces of Nerchinsk, Chita and Sakhalin, worked within a prison environment or, as a reward for good behaviour, in a 'free command' under more relaxed supervision. They undertook a wide range of tasks. Many worked, and then settled, as exiles or ex-convicts, on the land; others laboured on railway construction in the Murmansk, or mined gold in the Turukhansk or silver at Nertchinsk.

Conclusion

Transportation, then, was a global phenomenon in the nineteenth century and the penal settlements, scattered around the world, did not develop in isolation. There was communication and movement between them. Convicts followed the flag. A number of time-expired prisoners from Bermuda were sent to the Australian colonies as ticket-of-leave men and, when penal servitude ended on the island, some 200 prisoners were transferred to Western Australia. Those Indian convicts in the Straits Settlements not pardoned in 1873 were sent on to the Andamans. And when control of the Nicobar Islands passed from the Danes to the British in 1869 prisoners were transferred from Port Blair to pioneer a new penal colony.[35] Yet the forced transportation of convicts has been largely ignored by historians of nineteenth century migration. In the classic tome by Ferenczi and Willcox on *International Migrations* compulsory migration rates just five paragraphs in more than 1100 pages.[36] Even among those who have studied coerced or indentured labour, convicts rarely rate a mention. The suggestion made by Eric Williams more than 40 years ago that transportation might be viewed as an alternative to the slave trade, and that convicted Europeans and indentured Indians both represented responses to labour need, has not been developed.[37]

This is disappointing, for the forced migration of British, French and Russian convicts was a major component of international and intercontinental migration. One might argue that from Table 3.1 'only' about a quarter of a million convicts were shipped across oceans in the century after 1820, but this would distort the contribution that transportation made to the colonisation process. Australia, French Guiana, New Caledonia and Singapore could not have been effectively developed without such a labour inflow; and the growth of Gibraltar, Bermuda, Penang, Malacca and Mauritius would have been retarded without a source of bonded, criminal labour. Nor could the empty expanse of Siberia have been so rapidly populated without the forced migration and servitude of penal and political prisoners: until 1880 the majority of Russian migrants moving across the Urals did so compulsorily, and between 1800 and 1895 about half of Siberia's migrants had arrived involuntarily.

That is not to suggest that transportation was always promoted as a means to meet labour demand. The desire to establish penal settlements that were remote from home, thereby reducing the risk of recidivism, was clearly influential. Nevertheless, even in the Australian colonies, where penal considerations were most persuasive, economic concerns became increasingly important. Transportation, like the movement of indentured servants, was a means of recruiting labour through migration. The major difference was that while indentured workers signed their contract 'willingly' with private employers, transportees were selected by the state on the basis of their criminality. Convictism, like indenture, represented a half-way stage between a slave and free labour system; its bonded workers looked forward to freedom at a clearly defined point in the future. In short, transportation was — like the recruitment of contract labourers — complementary to the free migration of European peoples before the First World War.

NOTES

1. C. Erickson (ed.), *Emigration from Europe, 1815–1914*, pp.9–10.
2. D. Eltis, 'Free and Coerced Transatlantic Migrations: Some Comparisons', *American Historical Review* 88 (1983), 251, 255.
3. Eltis, 'Transatlantic Migrations', 255.
4. S. Engerman, 'Contract Labor, Sugar, and Technology in the Nineteenth Century', *Journal of Economic History* 43 (1983), 635–659; L. Engerman, 'Servants to Slaves to Servants: Contract Labor and European Expansion' in E. van den Boogaart and P.C. Emmer (eds.), *Comparative Studies in Overseas History* (forthcoming).
5. On the importance of indentured Pacific labour in Australia see P. Corris, *Passage, Port and Plantation*; K. Saunders, *Workers in Bondage*; A. Graves, 'The Nature and Origin of Pacific Island Labour Migration to Queensland, 1864–1906' in P. Richardson and S. Marks (eds.), *International Labour Migration: Historical Perspectives*, 112–139; and R. Schlomowitz, 'Melanesian Labor and the Development of the Queensland Sugar Industry, 1863–1906', in P. Uselding (ed.), *Research in Economic History* 7 (1982), 327–361.
6. S. Engerman, 'Contract Labor', 644.
7. Figures on contract labour are from Engerman, 'Contract Labor', Table 1, 642.
8. D.J. Hooson, *A New Soviet Heartland?*, p.29.
9. A.E. Smith, *Colonists in Bondage: White Servitude and Convict Labor in America, 1607–1776*.
10. E. O'Brien, *The Foundation of Australia (1786–1800)*.
11. R. Willock, *Bulwark of Empire; Bermuda's Fortified Naval Base, 1860–1920*, pp.44–5; R. Willock, 'Account of Life in the Convict Hulks' (3 parts), *Bermuda Historical Quarterly* 8 (1951).
12. H. Strobe, *The Story of Bermuda*, pp.64–5; T. Tucker, *Bermuda Yesterday and Today, 1503–1973*, pp.101–2, 109–110; H.C. Wilkinson, *Bermuda from Sail to Steam: The History of the Island from 1784 to 1901*, Vol. 2, pp.453–9, 588, 599–603, 658–60, 676–80.
13. E. Bradford, *Gibraltar: The History of a Fortress*, p.154; See also G. Hills, *Rock of Contention. A History of Gibraltar*; J. D. Stewart, *Gibraltar the Keystone*; E.R. Kenyon, *Gibraltar Under Moor, Spaniard and Briton*, pp.84–5.
14. For a detailed analysis of the ethnic diversity of Australia's convicts see S. Nicholas and P. Shergold, 'The Origins and Character of Transported Convicts' in J. Jupp (ed.), *Encylopaedia of the Australian Peoples*.
15. Quoted in H. Tinker, *A New System of Slavery: The Export of Indian Labour Overseas, 1830–1920*, pp.44–5.
16. P. Saha, *Emigration of Indian Labour (1834–1900)*, p.21.
17. Quoted in Tinker, *New System of Slavery*, p.45.
18. This section draws on C.M. Turnbull, *A History of Singapore, 1819–1975*, pp.45–6, 56–7 and 71–3; C.M. Turnbull, 'Convicts in the Straits Settlements, 1826–1867', *Journal of the Malaysian Branch of the Royal Asiatic Society* 43 (1970), 87–103; K.S. Sandhu, 'Tamil and Other Indian Convicts in the Straits Settlements, A.D. 1700–1873', in *Proceedings of the First International Conference Seminar of Tamil Studies*; K.S. Sandhu, *Indians in Malaya: Some Aspects of Their Immigration and Settlement, 1786–1957*, pp.132–140; S. Siddique and N. Shotam, *Singapore's Little India: Past, Present and Future*,

pp.8–13; N. Rajendra, 'Transmarine Convicts in the Straits Settlements', *Asian Profile* 11 (1983), 509–17; and an excellent first-hand description, J.F.A. McNair, *Prisoners Their Own Warders. A Record of the Convict Prison at Singapore.*

19.Sandhu, *Indians in Malaya*, p.138.

20.L.A. Mills, *British Malaya, 1824–67*, p.274.

21.D. M. Sein, *The Administration of Burma*, p.94.

22.See C. B. Kloss, *In the Andamans and Nicobars*, pp.193–99 for Temple's description of convictism.

23.Quoted in S. Vaidya, *Islands of the Marigold Sun*, pp.21–2.

24.*Report of the Indian Jails Committee*, Parliamentary Papers, 1919–20, I, Cmd1303, 274–312.

25.R. Pike, *Penal Servitude in Early Modern Spain*, pp. 43–4, 141–2, 152.

26.F. Renaudot, *L'histoire des Francais en Algérie, 1830–1962*, p.38.

27.S. Rodway, *Guiana: British, Dutch and French*, pp.139–152; M. Bourdet-Pleville, *Justice in Chains: From the Galleys to Devil's Island*, pp.155–59 and 178–187; R. Belbenoit, *Hell on Trial*, pp.13–19.

28.V. Thompson and R. Adloff, *The French Pacific Islands, French Polynesia and New Caledonia*, pp.240–2.

29.G. Griffith, *In an Unknown Land: An Account of Convicts and Colonists in New Caledonia*, pp.169–73.

30.Thompson and Adloff, *French Pacific Islands*, p.241.

31.McNair, *Prisoners Their Own Warders*, p.x; M. Simmington, 'Australia's Political and Economic Relations with New Caledonia, 1873–1945', Ph.D. thesis (University of New South Wales, 1978), 90–149.

32.F. Schroder, 'Die Deportation Mecklenburgischer Strafgefangener nach Brasilien 1824/25', *Deutschtum im Ausland* CII (1929), 497–8; E. Rosenfeld, 'Verschickung freiwillig auswandernder Insassen der Gefängnisse von Mecklenburg nach Brasilien in der Jahren 1824 und 1825', *Zeitschrift für die gesamte Strafrechtswissenschaft* XXIV (1903/4), 412–25.

33.J.A. Perkins and J. Tampke, 'The Convicts Who Never Arrived: Hamburg and the Australian Agricultural Company in the 1830s', *Push From the Bush* 19 (1985), 44–55.

34.See V.V. Obolensky-Ossinky, 'Emigration from and Immigration into Russia', in I. Ferenczi and W.F. Willcox, *International Migrations* II, pp.521–80; Great Britain, Foreign Office, Historical Section, 'Eastern Siberia', *Handbook No. 55*, pp.13–16; T. Armstrong, *Russian Settlement in the North*, pp.81–8.

35.J.L. Christian, 'Denmark's Interest in Burma and the Nicobar Islands (1620–1883)', *Journal of the Burma Research Society* 29 (1962), 229.

36.I. Ferenczi and W. F. Willcox, *International Migrations* 1, pp.102–3, 111–2.

37.E. Williams, *Capitalism and Slavery*, pp.9–12, 27, 141.

PART TWO

THE WORKERS

Chapter Four

Convicts as Migrants

Stephen Nicholas and Peter R. Shergold

Introduction

The convict settlers were Australia's first migrants. Surprisingly, few Australian historians have recognised that the transported convicts were not just criminals deported to a penal colony. One exception is Geoffrey Blainey whose analysis of the impact of 'the tyranny of distance' has done so much to focus attention on the importance to Australian economic growth of importing labour from overseas. By 1830 Australia's population, excluding Aborigines, was about 70,000 and nearly 90 per cent had been transported or were the children of those transported.[1] 'It is difficult to imagine', commented Blainey, 'that the population even under the most favourable conditions would otherwise have exceeded 10,000'.[2]

Peopling Australia with free immigrants would not have been easy. British North America and the United States were far more attractive destinations for free settlers. The cost of the passage from Britain to Australia, five to six times greater than that across the Atlantic, deterred migration. Even when the state intervened to subsidise the shipping fare, the long period of unemployment while at sea imposed a high opportunity cost upon free migrants in terms of the amount of earned income forgone. There was little chance of a migrant returning home. This led to Blainey's claim that transportation of convicts should be viewed as Australia's first immigration policy.

Historians have viewed the convicts as, quite literally, good for nothings. A.G.L. Shaw described them as 'ne'er-do-wells . . . quite unable to earn an honest living'.[3] The Irish, argued Patrick O'Farrell, were 'dishonest and cunning, often violent and dissolute'.[4] While Australian historians dismiss the transported convicts as 'human serpents', this book assesses the convicts as 'human capital'. The concept of human capital was developed as early as 1776 by Adam Smith in *The Wealth of Nations* when he compared an educated man to an expensive machine. Like a machine, the man who invested in education received higher wages over his life time as compensation for the initial costs of education. 'Capital' is simply any stock existing at a given moment which yields a stream of income over time.[5] That stock includes investments in education, training and work experience, skills, jobplace and locational adaptability and physical fitness. Capitalising the income flow at an appropriate discount (or interest) rate allows the value of the human capital to be measured at its present value. The greater the present value of a country's human capital, the higher and more rapid the growth of the nation's output and services.

Immigration can increase a country's stock of human capital when the migrants are skilled, educated, adaptable and fit. The country of origin loses the money value of these emigrants as a labour force. The Committee on Overseas Settlement in 1922 observed that 'A country from which emigration takes place bears the cost of maintaining the emigrants during the unproductive period of their lives'.[6] The Committee emphasised that 'it is the country to which they migrate which derives the direct benefit of their productive energies. It is . . . a costly business to bring up children who later migrate abroad'. This conclusion is relevant to transported convicts.

One test of the quality of convicts as migrants is to compare their attributes with Australia's current immigration standards. Contemporary immigration policy places great emphasis upon the age, health, skill, education and employability of newcomers. It is largely on the basis of such criteria that immigrants today are selected. There is a second test of the convicts' human capital which evaluates their contribution to colonial growth. The Irish and British who settled Canada and the United States were an obvious alternative source of human capital for Australia. How, then, did the transported convict compare to these free transatlantic migrants?

The data

The primary data source used to assess the human capital of transported workers was the convict indents. These records, prepared before embarkation, provided a detailed description of each convict's characteristics. Each convict's name and six measures of their human capital, namely age (Table A3), sex (Table A2), literacy (Table A7–8), occupation, height and deformities, were listed. Literacy was defined in terms of those who could both read and write, read only, or neither read nor write. Over 1000 separate occupations were specified, often involving two skills such as baker-confectioner, carpenter-joiner or soldier-cook. Variables on conjugal status, religion (Table A6), number of children, and colour of skin provided personal information on each convict. The regional location data, principally the town and county of birth and the county of trial allowed the country of birth and trial — England and Wales, Scotland, Ireland and foreign — to be identified (see Table A1). A rural or urban birthplace variable for each convict was constructed: convicts were defined as urban born when birthplace was given as a town and rural born when birthplace was given as a county. From the location data, intercounty mobility prior to transportation had occurred when the county of trial was different from the convict's county of birth. Each convict's criminal background included a detailed description of their crimes, such as stealing money, striking a sergeant or robbing a till; sentences (seven years, fourteen years or life); previous convictions and date of sentencing. Finally, the ship which transported each convict and the date of arrival in New South Wales was available in the indents. The data only include workers transported to New South Wales.

Ships arriving in 1817–18, 1820–21, 1825, 1827, 1830, 1833, 1835, 1839 and 1840 were sampled and data on 19,711 convicts were computerised, providing information on about one-third of the total post-1817 convicts sent to New South Wales or about a quarter of the total inflow. The data was transcribed alphanumerically (it was not coded) from the indents to computer coding sheets, then punched onto cards before being read into the computer. Altogether 16 boxes of computer cards translated into roughly half a million separate observations to make up the data set. Except for data on literacy before 1827 and Irish occupations in 1825, all the variables on the convicts' human capital, upon which our analysis is particularly reliant, were available for the whole 1817–40 period. Of course observations on particular variables were missing, but the missing information was randomly spread throughout the indents. The amount of missing data was remarkably low, a tribute to the careful collation of data by the British and Irish authorities on each convict before embarkation for New South Wales.

Once the data was fed into the computer, special FORTRAN computer programs were written to correct and analyse the data. A three year period of data 'cleaning' involved correcting spelling mistakes in the original indents and transcription errors which occurred in the copying of the indents onto coding sheets. All spellings, particularly of occupations and counties, were standardised. For example, over 1000 different job descriptions were standardised, then collapsed into 341 occupations as a prerequisite to empirical analysis. Once the data was cleaned and standardised, programs were written to analyse the data. The empirical results are presented not only in the tables in the text and in the appendix, but in the book's quantitative statements. Even the simplest statement, such as the proportion of literate English convict females, required a special computer program and many minutes of computer processing time. To answer more complex questions, for example how the convicts' occupations compared with those of English workers, separate computer programs were required to analyse not only the convict sample, but also the English 1841 census (which had to be computerised as well). A five-line table (such as Table 5.4) comparing the skills of convicts with those of English workers, involved many hours of work over several months.

This book is history written from the 'bottom up'. While the convicts were highly literate, they have been made inarticulate by history. An extensive literary record of their experiences no longer exists, and the books and pamphlets and letters which remain are unlikely to represent the everyday life of the average convict. But each convict did leave an extensive quantitative record providing a wealth of personal information. For example, the indents reveal that William Kilminster was a 22-year-old unmarried Wiltshire man who was found guilty of highway robbery at the county court in March 1826 and sentenced to life imprisonment. He had no previous convictions. Born in rural Wiltshire in 1805, Kilminster was a bricklayer before being transported to Australia, arriving in New South Wales aboard the *Midas*. He claimed to be able to read (but not write) and to be a practising Protestant; he was white, stood 172 cms tall and had no deformities. The 1828 census reports that Kilminster had been retained for government service, labouring at his English occupation as a bricklayer. From the extant records which all convicts left, our statistical analysis allowed us to reach new and startling conclusions about the convicts as workers and the efficiency of convictism as a labour system. The convicts speak not in words, but out of the dry dust of the statistics collected in order to regulate their convict life.

Regional origins

Table A1 presents the convict migrants' source countries by birthplace and place of trial. At the country level the variations between place of trial and place of birth appear small. Convicts born or tried in England comprised 60.1 per cent or 61.6 per cent of those transported to New South Wales, and for Scotland 4.9 per cent or 4.3 per cent. Even for Ireland the proportions of those born and tried were similar, totalling 33.9 per cent and 32.6 per cent respectively. Thus the considerable number of Irish-born who had migrated across the Irish sea before conviction was offset by the number of English and Scottish born, predominantly soldiers, tried and transported from Ireland. Similarly, a comparison of the convicts' origins according to their counties of birth and trial indicated few important differences. The urban counties at the forefront of British industrialisation tended to be a little more significant as places of trial than birth.

The geographical source of the transportees was measured by comparing the distribution of convicts' origins with that of the British population in 1831 and 1841. Most of the convicts came from the heartland of England and the east of Ireland. The 'fringe' counties of Cornwall, Devon and Dorset in the south and Northumberland, Cumberland, Westmoreland, Yorkshire and Durham in the north were underrepresented relative to the population, while Middlesex and Warwick were overrepresented. In Ireland there was an east-west split, with the backward agricultural counties of Mayo, Sligo, Galway, Clare, Donegal and Tyrone underrepresented; Dublin was overrepresented, accounting for a quarter of the transported Irish, but only 4.6 per cent of the population.

A large percentage of those transported came from the cities. About 45 per cent of all convicts were born in urban areas; 71 per cent of the Scots, 48 per cent of the English and 34 per cent of the Irish (see Table A4). The percentage changed over time. Before 1830 a majority of the convict migrants were urban born, changing to predominantly rural born thereafter (see Table A5). English migrants, accounting for 62 per cent of the sample, determined the pattern. The Irish migrants, except for 1817 and 1820, were mainly rural born, while the Scots were overwhelmingly city bred. At least after 1827 the typical convict had been born in and exposed to a rural environment, and, as a result, was more likely to satisfy the persistent calls by colonial administrators for workers familiar with agriculture.

At the country level, whether one uses birthplace or trialplace as the basis of comparison, it is clear that the proportion of English sent to New South Wales between 1817 and 1840 was higher than their proportion in the United Kingdom. The Scots and Welsh were underrepresented, while the Irish were sent to New South Wales in proportion to their share of the 1841 United Kingdom population. The reason for the relative absence of Scots does not reflect superior living conditions or a lower propensity to crime. What lessened their representation among the British urban poor transported to Australia was the fact that the Scots lived — and stole — under a different legal system than the English. The Scottish penal code based on Roman and canon law had fewer capital offences; provided lesser punishments for first offences; and took into account mitigating circumstances. Under this system petty offenders were less likely to be convicted than in England or Wales, and were less likely to be transported if found guilty. The rate of transportation was only about 20–25 per cent that of England.[7] If anything, those Scots transported were more likely to be hardened, persistent criminals than those sent from elsewhere in the United Kingdom. A recidivist rate of 61 per cent (against the average of only 39 per cent for the whole sample) confirms the criminal proclivities of the Scots.

Convicts tried in Ireland were also different from their English counterparts. Far more of them were women. More were married. Juveniles were fewer. The men were an average two years older than English, Welsh and Scots offenders. And the criminal records which they brought with them were more likely to be of a minor nature. Robbery and theft of animals were crimes in which the Irish were overrepresented.

Minor thefts predominated. Most significantly, those tried in Ireland were less likely to have been in trouble with the law prior to transportation. Seventy per cent of the Irish were first offenders, compared with some 59 per cent of the British. There was a strong element of social and political protest in the Irish crimes.[8] Quantitative analysis thus lends support to the famous statement of the contemporary Alexander Marjoribanks that 'a man is banished from Scotland for a great crime, from England for a small one, and from Ireland, morally speaking, for no crime at all'.[9]

Age and dependents

Current levels of Australian immigration have been justified, in part, to counter the greying of the Australian population. Without the entry of young adults from overseas Australia would face significantly higher levels of old age dependency. Immigration cannot reverse the process of ageing in the population, but it can retard that process. This appreciation of the beneficial impact that young adult migrants can have upon a host economy is not new. Throughout the history of planned immigration to the Australian colonies, governments have been keenly aware of the value in attracting youthful settlers whose costs of rearing had been borne overseas and who, upon entering the labour force at the beginning of their most productive years, would support more dependent members of society. Age became a criterion by which the state decided to select or reject immigrants. Today, potential migrants, excluding refugees, are awarded 15 points credit if they are aged 20–34 years, 10 points if they are aged less than 20 or 35–44 years, and no points if they are 45 years or older.[10] In 1986–87, only 46.5 per cent of the migrants were in the 16 to 35 age group, while nearly 30 per cent were under 15 years of age.[11]

In contrast with today's migrants, the convicts displayed a unique age distribution: over 80 per cent were aged 16 to 35 years, with 56 per cent aged 16 to 25 years (Table A2). The concentration of the migrants' ages in the prime age groups was uniform across the four major source countries, and also held for men and women. The heaping of the age distribution in the 16 to 25 years-old age band continued throughout the 1817–40 period (Table A3). What was missing from the convict inflow was the young and the old; less than 9 per cent was under 15 or over 39 years old.

Most early nineteenth century crime was committed by young adults and this natural age bias was exaggerated by the selection procedures used on board the hulks. In general 'old lags', deemed by the inspecting surgeon to be unlikely to survive the ordeal of a four-month voyage, were not transported. The surgeon inspectors were zealous in their task of choosing only the fit since they were paid, in part, on the basis of the number of live convicts landed in New South Wales. The selection procedures, coupled with rations which were, in the words of surgeon Peter Cunningham in the 1820s, 'both good and abundant' meant that shipboard mortality was remarkably low.[12] For the whole transportation period 1788–1868 the mortality was less than 1.8 per cent, and for the 1821–40 period it was only 1.5 per cent.[13]

The convict ships had a better health and safety record than the emigrant ships and the slavers, landing an extraordinary proportion of convict passengers fit and well in Sydney. The indentured Indians suffered heavy mortality on the Calcutta and Mauritius passage before 1850, but the most disastrous years began in the mid-1850s with the growth of heavy migration to the Caribbean.[14] Overall death rates were 8 per

cent, but in the worst year, 1856–57, the average mortality was 17.3 per cent and the
worst ship experienced a death rate of 31 per cent.[15] In the slave trade, high and variable
mortality among the blacks ranged between 3 per cent and 36 per cent for the 1712–77
French trade, between 6.5 per cent and 17 per cent for the 1675–1795 Dutch Caribbean
trade, and between 2 per cent and 25 per cent for the 1791–99 English Atlantic trade.[16]

More surprising was the low mortality on convict transports when compared with
ships carrying free emigrants. H.S. Klein concluded that the convict mortality was
'somewhat lower than the regular emigrant movements from Europe to America in the
same period'.[17] According to Bryan Gandevia, the convict ships were less crowded,
(measured by the tonnage divided by the number of passengers) and thus healthier
than migrant ships.[18] They also contained fewer children whose susceptibility to illness
pushed up the mortality of ships carrying free settlers. What makes these lower convict
death rates particularly impressive is that they were attained on much longer voyages
than the short transatlantic run, in spite of the fact that mortality was very sensitive to
passage time. Insofar as passage mortality was a reliable proxy for the healthiness of the
convicts on arrival, then there was no significant diminution in their physical fitness
during the voyage. The fitness of the convicts on arrival contrasts with the experience
of many bonded Indians who required hospitalisation upon landing in the West Indies
and the susceptibility to mortality by American slaves, which was rather crudely
described as 'seasoning'.[19] It seems that only fit convicts were embarked for the 'middle
passage', and that in most instances their fitness was not impaired on the long voyage to
Australia.

Prisoners in the pre-productive years were not sent to New South Wales. For
example, of the 7084 convicts received on board the prison hulks from British gaols in
1838 and 1839, 6 per cent were aged less than 15 years.[20] In contrast, the equivalent
figure for those sent from the hulks to arrive in New South Wales in 1839 and 1840 was
only 0.8 per cent. The selection criteria employed by the British and Irish authorities
effectively reduced the proportion of young dependents which the convict workforce
had to support.

The majority of convict migrants arrived in New South Wales unmarried and
unencumbered by offspring. Of the convicts who arrived in New South Wales only 20
per cent of the women and 28 per cent of the men admitted to being married or
widowed, and of that proportion 3127 had children. The average number of children
per convict parent was 2.8. On the basis of our sample the convicts sent to New South
Wales left behind 8882 children. Consequently the rearing cost for the convicts'
relatives left behind had to be borne by public aid, private charity or family support
networks in Britain and Ireland.

What New South Wales received was a supply of migrant labour with very few
dependents. That employers complained about the quality of the workers they had at
their disposal is not surprising: such statements of discontent are — like birth, death
and taxes — one of the few certainties of capitalist society. What is surprising is that
most historians have been blinded by such criticisms of the quality of the labour force
into ignoring the more obvious feature, namely that virtually all of those offloaded at
Port Jackson were fit and of working age. Where the youthfulness of the convict arrivals
is recognised, the economic implications are often missed. Thus Patrick O'Farrell,
noting that less than one-fifth of Irish convicts were over 30, bemoans the lack of an
'older and more responsible element'.[21]

R.B. Madgwick, analysing free immigration into the eastern Australian colonies before 1851, has emphasised that 'the people of Australia have always been alive to the danger of permitting large numbers of old people and young children to immigrate'.[22] Consequently when a systematic program of assisted migration was begun in 1832, colonial authorities limited financial assistance to productive workers only, imposed aged restrictions, and instructed selecting agents overseas to recruit families without young children. Such restrictions were only partially successful. Colonial officials frequently complained that they were deceived by fraud and misrepresentation into subsidising the migration of workers who were too young, too old or too weak. And the difficulty of attracting immigrants of the preferred age groups meant that the colonial authorities had little alternative but to extend the age limit for assistance from 30 to 35 years, and even up to 50 years if the immigrants had families of working age. The age structure of convicts forcibly transported to the Australian colonies was far better adapted to the population needs of a land of recent white settlement than that of migrants, assisted or unassisted, who chose to migrate. At most, 60 per cent of the assisted and 70 per cent of the unassisted fell in the most productive 16–35 age group; in contrast, 82 per cent of the convicts were in that age group (see Table A2).

It is easy to illustrate just how favourable was the absence of dependents among the convict migrants. Table 4.1 compares the proportion of young age dependents (aged under 14 years) in various migrant flows to the eastern Australian colonies in the first half of the nineteenth century. It is clear that the proportion of children was much lower among those transported. Since at the upper end of the age spectrum the proportion of dependent-age adults was relatively low, the differential between the convict and free migrant streams is explained largely by the absence of children. The instructions to selection agents in Britain to reject the older migrants appear to have been effective. Of the 56,659 assisted migrants to New South Wales between 1827 and 1850, only 2.2 per cent were aged 41 years or more.[23] Of course selection on the hulks also sought to exclude older criminals. In theory no man over 50 was sent, nor any woman over 45.[24] Among our sample of convicts the proportion aged 40 years or more at the time of transportation was only 8 per cent.

If we choose as the basis of comparison the unsubsidised migration of free workers in the transportation era, the low ratio of dependents among convict immigrants is equally pronounced. Analysis of 756,173 immigrants arriving in American ports between 1820 and 1840 suggests that 20 per cent were aged under 15 years, and about 10 per cent aged 40 years or more.[25] The equivalent figures for convict arrivals in New South Wales were 2 per cent and 8 per cent (see Table A2). A survey of 9620 British immigrants who landed at New York City in 1831 shown in Table 4.2, found that 48 per cent of the English and Welsh, and 41 per cent of the Scots, were aged under 15 years or over 40 years: for the English convict arrivals in New South Wales the figure was 7.8 per cent, and for the total convict intake 8.9 per cent. The superior age distribution of Irish convicts was equally pronounced. Of free Irish immigrants to New York City in 1831, 31 per cent were in the same dependent age brackets, compared to only 10.1 per cent of the Irish forcibly transported to New South Wales. Of the Irish arriving through the port of Boston between 1822 and 1829, 29 per cent were aged less than 14 years or 35 years or more: for the Irish convicts the equivalent statistic was only 15 per cent.[26] The relatively high dependency ratio for free British workers was not unusual. Most flows of European emigrants were similar. For instance, approximately 30 per cent of Swedish

Table 4.1: *Young Age Dependents in Immigrant Flows to the Australian Colonies, 1817–51*

Immigrant group	Number	Dependents 14 years old or less %
Government assisted migrants to New South Wales, 1837–40	10,976	42.9
Government assisted migrants to Port Phillip, 1839–50	1,274	33.0
Assisted migrants to Van Diemen's Land 1832–35	2,041	27.9
Assisted migrants to New South Wales, 1832–51	93,385	27.3
Bounty migrants to New South Wales, 1837–50	45,683	25.0
Unassisted migrants to Van Diemen's Land, 1829–35	5,729	23.9
Bounty migrants to Port Phillip, 1839–50	25,090	23.1
Unassisted migrants to New South Wales, 1829–51	31,946	20.8
Transported convict migrants to New South Wales, 1817–40	19,711	1.2

Sources: R.B. Madgwick, *Immigration into Eastern Australia 1788–1851*, pp.223–4; Convict Indents.

immigrants to the United States in the 1840s and 20 per cent of the Danes were aged under 15 years.[27]

The impact of convict migration upon increasing the supply of productive labour, and decreasing the relative burden of old and young-age dependency can be seen by examining the demographic structure of New South Wales on the eve of the abolition of transportation. At the 1841 census 26 per cent of the colonial population were children (aged less than 14 years), and 9 per cent were elderly (aged 45 years or more). In England, Wales and Scotland in that same year the equivalent figures were 33 per cent and 18 per cent. In short, those of productive age in the 'mother country' had to support a much higher proportion of their compatriots than was the case in Britain's distant and 'deformed' offspring. For each Briton in the high productive age group there was another in the low productive age groups; in New South Wales, by contrast, there were two persons in the high productive age group for each child or elderly person. Never again would the ratio be so favourable. By 1851, with a higher rate of natural increase, the ageing of the convict population and dependence on voluntary family migration, the proportion of young-age dependents had risen to 39 per cent and that of old-age dependents to 12 per cent. Even the massive immigration of ambitious young diggers in the gold rushes of the 1850s could not reverse the trend.

Table 4.2: *Comparative Age Distributions: Convicts to Australia and Free Immigrants to United States in 1831*
(percentages)

| | Nationality | | | | | |
| | Free immigrants | | | | Convicts | |
Age	English	Scots	Irish	Total	English	Irish
0–14	35.0	30.0	21.0	1.2	0.9	1.7
15–39	53.0	60.0	69.0	91.1	92.2	89.9
40+	13.0	11.0	10.0	7.7	6.9	8.4

Sources: C. Erickson, 'Emigration from the British Isles to the U.S.A. in 1831', *Population Studies* 35 (1981), 183; Convict Indents.

The unique age distribution and the absence of young and old dependents meant a migrant inflow biased towards productive-age individuals. As a result, the burden of dependent service provision, including education, training, medical and old-age care, was delayed for two generations. The colony was able to devote a considerable portion of its energy to building its infrastructure, ensuring its self-sufficiency in foodstuffs and basic manufactured goods, and developing export markets for the products of its oceans and sheep-runs.

Gender

Not only was the inflow of convicts into New South Wales marked by its low dependency ratio, it was also characterised by a high sex ratio. Most convict migrants were men. Overall, only 11.2 per cent of arrivals were women. However, there were marked variations by birthplace. Whereas just 6.4 per cent of convicts born in England were female, the figures for Irish born was 20.1 per cent (see Table A1). Consequently, while only 28.6 per cent of the male convicts sent to New South Wales were Irish, some 56.9 per cent of the female convicts had been born in Ireland.

The initial waves of emigrants from European countries in the nineteenth century were normally dominated by families and households moving in tightly-knit groups. Of English and Welsh male adult immigrants to America in 1831, one in two travelled as a member of a family. Seventy-seven per cent of English migrants travelled with their families and in the 1850s, 66 per cent of Swedish arrivals in America were family immigrants.[28] This free 'folk migration' of the early ninteenth century changed by the later decades of the century to a labour migration characterised more by young adults, predominantly unattached men. In 1881, only one in eight of the men arriving in America was attached to a family unit.[29] This shift towards males and away from young-age dependents, was typical of the Britons, Germans, Norwegians, Danes and Finns. By the early twentieth century, when the flow of these northern Europeans to America was being matched by a newer emigration from southern and eastern Europe, there were about two men entering for each woman. Of the 9.4 million immigrants to America between 1903 and 1912, for example, only 31 per cent were female.[30]

However, in only a few countries, and for particular ethnic groups, did the international flow of free labour in this later period match a sex ratio as high as that of the movement of convicts to New South Wales. In the early twentieth century only 20 per cent to 30 per cent of immigrants to Argentina were female, and the proportion of women migrating to Cuba, never more than 20 per cent, fell to just 10 per cent between 1916 and 1920. In the same period only 15 per cent of Italian emigrants, and 13 per cent of Portuguese emigrants, were female.[31] With these exceptions, the low proportion of convict women among those forcibly transported to New South Wales stands out as an exaggerated feature even of the typical male dominated labour migration at the end of the nineteenth century.

How did the sex ratio affect economic development in the penal colony? Women were imperfect substitutes for men in the physical occupations, such as road building, land clearing, ploughing, sawing, stonecutting and hauling, required in Australia. Had convict females accounted for 30 per cent to 40 per cent of the inflow like their free migrant counterparts, many of these muscle power tasks could not have been undertaken so efficiently. The level of agricultural output and the provision of infrastructure would have been lower, and economic growth and development slower.

One must be careful not to simplify the story. Perceptions and mores were as significant as physical processes in lessening the economic value of women in convict New South Wales. Unlike children or the elderly, women were 'supported' not because they were not able to work but because the patriarchal society of emerging capitalism did not allow them to work. For the women transported to New South Wales there was little evidence that female participation (except during the period around childbearing age) should have been lower than that of males. There was less young-age dependence; whereas 5.4 per cent of males were aged less than 16 years, the figure for females was only 1.8 per cent. The goods the women manufactured, such as clothing, often provided a substitute for imported goods. Katrina Alford has reminded historians that the economic value of female convicts as domestic servants has been underestimated, as has the value of their labour for the government.[32] But the fact is that because women's labour was undervalued, women convicts were also underemployed; females had few employment options and were always in excess supply.[33]

The increasing emphasis on the assignment of convicts to private masters during the 1820s and 1830s worsened the plight of women, with an increased proportion of female convicts remaining underemployed in government service. The rising number of such women led to Darling's request that the Colonial Office suspend female transportation for 12 months.[34] The failure to value the work of female convicts and to utilise their skills squandered a productive resource. Not only did women bring useful skills to the colony, but there was no retraining necessary for their use in Australia. Unlike men, the sewing, cooking, laundering and domestic skills of women were immediately adaptable without costly restructuring. But, given the attitudes of colonial administrations, a larger inflow of women would have compounded the problem of 'oversupply'. Australia was fortunate that an overwhelming proportion of the convict inflow were men, who were fully employed in New South Wales.

The sex imbalance also served to reduce the natural growth of population, giving the population and labour force in New South Wales a unique age and sex profile. Table 4.3 displays Butlin's recent estimates of the high proportion of workforce males in the total population and the overwhelming contribution of convicts and ex-convicts (as opposed to free immigrants and colonial born) to the male workforce. The exceptional ratio of male workforce to total population was a function both of the male convict flow and the

Table 4.3: *Male Workforce in New South Wales 1815–1840*
(percentages)

	Male workforce as % population	Civil status of male workforce		
		Convict and ex-convict	Free immigrants	Colonial born
1815	61.4	89.9	5.4	4.2
1820	71.3	94.4	1.7	3.9
1825	71.4	90.4	5.6	4.1
1830	69.4	87.7	8.2	4.1
1835	63.9	82.8	13.2	4.0
1840	55.2	71.3	24.0	4.7

Source: N. Butlin, 'White Human Capital in Australia 1788–1850'. *Australian National University Papers in Economic History* 32 (1985) 18–9.

small natural increase in the colonial born which, due to the low intake of female convicts, accounted for only 20 per cent of the population in the late 1830s. Until 1835, convict and ex-convict female workers dominated the potential female workforce. Thereafter, their proportion fell dramatically due to increasing free female immigration.[35] Throughout the period before 1840 the colonial born women accounted for a small stable 15 per cent of the female workforce. The peculiar shaping of the colonial population and workforce through the sex and age profiles of the convicts created an exceptional ratio of working males to the total population, providing a unique workforce base upon which to build economic growth.

Migrant experience

Uprooting from one's homeland is often a traumatic process. And the pain suffered can be expensive both to the individual and to the host society. Leaving the stability of one's own parish or town, cutting one's ties with a supportive network of family and friends, imposes non-pecuniary 'psychic costs' on an individual which offset to some extent the economic benefits to be derived from migration. Homesickness — for that is how the psychic cost is generally felt — weighs heavily in the heart of many migrants, increasing in intensity with the distance one has travelled from the security of home. Fear of personal dissatisfaction reduces the likelihood of migration: experience of dissatisfaction diminishes the value of a migrant to the host society. The migrant's productivity may be reduced. This applies equally to the convicts, many of whom missed home as well as freedom.

It is because of such feelings that free individuals approach the decision to migrate with caution. Perhaps only a minority of free migrants make a single, momentous decision to leave home for overseas. Migration often occurs by stages. Indeed it is more than a century ago that the statistician, E.G. Ravenstein, in attempting to formulate the laws of migration, posited a wave model in which the bulk of internal migration was perceived as a drift towards urban areas by successive steps.[36] There can be little doubt that this cumulating experience of migration can ease the traumas involved in moving overseas. The emigrant who has experimented with migration over short distances or for brief periods gradually learns to cope with separation and newness. It is therefore of significance that a large proportion of the convicts sent to New South Wales had experienced free migration before they were sentenced to forced migration, thus easing their adjustment to Australia.

By comparing the birthplace of convicts with their county of trial, the extent of pre-transportation migration can be easily calculated. We assume that crimes were committed in the offenders' county of residence. Undoubtedly some crimes were committed in counties contiguous to the criminals' place of residence, but such cross-border crimes were random and there is no evidence to suggest any systematic bias. True, the measure of intercounty migration is crude. It underestimates the incidence of mobility for two reasons. Firstly, intracounty movement cannot be ident-ified. Secondly, it cannot identify those born and tried in the same county, but who between their infancy and conviction had lived elsewhere. What one can calculate from the convict records is a minimum estimate of the convicts' intercounty migration before they were forcibly removed to Australia. The figures that emerge point to a highly mobile population. Analysis of the patterns of internal migration reveals that at least 38 per cent of the English and Irish convicts transported to New South Wales between 1817 and 1840 had already left their county of birth before finding themselves shipped to the other side of the world. This mobility does not reflect an over represen-tation of convict occupations in which travel was a requirement of the job — soldiers, sailors and seamen. All convicts, from unskilled labourers and general servants to artisans, experienced high levels of mobility before transportation. This is not true just for the English; the figures suggest that at least 57 per cent of Welsh-born convicts, and 58 per cent of Scots, had left their county of birth prior to their trial. In Ireland the figure was 41 per cent. Indeed the English were the least mobile with 'only' 35 per cent of those born in England having moved away from their native county.

Many convicts had, in the course of their pre-transportation lives, moved consider-able distances. Analysing the 3225 English men and women who had moved from their county of birth prior to conviction, the road distance travelled indicates that over one-half had travelled 70 miles or more. Table 4.4 reveals that most intercounty migration was over medium distances; 60 per cent of the convicts had moved between 30 and 110 miles. There was short-distance movement between Middlesex and the Home Counties; between Cheshire, Lancashire and Yorkshire; and between Shropshire, Staffordshire, Warwickshire and Worcestershire. But there was also con-siderable long distance movement into the manufacturing heartland of Lancashire and, more importantly, into the commercial metropolis of London — particularly from Yorkshire, Lancashire and Devon. More than half the English convicts who moved did so to a non-adjacent county; more than one-quarter had travelled in excess of 140 miles from their county of birth.

Irish convicts evidenced a similar pattern of mobility prior to their transportation. Table 4.4 shows that intercounty mobility for half of those who moved within Ireland involved distances of between 30 and 99 miles. Some two-thirds of the internal migrants had moved 35 miles or more, and a quarter had travelled more than 70 miles. Of the movers 61 per cent had moved to a non-adjacent county. The English and Irish convicts' experience of mobility at home eased their post transportation adjustment to New South Wales.

These are minimum estimates of mobility. The inclusion of figures on intercountry migration to and from Scotland, Wales and, in particular, Ireland, markedly increase

Table 4.4. *Distances Moved by English and Irish Workers Before Transportation*
(percentages)

Miles Travelled	English	Cumulative	Irish	Cumulative
10–19	10.8	10.8	9.2	9.2
20–29	3.0	13.8	17.5	26.8
30–39	12.1	25.9	9.9	36.7
40–49	5.7	31.5	18.0	54.7
50–59	6.4	37.9	9.2	63.8
60–69	7.9	45.8	8.7	72.5
70–79	4.7	50.5	4.9	77.4
80–89	3.5	54.0	6.3	83.7
90–99	5.0	59.0	3.0	86.7
100–109	5.0	64.0	3.3	90.0
110–119	3.5	67.5	3.5	93.5
120–129	2.1	69.6	1.8	95.3
130–139	3.6	73.2	0.9	96.3
140–149	2.7	75.9	0.8	97.0
150+	24.1	100.0	3.0	100.0

Source: Convict Indents.

the estimates of the median distance travelled. The Irish evidenced an especially high level of intercountry mobility. The indents suggest that 12 per cent of the Irish were resident in mainland Britain at the time of their conviction, representing almost one-third of those Irish who moved counties. Again this underestimated the extent to which the transported convicts had crossed the Irish Sea. Many Irish, paying as little as threepence for deck passage to Liverpool, had probably already been 'birds of passage', returning to Ireland after working in Britain as navvies or seasonal farm workers. The majority of the Irish emigrants to Britain had been born in Dublin (22.5 per cent), Cork (13.7 per cent) and Antrim/Armagh (7.6 per cent); most were convicted while resident in British cities, particularly in London, Liverpool, Manchester and Glasgow.

The number of Irish convicts sent from England and Scotland should not surprise us. Even before the potato blight and famine of the mid-1840s huge numbers of Irish had left their country of birth. Perhaps one million left for America and the empire; at least half that number crossed the Irish sea to Britain in search of work.[37] Contemporaries epitomised these Irish newcomers as unskilled, illiterate and profligate, sharing Thomas Carlyle's concern at the 'crowds of miserable Irish [who] darken all our towns'.[38] Even the positive view that the Irish workers in England contributed to the process of industrialisation characterises the Irish as unskilled and largely rural workers.[39] Whether viewed positively or as riff-raff, the verdict is the same: the Irish in Britain had little to offer but muscle power. This stereotypical characterisation found a distant echo in New South Wales. According to the Rev. Ullathorne, the Irish convicts sent from England were 'the poorest, worst and least educated portion of the poor Irish'.[40]

Yet there is no support for Ullathorne's claim.[41] If one examines the evidence contained in the convict indents on occupation and literacy it is clear that the Irish sentenced in British courts were significantly more skilled and educated than those convicts who remained behind in Ireland. Some 44 per cent of the Irish emigrant convicts could read and write, compared with 35 per cent of those sent directly from Ireland: conversely only 30 per cent of Irishmen sentenced in Britain were unskilled, compared to 51 per cent in Ireland. Our evidence suggests that the levels of literacy and occupational skills of Irish emigrant convicts in England were at least as high as native-born English convicts. Taking the two English counties (Middlesex and Lancashire) which transported more than 150 Irish emigrant convicts, the skill level of the Irish was not significantly different from the Middlesex-born convicts and the literacy level of the Irish in Lancashire was actually higher than that of the native-born convicts.

This greater investment in human capital of the Irish emigrants to Britain reflects a general trend. Irish and English-born movers were far more likely to be skilled and literate than those convicts born and tried in the same county. Using modern migration theory, we modelled intercounty mobility as a way in which individuals maximise their economic returns from investment in education and training. Briefly, each potential Irish or English migrant's probability of moving was described by a matrix, X_{ij}, of personal work-related characteristics, including age, sex, conjugal status, skill, literacy, urban-rural location and job classification. Since the choice of moving or staying occurs with some probability, that probability was estimated econometrically using logit analysis.

The logit model and the standard results are given in Table 4.5. The English migrants' education and skill variables in Table 4.5 are positive and statistically significant. For both male and female convicts the greater the degree of occupational skill and the higher the level of literacy, the greater the likelihood of intercounty movement. The positive skill coefficients are explained by the lower job search costs and greater job opportunities for individuals with general training. Irish migrants also displayed higher levels of skill than Irish stayers. Education, proxied by literacy, allowed English migrants to adapt more easily to alternative locations, reducing the nonpecuniary psychic costs of leaving family and community. Further, education reduced the real costs of information. English women were more mobile than men and there were higher real costs of moving for married as opposed to single individuals.

For the Irish, the sex, conjugal status and education variables were not statistically significant and are not included in the preferred equation in Table 4.5. The absence of a statistical relationship between mobility and education for the Irish can be explained by the bimodel pattern of mobility for pre-industrial societies. Urban opportunities attract both the innovative and ambitious farmers and the rural failures. In a backward and rural economy, subject to conflicts over landholding, there was a tendency for exogeneous economic and political factors to sweep the illiterate out of the countryside into the cities along with their more educated neighbours.[42]

Location, the rural-urban dummy, had a negative and significant effect on the probability of moving, reflecting the fact that the greater job opportunities of urban locations discourage movement. The probability of moving also depended on the industrial sector in which migrants found employment. English workers in dealing, industrial service and public service had the highest odds of moving while domestic service and labour, not elsewhere classified, had a lower, but positive, probability of migrating; workers in manufacturing had a negative (and significant) probability of moving, indicating a disincentive to separate from the most rapidly expanding indus-

Table 4.5: *Pre-Transportation Mobility: Logit Equations for Stayers-Movers*
Model $P_{ij} = \exp(B_j X_{ij}) / \Sigma \exp(B_j X_{ij})$

English		Irish	
Sex (0=female, 1=male)	−0.24 (−2.17)		
Education (0=illiterate 1=literate	0.35 (5.44)		
Skilled	0.47 (4.39)	Skilled	0.34 (2.35)
Semi-skilled	0.28 (2.55)	Semi-skilled	0.14 (1.02)
Age	0.01 (3.15)	Age	0.02 (5.56)
Location (0=rural 1=urban)	−0.24 (−0.42)	Location	−1.26 (−13.16)
Conjugal (0=single 1=married)	−0.10 (−1.30)		
Manufacturing	−0.16 (−1.30)	Domestic service	0.38 (2.98)
		Building and mining	0.45 (1.69)
Dealing, industrial and public service	0.39 (4.25)	Manufacturing	0.37 (2.07)
Domestic service and other labourers	0.17 (1.50)	Transport	0.51 (2.07)
		Dealing, industrial and public service	0.95 (4.91)
		Other labourer	−0.13 (−0.76)
Constant	−1.46 (−8.27)	Constant	−1.51 (−7.50)
X^2	165.20	X^2	345.94
D.F.	10	D.F.	10
Sample Size	6684	Sample Size	3994

Asymptotic t- ratios in parentheses.
Source: Convict Indents.

trial sector. Excepting other labourers, Irish workers in all industrial sectors had a positive and significant probability of moving. The constant in both equations captures agricultural workers and these individuals had a negative probability of moving. The X^2 statistic allowed the null model, with all the coefficients equal to zero, to be rejected for both equations.

These statistical results disprove the traditional historical stereotype of convicts as a wandering criminal class, a species of travelling thief in search, not of work, but of criminal opportunity. The transported workers sent to found a penal colony on the far side of the world were well-suited to the task of transforming that open prison into a capitalist economy. Marjorie Barnard was quite right when, examining the bonded arrivals at Port Jackson, she emphasised that it 'takes peculiar qualities of mind and character to face up to a new life'.[43] Where she was wrong was in assuming that the arrivals were forced to face their circumstances 'willy-nilly'. Many were already experienced migrants. The quantitative and statistical work suggests that the convict migrants had moved prior to transportation in order to seek economic opportunity for their skills. They were well-adapted to building a new life. Their pre-transportation migratory experiences reduced the psychic costs of migration, easing the transition into work and life away from established family and community relationships. For many of those uprooted and enchained, imprisonment and transportation may have been a trauma. Migration was not.

Migrant costs

The fact that the majority of settlers in New South Wales before 1840 were bonded to a period of penal servitude lowered some costs usually attached to migration. Immigration policy today is concerned with 'migration effectiveness'. Australia, since the convict period, has always sought long term settlers and expressed concern at the relatively high proportion of immigrants who return to their homeland: between 1982 and 1987 net migration was only 67 per cent of immigrant arrivals.[44] To the extent that the state has subsidised the passage of immigrants and met their initial settlement costs, and to the extent that returning migrants need to be replaced, then low levels of net migration are inefficient. This concern acknowledges the fact that for most migrant flows there is a substantial return rate, and that net migration is far less than gross migration. Migration efficiency is generally estimated by using a ratio which compares the net number of moves of individuals between areas, to the gross number of moves that take place: the higher the ratio, the more 'efficient' the migration process.

Convict migration was highly efficient. Britain bore the cost of transporting the convicts, a sum estimated at about £57 per person in the early nineteenth century. This was a substantial amount. In 1835 it would have taken a male agricultural labourer or a female spinner two years to earn such a sum; an unskilled London messenger, a Manchester porter or Durham miner just over one year; a Manchester ironworker or London carpenter about 10 months; and even that most aristocratic of skilled artisans, a printer, at least seven months.[45] It would have taken these workers much longer to have saved such a sum from their weekly earnings. The cost of transportation, then, represented a substantial investment for the state. In terms both of Britain's desire to rid itself of criminals, and of New South Wales' need to acquire labour, it was important that return migration should be low. The years of forced labour which had to be served; the geographic constraints placed on movement by tickets-of-leave and conditional pardons; and the high personal cost attached to returning home by 'the tyranny of distance' combined to prevent or deter return migration. Most of those forced overseas stayed overseas. Less than 5 per cent of the convicts ever saw Britain or Ireland again.

Moreover the costs attached to initial settlement were lower for convicts than free migrants. To the extent that the migrant-receiving country has to divert capital from the production process to providing infrastructural support for newcomers and their dependents, immigration imposes short term costs. The selection of convict migrants on the basis of age and health meant that the costs of hospitals and schools was relatively low. The fact that most convicts were unattached males, and that they were subject to penal discipline, meant that they could be housed efficiently in barrack accommodation not generally acceptable to free migrants nor suitable for families.[46]

Another potential cost of immigrants is that they settle in areas and take jobs which are most beneficial to themselves but may not be in the best interests of the economy as a whole. Throughout Australia's white history free immigrants have preferred to settle in established urban communities. To control the location of migrants has been a dream of Australian policy planners. One aim of inter-war immigration was to select farm workers, farm lads and young girls for settlement on the land. In 1923 Prime Minister Hughes caught the essence of the scheme when he stated, 'As the people advance, the desert recedes'.[47] However, few migrants actually settled on the land; in New South Wales only 38 migrants found their way to the frontier marked by the receding desert. Only occasionally has the Australian government directly influenced the immigrants' choice of location. Perhaps the most direct intervention occurred after the Second World War when displaced persons accepted from northern Europe were obliged to sign a contract by which they agreed that Australian authorities could direct them where to work for up to two years. Under this agreement most were dispersed into the Australian countryside where, Geoffrey Sherrington has noted, 'they often found that they had exchanged one form of forced labour for another'.[48]

So too with the convicts. The men and women of the convict ships arrived as forced labour, able to be directed as the state desired. The preponderance of males, and the limitations placed upon family formation by the skewed sex distribution, made it possible to distribute transported workers without incurring the moral wrath faced by Mississippi plantation owners who broke up slave families in pursuit of profits. The fact that convicts could be assigned in the interests of colonial development, and that geographic constraints were placed on them even after they had been awarded tickets-of-leave, meant that the social costs of immigration could be minimised. The shepherds and hut-keepers assigned to the bush frontier of colonial Australia may have hated and feared the isolation of their existence, but there was little they could do about it. Until the expiry of their sentence, they suffered: New South Wales benefited.

Conclusion

The transported convicts were Australia's first migrants, and transportation can be viewed as Australia's first immigration policy. The convict workers had a unique age distribution, with over 80 per cent bunched in the most productive 16 to 35–year-old age group. Only 36 per cent of today's migrants, and 60 per cent of the assisted and 70 per cent of the unassisted migrants in the 1830s and 1840s arrived in Australia in this most preferred age category. Not only were Australia's first migrants young, they were also fit. Stringent medical checks on the convicts' health before embarkation, and lower mortality during their long passage to New South Wales than emigrants and slaves on the shorter North America route, guaranteed a physically fit workforce for the new colony. It was also a workforce without dependents. Free emigration in the early nineteenth century was family migration, dominated by families and households moving in tightly-knit groups. In contrast, the convicts were overwhelmingly male (89 per cent), only one-quarter were married, and fewer still (less than 15 per cent) were parents. Even those who had dependents left them at home, with little ability to transfer remittances from New South Wales for their support. Not only was the cost of maintaining the convicts during the unproductive period of their lives borne by Britain and Ireland, so too was the cost of caring for dependent wives and children.

Since the population was overwhelmingly male convict and ex-convict, males were disproportionally represented in the workforce. The exceptional ratio of male workforce to total population was a function both of the convict inflow and the small natural increase in the colonial born, due to the low intake of female convicts. Depending on their human capital skills and the work organisation used to extract labour, the convicts offered an exceptional workforce upon which to build economic growth.

Transportation was not the first experience of migration for many convicts; over 35 per cent of all the convicts had moved from their county of birth before being sent to New South Wales. The econometric results of our migration model suggest that the convicts had moved to maximise the economic returns on their investment in education and training and not to engage in criminal activity. Their pre-transportation migratory experiences reduced the psychic costs of forced migration to New South Wales, easing the transition into work and life away from established family and community relations. Finally, the transportation of forced migrants meant high levels of migration effectiveness: unlike free emigrants, the convicts were assigned to jobs and sent to locations chosen by colonial administrators, few ever returning home. For all these reasons the convict settlers offered an exceptional workforce in terms of age, sex migratory experience and effectiveness by the standards of nineteenth and twentieth century free migrants.

NOTES

1. N. Butlin, 'White Human Capital in Australia 1788–1850', *Australian National University Working Papers in Economic History* 32 (1985), 8–14.
2. G. Blainey, *The Tyranny of Distance*, p.149.
3. A.G.L. Shaw, *The Convicts and the Colonies*, p.164.
4. P. O'Farrell, *The Irish in Australia*, p.24.
5. M. Blaug, *An Introduction to Economics of Education*, pp. 2–8.
6. Report of the Committee on Overseas Settlement, Parliamentary Paper, 1922, XII, Cmd. 1804, 217–8.
7. Shaw, *Convicts*, pp.164–5.
8. Shaw, *Convicts*, pp.182–3.
9. A. Marjoribanks, *Travel in New South Wales*, p.154.
10. Secretariat to the Committee to Advise on Australia's Immigration Policies, *Understanding Immigration*, p.35.
11. Department of Immigration and Ethnic Affairs, *Statistics Monthly*, October (1987), 10.
12. C. Bateson, *The Convict Ships 1787–1868*, p.63.
13. Calculated from Shaw, *Convicts*, pp.363–8 and Bateson, *Convict Ships*, pp.379–80.
14. H. Tinker, *A New System of Slavery: The Export of Indian Labour Overseas, 1830–1920*, p.161.
15. Tinker, *New System of Slavery*, pp.162–3.
16. H.S. Klein and S.L. Engerman, 'A Note on Mortality in the French Slave Trade in the Eighteenth Century' in H.A. Gemery and J.S. Hogendorn (eds.), *The Uncommon Market: Essays in the Economic History of the Atlantic Slave Trade*, p.264; J. Postma, 'Mortality in the Dutch Slave Trade, 1675–1795' in Gemery and Hogendorn (eds.), *Uncommon Market*; H.S. Klein, *The Middle Passage: Comparative Studies in the Atlantic Slave Trade*, p.232.
17. Klein, *Middle Passage*, p.90.
18. B. Gandevia, 'Medical History in Its Australian Environment', *Medical Journal of Australia* 18 (1967), 943.

19. Tinker, *New System of Slavery*, pp.158, 161–2; Klein, *Middle Passage*, p.237.
20. *Reports of J.H. Capper*, 'A General Statement of the Convicts Received on Board the Hulks in England', Mitchell Library, Q365/G.
21. O'Farrell, *Irish in Australia*, p.24.
22. R.B. Madgwick, *Immigration into Eastern Australia 1788–1851*, p.222.
23. Madgwick, *Immigration*, pp.224–8.
24. *Report from the Select Committee on Convict Establishments*, Parliamentary Paper (hereafter P.P.), 1810, IV, C348, 16.
25. Calculated from *Historical Statistics of the United States: Colonial Times to 1970*, Part I, Series C120–137.
26. C. Erickson, 'Emigration from the British Isles to the U.S.A. in 1831', *Population Studies* 35 (1981), 183–4.
27. Erickson, 'Emigration', 184.
28. Erickson, 'Emigration', 184.
29. Erickson, 'Emigration', 184.
30. Erickson, 'Emigration', 185.
31. Erickson, 'Emigration', 185.
32. K. Alford, *Production or Reproduction? An Economic History of Women in Australia 1788–1850*, pp.163–4.
33. Alford, *Production or Reproduction?*. pp.78–80; 161–4; A. Salt, *These Outcast Women: The Parramatta Female Factory 1821–1848*, p.87; M. Perrott, *A Tolerable Good Success: Economic Opportunities for Women in New South Wales 1788–1830*, pp.28–43..
34. Alford, *Production or Reproduction?*, p.79.
35. Butlin, 'White Human Capital', p.21.
36. E.G. Ravenstein, 'The Laws of Migration', Part I, *Journal of the Royal Statistical Society* 48 (1885), 167–227.
37. J. Mokyr and C. O'Grada, 'Emigration and Poverty in Pre-Famine Ireland', *Explorations in Economic History* 19 (1982), 360–2.
38. Quoted in R. Swift, 'Anti-Catholicism and Irish Disturbances: Public Order in Mid-Victorian Wolverhampton', *Midland History* 9 (1984), 87.
39. J.A. Jackson, *The Irish in Britain*; J.H. Clapham, *An Economic History of Modern Britain* I, pp.57–8; S. Pollard, 'Labour in Great Britain' in P. Mathias and M.M. Postan (eds.), *The Cambridge Economic History of Europe: The Industrial Economies: Capital, Labour and Enterprise*, Part I, VII, pp.113–5.
40. Evidence of Rev. William Ullathorne, *Report from the Select Committee on Transportation*, P.P., 1837–38, XXII, C669, 33.
41. The rest of this section relies on S. Nicholas and P. Shergold 'Human Capital and the Pre-Famine Irish Emigration to England', *Explorations in Economic History* 24 (1987), 158–77; 'Intercounty Labour Mobility During the Industrial Revolution: Evidence from Australian Transportation Records', *Oxford Economic Papers* 46 (1987); 'Internal Migration in England, 1818–1839', *Journal of Historical Geography* 13 (1987), 155–68; 'Irish Intercounty Mobility Before 1840', *Irish Economic and Social History* 14 (1987).
42. L. Bouvier, J. Macisco and A. Zarate, 'Towards a Framework for the Analysis of Differential Migration: The Case of Education' in A.H. Richmond and D. Kabat (eds.), *Internal Migration: The New World and the Third World*, pp.31–3.
43. M. Barnard, *Macquarie's World*, p.111.
44. Department of Immigration, *Statistics Monthly*, October (1987), 4.
45. J.G. Williamson, 'The Structure of Pay in Britain, 1710–1911', in P. Uselding (ed.), *Research in Economic History* 7 (1982), 1–54.
46. See Chapter 13 for a discussion of housing.
47. D. Pope, 'Assisted Immigration and Federal-State Relations, 1901–30', *Australian Journal of Politics and History* 28 (1982), 25.
48. G. Sherrington, *Australia's Immigrants 1788–1978*, p.136.

Chapter Five

Convicts as Workers

Stephen Nicholas and Peter R. Shergold

Introduction

Most historians acknowledge that many of those convicts who rose to pre-eminence in New South Wales society did so on the basis of occupational skills acquired prior to their transportation: Francis Greenway, the west country architect sentenced for 'counterfeiting' (concealing assets in bankruptcy) made his mark as colonial architect; William Redfern, the naval assistant surgeon recognised by Macquarie as the most skillful medical man in New South Wales, became the colony's assistant surgeon; and the creole from St Kitts, George Howe (alias Happy George), transported for shoplifting, had experience as a printer on the *London Times* which made him ideally suited to become the New South Wales Government printer and editor of the *Sydney Gazette*. But most historians imply that these are the exceptions, and that most transported convicts possessed few work skills.

A single reference is often enough to tar two generations. Thus an early complaint of Governor Phillip about 'how difficult it is to make men industrious who have passed their lives in habits of vice and indolence' became the basis for assessing the quality of the convicts' human capital as poor. Historians, dismissing the convicts as 'a disreputable lot' have simply repeated the complaint.[1] There is no need to rely on indirect and contemporary evidence on the workers' human capital; the skills of each transported worker can be evaluated directly from the indents which provide a listing of occupations for each convict arrival in New South Wales. Historians have tended to dismiss the occupational data as unreliable. Lloyd Robson's rejection of the occupational skills of the convicts is the most regrettable since he provided (until now) the only large statistical sample of convict attributes.[2] A.G.L. Shaw barely mentioned the convicts' occupational background. Dubious of the occupational statistics, J. Tobias argued that new prison arrivals in Britain described themselves as of whatever occupation was most convenient for that prison.[3] Two historians, V. Gatrell and T. Hadden, suggested that occupational data were the 'least reliable material' on nineteenth century British convicts. They cite the opinion of the criminal registrar in 1857 that 'as it would be desirous [for prisoners] to claim some honest employment, the numbers classed as in employment would probably be overstated'.[4]

The occupational data, then, has been mostly ignored or dismissed on the basis of contemporary comment. In contrast, we describe the occupational data contained in the indents and provide several tests of its reliability. On the basis of this analysis we find the convicts' stated occupations provide a reliable guide to their skills. Using the indent occupations, and the data on literacy and height which is also available in the indents, the transported workers' human capital is compared with the skills of the workers who remained at home. We discovered that convicts, in terms of their human capital, were a cross-section of the English and Irish working class.

Reliability of the data

The relatively little written evidence left by transported convicts — their narratives, letters and petitions — suggests that the occupational skills brought to Australia by Greenway, Redfern and Howe were not unusual. Indeed the crimes for which convicts were transported bore testimony to their work skills. Thomas Watling, for example, was transported from Dumfries in 1789 for forgery. Described as 'by trade a painter or limner', he was also an engraver who taught drawing to ladies and gentlemen at his own academy.[5] In New South Wales he found employment painting 'the nondescript productions of the country'. He did not think much of his efforts. 'The performances are . . . such as may be expected from genius in bondage, to a very mercenary sordid person [his master]'.[6] No doubt his careful copying of Bank of Scotland guinea notes had been accomplished with more enthusiasm.

William Derricourt, born in 1819 in Kings Norton, was, like so many other Worcestershire lads, apprenticed in the gunmaking trade. His first apprenticeship, to a gunlock filer, ended in a severe beating.[7] He ran away, was caught, and served a month's gaol for desertion. He was then apprenticed a second time to a gunsmith, but claimed that he fled after his master's son killed a lad in a fight in which he too was involved. He then worked as a barge hand on the flyboats that plied the Black Country canals around Birmingham before serving with a hawker of small hardware. It was after the pedlar died, and he pretended to be his son in order to keep his money, that he found himself sentenced to 10 years transportation for theft.

Or take the case of William Buckley. He is remembered in history as the 6 feet 5 inch giant who fled to the bush, living with the Aborigines for 32 years in the unexplored country around Port Phillip. But to us it is his youth that is interesting. Born in Macclesfield, Cheshire, in 1780, he was taught to read and, at age 15, apprenticed to a bricklayer 'to be taught the art and mystery of building houses'.[8] Like Derricourt, his apprenticeship days were unhappy and at 19 he enlisted in the King's Own Regiment of Foot. Court-martialled for 'riotous dissipation' — actually, he admitted, receiving stolen property — he was sentenced to confinement on the Woolwich hulks. His four years of experience as an apprentice bricklayer were not lost. In 1802, when it was decided to form a new penal settlement at Port Phillip, he was chosen: 'Being a mechanic, I, with others, was selected'. Acknowledging that his treatment on the voyage out was 'very good', and that the initial terms of his servitude were relaxed, he emphasised that a 'distinction was made between the mechanics and the rest of the prisoner people'.[9]

Even the most unlikely convicts often had years of training. Consider Charles Adolphus King whose narrative was designed to be a 'warning voice from a penitent convict'.[10] Here was a lad who, in 1818, aged 17, was sentenced to 14 years for burglary. He had, by his own admission, run away to London and lived a wild life in St Giles. Yet even the illegitimate King does not prove to have been a criminal trained from the cradle. Rather, he had been employed as a 'boy' to a firm of calico printers from his ninth to thirteenth year, and even his spree as a juvenile delinquent was short-lived. After 12 months living on the streets he signed up for four years at sea, and was transported only when he deserted a year before his term was up.

Such qualitative testimony suggests that the quantitative evidence on convict skills needs to be assessed with greater care. Certainly the evidence is massive. Of the 19,711 convict arrivals examined, some 95 per cent had an occupational status recorded. It was entered in remarkable detail, with over 1000 separate occupations identified. Many convicts had two skills noted. Often they were closely allied, such as carpenter-joiner or baker-confectioner. But often they served to describe the occupational status of a convict more accurately: soldiers were listed not as mere foot-sloggers and cannon-fodder but servants (often foreign-born), cooks and bakers. Even the young 14 and 15-year-old transportees usually possessed trade attachments: a few as apprentices or helpers, but the majority as 'boys', such as errand boy, bricklayer's boy and bootmaker's boy.

The specificity of the listed occupations engenders immediate confidence in their reliability. What is noteworthy about the recorded jobs is their sheer variety. The occupations were recorded with a level of accuracy and detail far superior to the contemporary census. While convicts stating their occupation as weaver or jeweller may have been exaggerating their craft status, such a claim is difficult to countenance for convicts who recorded their occupations as mule-twisters, muslin singers, watchchain gilders, gunflint makers, sword polishers, strawplaiters, fishhook makers, harpstring makers, equestrians or cricketball stitchers. Can such jobs be merely the exaggerated figment of a criminal mind? How workers believed claims to occupational prowess in these crafts would alleviate their prison conditions in England or New South Wales is difficult to discern.

A quantitative test of the reliability of the indent occupations involves cross-tabulating the convicts' county of trial with regional occupational skills. Workplace characteristics recorded in the indents were not randomly distributed. Table 5.1 shows that the regional distribution of jobs accords with our knowledge of the British economy in the first half of the nineteenth century. Most cutlery makers were tried in Sheffield, knitters and stockingmakers in Nottingham, potters in Staffordshire, and weavers in Lancashire. A second quantitative test of the reliability of the data involves correlating literacy rates with occupations. The results in Table 5.2 are again consistent with *a priori* expectations: those who stated that they were unskilled urban and rural labourers were least likely to possess reading or writing skills; whereas those who claimed to be white-collar workers (clerks or teachers) or artisans (ironfounders, bookbinders, cabinetmakers or jewellers) had high levels of literacy.

Turning to a quantitative assessment of crime and occupation, Table 5.3 calculates for each occupation with over 30 observations, the proportion of theft which was work related. The detailed description of each crime in the indents allowed three categories of work related theft to be defined: stealing tools, stealing goods and stealing from the worker's master, mistress or employer. Theft of tools included tools which were specific to the job, for example, a sawyer stealing a saw, and all thefts which were listed as 'tools' on the indents. The theft of goods involved stealing moveable property and foodstuffs related to the job, such as iron by a blacksmith, sheep by a butcher, or livestock and small farm animals by farm servants and farm labourers. Stealing from one's master included all thefts where the indents specified master, mistress or em-

Table 5.1: *Regional Basis of Convict Occupations*
(Percentages)

Occupation	Warwick	Lancs.	Stafford	Middlesex	Cheshire	Worcester	Notts.	Yorks
Brassfounder	66.6					3.9		
Brazier	25.0		18.8					
Buttonmaker	70.8		12.5					
Cabinetmaker				40.5				
Clerk				44.6				
Clothier								53.8
Cottonspinner		48.8			22.0			
Cottonweaver		56.3			18.7			
Cutlerymaker								
Dressmaker				34.3				
Dyer								31.0
Factory labourer		61.7						
Gunsmith	45.0		10.0					
Ironmoulder	4.1	37.5	4.1					
Jeweller	47.8		4.3			4.3		
Knitter		31.6					57.9	
Locksmith	5.9		52.9					
Milliner				33.3				
Miner		14.4	21.6		8.1			13.5
Nailmaker			11.9			35.7		
Potter			70.4					
Printer				50.0				
Spinner		53.8			23.1			
Stockingmaker							32.1	
Upholsterer				50.0				
Weaver		24.1			24.1			12.5

Source: Convict Indents.

ployer and all thefts by nursemaids, general servants, housemaids and kitchen hands which were listed as theft from inside the house. On this basis about 10 per cent of the thefts were work related, ranging from 0.7 per cent for general servants to 40 per cent for butchers and farm servants. These are lower bound estimates because most thefts were listed in the indents simply as stealing money or stealing clothing without any indication of whether they were work related. While some work related thefts were easily identified, such as horses or saddles stolen by grooms, the indents rarely tell one if the theft of money, clothes, trunks, spoons, watches, food, and handkerchiefs was from employers. Table 5.3 provides upper bound estimates of work related theft for each occupation, where all theft that could be work related was assumed to be connected with the worker's job. If the lower bound underestimates work related crime, then our upper limit percentages, showing about 95 per cent of thefts as work related, are overestimates. What is clear from Table 5.3 is that a significant proportion of crime was related to the worker's employment, which confirms our confidence in the accuracy of the occupational skills in the indents.

An analysis of the 1828 muster, discussed in detail in Chapter 8, links the convicts' jobs in New South Wales with their occupations in Britain. Most bricklayers, bootmakers and blacksmiths, clerks and carpenters, plasterers and ploughmen, were

Table 5.2: *Literacy Rate for Major Occupations*
(Occupations with more than 20 Observations)

Occupation	Read and/or write Literacy rate (%)	Number	Occupation	Read and/or write Literacy rate (%)	Number
Sweep	41	97	Groom	77	435
Caneworker	57	23	Furnituremaker	77	28
Miner	58	130	Generaliser	78	580
Labourer	60	4173	Mason	78	111
Farmlabour	60	403	Ironmoulder	78	35
Ropemaker	60	53	Waiter	79	35
Cook	60	65	Soldier	80	418
Boatman	61	443	Seaman	80	278
Ploughman	62	562	Sawyer	81	157
Brickmaker	64	142	Butcher	81	300
Factory labourer	64	74	Coachman	82	95
Woolcarder	64	29	Cabinetmaker	83	65
Carrier	65	196	Cornmiller	83	55
Locksmith	65	23	Printer	83	65
Herdsman	66	226	Sailor	84	130
Nailmaker	67	60	Whitesmith	84	97
Tanner	67	59	Gardener	85	201
Fisherman	67	24	Barber	85	35
Spinner	69	58	Cooper	86	37
Messenger	69	636	Bootmaker	87	578
Plasterer	70	90	Porter	87	58
Bargeman	70	157	Buttonmaker	88	29
Livestock Dealer	70	22	Brassfounder	88	62
Stockingmaker	71	34	Baker	88	217
Dyer	72	104	Cutlerymaker	89	69
Dresser	73	202	Saddlemaker	89	54
Hawker	73	69	Tailor	89	297
Silkweaver	74	34	Painter	90	146
Weaver	74	541	Cottonspinner	92	47
Brewer	74	22	Carpenter	93	265
Blacksmith	75	212	Greengrocer	93	36
Brazier	75	20	Watchmaker	94	47
Bricklayer	75	162	Coachmaker	96	95
Engineer	75	21	Shopman	96	40
Potter	76	36	Clerk	99	136
Stableman	77	257	Jeweller	100	36

Source: *Convict Indents.*

working in those occupations in which they claimed expertise prior to conviction. Overall, 70 per cent of the skilled urban workers and 60 per cent of the skilled builders were labouring in the same jobs in Australia as they held in Britain. Even 33 per cent of the unskilled urban workers, whose skills seemed a poor match for the employment needs of an agricultural colony, found similar jobs to those held at home. Further corroborating evidence for the accuracy of the indents is provided by the extant bench books. These books reveal that at least a minority of artisans and mechanics appealed to authority when they were assigned to jobs not commensurate with their labour skills.[11] Finally, a recent survey of mid-nineteenth century Black Country trials found that

Table 5.3: Work Related Theft: Occupations with at least 30 Observations
(Percentages)

Occupation	ENGLAND				IRELAND			
	Lower bound estimates Type of crime			Upper bound estimates	Lower bound estimates Type of crime			Upper bound estimates
	Tools	Goods	Master	All theft	Tools	Goods	Master	All theft
Allwork			6.0	42.0			1.5	92.7
Baker		5.8	2.9	98.1		3.2		96.8
Bargeman		2.4	2.4	94.1				
Blacksmith	3.1	4.12		96.9		7.2		84.6
Boatman	2.2	2.2		95.7				
Bootmaker	0.4	6.9	2.4	94.7	1.9	3.8	1.0	75.0
Brassfounder		2.6		94.7				
Bricklayer		2.0		96.7				
Butcher	1.5	40.8	0.8	95.4	1.7	38.3		86.7
Carpenter	4.3			91.4	1.9	3.8		81.7
Clerk	2.5	5.0	2.5	95.0				
Coachman	2.9	2.9	5.9	85.3				
Cook	3.8	3.8	7.5	96.2		9.8	2.4	95.1
Cottonspinner	6.1	9.1	3.0	93.9				
Dairyhand						3.73	0.9	97.2
Dyer		6.3		95.2				
Factory labourer			2.0	96.1				
Farm labourer		41.1		94.7		33.2	0.5	83.9
Farm servant	0.8	40.9		96.9		31.1		46.7
Gardener		16.2		85.7				
General servant			0.7	93.4			4.82	88.7
Groom		9.4	1.0	93.1		9.6	2.1	86.2
Herdsman		33.3		95.5		42.2		
Housemaid			6.7	95.3	0.5		2.1	93.2
Iron moulder		6.7	6.7	96.7				
Kitchenhand		1.3	2.7	94.7	0.5	8.7		92.3
Labourer	0.9		0.6	91.4	0.5		0.2	73.4
Laundress		20.0		97.1		32.2	1.1	96.7
Mason	2.0	2.0	2.0	98.0				
Messenger	0.4		0.9	98.7	0.4			94.9
Miner	1.0	4.1		95.9				
Nursemaid		5.9	2.0	88.2		1.9	1.0	85.6
Painter	1.3	2.5	1.3	95.0				
Plasterer		2.2	2.2	95.7		11.2	0.7	77.6
Ploughman	1.4	11.5	0.3	98.4				
Sawyer	2.5	3.7		93.8				
Seamstress						32.4	3.0	97.1
Silkweaver		6.5		90.3				
Stableman	1.7	4.2	0.8	98.3		9.4		90.6
Sweep		2.1		100.0				
Tailor	0.9	12.3	5.7	96.2		16.0		65.3
Weaver	0.5	7.3	0.5	95.6		6.4		89.4
Whitesmith			2.3	95.3				

newspaper accounts consistently bore out the accused's statement of his occupation. From this, David Philips argued that 'most of the people claiming a certain occupation when appearing in court had at least practised, or did practise, that occupation at some time'.[12] On the basis of the above reliability tests the occupations claimed by convict workers in the indents can be treated with a great deal of confidence.

What were the convict workers' skills?

What then does a study of the occupations recorded on the indents reveal? The occupations of the convicts were grouped and reduced in number to 341 separate categories. The difficulty was, of course, to balance the need to make the data manageable while preserving the significant identity of trade skills possessed. The decision to include within the 'bootmaker' category shoemakers, lasters, cordwainers and cobblers was straightforward; in contrast, the decision to include blademakers and scissormakers under the generic designation 'cutlery maker' was harder, and largely determined by the fact that each separate occupation was represented by only a few individuals.

Table 5.2 presents the data in a detailed but easily comprehensible form. The single largest male group was, not surprisingly, labourers. Over 4000 were classed as labourers or road or factory labourers and another 400 as farm labourers. What is surprising is how few this number was as a proportion of the total intake — a mere 28 per cent. Even adding to that total other 'presumably' low skill occupational groups such as allwork, carriers, cleaners, drifters, gipsies, hawkers, lamplighters, messengers, porters, newsboys, slaves, sweeps, warehousemen and vermin destroyers, the total increases only to 34 per cent. Moreover, the assumption that these groups were 'low skilled' was not always supported by further testing. It might be supposed that those who worked as messengers and porters required little beyond basic common sense and muscle to perform their jobs, but the literacy data indicated that in educational terms these occupations were quite distinct from labourers. From Table 5.2 it can be seen that only 60 per cent of labourers were able to read and/or write, while the equivalent figure for messengers was 77 per cent and for porters 87 per cent.

There are two other main occupational groups which might be placed near the bottom of the skill and economic pyramid — military rank-and-file and domestic servants. Seamen and sailors, excluding officers, totalled 408; the number of soldiers was 418, again excluding officers. Five hundred and eighty male convicts were general servants. Adding to that the more specific trades of butler, coachman, cook, gamekeeper, gardener, groom and valet (not all of whom may have been employed in domestic service), the number reaches 1378 or 8.3 per cent of the total. Even the most generous overestimate of the proportion of low skilled among the convicts transported, including labourers, porters, messengers, military and domestic servants, brings the total to less than half. The occupational data provide no support for the traditional view that the convicts were without useful skills.

In fact, the data reveal a deep reservoir of labour skills, virtually ignored by historians. Some, such as thatcher, are clearly rural. Some others may be rural; for example, at least a proportion of those recorded as blacksmiths were rural workers who made a living shoeing horses and mending ploughs. Grouping together the major agricultural occupations — farmers, farm bailiffs, farm servants and farm labourers, as well as the more specific designations of ploughman, cowkeeper, dairyhand, herds-man, horsebreaker, reaper and shearer — the number approaches 2000 or just 12 per cent of total male workers. Even if one adds nurseryman, gardener, woodman and gamekeeper to the rural occupations, the figure increases only to 13 per cent. Clearly, the majority of skills were urban in orientation. Certain skills predominated: bootmakers, who alone composed 3.5 per cent of the total intake; bakers and butchers; blacksmiths and whitesmiths; tailors and tanners; knitters, spinners and weavers; dyers and carders; brassfounders and ironmoulders; cabinetmakers and coopers; makers of ropes, saddles, sails, pottery and cutlery. Construction trades were particu-larly well represented. Bricklayers and masons, carpenters and sawyers, plumbers, glaziers, painters, plasterers and paperhangers together represented over 6 per cent of the total male convict arrivals. In addition, there were 136 clerks, or about one per cent of total, who operated the state bureaucracy in the colony.

To evaluate this reservoir of convict skills on a quantitative basis, some comparative standard is required. That standard for Australian historians, focusing on the crimi-nality of the transported workers, was the unskilled section of the British and Irish working class. To test this proposition we compared our convict sample with the employed population in England as recorded in the 1841 census. In short, we asked: were the convicts exiled to New South Wales representative of the working class population left behind in industrialising England?

Two skill classification schemes were used to standardise the 341 convict occu-pations and to compare them with the 1024 separate occupations in the 1841 census. The five-skill Armstrong scheme defined workers as professional, middling, skilled, semi-skilled and unskilled (see Appendix A15).[13] The English and Irish male convicts were more skilled and unskilled than the females who were more heavily represented in the semi-skilled class 4 (see Table A11). Similarly, both English and Irish urban convicts were more skilled than their fellow workers from rural locations; over 53 per cent of the urban, but only 37 per cent of the rural English convicts, were skilled (see Table A12). Foreign and Scottish-born workers were the most highly skilled convicts, with only 12 per cent of the foreign-born unskilled. The English convicts were signifi-cantly better endowed with skills than the Irish convicts; 46 per cent of the English were skilled compared with 34 per cent of the Irish. Forty-two per cent of the Irish were unskilled, but only one-quarter of the English. Over the sample period, there was a tendency for the semi-skilled and unskilled English and Irish intake to rise (see Table A13). By the end of transportation, the convict arrivals were less skilled than at the be-ginning.

A second classification divided workers into urban and rural skilled and unskilled, skilled construction, military, professional, dealer and domestic service to gain a finer grading of skill and industrial category (see Appendix A18). Sixty-four per cent of the English males held urban jobs, and two-thirds of them were skilled. The next two largest categories of English convicts also held skilled jobs, with 8.6 per cent of the male convicts being building tradesmen and 7.5 per cent skilled rural workers. The same pattern held for the Scots, except for a large share of workers (7 per cent) from a public service background. The differences between the Irish and English males in our sample is particularly evident in Table A16: 40 per cent of the Irish were unskilled urban workers and only 26 per cent were skilled, with another 9 per cent in domestic service. The women convicts were concentrated in domestic service jobs which accounted for three-quarters of female employment. Only at the very end of the period did the number of unskilled urban workers rise substantially, reaching 40 per cent of the total intake in the last three years of transportation (see Table A17). Until then, rural skilled and unskilled workers and urban skilled and building workers accounted for almost 60 per cent of the male workers. The two skill classifications show that the convicts included a very high proportion of skilled workers, although biased towards urban occupations.

Skilled craftsmen were in demand in the colony, not only in building and construction, but in metalworking, food, woodworking, tanning and leatherworking. It was these building and industrial trades which private masters sought so assiduously through assignment and about which they complained so bitterly when the government harboured the artisans for its own use. It was the skilled industrial worker, too, who most easily earned additional income working on his own account at his trade. Butlin has warned that early New South Wales should not be treated too readily as rural-orientated.[14] The standard of living, tastes of the settlers and the isolation of the colony created a strong inducement to utilise special non-rural occupations. For example, the colony's consumer and producer good requirements, including demand for tools, furniture, clothing, leathergoods, soap and utensils, easily supported an extensive system of artisan workshop production. The transported convicts brought a reservoir of such skills which were tapped to develop the economy. Only at the end of the transportation period were many locally made consumer and producer products subject to strong competitive pressure from cheap mass produced imports from overseas.[15] By 1840 considerable structural adjustment involving the decline of some types of workshop production must have been required. For example, the women who spun and wove in the Female Factory in the 1820s saw their products displaced by imported textiles in the 1830s, replicating in Australia the painful process of decline experienced by spinners and handloom weavers in Britain. Until the triumph of British machine-made goods however, the colony relied on the large number of skilled convicts to guarantee a high level of per capita consumption and rapid economic growth. Of course, this does not mean that there was not a measure of job restructuring and retraining necessary to adapt British skills to fill rural-based job requirements. However, such restructuring should not be exaggerated.

How did the transported convicts' skill compare to those in the 1841 English census? Transported English convicts were, not surprisingly, underrepresented in professional, managerial and supervisory jobs. Whereas 1.2 per cent of the English labour force was located in the 'professional and upper class' category and 8.7 per cent in the frustratingly amorphous 'middling' class, the equivalent convict figures were 0.3 per cent and 2.8 per cent respectively. Over three times as many English workers as Australian convicts were in Armstrong's skill classes 1 and 2 which marks the major differences between the English workforce and the convict sample. At first sight it appears from Table 5.4 that English workers were signficantly more skilled (53.1 per cent) than their convict counterparts (45.2 per cent). This apparent difference is due to the convict sex bias. Only 6 per cent of the English convict labour force included women, while 35 per cent of the English workforce were female. England's female workers were heavily represented in skill classes 3 and 4. Adjusting each female skill category in the 1841 census to correspond with the proportion of convict women in that category, the differences remaining in the distribution of skills between English

Table 5.4: *Armstrong Skill Classification of English Workforce and English Convicts*
(Percentages)

Armstrong Classification[a]	Total	English 1841 census		English convict sample	
		Adjusted total	Male only	Total	Male
1. Professional	1.2	1.6	1.7	0.3	0.3
2. Middling	8.7	9.1	9.2	2.8	3.1
3. Skilled	53.1	48.3	47.9	45.2	45.6
4. Semiskilled	21.2	25.5	25.7	27.4	26.3
5. Unskilled	15.9	15.5	15.5	24.3	24.7

a. See Appendix Table A15 for detailed description

Sources: Great Britain 1841 Census, Parliamentary Paper, 1841, XIV, C52; Convict Indents.

workers and English convicts in Table 5.4 are not significant. The proportion of male convict and male English workers across the five classes in Table 5.4 is roughly comparable, although there were more unskilled workers among the convicts than in the English working population as a whole.

Overall, the skills that convicts brought to Australia were broadly representative of the skills across the working classes in England. There is no evidence that convicts were unskilled class 5 workers or professional criminals, even if class 5 could be considered a proxy for the criminal class. In fact, the proportion of unskilled convicts was almost the same as the 22 per cent of unskilled migrants admitted to Australia in 1987.

The Armstrong scheme tends to underestimate the skill component in the convict sample. There are obvious problems in some of the classes when used as economic indicators. All farmers, for example, are class 2 'middling', no matter what the scale of enterprise or what their property relationship to the land they till; agricultural labourers are placed in class 4 'semi-skilled', whereas all other labourers are placed in class 5 'unskilled'. In consequence, an urban-industrial population is adjudged less skilled and lower in class than a rural-agricultural one. This effect biased the convict sample (with its high proportion of urban occupations) downwards towards an unskilled workforce. The degree of difficulty in ascribing class characteristics to occupations can be appreciated when one takes a different approach and attempts to assess the quality of those workers who — on the basis of their skill, income, education and work autonomy — have been portrayed as the 'aristocrats' of British manual labour. Using Geoffrey Crossick's definition of Kentish London wage-earning aristocrats, Chapter 7 shows that the proportion of artisan workers in the 1841 English census coincided closely with that of transported convicts (see Table 7.2) All this suggests that the proportions of convict workers in the skilled and semi-skilled categories of Armstrong's scheme is a lower bound or minimum estimate.

In Table 5.5 the English and convict workforces are compared using the alternative nine category scheme which highlights skilled and unskilled trades. The convict indents contain many more urban unskilled (category 1) and many fewer unskilled farm occupations (category 2) than the 1841 English census. There were fewer convict dealers and professionals, but many more domestic servants. Skilled building trades

Table 5.5: *Nicholas-Shergold Skill Classification of English Workforce and English Convicts* (Percentages)

Nicholas-Shergold Class[a]	1841 English census	English convicts
1. Unskilled urban	8.2	21.6
2. Unskilled rural	20.3	4.9
3. Skilled building	7.9	8.1
4. Skilled urban	32.4	39.2
5. Skilled rural	6.9	7.0
6. Dealers	5.2	2.6
7. Public service	5.7	4.0
8. Professional	2.9	1.5
9. Domestic service	4.6	11.2
10. Occupations not elsewhere classified	5.9	—

a. See Appendix Table A18 for detailed description.

Sources: Great Britain 1841 Census, Parliamentary Paper, 1841, XIV, C52; Convict Indents.

(category 3) and urban artisans (category 4) were represented in proportion to the English workers in those categories. This confirms the urban trade bias of the convict inflow. However, the proportion of skilled convict farm workers (category 5) was almost identical to that in the census. In the crucial area of rural job requirements, Australia was well supplied from England with skilled rural trades requiring years of training. This greatly reduced the costs of job restructuring, since the retraining involved in turning an urban unskilled worker or domestic servant into a rural, unskilled farm labourer was much less than that required to train skilled ploughmen, farmers, farriers, shearers and reapers. Unskilled workers, whether urban or rural, undertook tasks requiring muscle power. While an urban labourer required 'breaking in' to rural work, such retraining was comparatively easy — and rapid — for fit, young men.

The urban bias in the convict sample is also evident when compared with the free migrant flow from England to America in 1831. Erickson found that 25 per cent of the English emigrants claimed to have had agricultural occupations and only 10 per cent were urban labourers.[16] However, these free English emigrants to Boston included a high proportion of pre-industrial craft workers (34.9 per cent) and commercial and professional occupations (12.4 per cent) less well-suited to forging a new economy than were the convict labourers.

A major problem with both the Armstrong and the nine category scheme was the necessity to group occupations on the basis of pre-conceived perceptions of class and status. Avoiding this constraint, a rank correlation test allowed the range of occupational structures in the census and convict sample to be compared directly. Firstly, we reduced the number of individual job descriptions to 83 of the most important occupations — essentially all English occupations which had more than 5000 workers in 1841. Next, each occupation was ranked in order of numerical importance, in the case of the 1841 census from farm labourers to buttonmakers. Finally the two rankings were compared. The overall rank order of the 83 occupations had a high degree of similarity, as Spearman's rank coefficient of 0.71 shows. If the occupational structure included only urban jobs then the coefficient would be considerably higher. The relationship between the census and sample improved when those occupations not generally perceived to be working class were excluded. Very few clergymen, policemen and customsmen made it into the ranks of convicted criminals. If one excludes eight professional groups from the analysis, the rank correlation of the remaining 75 working class occupations rises to 0.75. Another statistical test, the Mann-Whitney, was applied to the occupational statistics. This is a two-sample rank test suitable for non-parametic data, in which the null hypothesis is that the two compared samples derive from the same population. Mann-Whitney showed a 95 per cent probability that the two groups — transported convict and free workers — came from the same occupational population.

It is also possible to compare broadly the occupations of the Irish convicts with the 1841 Irish census. Details of 183 Irish convict occupations were grouped into the six broad occupational categories as indicated in Table 5.6. For males, the convict sample and the Irish census differ with respect to farmers, category 3. The differences are not as great as they might appear at first sight. In preindustrial Ireland, the border line between farmer, cottier, and farm labourer was not well-defined. Joel Mokyr has noted that, 'Both rich and poor were landholders in Ireland, and terms like 'farmer' and 'labourer' had become fuzzy'.[17] Many 'farmers' had no capital, owned little land, and frequently worked as wage labourers. Although the misreporting of farmers as farm labourers in the convict sample biased downwards the skilled occupational categories, there is no adjustment attempted here to reapportion some of category 1, farm labourers, as farmers. Overall, some 72 per cent of male Irish convicts were recorded as

Table 5.6: *Occupational Breakdown of Irish Workforce and Irish Convicts* (Percentages)

	Occupational category					
	1	2	3	4	5	6
Irish convicts						
Male	71.1	5.9	1.1	16.0	2.6	3.3
Female	91.8	5.2	0.0	1.0	0.0	2.2
1841 Irish census						
Male	55.4	7.1	20.7	10.5	4.9	1.5
Female	33.7	59.9	1.9	0.7	3.4	0.4

1. Labourer
2. Textile worker
3. Farmer
4. Other artisan
5. White collar workers
6. Other

Sources: Convict Indents; Report of the Commissioners Census of Ireland, Parliamentary Paper, XXIV, 1843 C504; J. Mokyr and C. O'Grada, 'Emigration and Poverty in Pre-Famine Ireland', *Explorations in Economic History* 19 (1982), 379.

farmers or labourers, compared to 76 per cent of the 1841 Irish population. The proportions of textile, artisan, and whitecollar workers were similar. Female workers were concentrated into two categories, labourer and textile worker, while the female convicts were classified as labourers. The apparent differences in Table 5.6 disappear once it is remembered that female textile workers identified in the census worked at home as domestic workers and were classified as female farm servants (labourers) in the indents. Generally, the Irish convicts, like their English counterparts, are broadly representative of the Irish workforce at home.

Convicts, the English prison population and a criminal class

While Australian historians have never compared the convicts to the English working class, they have argued that transported workers were simply English prisoners in an 'open gaol'. Of course, it is not strictly accurate that convicts were an unbiased sample from the English prison population: the convicts were younger, fitter and included more males than the prison population at home. How do the convicts at home and in New South Wales compare on occupational grounds? Computerising the occupations of convicts serving their sentences in 1844 in Pentonville prison, we found that the English prisoners and transported convicts had a Spearman rank coefficient of 0.91 and the Mann-Whitney test showed the two samples were drawn from the same population at almost any level of significance. This is consistent with recent work by British historians working on Victorian criminality. David Philips gave the 1844–45 occupational breakdown of Black Country offenders as 58.8 per cent unskilled and semi-skilled; 38.4 per cent skilled; and the upper and middle classes accounting for the remaining 2.8 per cent of the offenders. The breakdown for the English convict sample was 51.7 per cent unskilled and semi-skilled, 45.2 per cent skilled and 3.1 per cent middle and upper classes.[18] On this basis, transportees were better skilled than those criminals who remained in England.

The research work by historians of Victorian crime has rejected the idea of a criminal or dangerous class, born and bred to a life of crime and operating as organised gangs. Since the convicts and English prisoners can be treated as the same population, the finding by British historians of Victorian crime that the offenders at home were ordinary working men and women also applies to the convicts sent to New South Wales. David Jones found that in the great metropolis of casual labour, London, convicted offenders who committed the occasional petty crime were little different from the rest of the working population.[19] The same held for Manchester. In a recent study of crime and society in early nineteenth century England, George Rude found no case for the existence of a 'criminal class'.[20] Philips argued that Black Country crime was committed by people who worked at jobs normally, but stole articles on some occasions.[21] What was noticeable about Black Country crime was its casualness and lack of planning, characteristic of ordinary men and women not full-time professional criminals.There was no criminal class in England to transport to Australia. The convicts sent to Australia were ordinary working men and women.

Education

All the quantitative and qualitative evidence on occupations points to one conclusion:

the convict workers sent from England were broadly representative of the English and Irish working class. But occupation alone does not fully describe the human capital that convicts brought to Australia. Their levels of education and their fitness also determined the contribution they would make to developing the new colony.

The quality of the labour force is improved by education. Education can be gained by formal training in school, apprenticeship and on-the-job training, either under supervision or merely through learning-by-doing. Education is an investment in human capital, which yields an individual worker higher lifetime earnings. Those returns accrue not only to the individual, but also to the economy through higher output. The convicts' investment in education was higher than that of the population at home.

Literacy, the ability to both read and write, read only, or neither read nor write, is a good proxy for education. Tables A7 and A8 present the basic data on literacy for each country and for males and females. In summary, half the English male convicts could read and write, and somewhat less than one-half of the Irish male transportees. Scottish convicts were the best educated, with about 65 per cent being able both to read and write: the foreign-born were the least educated with only 37 per cent being able both to read and write, although this figure excludes literacy in their first language. A higher percentage of males were able to read and write than females, and urban convicts were more literate than rural workers. There was no long run trend toward a better or poorer educated workforce between 1827 and 1840, although there were yearly fluctuations (see Table A9). These fluctuations were due largely to the changing age, sex, industrial and skill components in the yearly inflow.

Table 5.7 suggests that convicts transported to New South Wales were better educated than the 'average' English worker left behind in Britain. Three-quarters of the English convict workers could read, or read and write; the convicts' literacy was significantly higher than the average for all English counties (58 per cent), and higher than that of English workers (65 per cent) after adjusting the registrar-general's average national figures for county population size. As an independent check, Roger Schofield's random sample of 274 English parish registers yielded an estimate that 58 per cent of persons could sign their marriage certificates in 1840.[22] The Irish convict literacy rate was not significantly different from that in the Irish census of 1841. At the micro level,

Table 5.7: *Literacy Rates of Convicts, Irish and English Workforces: Ability to Read and/or Write* (Percentages)

| | Convicts | | Total working population 1839–42 | |
	County of birth	County of work	Average across counties	Adjusted for county population size
England	75.0	75.0	58.0	65.0
Ireland[a]	62.0	61.0	54.0	—

a. Ireland 1841

Source: Convict Indents; Annual Report of the Registrar-General: Births, Deaths and Marriages in England; Report of the Commissioners Census of Ireland, Parliamentary Paper, 1843, XXIV, C504.

the literacy rates of the English convicts calculated on a county of birth basis diverged noticeably from the registrar-general's county literacy rates. For example, Leicester, Worcester and Warwick have high literacy rates using the convict sample, but low literacy levels using the registrar-general's data. There is one uniform pattern: every English county sent convict workers who were, on average, more literate than the population which remained at home.

Differences between the registrar-general's estimates of literacy and the convict sample are due to the measurements of literacy, gender, urban-rural mix, skill base and the composition of trades which made up the two data sources. The registrar-general measured literacy by the ability to sign one's name on the marriage registers; like most modern surveys the convict indents depended on answers to questions about literacy rather than on a direct test. The two measures are not identical. However, even large margins of error in the convict indents do not explain the 17 point higher literacy rate for convicts. The higher convict literacy rates are explained by the sex, skill and urban bias of the transported workers. About 94 per cent of the English convict sample were male, who were, on average, 10 percentage points more educated than the females. The convict sample was biased towards urban workers. Almost 50 per cent of the English convicts were urban (see Table A4) and urban literacy rates were seven percentage points higher than rural rates (see Table A7). Finally, the convict sample was underrepresented in the low literacy trades, such as agriculture, mining and industrial service, but overrepresented in skilled urban trades, such as whitesmiths, cutlery makers, brassfounders and plasterers. As a result, the convict workers transported to Australia were better educated than the men and women left behind in England.

The convicts sent to Australia were also better educated than the English prison population. From a sample of 23,172 male and female prisoners between 1837 and 1839, R.K. Webb found that 65 per cent were literate.[23] While this is a good match with the registrar-general's estimates for the general population, Webb did not think that the prison population was a good proxy for working class literacy. He rejected the prison population as an accurate cross-section of the working class on the grounds of its 'criminality'. Webb preferred a special sample of working class prisoners from the manufacturing areas in Lancashire, Cheshire and Stafford tried before a special commission in 1842. It is doubtful that the literacy rate of politically conscious men before a special commission was more representative of working class educational levels than the general prison population. As we have seen, the prison population consisted of ordinary working men and women. The balance of probability suggests that the prison literacy rate was a good proxy for the general population as indicated by the registrar-general's literacy estimates. Interestingly, the literacy rate of 73 per cent among the men in Webb's special sample corresponds almost exactly with a literacy rate of 74 per cent for the convict transportees from those three industrial counties. It is tempting to argue that the higher literacy rate of convicts sent to New South Wales reflected the 'cream' of the English prison population.

This conclusion needs to be modified in light of the 'schooling' of convicts in reading and writing on the hulks. From the end of the Napoleonic Wars schools were established on the hulks, although attendance was voluntary. It is difficult to judge what effect the schooling had on literacy rates. On the hulk *Stirling Castle* in 1841, 75 per cent of the 331 prisoners could already read and/or write, while only 80 were illiterate; however only 70 attended the school, and some of these were improving their literacy.[24] From the yearly reports on the hulks, *Stirling Castle* seems to be typical of the proportion of convicts attending schools on the hulks generally.[25] The quality of the teaching was variable, with teachers selected from among the convicts. Chaplain Price's complaint to the superintendent of the hulks that it was 'a very difficult matter to give anything like an accurate account of the prisoners sent to this place, in consequence of their continual changing state' reflected the transient nature of the hulk population; in 1838 there was a 50 per cent turnover in the population on the Woolwich hulks.[26] In such an environment there would have been little continuity of education. While schooling on the hulks would have improved the level of literacy, it was unlikely to have been a decisive factor in accounting for the higher literacy of the convicts when compared with the prison population in England. For whatever reason, those workers on the hulks who had the highest educational attainment appear to have been selected for transportation.

Economists who have viewed education as a process of human capital formation requiring social investment have made international comparisons of literacy rates and economic growth.[27] A 40 per cent literacy rate seems the threshold level for economic development, and an increasing literacy ratio a necessary condition for economic growth.[28] With a read and/or write literacy rate of 75 per cent, and a read and write rate of 46 per cent, the convicts provided New South Wales with the threshold education level needed for sustained growth. As Table 5.8 shows, the convicts' literacy compares

Table 5.8: *Literacy Rates of the Convicts Compared with the Population in Today's Less Developed Countries: Ability to Read and/or Write* (Percentages)

Country	Year	Literacy Rate
Convicts	1817–38	70.5
Afghanistan	1976	12.0
Algeria	1976	24.0
Angola	1972	3.0
Bangladesh	1976	22.0
Egypt	1975	48.0
Ethiopia	1974	6.0
Ghana	1976	31.0
Haiti	1976	24.0
India	1976	33.0
Iran	1976	37.0
Iraq	1971	24.0
Jordan	1976	32.0
Liberia	1972	9.0
Libya	1976	22.0
Mali	1975	2.0
Morocco	1976	22.0
Nicaragua	1975	2.0
Niger	1973	15.0
Pakistan	1975	15.0
Senegal	1975	6.0
Sudan	1976	15.0

Source: Statistical Abstract of the United States 1979, pp.873–4; Convict Indents.

favourably with that of many of the world's less developed countries today. On this basis it is not surprising that New South Wales experienced rapid economic growth.

Height and productivity of convict workers

It is only in the last decade that historians have come to appreciate that data on human height provide a good indicator of the standard of living prevailing in past societies, and a valuable guide to changes in social welfare over time. In 1978 the National Bureau of Economic Research and the Centre for Population Economics sponsored a major collaborative project to develop time series on the average adult stature of national populations.[29] The on-going project reflects an increased recognition by economic historians and economists of the implications of medical research on the relationship between anthropometric measures, nutrition and labour productivity. The project found, contrary to popular opinion, that genetic influences appear to have very little impact on the mean heights of people in different societies. Rather, according to P.B. Eveleth and J.M. Tanner, measures of height-by-age, the age at which the growth of stature terminates and attained final height 'reflect accurately the state of a nation's public health and the average nutritional status of its citizens'.[30] Employing a some-what different definition, W.M. Moseley and L.C. Chen argued that height-by-age statistics provide 'generalised indexes of health' and 'non-specific indicators of health status'.[31]

If these hypotheses are correct, and a great deal of recent medical and historical research appears to substantiate them, then they have important implications for our study of convict labour. The fact that all transported convicts were measured, and the information recorded on the indents to the nearest quarter-inch, provides a reliable indicator of the nutritional history and health of the bonded labour that arrived in New South Wales. In addition, the convict height statistics are far superior to many other data sets on height used by historians. Most historical information survives from the recruitment of men into military organisations that rejected shorter applicants. Consequently, these military data are biased, and estimates have to be made of the truncated left tail of the height distribution. In contrast, the height-by-age data for transported convicts reveals a normal distribution, with standard deviations around the mean of no more than the range of 5.0–6.5 cms which is usual in height distributions. Moreover, convict data are unusual in providing information on women.

The height statistics are important not only as a measure of the accumulated past nutritional experience of convicts, but also as an estimate of the convicts' potential contribution to economic growth in Australia. In general, the better the nutritional status of an individual, the higher that individual's labour productivity, especially in a society in which work was largely accomplished by physical effort. Moreover, social scientists have revealed a strong correlation between height and mortality.[32] The taller a convict the better his/her health, the greater his strength and the more years of useful toil he/she was likely to be able to perform.

The assertion, made most recently by Robert Hughes, that transported convicts were 'runts' is therefore of considerable interest to economic historians. Examining a list of 465 escaped adult convicts, Hughes notes that more than 80 per cent of the men were less than 5 feet 8 inches (173 cm).[33] Our data substantiate this claim: of 14,946 adult male convicts in our sample, 83.3 per cent were below that height. But to assess the shortness of convicts by contemporary Australian standards is ahistorical and incorrect. The key question is how the average height-by-age of transported convicts compared with that of contemporary British and Irish workers left at home. Only if the height and nutritional status of bonded labour in New South Wales was less than that of free British and Irish workers would the convict workforce be likely to have had lower productivity, and its members a lesser life expectancy, than workers in the United Kingdom.

Some contemporary evidence appears to support the contention that the transported convicts were shorter than their cohorts at home. Edwin Chadwick, for example, wrote in 1844, on the basis of personal observation, that 'adult prisoners from the towns and convicts in the hulks ... are in general below the average standard of height.[34] The pioneering studies of convict stature, undertaken by the medical historian Bryan Gandevia, develop this hypothesis in unequivocal terms. The major arguments propounded by Gandevia with regard to convict height may be summarised as follows: that 'the convict boys transported from Britain in about 1840 were of very short stature'; that their 'heights were low even for contemporary Britain'; that 'the maximum height of adult male convicts was not attained until the age of 25–29 years; and that 'the adults were of small stature by comparison with their British contemporaries', implying that their 'growth potential was never achieved'.[35]

Gandevia analysed the indents of convict boys who were transported in special ships designed for youthful offenders, and who arrived between 1837 and 1842. Data on 452 boys aged 10–18 years were recorded, of which 435 were aged 13 years or over. In contrast, we analysed the statistics of 1142 boys aged 13–18 years. Table 5.9 indicates that the 'very small stature' recorded by Gandevia was not common. Our estimates suggest that for each age group, mean height was considerably higher than that previously indicated. The evidence shows that 14-year-old boys were, on average, 3 cm higher than the figure proposed by Gandevia, and that 15-year-olds were no less than 9 cm taller.

Gandevia also argued that convict boys, because they came from the lower social classes and the more disadvantaged areas, were small in stature even by the standards of contemporary British society. The basis of the British statistical data for this claim, Gandevia acknowledged, came from three of four decades after the arrival of the convicts. Thus the comparative tallness of British boys at home may simply have reflected a secular increase in height over time. We believe this to have been the case, and using data from the same period show that the convict boys were as tall as their urban contemporaries of similar socio-economic status.

The stature of the convict boys can be compared to that of London lads recruited into the Marine Society in the early nineteenth-century. Although the Society was a charity which sought to provide employment to indigent boys, Roderick Floud argued that their heights 'are not misleading as a guide to the average heights of working-class Londoners'.[36] Table 5.9 reveals that the stature of the boys transported to New South Wales between 1818–1840 (who were born between 1802 and 1827) were considerably taller at every adolescent age than that of the Marine Society recruits born between 1756 and 1799, and at least as tall as those born between 1815 and 1829.[37] Moreover the heights, and velocity of growth, of the convict boys is remarkably similar to the data collected by Horner on Manchester factory children in the 1830s (see Table 5.9).[38] The

Table 5.9: *Height-by-age of Convict, Poor London and Manchester Factory Boys*

	1	2	3	4	5
	Transported convict boys		Poor London boys		Manchester factory boys 1830s
Age (years)	Gandevia estimate mean height (cm)	Nicholas/ Shergold estimate mean height (cm)	Born 1756–99 mean height (cm)	Born 1815–29 mean height (cm)	mean height (cm)
13	136	140	131	-	138
14	140	143	136	145	144
15	145	154	142	147	152
16	150	155	147	154	157
17	153	160	—	—	159
18	156	162	—	—	—

Sources: 1. B. Gandevia, 'A Comparison of the Height of Boys Transported to Australia from England, Scotland and Ireland, c.1840, with Later British and Australian Development', *Australian Paediatric Journal* 13 (1977), 91–96.
2. Convict Indents.
3. & 4. R. Floud and K.W. Wachter, 'Poverty and Physical Structure: Evidence on the Standard of Living of London Boys 1700–1870', *Social Science History* 6 (1982), 440–50.
5. Floud and Wachter, 'Poverty and Physical Stature', 445.

transported youths appear to have grown at least as tall and as fast as other working-class children.

There is considerable evidence that the age at which adult stature is achieved has fallen. Today adult height is reached by 17 years of age. In contrast, Gandevia has hypothesised that convict boys transported to Australia did not reach full adult stature until 25–29 years of age.[39] Our own calculations, based on age-specific heights through to 25 years, indicate that Gandevia's estimate is far too high. Our data suggest that the initial adolescent growth spurt occurred between 13 and 15 years of age. Age-specific heights continued to rise rapidly until 19 years of age, at which time average stature was from 98.6–98.8 per cent of the adult (24 year old) height. Terminal height, or the attainment of skeletal maturity, seems to have been reached soon after 20 years of age, the same as has been recorded for working-class Britons in the first half of the nineteenth-century.

What, then, was the terminal stature of the convicts transported to New South Wales? Gandevia originally estimated the average height of adult male convicts transported to Australia to be 'about 165 or 166 cm'. In contrast, British male criminals in 1870 were about 168–170 cm tall. He therefore hypothesised that 'the growth potential of the juvenile convicts was never achieved'. Gandevia also calculated the average height of adult female convicts which he put at 155 cm.[40] Our estimates suggest that Gandevia's figures are too low. Table 5.10 indicates that male convicts born between 1781 and 1815, who were 25 years of age or over, had a mean height of just over 167 cm and their female counterparts a mean height of slightly more than 156 cm. The

Table 5.10: *Height of Convicts by Date of Birth, Birthplace and Sex*[a]

| Year of Birth | Male | | | | Female | | | |
| | Urban-born | | Rural-born | | Urban-born | | Rural-born | |
	(no)	(cm)	(no)	(cm)	(no)	(cm)	(no)	(cm)
1724–89	738	167	987	168	35	156	89	156
1790–99	1043	167	1351	167	78	155	174	156
1800–09	694	166	1811	168	185	155	316	157
1810–19	605	167	1529	168	159	155	253	156
Total	3080	167	5678	168	547	155	832	156

a. Mean height in centimetres of those aged 24 years or over. The Table excludes convicts whose date of birth was not known.

Source: Convict Indents.

figures do not reveal a population of runts. The average height of adult men, about 167–168 cm, indicates that transported convicts were not small by the standard of contemporary British males recruited into the British army.

Certainly most convicts sent to New South Wales were short compared with citizens of the newly independent United States. North Americans enjoyed diets that were remarkably nutritious by European standards, and particularly rich in protein. The mean final height of native-born white males born between 1780 and 1840 approached 173 cm. Even black American male slaves, who were malnourished during childhood, attained an adult stature of 171 cm.[41] The adult height of Britons was markedly lower. A combination of intra-uterine malnutrition, poor childhood diet and the consumption during infancy of injurious substances, notably the opium, laudanam and morphia that were the ingredients of popular patent medicines for children, stunted the physical development of British workers. Floud has estimated that the adult height range of poor Londoners was only 163–168 cm in the early nineteenth century.[42] So while not as tall as Americans, the convicts sent to New South Wales were probably taller than London labourers.

But to compare data from London with those derived from the whole of the United Kingdom is wrong. There existed significant regional and occupational differences in height. The convict data support the arguments of Floud that rural-born Britons were taller than urban-born; that manual workers and labourers were smaller than professionals and tradesmen; and that Englishmen were smaller than Scotsmen.[43] Male convicts born in urban areas of Middlesex, Surrey, Sussex and Essex (predominantly London) attained the lowest adult stature of 164.5 cm; those born in the city of Dublin reached 166.4 cm; and the tallest were rural-born Scots who averaged 170 cm. Variations in the final height of convicts matched those for the population as a whole within the British Isles.

If the British population had a nutritional status markedly lower than that across the Atlantic, it was significantly superior to the standard that prevailed across the English Channel. British workers, and New South Wales convicts, were taller than other European workers. A study of white native-born male American farmers recruited into the army in New England in the 1820s, estimated the height of American recruits at 172 cm. In contrast, white immigrant recruits born in England were almost 2 cm shorter.

But immigrants from continental Europe were a further 3 cm smaller.[44] Similarly, data on army conscripts recruited in Norway, Italy, Belgium, France and Spain suggest that the mean final male height for European national populations in the nineteenth century was just 165 cm, with most European nations averaging less than 166 cm.[45]

The convicts transported to New South Wales were not short by contemporary British and Irish standards.[46] The height-by-age data on the New South Wales convicts indicate that their nutritional status was at least as good as that of the free British workers from which they were selected. The nutritional level reflected in the convicts' height has important implications for labour productivity. The level of nutrition measured by height is a good proxy for the ability to undertake physical work. Since convicts were, on average, as tall at all ages as those free workers at home, their levels of labour efficiency were equivalent to those that existed in Britain. In Australia where a premium was placed on the ability to perform hard physical labour, the transported convicts were well-suited to the task of forging a new economy.

Conclusion

The indents provided a detailed listing of each convict's occupation. This data is reliable: occupations were listed in great detail; occupational skills correlated with the specialised geographic location of British industry; a large proportion of crime was work related; and the jobs convicts were assigned to in the colony often corresponded with the trades they practised in Britain. Comparing the convicts' occupations in the indents with the occupations of the workforce in the 1841 English census, we found that the transported convicts were a cross-section of the English working class. This result was confirmed by several different statistical tests. Performing a similar exercise for the Irish convicts, the skills of the transported Irish were consistent with those skills for the workforce in the 1841 census for Ireland. These findings are supported by the research work of historians studying Victorian crime which rejects the idea of a criminal class in Britain. Crime was committed by ordinary men and women who worked at jobs normally, but stole articles on some occasions.

There were two other measures of the convicts' human capital — educational attainment and height. Measuring literacy by the ability to read and/or write, the convicts were better educated than the English working population (whose literacy was measured by the ability to sign the marriage register). The higher literacy level among the convicts was due to the higher proportion of males and urban workers among the transportees than in the English working population. The productivity of a country's workforce depends on the nutritional level of the society. One proxy for the standard of living of a population is its height. The convicts were of the same stature as the recruits into the Marine Society and the British army in the early nineteenth century. On this basis, the convicts transported to Australia had labour productivity levels equivalent to the male workforce left in Britain. All three of our separate measures of the convict workers' human capital — their occupations, literacy and height — point to the same conclusion: the convict settlers sent to New South Wales were ordinary members of the British and Irish working classes.

NOTES

1. A.G.L. Shaw, *Convicts and the Colonies*, p.264.
2. L.L. Robson, *The Convict Settlers of Australia*.
3. J. Tobias, *Crime and Industrial Society in the 19th Century*, p.18.
4. V.A.C. Gatrell and T.B. Hadden, 'Criminal Statistics and Their Interpretation' in E.A. Wrigley (ed.), *Nineteenth Century Society: Essays in the Use of Quantitative Methods for the Study of Social Data*, pp.336–396.
5. G. Mackaness, 'T. Watling', in G. Mackaness (ed.), *Letters from an Exile at Botany Bay*, 6.
6. Mackaness, 'Watling', 36.
7. L. Becke (ed.), *Old Convict Days*, pp.71–4.
8. W. Buckley, *Life and Adventures of William Buckley*, p.2.
9. W. Buckley, *Life and Adventures*, p.5.
10. C.A. King, *A Warning Voice from a Penitent Convict*, no pages.
11. A. Atkinson, 'Four Patterns of Convict Protest', *Labour History* 37 (1979), 36–7.
12. D. Philips, *Crime and Authority in Victorian Britain*, pp.152–3.
13. W.A. Armstrong, 'The Use of Information About Occupations' in E.A. Wrigley (ed.), *Nineteenth Century Society: Essays in the Use of Quantitative Methods for the Study of Social Data*, pp.215–23.
14. N. Butlin, 'White Human Capital in Australia, 1788–1850', *Australian National University Working Paper in Economic History* 32 (1985), 30–7.
15. W.G. Rimmer, 'Hobart', in P. Statham (ed.), *The Origins of Australia's Capital Cities*.
16. C. Erickson, 'Emigration from the British Isles to the U.S.A. in 1831', *Population Studies* 35 (1981), 186.
17. J. Mokyr, *Why Ireland Starved: A Quantitative and Analytical History of the Irish Economy, 1800–1850*, p.17.
18. D. Jones, *Crime, Protest, Community and Police in Nineteenth Century Britain*, pp.132, 178–98.
19. G. Rude, *Criminal and Victim: Crime and Society in Early Nineteenth Century England*, p.126.
20. Philips, *Crime and Authority*, p.287.
21. R.S. Schofield, 'Dimensions of Illiteracy, 1750–1850', *Explorations in Economic History* 10 (1973), 445.
22. R.K. Webb, 'Working Class Readers in Early Victorian England', *English Historical Review* 65 (1950), 335.
23. Chaplains (H. Winter) *Report on Fortitude*, attached to *J.H. Capper's Report No. 1*, 26 July 1841, Mitchell Library (hereafter ML), Q365/G.
24. *Reports of J.H. Capper*, ML, Q365/G.
25. Chaplains (T. Price) *Report on Justitia*, attached to *J.H. Capper's Report No. 2*, 24 February, 1841, ML, Q365/G.
26. C.A. Anderson and M.J. Bowman (eds.), *Education and Economic Development*, Chapter 17–8, 20.
27. Schofield, 'Dimensions of Illiteracy', 431–7.
28. Schofield, 'Dimensions of Illiteracy', 431.
29. For details of the project, entitled 'Secular Trends in Nutrition, Labor Welfare and Labor Productivity', see R.W. Fogel, 'Nutrition and the Decline in Mortality Since 1700: Some Preliminary Findings', *National Bureau of Economic Research Working Paper* 1402 (1984); and R.W. Fogel et al., 'Exploring the Uses of Data on Height: The Analaysis of Long-term Trends in Nutrition, Labor Welfare and Labor Productivity', *Social Science History* 6 (1982), 401–20.
30. P.B. Eveleth and J.M. Tanner, *Worldwide Variations in Human Growth*, p.1.
31. W.M. Moseley and L.C. Chen, 'An Analytical Framework for Study of Child Survival in Developing Countries' (mimeo, 1983) cited in Fogel, 'Nutrition and the Decline in Mortality', 32.
32. See, for example, A.M. John, 'The Demography of Slavery in Nineteenth-Century Trinidad', unpublished Ph.D. thesis (Princeton University, 1984).
33. R. Hughes, *The Fatal Shore*, p.174.
34. Cited in R. Floud, 'A Tall Story? The Standard of Living Debate', *History Today* 33 (1983), 36.
35. B. Gandevia, 'A Comparison of the Heights of Boys Transported to Australia from England, Scotland and Ireland, c.1840, with Later British and Australian Developments', *Australian Paediatric Journal* 13 (1977), 91–6; 'Some Physical Characteristics, Including Pock Marks, Tattoos and Disabilities, of Convict Boys Transported to Australia from Britain c.1840', *Australian Paediatric Journal* 12 (1976), 6–12; 'The Height and Physical Characteristics of Convicts Transported to Australia c.1820–1850', *Australasian Association for the History and Philosophy of Science-Proceedings* 11 (1975), 2–8; and *Tears Often Shed: Child Health and Welfare in Australia from 1788* pp.48–67.
36. Floud, 'A Tall Story?', 38.
37. R. Floud and K.W. Wachter, 'Poverty and Physical Stature: Evidence on the Standard of Living of London Boys 1770–1870', *Social Science History* 6 (1982), 445.
38. Cited in Floud and Wachter, 'Poverty and Physical Stature', 445.

39.Gandevia, 'Height of Boys Transported to Australia', 91–6.

40.Gandevia, 'Height of Boys Transported to Australia', 91–6.

41.Fogel, 'Nutrition and the Decline in Mortality Since 1700', 43–56; and R.W. Fogel et al., 'The Economics of Mortality in North America, 1650–1910: A Description of a Research Project', *Historical Methods* 11 (1978), 84.

42.Floud and Wachter, 'Poverty and Physical Stature', 447.

43.Roderick Floud, 'Measuring European Inequality: The Use of Height Data' (mimeo, Conference of the Social Science History Association, 1986), 24.

44.K.L. Sokoloff and G.C. Villaflor, 'The Early Achievement of Modern Stature in America', *Social Science History* 6 (1984), 453–81.

45.Floud, 'Measuring European Inequality', 20.

46.For a more detailed discussion of convict height see S. Nicholas and Peter R. Shergold, 'The Height of British Male Convict Children Transported to Australia, 1825–1840 Part I and Part II', *Australian Paediatric Journal* 18 (1982), 1–11.

Chapter Six

Female Convicts

Deborah Oxley

Introduction

Who were the female convicts? The female convicts have not been subsumed within any universal set of 'convicts' for two reasons. Firstly, in a patriarchal society the attributes attained by women and men frequently differ; as there were so few females among the convicts transported to New South Wales such differences are easily swamped in a statistical sample which reflects this sex imbalance, that is, in which males predominate. To avoid this loss it is therefore necessary to look at women separately. There is also a second reason for making this division, and that is because the division has already been made by historians and contemporaries of the convicts who condemned the male convicts for their crimes but the female convicts for their sex. In spite of the fact that prostitution was not an offence punishable by transportation it is the alleged crime for which the female convicts have been made to pay. Commentators have responded to the complex question of 'who?' with the simple answer of 'whore', in their eyes making further analysis redundant. In this chapter a more comprehensive answer is sought and two questions in particular are addressed: what sort of criminals were these women, and what sort of workers?

Damned whores and criminal classes

The view that presented the convicts as the victims of an oppressive economic and social system in which, as Arnold Wood has it, the real villains were left behind on the court benches and in the House of Lords has been put asunder by the onslaught of Manning Clark, Lloyd Robson and A.G.L. Shaw.[1] Robson's statistical analysis of convicts included 1248 women transported to the eastern colonies. In the present work 2210 of the female convicts arriving in New South Wales between 1825 and 1840 are investigated. Although the two samples are based on the same source of information — the convict indents — the conclusions reached differ considerably.[2] Using statistics, Robson has located the convicts' origins in the criminal class, a point subsequently accepted by many historians and popularists as fact 'established beyond reasonable doubt'.[3] To the proponents of this view the vast majority of the convicts were aberrant and evil, 'idle and depraved'.[4] The women were considered no exception.

While the female convicts were classified as members of a criminal class, they were, unlike the men, located there less for the transportable offences of which they had been found guilty than for the belief that they were prostitutes. An official reporting to the 1837 Select Committee on Transportation claimed that the female convicts were 'all of them, with scarcely an exception, drunken and abandoned prostitutes'.[5] Such accusations abounded. Ever since the label 'damned whore' was uttered by Lieutenant Ralph Clark, supposedly on sighting the female convict ship the *Lady Juliana* in June 1790, the prostitution of the females who were transported to Australia has become a truism. These women, claimed contemporaries and historians alike, had chosen to sell their womanly virtues upon the open market rather than to fulfil the worshipped role ascribed to them by society. In doing so they damned themselves. Or more correctly, they have been damned for it.[6]

In spite of the fact that we cannot know how many of the female convicts had ever practised prostitution in the United Kingdom, the accusation alone has been enough to taint popular and historical opinion. When Robson attempted to assess the extent of prostitution, relying on reports made by gaolers and surgeon-superintendents (who frequently confused promiscuity with prostitution) and occasionally on the word of the woman herself, he estimated that about 20 per cent of the female convicts transported to Van Diemen's Land (the only ones for whom this information was recorded) had been prostitutes. Overlooking the four-fifths who were not prostitutes by his own estimation, and the insignificance of the women's crimes as he reported them, Robson wrote, surprisingly, that 'the picture presented of the women convicted and transported to Australia is not an attractive one'.[7] Similarly, Shaw wrote that although 'how many were prostitutes will never be known, almost all contemporaries regarded them as particularly "abandoned"'; and even if these contemporaries exaggerated, the picture they presented is a singularly unattractive one'.[8] Even in the most recent works the claim persists, without explanation or source, that 'many were prostitutes', at least among the Irish female convicts.[9] The belief in the prostitution of the female convicts has become so intertwined with their criminality that the two have become synonymous.

Arithmetic inflation apart, the very definition of prostitution has been assumed unquestioningly by those who have sat in judgment on the female convicts. This class-biased label has been accepted as correct. A woman living in a de facto relationship — a common working-class practice — was defined as a prostitute, whereas with the sanctity of marriage her morality would have been secured.[10] A domestic servant was prone to be stigmatised in this way, both because her employment was often predicated upon her remaining 'single' and thus limited her to de facto relationships, and because she was an easy target for the sexual advances or sexual attacks of men in her master's family or employ — men who, having seduced or raped her, then proceeded to condemn her as a whore. Rather than investigating the economic motives that may have led to the decision to become a prostitute, or the sort of system it was that created prostitution as an occupation for women, or even what the term 'prostitute' actually meant, many historians have accepted the contemporary view that prostitution was evidence of the morally corrupt nature of the female convicts. It has become a basic tenet by which the female convicts have been judged, often to the exclusion of all other criteria. Labelled as 'damned whores' by the members of another class and of another sex, some of whom were also from another time, the supposed prostitution of the female convicts was not perceived as an index of working class poverty but as adequate qualification for membership of an outcast criminal class.

Robert Hughes has noted how 'In the mouths of Authority, the word "prostitute" was less a job description than a general term of abuse'.[11] The accuracy of the decision to locate prostitution in the criminal sphere rather than in the capitalist economy would in itself seem doubtful. To what extent is prostitution an act committed beyond the realm of the capitalist economy and in contempt of capitalist work practices? A woman who sells her sex is selling a commodity, perhaps a unique form of labour power, and is therefore complying with capitalist ideology and practice. Taking the analysis onto a slightly more sophisticated plane, the system under consideration is more accurately defined as a capitalist patriarchal one. Capitalist exploitation is mediated through the pre-existing sexist hierarchy which creates for working class women a role which entails not only exploitation as a worker but exploitation conditioned by her oppression as a woman. A woman's participation in the paid labour market is conditioned by her responsibility for the reproduction of the working class, future, past and present (that is, for childcare, care of the aged, the sick, fathers, husbands and sons). This limits the availability and timing of her paid working hours while simultaneously creating another sphere of work (the reproduction of the working class) as either not paid or low paid. Under this system women act as service centres.

Another aspect of this is sexual servicing, through enforced fidelity and fecundity, or through rape, or through prostitution: woman as a service centre to be obtained through marriage, force, or payment. Prostitution is thus a structural aspect of capitalist patriarchy, as under its capitalist component sex is commercialised and turned into a commodity. In the eighteenth and nineteenth centuries prostitution was of particular importance given the heightened use of the dual but complementary roles created for women as either God's police or damned whore: as a 'good' woman or a 'bad' woman, as virginal or sexual.[12] Therefore even those female convicts who were professional prostitutes prior to their transportation do not qualify for membership of a criminal class. Rather, the location of prostitution within the criminal sphere would seem to be more the result of moral, religious and class biases than of conscious analysis. A different moral framework would in fact perceive prostitution as an occupation, quite receptive to reclassification as legal, and thus as evidence of a woman's working class origins.

Both because there is insufficient evidence to determine how many of the female convicts ever engaged in prostitution and because such information is irrelevant for our purposes, other than to help prove that these women were workers, it seems fair to assess whether the women were outcast criminals or not according to the same criteria that were applied to the men. From the literature there appear to be two major characteristics which define the criminal class: its professional status and the behavioural deficiencies of its members.

Defined as professionals, criminals formed a third and independent class. Its members neither owned nor controlled the means of production as did the capitalist class, nor sold its collective labour power as did the working class, but instead had chosen to exist beyond the realm of the capitalist economy in a parasitic fashion. They were, according to Clark, part of the working class only to the extent that 'crime is an occupation just as plumbing, carpentering, etc., are occupations for other members of the working classes'.[13] They were not casual criminals but 'professional and habitual criminals', not workers who occasionally committed crimes but individuals who supplied their needs and wants entirely through crime — witness Henry Mayhew's division of his subject into 'Those That *Will* Work, Those That *Cannot* Work, And Those That *Will Not* Work comprising prostitutes, thieves, swindlers, beggars'[14]. These individuals had, according to the 1837 Royal Commission on The Constabulary, succumbed to 'the temptations of the profit of a career of depredation' rather than choosing the presumably more arduous task of wage labouring (given the options, one may speculate as to what motivated any individuals to resist this supposed temp- tation).[15] Thus a dichotomy existed between the working class and the criminal class, and never the twain did meet, for the latter was 'the true underworld of professional pickpockets, thieves and prostitutes. These people knew what a good servant was but their whole lives turned on outraging that ideal — only the suckers worked and touched their caps to the masters, the flash man tricked and robbed them', wrote John Hirst in 1983.[16]

The second defining characteristic of an alleged criminal class is the behavioural deficiencies attributed to its members. It was because of these deficiencies that individ- uals supposedly chose to reject paid employment. The collective absence of the criminal class from what was considered to be the legitimate economy was not by and large the result of an inadequate demand for labour power: 'The notion that any considerable proportion of the crimes against property are caused by blameless poverty or destitution we find disproved at every step' wrote the Constabulary Commissioners.[17] Rather, this absence was considered to be a conscious rejection of capitalist work practices stemming from behavioural deficiencies such as laziness and immaturity, and even lack of intelligence. These were people who, according to Shaw, preferred to be wanderers and vagabonds roving the countryside committing crimes rather than paid workers contributing to the good of the economy.[18] According to Clark, they were 'men [sic] with a deep-seated resistance to work' who were 'characterised by mental imbecility and low cunning. Many of them were lazy in disposition and lacked energy both of body and mind'.[19] The criminal class was not, then, the product of larger social and/or economic forces, or even of a politically-based rejection of capitalist work practices. It was the product of behaviourally deficient (and morally reprehensible) individuals. According to this argument, the individual is not the product of class; rather, class becomes the product of the individual.

A stereotype has thus been established of the professional criminal and of the transported convict as an individual who had chosen to stand outside the capitalist economy in contempt of capitalist work practices and who instead maintained herself or himself entirely through crime. How well does this image fit that of the female convict? If the image is correct then certain characteristics with regard to crimes and occupations would be expected. Goods stolen should have been either of a sufficiently high quality or quantity for resale to generate a substantial income, or diverse enough to satisfy the consumption of the criminal directly. Furthermore, stealing would have had to have been done constantly and would most likely have been reflected in a high number of previous convictions, unless the thief was very artful which seems unlikely given their behavioural flaws of 'mental imbecility and low cunning'. Also, sentences should have been heavy due to the severity of the crime and the previous criminal record. As for occupational skills and other forms of human capital investment, a 'professional and habitual' criminal would neither need any — not in a utilitarian bourgeois sense — nor possess the stamina of character required to attain them. How, then, does the evidence compare with this?

Professional criminals or casual pilferers?

Overwhelmingly the female convicts committed crimes against property — 96.2 per cent of the 2191 women whose crime we know. What is surprising about the offences committed by the female convicts is their apparent aversion to crimes which brought them into direct contact with their victims or other people.[20] Among property offences only 18.5 per cent necessarily entailed direct personal contact, namely highway robbery, pickpocketing, robbery with assault and one incidence of a woman who sold her child. Above this, one-tenth (10.2 per cent) were involved in crimes which potentially may have involved confronting another person, for example, burglary, stealing from premises (place of work, lodgings etc.), shoplifting and housebreaking. Only 1.8 per cent of the known sample committed violent crimes and when violence did occur it is not always clear that it was motivated by possible financial remuneration. For example, infanticide more likely resulted from a fear of losing employment as a domestic servant than from the hope of earning an illegal income. If these women were trying to derive an income from crime they seem to have limited their activities considerably by avoiding confrontation and the use of violence.

Was it true that these women were professional and habitual criminals living entirely off their illegal earnings? If the answer is yes, then an analysis of the property thieved should reveal this. When the offence leading to transportation was stealing — as it was for 60.8 per cent of the women — the convict indents recorded what item or items had been stolen. This was also done occasionally when the crime was robbery. Were the goods stolen of adequate quality, quantity or diversity to produce an income on which a person might survive, or the families of the 618 women known to have children? Seemingly not. There was diversity among the stolen goods, with over 200 different items being specified, although only 20 of these appeared as the object of criminal desires with any regularity. Money was the single most prevalent item stolen. However, it should be noted that the theft of only one shilling led to transportation — a sum hardly likely to purchase much of the good life. The information is most revealing when the stolen goods are classified into a few basic groups. The results are presented in Table 6.1. Had the thieves been targeting the valuable, marketable items, then the categories of jewellery, metals and possibly miscellaneous goods should have been the largest. Instead, those items which were more suited to immediate consumption — many of them the basic necessities of life — predominated: together clothes, cloth, household goods (for example candles, pots and pans), bedding and foodstuffs accounted for nearly three-fifths of the items stolen. The female convicts from England and Wales stole less of the items designated as immediately satisfying basic needs, the Irish less of items requiring resale before such needs could possibly be met, and the Scottish women less money, but in all three regions the most prevalent theft was the same, that of items capable of satisfying needs directly, that is without resale or in the case of money, without purchasing. By and large the items that were stolen were petty, far from valuable, and were taken in small numbers — a blanket, a pair of gloves, a loaf of bread, a shirt, even a prayer book. Of course such items could have been resold to gain money to spend on what the ruling class considered to be frivolous luxuries — yet luxuries that they were entitled to enjoy — such as gambling and alcohol and expensive dresses, activities which were not only detrimental to the obedience and regimentation of the workers, but a threat to social order as well. But equally such items could

Table 6.1: *Classification of Items Stolen*

Item	Frequency	Adjusted
Animals	5.0	5.4
Bedding	4.0	4.2
Cloth and yarn	10.4	11.2
Clothes	33.1	35.4
Foodstuffs	3.1	3.3
Household goods	4.6	5.0
Jewellery	6.3	6.7
Metals	0.9	0.9
Money	22.2	23.7
Miscellaneous	4.0	4.2
Unspecified	6.4	—
Total	100.0	100.0
Number of cases	1408	1318

Source: Convict Indents.

have been stolen in order to alleviate suffering: such thefts might supplement income, or be useful in themselves, although they seem inadequate to sustain life for more than the briefest time. In either case it would seem unlikely that the theft of a loaf of bread or a single cloak represented a way of life commensurate with the expectations of a professional criminal element which believed it could gain more through crime than wage labour.

Nor can the women be said to be well-known criminals. If they habitually thieved they certainly did not get habitually caught. Of the female convicts born in England and Wales only 39.8 per cent had a recorded prior conviction, and among the Irish-born the figure was fractionally lower at 33.5 per cent, indicating that the 'typical image of the English convict as an urban pickpocket, convicted many times before, does not apply in Ireland' nor for that matter in England.[21] These figures are notably lower than those for Robson's known sample (70 per cent of the English and 51.7 per cent of the Irish female convicts had previous convictions), probably resulting from the larger number of second offenders transported to Van Diemen's Land — a region represented in Robson's sample but not the present one. However, the reputation that the Scottish female convicts had of being particularly hardened criminals, described by Robson as 'the worst of a bad lot', was predicated upon their tendency to have been convicted previously and the present sample does little to refute this.[22] It is the same pattern found for men in Chapter 4. Whereas in Robson's sample 92.9 per cent of the female convicts born in Scotland had previous convictions, the present finding is 77.2 per cent. Of those tried in Scotland in the present sample the figure rises to 83.5 per cent, supporting the belief that judicial sentencing patterns were responsible for the apparently greater criminality of the Scottish women. Nor does it seem that the existence of a criminal record was a good measure of 'criminality' — of the professional status of the convict — when it is realised that the women tended to have been previously convicted for the same type of small-scale crime as that that had led to their transportation.[23] To have a previous conviction for stealing a loaf of bread before being transported for stealing butter does not make the woman socially aberrant and criminal, merely human, with human needs, living in a capitalist economy where legal access to subsistence can only be bought with money obtained in a limited number of ways.

Judicial sentencing patterns were also likely to have been responsible for the discrepancies between the sentences received by the female convicts from different regions. Ninety-four per cent of the Irish were sentenced for the minimum seven years, 83.3 per cent of the Scottish and 70.7 per cent of those women born in England and Wales, revealing the same pattern as that found by Robson.[24] Interestingly, no statistically significant relationship existed between the length of sentences and the absence or presence of prior convictions. Such a correlation would have been expected if these two variables were true indicators of the seriousness of the crimes involved rather than just idiosyncratic judgments.

Thus the majority of the women convicts in the present sample were first offenders guilty only of very small scale crimes. It seems unlikely on the basis of this information that the female convicts were professional and habitual criminals. The first defining characteristic of the criminal class is therefore absent among the female convicts. What then of the second defining characteristic? Did the female convicts display traits consistent with laziness and an 'unwillingness to accept the personal investment and self-discipline implied by continuity of work and purposeful action'?[25] Had the women been indolent vagabonds roaming the countryside in search of criminal mischief? This can be measured in terms of their human capital investment — that is, by the amount of effort they put in to enhancing the value of their labour power, and in terms of their mobility. If the criminal class theory is correct, then the women should have displayed few skills and little education — particularly those who were mobile.

Occupations, skill and literacy

The contention that the female convicts were professional criminals, rather than ordinary workers who either through low wages or unemployment felt the need to supplement their incomes through occasional crime, is further strained by the finding that 95 per cent of the women in the present sample had occupations recorded against their names in the indents. In addition, 6.5 per cent of the women had recorded a second job. Only one woman was listed as unfit for work. Their skills ranged over 36 different trades, from general categories such as allwork and general servant through to more specific skills such as upholsterer and jeweller. From Table A15, female convicts fell into four skill categories: domestic service (77 per cent), unskilled urban (9.4 per cent), unskilled rural (6.7 per cent) and skilled urban (6.6 per cent). The vast majority of the women were concentrated into just 13 occupations as can be seen from Table 6.2, and of these, three dominated: general servant, housemaid and kitchenhand. The same pattern existed in all three regions. It is unclear whether the information on occupations included women's work in the domestic industry or the unpaid work of women in the home; it seems most likely that these tasks were excluded, thus understating the variety of the women's skills. It is apparent, however, that the female convicts came to New South Wales with a selection of immediately useful skills.

If the 13 major occupations are categorised according to Armstrong's social-skill classification then the significant stock of skills among the convicts emerges. As Table A11 in the Appendix illustrates, rather than being primarily unskilled, 71.2 per cent of

Table 6.2: *Occupations of Female Convicts Prior to Transportation*
            (Number)

	First recorded occupation	Second recorded occupation
General servant	444	20
Housemaid	389	20
Kitchenhand	317	3
Allworker	192	3
Nursemaid	189	14
Laundress	141	4
Dairyhand	127	6
Cook	87	15
Seamstress	63	11
Nurse	42	
Dressmaker	32	8
Milliner	18	2
Farm labourer	14	
Bootmaker	6	
Confectioner	6	
Housekeeper	6	4
Bar attendant	4	
Chambermaid	4	1
Governess	3	
Silk weaver	3	
Caneworker	2	
Cotton spinner	2	
Dairy producer	2	
Factory labourer	2	
Hawker	2	
Baker	1	
Embroiderer	1	
Gipsy	1	
Jeweller	1	
Lace manufacturer	1	
Laundrymaid	1	24
Servant		2
Tape weaver	1	
Tobacco maker	1	
Upholsterer	1	
Wool spinner	1	
Unfit	1	
Number of cases	2108	137

Source: Convict Indents

the females were semi-skilled or skilled working class or 'middling' and professional. This result is hardly consistent with the image of the convicts as 'the dregs of society'. If the female convicts were not members of a distinct criminal class whose only profession was crime but were instead members of the working class, then the occupational structure of the female convicts should resemble that for the female population of the domestic economy, although some variations could result from greater poverty associated with a decline in a particular industry. Bearing in mind that there are only 763 English female convicts in the sample, 19.6 per cent of these convicts were unskilled workers compared with 17 per cent of the English women in the 1841 census. On this basis it appears that the female convicts' occupations were broadly representative of the occupational structure at home.

The social-skill classification of an occupation correlates closely to the percentage of literate female convicts recorded as belonging to that occupation; 81 per cent of the skilled could read and write but only 51 per cent of the unskilled. B.M. Penglase found the same correlation for a different sample of 329 female convicts arriving in New South Wales in 1838.[26] The levels of literacy varied not only occupationally but regionally as well. The rural-born women were less literate than the urban-born, and clearly this had implications for the levels of literacy attained within the predominantly rural pre-industrial Irish economy: the Irish were far more illiterate than the female convicts from England and Wales, and all were inferior to the Scots with their more advanced system of education (see Table A7).

Numeracy can also be measured in a very approximate way by using a technique known as age-heaping or clustering. A cluster exists when an unusually large number of people claim to have rounded ages, for example 20 or 30 years rather than 19 or 31 years. It is believed that this in part reflects guessing by innumerate individuals and that a higher proportion of the women with rounded ages tended to be innumerate than those with non-rounded ages. Using this indicator of numeracy a pattern similar to that for literacy emerges: the Irish convicts displayed age-heaping (one-quarter giving rounded ages) while the English and Scottish did not, thus augmenting the finding that the British female convicts had on average received more human capital investment than their Irish counterparts.

How representative were the Irish female convicts of the Irish female population? Using census data the two groups appear very similar, with illiteracy rates of 52 per cent and 55 per cent respectively, although fewer convicts could both read and write. Nor did rates of numeracy differ substantially. For that small group of 140 Irish female convicts who had moved country a quite different literacy profile emerges — one quite consistent with the brain-drain thesis which suggests that the best skilled workers were the migrants. Of those tried in England only 34 per cent were illiterate and for those in Scotland the figure fell to 22 per cent. If the Irish female convicts who moved to England and Scotland were representative of Irish emigrants generally, then this result does much to reverse Joel Mokyr and Cormac O'Grada's assertion, based on evidence of age-heaping calculated from the passenger lists of Irish free emigrants to America, that Ireland lost the 'less educated and less able'.[27]

The comparison of literacy rates between the two English and Welsh female populations, convict and native, is more problematic. The female convicts were categorised into three levels of literacy according to their own testimony (hence casting some doubt on the validity of this data if there was a motive to lie) whereas the measure for the literacy of the adult female population was dichotomous and empirically derived based upon the ability to sign the marriage register (hardly a sophisticated test of the ability to write). Roger Schofield noted that 'the proportion of the population able to sign was less than the proportion able to read and greater than the proportion able to write' which raises the problem of the basis of the comparison to be made with the convict data.[28]

Firstly, defining female convict literacy as the ability to both read and write, it appears that the English and Welsh female convicts were educationally atypical, being inferior to their native adult female population. Whereas approximately half of the native population could sign the marriage register, only 35.4 per cent of the female convicts from England and Wales were 'literate' (see Table A7). The picture changes dramatically when convict literacy is redefined as the ability to read or write. Instead of a literacy rate of 35.4 per cent, the figure jumps to a massive 82.8 per cent. Assuming that the comparable literacy rate lies somewhere between the figures of 35.4 per cent and 82.8 per cent, the female convicts were at least as literate (and probably more literate) than the female population left behind. Both skill and literacy indicate equal or greater human capital investment among the convicts compared with the female population at home, dispelling the Schedvins' notion of the convicts' 'restlessness and unwillingness to accept the personal investment and self-discipline implied by continuity of work and purposeful action'.

Mobility

The female convicts appear to have been quite highly skilled and highly literate members of the working class, and the 'restlessness' of which they have been accused may even indicate that the convicts were part of a talented and mobile source of labour power. Certainly there was a high degree of mobility among the female convicts. Almost one-half of the female convicts were mobile — 43.5 per cent of the known sample. They migrated from a variety of counties, with five major migration routes: Kildare and Wicklow to Dublin, Dublin to Lancashire, and Limerick and Cork to Middlesex — the latter route being the largest single flow, accounting for 2.7 per cent of those women who were mobile. However, taken together these five routes only accounted for 8 per cent of the migrants. Given that Dublin, Lancashire and Middlesex attracted 36.2 per cent of the female migrants, the diversity of the counties of origin is evident.

The tendency to migrate was not uniform. Sixty-nine per cent of migrants were rural born. Given the composition of the rural-born population in the present sample, in which widows and married women are proportionally more prominent than in the urban-born population, the set of mobile women tended to display many similar characteristics: the female migrants were marginally older than nonmigrants, fewer were single, and more had children. They were also less likely to have had prior convictions.

Convict women who had moved prior to conviction also differed in important ways from the rural-born population and from the stayers in both rural and urban areas. The most important contrast was their level of literacy. While 43.4 per cent of the rural-born female convicts were illiterate, only 32.2 per cent of those who had moved were. Comparing stayers and migrants, 50.7 per cent of rural stayers were illiterate but only 36.3 per cent of rural migrants. Likewise, urban stayers were more illiterate than were the urban migrants — 29.5 per cent as opposed to 23 per cent. Mobility also bore a relationship to skill. The women from some of the occupations exhibited higher levels of mobility than average, while others exhibited less. To illustrate, the categories of cook and dressmaker — both of which belonged to the skilled and highly literate class — had mobility rates of 52.9 per cent and 53.1 per cent respectively. By comparison the less skilled categories of housemaid, kitchenhand and nursemaid were less mobile at 39.4 per cent, 39.9 per cent and 32.8 per cent respectively. Such differences could have resulted from the nature of employment if, for example, employment involved travelling. It could indicate that those who migrated were more likely to attain skills than those who did not, or that more highly trained workers were more likely to migrate in search of employment or better conditions and pay. It does not, however, suggest an 'aversion to continuity and steady work' among those that the Schedvins' named the 'nomadic tribes of urban Britain', nor that they were especially idle and worthless or wanderers and vagabonds as Shaw has claimed.[29]

Conclusion

The female convicts transported to New South Wales were not members of a professional criminal class. No such class existed.[30] Maybe a few individuals chose to live by crime but crime did not represent a better way of life or an easier one than wage labouring; what crime did offer was a supplement to income for those in low-paid employment and an alternative to the highly stigmatised workhouses for those out of work. Such parlous conditions were not unusual. Structural changes had been taking place within the British economy which heightened vulnerability. The safety-net provided by the local production of basic necessities which could be obtained through the exchange of goods or obligations crumbled as production was organised around trade and urbanisation intensified. Previously common property was defined as private, and traditional wage supplements such as gleanings and sweepings were reconstructed as property crimes.[31] Labour power had become a commodity but a highly heterogeneous one not always in demand.

The position of women was particularly precarious. Their labour — when it was financially rewarded — received even less remuneration than that of their poorly-paid male counterparts,[32] and the recasting of the sexual division of labour that was in process at this time led to a contraction in the demand for paid female labour power. Female labour was not only low-paid, it was often erratic as well, whereas women's responsibilities were not. Labour power that was paid below its cost of reproduction resulted necessarily in poverty. Not surprisingly some women probably cushioned the impact of economic fluctuations by turning to prostitution. Not surprisingly some women committed crimes in an attempt to gain momentary relief from poverty, or in protest. Not surprisingly, given the exalted status of private property, this rebellious and often surplus labour was exported. The only thing that is surprising was that not more women turned to crime.

So, transported to the other side of the world after what was often but a single conviction for the theft of an item of inconsiderable value, were the women who would help found the White Australian economy and society. In a colony where so few white women came voluntarily, these unwilling migrants bore a substantial responsibility. So few, they were valued less — a violation of the classical law of supply and demand determining price.[33] They were used, abused, undervalued and ridiculed by many of their contemporaries, and they fought back. They could not, however, repel the assaults made by their historians, men who have downgraded these women's importance and whose main interest lay in speculating about one aspect of the women's sexuality or employment. Historians of the 1970s and 1980s — Katrina Alford, Beverly

Kingston, Portia Robinson and others[34] — have demonstrated how erroneous the classification was that labelled these women simply as prostitutes who contributed nothing other than vice after their arrival in Australia. I have shown how prior to transportation the appellation 'damned whore' was also totally inadequate. The female convicts were not the professional members of a criminal class. These women were talented and skillful workers, many with an experience of migration attained within Britain and Ireland that aided them in their transition to what was for them a new land. As well, these mainly young women brought with them the ability to bear children and to create and perpetuate the future labour force. While Britain did without these women, White Australia could not.

NOTES

1. G.A. Wood, 'Convicts', *The Royal Australian Historical Society Journal and Proceedings* 8 (1922) 177–208; M. Clark, 'The Origins of the Convicts Transported to Eastern Australia, 1787–1852', *Historical Studies: Australia and New Zealand* 7 (1956), 314–27; L.L. Robson, 'The Origin of the Women Convicts Sent to Australia, 1787–1852', *Historical Studies Australia and New Zealand* 11 (1963), 43–53; L.L. Robson, *The Convict Settlers of Australia*; A.G.L. Shaw, *Convicts and the Colonies*.
2. The female convicts were collected as part of the sampling of selected years described in Chapter 4. Also see H.S. Payne, 'A Statistical Study of Female Convicts in Tasmania, 1843–53', *Tasmanian Historical Research Association Papers and Proceedings* 9 (1961), 56–59; J. Williams, 'Irish Female Convicts and Tasmania', *Labour History* 44 (1983), 1–17; D. Oxley, 'Who Were the Female Convicts?', *Journal of the Australian Population Association* 4 (1987), 56–71.
3. See J.B. Hirst, *Convict Society and its Enemies*, p.33; R. Hughes, *The Fatal Shore*, pp.158–63; H. McQueen, *A New Britannia*, p.126; M.B. Schedvin and C.B. Schedvin, 'The Nomadic Tribes of Urban Britain: A Prelude to Botany Bay', *Historical Studies: Australia and New Zealand* 18 (1978), 254.
4. P. Colquhoun, *A Treatise on the Police of the Metropolis*, preface.
5. Cited in R. Perkins, 'Push and Pull Politics: Prostitution, Prejudice and Punishment', *Arena* 74 (1986), 92.
6. See A. Summers, *Damned Whores and God's Police*, esp. p.286.
7. Robson, 'Origin of the Women Convicts', 46–7, 53.
8. Shaw, *Convicts and the Colonies*, p.164.
9. P. O'Farrell, *The Irish in Australia*, p.24.
10. M. Sturma, 'Eye of the Beholder: The Stereotype of Women Convicts, 1788–1852', *Labour History* 34 (1978), 7.
11. Hughes, *The Fatal Shore*, p.244.
12. See E. Trudgill, 'Prostitution and Paterfamilias' in H.J. Dyos and M. Wolff (eds.), *The Victorian City, Images and Realities* II, 693–706; Perkins, 'Push and Pull Politics', 94–6.
13. Clark, 'Origins of the Convicts', 133.
14. Shaw, *Convicts and the Colonies*, p.165; H. Mayhew, *London Labour and the London Poor*, title page.
15. Cited in V.A.C. Gatrell and T.B. Hadden, 'Criminal Statistics and their Interpretation' in E.A. Wrigley (ed.), *Nineteenth-Century Society: Essays in the Use of Quantitative Methods for the Study of Social Data*, 381.
16. Hirst, *Convict Society and Its Enemies*, p.32.
17. Cited in Gatrell and Hadden, 'Criminal Statistics', 381–2; also see Clark, 'Origins of the Convicts', 125; Schedvin and Schedvin, 'The Nomadic Tribes of Urban Britain', 261.
18. Shaw, *Convicts and the Colonies*, p.160.
19. Clark, 'Origins of the Convicts', 314.
20. See J.M. Beattie, 'The Criminality of Women in Eighteenth-Century England', *Journal of Social History* 8 (1975).
21. Williams, 'Irish Female Convicts', 7.
22. Robson, 'Origin of the Women Convicts', 46.
23. Williams, 'Irish Female Convicts', 7.
24. Robson, *The Convict Settlers of Australia*, p.200.
25. Schedvin and Schedvin, 'The Nomadic Tribes of Urban Britain', 275.

26.B.M. Penglase, 'An Enquiry into Literacy in Early Nineteenth Century New South Wales', *Push From The Bush* 16 (1983).

27.J. Mokyr and C. O'Grada, 'New Developments in Irish Population History, 1700–1850', *Economic History Review* 37 (1984), 374–7.

28.R.S. Schofield, 'Dimensions of Illiteracy, 1750–1850', *Explorations in Economic History* 10 (1973), 440.

29.Schedvin and Schedvin, 'The Nomadic Tribes of Urban Britain', 255–7; Shaw, *Convicts and the Colonies*, p.160.

30.D. Jones, *Crime, Protest, Community and Police in Nineteenth- Century Britain*; D. Philips, *Crime and Authority in Victorian England*; G. Rude, *Criminal and Victim: Crime and Society in Early Nineteenth Century England*.

31.Jones, *Crime, Protest, Community and Police in Nineteenth-Century Britain*, pp.11–2.

32.N. McKendrick, 'Home Demand and Economic Growth: A New View of the Role of Women and Children in the Industrial Revolution' in N. McKendrick (ed.), *Historical Perspectives: Studies in English Thought and Society*, 170, 152–210.

33.M. Dixson, *The Real Matilda, Women and Identity in Australia, 1788–1975*.

34.K. Alford, *Production or Reproduction? An Economic History of Women in Australia, 1788–1850*; B. Kingston, *My Wife, My Daughter and Poor Mary Ann*; P. Robinson, *The Hatch and Brood of Time, A Study of the First Generation of Native-Born White Australians 1788–1828*.

Chapter Seven

A Labour Aristocracy in Chains

Stephen Nicholas and Peter R. Shergold

Introduction

The identification of the convicts with the criminal class has denied the transported workers membership of the ordinary working class. Not surprisingly, few Australian historians have asked if elite workers, members of a skilled upper stratum of labour aristocrats, were transported to New South Wales. True, Lelia Thomas, in 1919, identified among the convicts a 'labour aristocracy [which] was exceedingly independent and often insolent, creating a danger centre in the labouring classes which the government viewed with uneasiness'.[1] According to Thomas, 'For the germ of the labour movement, we do not look to the freeman, but to the government convict, particularly to the mechanic .... This restless and favoured labour aristocracy was already instinct with a strong labour consciousness'.[2] But more recent labour historians have not shared this view. R.W. Connell and T.H. Irving agreed that there was an educated and skilled convict elite, but argued that they were divided from the rough, uneducated and vice-ridden mass of labouring convicts.[3] First and foremost they were divided along ideological lines from the convict lumpenproletariat.[4] This division was reinforced by the authorities, who provided privileges for skilled workers and sometimes physically segregated the educated convicts (because they were regarded as especially threatening). As a result Connell and Irving argued that the literate and skilled convicts failed to provide the leadership necessary to resist the excess of the penal system and to organise convict workers into 'combinations'.[5] While there were convict movements, they were short-lived and did not accumulate the experience of organisation. It was to the free immigrants, not the educated convicts, that Connell and Irving looked for the foundation of the labour movement.

On the source of working class institutions, Thomas pointed to their 'natural origin' in response to the economic pressures within colonial society.[6] The trade unions and benefit societies were not brought to Australia from England. Here there is unanimous agreement — L.J. Hume, Max Hartwell, Connell and Irving concur that the origin of the labour organisation in Australia was an autonomous local development.[7] Hume saw the 'solid core of free, skilled employees in the urban crafts' with a 'positive outlook and set of values' as the creators of the trade societies which allowed them to reap the benefits of years of apprenticeship training.[8] In contrast, Connell and Irving deny that the labour organisation was produced by craft exclusiveness. They argue that the illegal and informal organising among ordinary working men was the first labour movement in Australia. Such activities lay behind the craft societies of the 1830s and continued alongside them.[9] They acknowledge their case is built on inferential grounds since so little hard evidence on labour organisation exists. But whatever the backdrop to the trade unions and benefit societies, they drew their membership, as Connell and Irving readily admit, from the skilled and literate craftworkers wishing to regulate their particular trade. The trade and benefit societies were formed by the highly skilled urban crafts, the tailors, shoemakers and printers; the coachmakers and saddlers; the weavers, bakers and engineers; the shipwrights and cabinetmakers; and bricklayers, painters, carpenters and joiners.[10] Whether benefit society, providing sickness and funeral expenses, or trade union, the organisation fixed wages, collectively bargained and occasionally went on strike.[11] While covering only a fraction of the workforce, they represented craftsman-cum-entrepreneur as well as craftsman-cum-employee, emphasising the values of independence and co-operation.[12]

The role of the time-expired skilled convict in the growth of the benefit and trade societies is unclear. While the form and colour of the labour movement had been set in convict moulds, Thomas looked to the free skilled emigrant for the growth of unions in the 1830s.[13] So too do Connell and Irving. However, the membership of the Trade Union Benefit Society of 1835 included emancipists.[14] Sandra Blair's study of the print workers found the convicts split along lines of status, with the skilled and educated divided from the ordinary convicts, but working alongside free printers and compositors. So too, did the skilled turners in the bigger furniture workshops. For these skilled workers there was no separate self-contained convict community.[15] Convicts even became reporters and editors of Sydney newspapers. More importantly, the print trade aristocrats were involved in the early formation of the printer's union and took part in the strike of 1839 which began in the *Sydney Herald* office.[16] For the printers, then, the trade training which created a labour aristocracy in Britain was transported to colonial Australia, where the printers found newspaper jobs and, while still convicts, were founding members of the printers' union. Were the printers an exception, both in being labour aristocrats and actively contributing to the growth of artisan organisations in Australia? This chapter places the growth of labour aristocrats within the changing labour processes in industrialising Britain, arguing that skill, job autonomy and control over the organisation of work defined a coterie of elite skilled workers. Using literacy as a proxy for these labour process values, a labour aristocratic elite was reconstructed from our sample of transported workers. In the conclusion we pose some tentative hypotheses concerning the contribution of the convict labour aristocrats to colonial society, particularly the establishment of the Sydney Mechanics School of Arts.

Historical specificity of a labour elite in Britain before 1840

'Labour aristocracy' is a concept in search of a theory. Originally the term was a useful metaphor to describe divisions within the British working class. The labour aristocrat, as the name implies, was the upper stratum of the working class. However, historians have disagreed over how that upper stratum should be defined and on its effects on class, economy and society in nineteenth century Britain.

The paradigm for research on the labour aristocracy starts with Eric Hobsbawm's often quoted list of criteria for identifying an elite: a high level and regularity of earnings, social security, superior conditions of work (including treatment by foremen and masters), work relations and personal relations with social strata above and below, general living conditions and finally, prospects for advancement for himself and his children.[17] One strand of the new work on an elite hierarchy has argued that the concept of labour aristocracy implies an ideology and cultural cohesion broader than mere craft consciousness.[18] Rather than apeing middle class values, style of life and aspirations, the labour aristocrat evolved — within a specific working class socio-economic situation — artisan values of status, respectability and independence.[19] These values were rooted in artisan dominated institutions such as chapels, co-operative movements, friendly societies, mechanics institutes, building societies, and trade unions and were displayed through a popular culture within a well-defined community. Of course, these socio-ideological values cannot be comprehended outside the context of capitalist development and the work experience of the artisan. For those studies based on local data — Kentish London, Edinburgh or Oldham — the labour aristocracy was linked to each locality's occupational and industrial structure. Classifying workers by occupation and industrial structure provided a quantitative means of identifying labour aristocrats in terms of Hobsbawm's standard of living, wage and economic security criteria. More importantly, the quantitative analysis of occupations focused attention on authority at work, and on work conditions which were also key elements in Hobsbawm's definition.

Rejecting the idea that the creation of a labour aristocracy coincided with the emergence of skilled unionism at mid-century, E.P. Thompson identified an old and a new elite in the years before 1850.[20] The old elite was tied to the traditional handicraft trades, while the new arose in the iron, engineering and manufacturing industries that required new skills. Such a scheme is compelling; it introduces historical change in terms of a shift from an old to a new elite as an explanation for the historical continuity of a labour aristocracy before and after 1850. Against a background of changing technology and increasing mechanisation, the shift between elites was a life and death struggle as much between artisan and outworker as between the handicraftsman and the newly skilled mechanic and as much in defence of cultural values and status as to protect real wages and income. However, Thompson's magnificent survey of London artisan life during the industrial revolution is a description, and not a model, of a shifting labour aristocracy. From a microcosm of coopers, shoemakers, hatters, carriers, brassfounders, leather dressers, sawyers and gold beaters, occupational groupings of privileged London artisans can be constructed. But only detailed local studies, like those of R. Gray and Geoffrey Crossick on Edinburgh and Kentish London, can hope to analyse occupational hierarchies in terms of the industrial structure, the workplace, culture and ideology and the wider socio-political environment.

Further, occupational groupings vary from one geographical area to another, across trades and within trades. As Thompson readily admits, the Sheffield cutlery and the Birmingham smallware trades are scarcely represented in the London occupational structure.[21] Finally, John Foster's attempt to tie the labour aristocracy to specific subcontract and pace-making labour processes in capitalist development set the parameters for future studies of a labour aristocracy.[22] If the concept of a labour aristocracy is to have meaning wider than mere social stratification, then the labour aristocrat must be analysed within specific work organisations.

Deciding who were the labour aristocrats in any particular historical period is, at least in part, a quantitative exercise. They have to be counted. Such arithmetic presupposes the ability to identify the object to be counted according to some agreed characteristics. The work organisation approach to a labour aristocracy relies on a cluster of characteristics including wages, authority at work, status, skill, independence, and economic security. Some characteristics are themselves quantitative, such as wages, while qualitative characteristics, for example skill or work authority, can only be proxied by quantitative variables such as years of training or level of education or literacy. Here the labour aristocracy in our sample of convicts is reconstructed by choosing a quantitative variable which proxies the work organisation of the elite worker in a particular period. As a prerequisite to defining a quantitative proxy, the basic theoretical framework for pre-1840 labour processes is sketched.

Labour processes or work organisation are easy to identify in theory, but difficult to measure in practice. The labour process is the work structure and controls which capitalists develop to extract work power from labour. The labour aristocrat had control over the work process. Of course, the work autonomy of the labour aristocrat should not be overemphasised. Even in putting-out, the artisan was subject to some control by the capitalist. For example, the division of labour in putting-out was instituted by the capitalist. While work was unsupervised directly, the capitalist indirectly monitored the worker through examining the quality of the product, through setting work targets and by paying by output. Capitalists' authority over work was exercised through ownership of physical capital and control of product assortment and raw inputs. It was the capitalist who determined the nature of the final product. It was the capitalist too who decided the level of output to be achieved. Capitalist control over the type and regularity of work was reflected in the internal organisation of the artisan's workshop. Regularity and standard work meant that the putting-out workshop was hierarchical with a pyramid of journeymen, family members and apprentices hired by the artisan and supervised by the artisan in such matters as training and work performance.[23]

When indirect supervision and discipline of work in putting-out was found inadequate by the capitalist (but not by the worker) there was an incentive to shift to a system which offered the capitalist more control.[24] The factory allowed the capitalist direct control of the work process both through the extensification and intensification of work. In the early factory, time-keeping in the form of fixed work weeks and fixed work days was a common example of the extensification of work. Work intensification procedures in the period before 1840 involved direct supervision of workers including rules, fines, corporal punishment, wage rises, kindness, promotion and premiums and the continued monitoring of the product.[25] Through the intensification of work within the hierarchical factory, capitalists could more easily exploit the worker. The factor limiting capitalists' intensification of work was skill. The greater the specialist job knowledge and experience involved in jobs, the more likely it was that the worker could determine the pace and organisation of work.[26] Skilled work meant that the artisans determined how the task was carried out while the capitalist with considerably less job knowledge simply set the task. Closely related to job knowledge as a measure of skill is the concept of job autonomy. Skilled jobs are likely to involve discretionary work in contrast to unskilled jobs where work is prescribed. Skill limited the system of control capitalists could employ over workers. Skilled jobs requiring knowledge and offering job autonomy meant a division of labour based on exclusivity, status, high wages and employment security.

In terms of work processes, the factory and the putting-out system overlapped. Putting-out was a type of subcontract system where the capitalist had greater or lesser control depending on the particular relationship with the artisan. This also applied in the factory organisation where the absence of direct control was reflected by subcontracting in the factory. Under this system the artisan might own his intermediate inputs (including capital) and sell his processed output, thus experiencing less control than in putting-out. Alternatively, direct supervision in the factory might be exercised through a hierarchy of superintendents, timekeepers and foremen offering the capitalist much more control over work than any form of putting-out. Internal subcontract in the factory made transparent the relative power relationship between worker and capitalist in a more direct way than external subcontract (putting-out). Independence at work, either in the factory or in putting-out, was shaped by the relative bargaining strengths of artisan and capitalist. Skill was one advantage which gave workers power in their negotiations with capitalists over employment and work performance. Skill more than any other variable identified the labour aristocrat. If a proxy can be found for skill, then the labour aristocracy can be quantitatively identified.

Quantitative reconstruction of the labour aristocracy before 1840

While wages and living standards by themselves do not define a labour aristocracy, they are frequently used as proxies for skill. Gray objected that wage rates are poor proxies for labour elites since wages tell nothing about unemployment, regularity of earnings, piece rates and bonuses.[27] Besides these problems, the paucity of reliable wage data constrains their use as a proxy for skill. Another long standing proxy for skill and a major characteristic of the artisan elite is literacy. Correlating literacy with the labour aristocracy, Hobsbawm related high literacy areas (such as Birkenhead, York and Doncaster) with the existence of a skilled artisan elite in shipbuilding and railway repairs.[28] In contrast, low literacy prevailed in the west Midlands where semi-skilled, semi-domestic industry was concentrated. Gray in his study of Edinburgh noted that education differentiated the labour aristocrat from the nominally literate and illiterate workers.[29] In a discussion of supervisory workers, J. Melling argued that the artisan elite of supervisory workers had a superior education.[30] For G. Stedman Jones the breach in craft control after 1840 was characterised by new skills requiring only a modest level of literacy, a fact which differentiated the new elite from the old craft labour aristocracy.[31] According to Crossick, education was a key variable in fixing the status of the skilled artisan in Kentish London.[32] When discussing the failure of the artisan elite to lead the labour movement in colonial Australia, Connell and Irving identify that elite in terms of literacy.[33] While all these studies hypothesised a relationship between education and the labour aristocracy, the absence of literacy levels by occupation prevented any empirical application of the relationship. However, the convict indents which identify the ability to read and/or write for each occupation, allow the pre-1840 convict artisan elite to be reconstructed. To test the validity of using literacy to proxy the labour aristocracy, a simple econometric model was estimated. Labour aristocrats were identified from Crossick's detailed study of Kentish London elites.[34] For all occupations with 20 or more observations a limited dependent variable; 1 if the occupation was one of Crossick's elite, 0 otherwise; was formed. Estimating a logit model, the dependent qualitative variable was regressed against the average level of writing ability for each occupation:

Labour Aristocracy = -2.45 + 0.036 Literacy $X^2 = 6.40$
(-2.58) (2.36)

X^2 and t-tests (displayed in brackets above) indicate that literacy was a significant determinant of the labour aristocracy, supporting recent qualitative work by British and Australian historians on elite workers.

Since the literacy of each occupation was used to proxy skill, all non-working class occupations and their corresponding literacy levels, essentially Armstrong's class 1 and 2 professional and intermediate occupations, were excluded from the data set. So too were the data on the Irish and the female convicts. The concept of a labour aristocrat is one of a male worker in an emerging capitalist economy, not applicable to women workers or workers in backward agricultural economies. The reduced sample included 229 of the original 342 occupations.

For occupations with more than 20 observations the mean literacy rate was probably an unbiased estimate for the educational level of the transported workers. However, the highly specific occupational descriptions in our sample meant that many occupations had only a few observations and even a couple of extreme observations could bias the mean literacy rates. Unfortunately, there are no independent checks on occupational literacy allowing the accuracy of our mean literacy rates to be compared with similar data. If the mean literacy rates were biased, then the labour elite would be over or underestimated. To overcome this problem a form of sensitivity analysis was employed. Literacy rates were calculated for each occupation using four different observational sizes, 25+, 18+, 10+ and 5+. The number of occupations used to calculate the labour aristocracy varied with each observational set. Nearly all 229 occupations were utilised for 5+ observations but fewer occupations for 25+ observations. Table 7.1 shows that by choosing a literacy rate of 80 per cent to define the labour aristocrats, the elite accounted for 6, 7, 8 or 9 per cent of the workers depending on whether the number of observations for each occupation used to calculate literacy was 25+, 18+, 10+ or 5+. The remarkable stability of these percentages across observational sizes supports the integrity and accuracy of the mean literacy rates.

There was a similar problem involved in the choice of the level of literacy to differentiate labour aristocrats from all other workers. In the absence of any agreed absolute literacy rate which defined a labour aristocrat, Table 7.1 also provides a range of literacy rates varying between 70 per cent and 90 per cent to define elite workers. The definition of an elite in Table 7.1 was sensitive to the literacy rate chosen, varying between 4 per cent and 14 per cent for all workers using an observational set of 25+ and 1 per cent and 9 per cent for 5+ observations.

Based on the ability to write, the labour elite reconstructed in Table 7.1 using 25+ observations accounted for between 6 per cent and 14 per cent of all convict workers sent to New South Wales. Defining literacy in terms of the ability to read or write, Table 7.2 shows that the labour aristocrats ranged between 8 per cent and 26 per cent of all convicts. Requiring a much greater investment in human capital by the workers, the ability to write provides a more rigorous test of skill than the ability to read. While not all skilled jobs required the ability to write, reading was a skill widely spread throughout the working class, weakening it as a proxy for job autonomy. Using the ability to

Table 7.1: *Reconstruction of the Convict Labour Aristocracy: Ability to Write*
(Percentages)

No. of observations	Able to write	Convict elite as percent of convict sample	Occupations common to convict sample and 1841 English census	
			Convict elite as percent of convict sample	English elite as percent of English census
25+	85	4	6	—
25+	80	6	8	17
25+	75	8	11	25
25+	70	14	16	32
18+	90	2	6	4
18+	85	3	5	7
18+	80	7	8	18
18+	75	9	11	25
10+	90	2	2	4
10+	85	4	5	8
10+	80	8	8	17
5+	90	1	2	4
5+	85	5	5	8
5+	80	9	9	18

Source: Convict Indents

write as the proxy for skill, this study suggests that an elite stratum of transported labour aristocrats brought to New South Wales the experience of job autonomy and work discretion and the value of independence and respectability developed in Britain.

Table 7.1 also compares the proportion of labour aristocrats in the convict workforce to the proportion of English aristocrats in the 1841 census. For all convict occupations identified as labour aristocrats on the basis of literacy, the percentage of English workers in those same occupations was calculated. The percentage of English workers in Table 7.1 who were labour aristocrats was roughly twice that of the reconstructed convict elite. This reflects, in part, a smaller percentage of elite than ordinary English workers who committed crimes and were eligible to be transported. The values of the English labour aristocrats and the less pressing economic and social necessity to engage in crime meant elite workers formed a relatively small percentage of convicted workers. Further, the convict occupations aggregated workers who laboured between 1780 and 1840 and is not strictly comparable with a census of workers in a single year. Coupled with rapidly changing occupational structures during the industrial revolution, the convict elite are likely to have been biased downward, relative to the 1841 English census elite. For these reasons it is not surprising that there was a smaller percentage of elite workers in the convict workforce than in the 1841 English population.

Although the elite formed a smaller fraction of the working class in New South Wales than in England, the transported workforce did provide an elite hierarchy perched on the broadbase of semi and unskilled workers. This is confirmed when Crossick's Kentish London artisan occupations, as a proportion of the convict sample, is compared to the proportion of those same occupations in the 1841 census in Table 7.3. Kentish

Table 7.2: *Reconstruction of the Convict Labour Aristocracy: Ability to Read or Write*
(Percentages)

No. of observations	Able to read and/or write	Convict elite as percent of Convict sample	Occupations common to convict sample and 1841 English census	
			Convict elite as percent of Convict sample	English elite as percent of English census
18+	90	8	11	25
18+	85	24	29	47
10+	90	9	11	25
10+	85	25	30	46
5+	90	10	12	26
5+	85	26	29	46

Source: Convict Indents

London's artisan occupations accounts for 11.9 per cent of the convict sample workers and 11.7 per cent of the 1841 English census workers. When we compare the urban convict workers with those occupations in an urban environment similar to that from which the convicts came, then the proportion of elite convict workers in the total population is (11.9 per cent), remarkably close to that at home (11.7 per cent).

Conclusion: English labour aristocrats and New South Wales

The convict workers transported to New South Wales were not only a cross-section of the British working class, but included an upper stratum of elite workers. In Britain, skill gave the elite worker greater power to bargain with employers, exercise job autonomy and resist many of the work controls which extensified and intensified the work process. Skill, more than any single variable, defined a worker's relationship with his fellow workers, determined his wages and work conditions and allowed social advancement. Whatever other characteristics might have defined a labour aristocrat, skill was the most important. While skill levels can be studied using qualitative sources for particular occupations, to evaluate elite workers across the full spectrum of working class occupations, a quantitative proxy is required. The ability to write is one commonly used proxy for skill. Since the convict indents include both the occupation and literacy level for each convict, it was possible to reconstruct the labour aristocracy transported to New South Wales. Based on literacy by occupation, between 6 per cent and 14 per cent of all convict workers were labour aristocrats.

What impact did the labour aristocrats have on the society and economy of colonial New South Wales? The labour aristocracy retained their group cohesion in Australia. They were separated from other workers on the basis of their skills and literacy. In 1826 Sir Robert Peel ordered the colonial authorities to isolate the 'educated' convicts from the rest of the transported workers by sending them to the remote agricultural outstations.[35] At best, this order was carried out intermittently, since colonial governors came to value the skills of the transported 'educated' convicts. If geographical isolation was incomplete, then job segregation more than compensated. The next chapter will reveal that over 70 per cent of the transported urban craftsmen were appointed to jobs

Table 7.3: *Comparison of Crossick's Kentish London Labour Aristocrats/Elites with 1841 Census and Convict Sample*

Crossick's Kentish London occupations	Total number of workers	
	1841 census	convict sample
Millwright	8,870	13
Shipwright	20,413	11
Brassfounder	6,349	63
Engineer	25,258	21
Locksmith	5,478	23
Toolmaker	4,847	17
Cutler	8,030	69
Bricklayer	39,699	162
Carpenters and joiner	162,525	334
Sailmaker	3,758	24
Boatbuilders and bargebuilder	2,904	11
Boilermaker	3,473	4
Riveter	0	9
Plater	1,566	0
Rigger	0	2
Sawyer	29,573	157
Smith	108,304	407
Draughtsman	196	0
Mason	82,462	133
Plumber (painter and glazier)	13,358	192
Plaster	13,358	91
Lightermen and waterman	24,057	162
Pattern maker	1,718	1
Ironfounder	0	14
Moulder	4,337	35
Firemen	1,096	1
Turner	7,054	0
Coppersmith	1,310	8
Fitter	1,096	1
Sub-total	614,435	1,984
Total census population and convict sample	5,230,740	16,685
Percentage of labour aristocrats in census and convict sample	11.7	11.9

Sources: Convict Indents; G. Crossick, *An Artisan Elite in Victorian Society: Kentish London 1840–1880*, Chapter 7.

which utilised their English skills: in contrast, only 33 per cent of the unskilled urban labourers and 27 per cent of the domestic servants found the same jobs in New South Wales that they held at home. More than anything else, it was the skills of elite workers which acted to keep the labour aristocracy together as a distinct group in the colony. A large proportion of the skilled workers were assigned to government service in the lumber and dockyards, where several hundred craftsmen in over 40 different occupations were gathered together within separate workshops or departments consisting of 10 to 60 artisans. Work organisation in the New South Wales lumberyard corresponded closely to that in English workshops, providing the labour aristocrat with a familiar degree of job autonomy and independence.[36] Indeed, in the colony where skills were scarce, convict artisans might have exercised an enhanced level of independence and felt a higher level of self-importance than they did as free workers in England. Certainly the need to train apprentices required the co-operation of skilled craftsmen, giving the labour elite a measure of greater power, for it was on convict or emancipist labour aristocrats that the state had to rely to provide manual training.

Literacy and skill acted to separate the convict artisan from the bulk of the convict population by more than physical space. While values and ideas of one's worth are difficult to maintain in isolation, these self-proclaimed values were reinforced and strengthened in the group solidarity of the workplace. Firstly, by working together in the shops or the lumberyard, the artisans honed and exaggerated their values, differentiating themselves from what some of the elite saw as the rough, uneducated and vice-ridden mass of convicts.[37] Secondly, skills separated the elite from the bulk of the convicts because the labour aristocracy did well out of the penal system.[38] The skilled craftsman was favoured at work, and the indulgence of working on one's own account meant that labour aristocrats were able to earn substantial sums through private employment beyond their hours of enforced servitude. The attitudes of the labour aristocrat might have been strengthened in Australia. At the very least, the physical separation, group solidarity and special privileges maintained the elite worker's values and self-perceptions within the convict labour market.

Besides contributing to the membership of the Trade Union Benefit Society and the printers' union, the convict mechanics were represented in the Sydney Mechanics School of Arts. Checking the school's 1835 membership lists against our sample of convicts, 59 convict names matched those of institute members.[39] Unfortunately, there is no way of telling for certain whether the names on the membership lists and the indents refer to the same individual. However, 82 per cent of the 55 convicts whose occupations were known, were labour aristocrats, including instrument makers, wheelwrights, carpenters, whitesmiths, painters and bricklayers. Most of those identified as possible institute members had arrived in Australia between 1816 and 1828, and would have been free by 1835 and eligible to join the society. While there were many Clarkes and Jones that both came free and were transported, there must have been few Thomas Bodenhams, J.C. McDougals and James Goldies. Clearly, the labour elite participated in the Mechanics Institute, finding in New South Wales an expression for the their values in the same institutions they used at home.

Mateship, fatalism, contempt for do-gooders and God-botherers, harsh humour, opportunism, survivors' disdain for introspection, and an attitude to authority in which private resentment mingles with ostensible resignation was, according to Robert Hughes, the meagre baggage of values the convicts brought with them to Australia.[40] Humphrey McQueen dismissed the convicts' value system as lumpenproletarian, characterised by individual acquisitiveness and honour of thieves.[41] This is certainly wrong. A labour aristocracy, with its self-proclaimed values of independence, respectability and status, was transported to Australia. The elite retained its values and identity at work and through participation in the same institutions which it had created for itself at home, the benefit societies, trade unions and mechanics institutes.

108   PART 2 — THE WORKERS

NOTES

1. L. Thomas, *The Development of the Labour Movement in the Sydney District of New South Wales*, p.11.
2. Thomas, *Labour Movement*, p.12.
3. R.W. Connell and T.H. Irving, *Class Structure in Australian History: Documents, Narrative and Argument*, pp.48–9.
4. Connell and Irving, *Class Structure*, p.49.
5. Connell and Irving, *Class Structure*, p.49.
6. Thomas, *Labour Movement*, p.38.
7. L.J. Hume, 'Working Class Movements in Sydney and Melbourne Before the Gold Rushes' in M. Beever and F.B. Smith (eds.), *Historical Studies: Select Articles*, p.32; R.M. Hartwell, *The Economic Development of Van Diemen's Land 1820–1850*, p.93; Connell and Irving, *Class Structure*, p.57.
8. Hume, 'Working Class Movements', 33–4.
9. Connell and Irving, *Class Structure*, p.57.
10. See Hume, 'Working Class Movements', 34; Hartwell, *Economic Development*, p.90; Connell and Irving, *Class Structure*, pp.68–71; Thomas, *Labour Movement*, pp.28–31.
11. W. Nichol, 'Medicine and the Labour Movement in New South Wales, 1788–1850', *Labour History* 49 (1985), 29–31.
12. Hume, 'Working Class Movements', 32; Thomas, *Labour Movement*, p.26.
13. Thomas, *Labour Movement*, p.14.
14. Thomas, *Labour Movement*, p.22.
15. S. Blair, 'The Felonry and the Free? Divisions in Colonial Society in the Penal Era', *Labour History* 45 (1983), 3–7; A. Atkinson and M. Aveling, *Australians 1838*, pp.135–6.
16. Blair, 'Felonry and the Free?', 13.
17. E. Hobsbawm, 'The Labour Aristocracy in Nineteenth Century Britain', in E. Hobsbawm (ed.), *Labouring Men*, 273.
18. G. Stedman Jones, 'Class Struggle and the Industrial Revolution', *New Left Review* 90 (1975), 35–69.
19. G. Crossick, 'The Labour Aristocracy and Its Values: A Study of Mid-Victorian Kentish London', *Victorian Studies* 19 (1976) 301–28; G. Crossick, *An Artisan Elite in Victorian Society: Kentish London 1840–1880*, Chapter 7; R. Gray, *The Labour Aristocracy in Victorian Edinburgh*, Chapters 6–7; J. Foster, *Class Struggle and the Industrial Revolution: Early Industrial Capitalism in Three English Towns*.
20. E.P. Thompson, *The Making of the English Working Class*, p.237.
21. Thompson, *English Working Class*, p.235.
22. Foster, *Class Struggle*.
23. See M. Berg, *The Age of Manufactures 1700–1820*, especially Chapters 3, 5, 7.
24. S. Marglin, 'What Do Bosses Do?' *Radical Review of Political Economics* 6 (1974), 33–60.
25. S. Pollard, *The Genesis of Modern Management: A Study of the Industrial Revolution in Great Britain*, pp.181–92.
26. C. Littler, *The Development of the Labour Process in Capitalist Societies*, Chapter 1–3; H. Braverman, *Labour and Monopoly Capital: The Degradation of Work in the Twentieth Century*, pp.70–137; D. Clawson, *Bureaucracy and the Labor Process: The Transformation of U.S. Industry 1860–1920*, Chapter 4.
27. Gray, *Labour Aristocracy*, Chapter 2.
28. Hobsbawm, 'Labour Aristocracy', 310–2.
29. Gray, *Labour Aristocracy*, p.130.
30. J. Melling, 'Non-Commissioned Officers: British Employers and Their Supervisory Workers, 1880–1920', *Social History* 5 (1980), 196.
31. Stedman-Jones, 'Class Consciousness', 66.
32. Crossick, *Aristan Elite*, p.60.
33. Connell and Irving, *Class Structure*, pp.49–50
34. Crossick, *Artisan Elite*.
35. Blair, 'Felonry and the Free?', 5.
36. See Chapter 11.
37. Connell and Irving, *Class Structure*, p.49.
38. Connell and Irving, *Class Structure*, p.49.
39. Sydney Mechanics School of Arts, *Third Annual Report for the Year 1835*, Mitchell Library, 374/95, pp.25–7.
40. R. Hughes, *The Fatal Shore*, p.175.
41. H. McQueen, 'Convicts and Rebels', *Labour History* 15 (1968), 25.

PART THREE

THE SYSTEM

Chapter Eight

The Convict Labour Market

Stephen Nicholas

Introduction: free, slave, or capitalist society?

Colonial New South Wales has been characterised as a slave society and convictism as a slave labour system. While inexorably bound together, the two concepts of convictism and slavery are not identical, a point which has escaped both contemporary observers and historians. Contemporaries asserted that assignment was slavery. Governors Arthur, Darling, Gipps and Fitzroy believed that assigned convicts were slaves, all governors having had previous experience in colonies where other forms of slavery existed.[1] Quoting Governor Bourke, Lord John Russell declared that convict and slave labour was identical, whether the convict was assigned or in government service. Even Macquarie thought that transportation, with every indulgence, was slavery.[2] The most vehement anti-slavery document, the Molesworth Report of 1838, declared unambiguously that 'Transportation . . . is much more than exile; it is slavery as well'.[3] Contemporaries identified convicts with slaves not just because of their brutish treatment at work but because they faced restraints on their freedom of action in the labour market. Similarly, historians have identified convict punishment and the work system with slavery. Ken Macnab and Russel Ward did not differentiate between slave and convict labour and K.M. Dallas viewed convicts, particularly those on assignment, like any other slave category.[4] The fact that convicts might gain a higher living standard than free workers spoke of the efficacy of any slave system, but did not alter the basic fact that convictism was slavery. Both Dorothy Cubis and A.G.L. Shaw saw convicts as a substitute for slaves in colonial Australia, but provided no detailed analysis of the similarities between the two types of forced labour.[5]

In an early attempt to incorporate capital as well as labour in a model of the Australian economy, Frank Driscoll identified a 'sheep aristocracy based on convict slave labour' as the basis of the labour system in New South Wales.[6] With Driscoll the debate widened to include not only convictism and slavery, but the origins of capitalism. Perhaps the clearest statement of the rise of colonial capitalism is K. Rowley's thesis of pastoral capitalism.[7] While Driscoll thought pastoralism depended on slave labour, Rowley argued that it depended on wage labour. Reacting to Rowley, Michael Dunn argued that Australia was a slave society, and provided an explicit definition of convictism as slavery.[8] To Dunn, capitalism and slavery are alternative production modes by which labour is exploited by a dominant class. Under the condition of slavery the whole product of labour is the master's, who then distributes part of the product to the slave for maintenance. Under capitalism, labour is a commodity, and appropriation of the labour surplus takes place in the labour market, in the act of exchange, before production. Rejecting the 1820s as the decade in which colonial capitalism arose, Dunn argued that New South Wales remained a slave society until the end of transportation in 1840 when the slave owning class finally ceased to dominate over capitalists.

For all its sharpness and simplicity, Dunn's labour market model approach to convictism is flawed by the fact that landowners did not have private property rights in convicts; ownership rights over convicts were vested in the government. Assignment was a commodity exchange when private employers paid a quasi-wage, a mix of maintenance in kind and money, for convicts allocated by the state controlled labour market. Convicts in government employment were not integrated into Dunn's conception of the labour market. According to Dunn, government service acted as a supplement both to slavery and capitalism and was not itself part of a mode of production.[9] Within the same Marxist framework, W. Nichol presents a more empirical, and useful, typology of labour relations.[10] Concerned with the ideology of paternalism in maintaining the colonial class structure, Nichol matched the ownership relation to the forces of production of public service, assigned and ticket-of-leave convicts to slaves, serfs and proletarians respectively. While presenting a spectrum of slave to wage relations, Nichol never places these labour relations into the context of the labour market. From his assertion that the government stifled the free workings of the market by restricting wages, prices and spatial mobility, it is difficult to discern whether Nichol saw two or more interacting labour markets or just one.[11]

Reacting to Dunn's slave mode of production, R.W. Connell and T.H. Irving found the origins of Australian capitalism in the dynamic formulation of the colonial labour market.[12] They saw two distinct labour markets by the 1820s: a private labour market based on propertyless labourers and a muted labour market within the penal framework of assignment.[13] They share with Dunn the clear distinction between assignment and the private market. Assignment created a muted labour market when capitalists competed for craftsmen whose rare skills were central to colonial development and when pure coercion was bad business. This led to capitalists supplementing the lash with incentives. Wage payments, whether in kind or money, made convict labour power a commodity, and part of the labour market. Connell and Irving do not romanticise the government's control of public labour as public enterprise; it was forced labour for penal purposes.

Recently John Hirst declared that historians, by asking when Australia became a free society, have been posing the wrong question.[14] Colonial New South Wales was not a society which had to become free; its freedoms were well established from the earliest times. The convicts were not like slaves, and their masters were not corrupted by power. By focusing on the convicts' legal rights and limited sentences, and the fact that their children were born free, Hirst differentiated between slave and nonslave societies.[15] Criticising Hirst, David Neil argued that the day-to-day coercion and severe corporal punishment distinguished slaves and convicts more from free workers than from each other.[16] The domination of the convicts, particularly their feelings, emotions, dignity and culture, made New South Wales a slave society, even though incentives, rations and living conditions of convicts might have been superior to that of free Englishmen. In Neil's phrase, even a dog knows the difference between being kicked and being tripped over.[17] Molesworth understood the point: 'The physical condition of a convict is generally better than that of an agricultural labourer [in England] . . . it is the restraint on freedom of action, the degradation of slavery and the other moral evils, which chiefly constitute the pains of transportation . . . '.[18] Nor was the point entirely missed by Hirst who conceded that 'convict labour was forced labour'.[19]

The debates about whether colonial New South Wales was strictly free from the beginning, or whether social relations were strictly capitalist, are both 'a trifle academic'.[20] The historical argument has obscured the main issue. While much energy has been expended on whether Australia was free or capitalist, two prior underlying assumptions about convictism have received unanimous assent; that convict forced labour differed significantly from free labour and that it was inefficient. Neither assumption has been explicitly tested. To test the efficiency of convictism, three distinct elements in colonial labour relations need to be evaluated: the labour market, the system of assignment and the nature of the work process. In the labour market, wages in money or kind equate the supply and demand of labour power in the form of a set of employment contracts between employers and workers. Accepting the existence of a capitalist labour market, including the system of assignment, this chapter explicitly models the New South Wales labour market. Based on the stylised 'facts' of the colonial labour market, the purpose of the model is to generate hypotheses which are subjected to historical testing and refinement in the rest of the book. Secondly, assignment by the state is part of the capitalist labour market but also forms a distinct and separate allocative mechanism. The efficacy of assignment has been much criticised, but not explicitly evaluated. Thirdly, the work process, particularly in the public sector, has been described mainly in terms of coercion, and coerced labour has been assumed inferior to the work organisation of free labour. There is no greater symbol of inefficiency at work than the lash. Part Three of this book examines each of these alleged failures, finding that the comparative evidence across labour systems provides little support for the view that convictism was inefficient.

Modelling the colonial labour market

Convict labour was coerced or forced labour. Coerced labour is usually defined negatively as unfree labour. Free or self-owned labour has private property rights over its own labour power. Specifically, free labour excludes others from directing its use, exclusively appropriates income from its use and can transfer or exchange both these rights.[21] Through an employment contract in the labour market, free labour exchanges the rights to determine the use of its own labour power and to gain income from its own labour for a wage. Such contracts, subject to agreed wage payments, work procedures and termination conditions, are entered into voluntarily and for a fixed duration. Coerced labour, including convict labour, slavery, serfdom, military draftees and Nazi and Soviet forced labour, also enter implicit or explicit contracts, but the contracts are determined exclusively by another party (a private individual or the state), denying the worker most property rights over his own labour. Coercive contracts, like other employment contracts, specify behaviour for both parties and are subject to enforcement through the market or the law.[22] In the convict system British and Irish courts determined the duration of the employment contract, while the colonial government regulated the type and location of work, payment, punishment and remission. While the degree of coercion varies across different classes of forced labour, all coercive contracts share two common characteristics: they compulsorily deliver labour power, and they set a wage (in terms of a consumption basket) below the workers' marginal revenue product.[23] Expressed differently, convict workers were forced to supply labour power (for which they were paid in kind or money) below the wage they could have earned if they had been free.

The supply of convict workers uniquely shaped the colonial labour market. To the usual supply and demand for free workers, a model of the colony must be augmented not only by the supply and demand for convicts, but by a public sector employing convict labour and a private sector using both free and convict workers. Below, a simple model of the Australian labour market is presented. The model generates a number of testable hypotheses concerning the issues of labour scarcity, wage levels and income transfers between free and convict workers and between the public and private sectors. Readers uninterested in the derivation of the formal labour market model or in the rather technical arguments can turn directly to the basic conclusions at the end of this section.

In colonial New South Wales, the government and private employers formed two separate but interdependent markets for labour. In both markets the demand curve sloped downward to the right: that is, more labour power was demanded as the wage rate fell relative to the price of all other goods. The supply side was more complicated: the private market employed both free and convict workers while the government employed convict labour almost exclusively. The stock of free labour was augmented by natural increases (or decreases), net immigration, and time-expired, pardoned or ticket-of-leave convicts. Since the labour force participation rates tended to be high for resident free labour, and because the opportunity cost of travel to Australia deterred free migration, even large wage rises were able to call forth only relatively small increases in labour. Consequently, the supply curve for free labour was fairly inelastic. This was particularly true of time-expired convicts who recouped income losses during their period of forced labour by high levels of participation once free. In the first years of the colony, shifts in the free labour supply were due largely to the release of time-expired convicts, but by 1835 net immigration of settlers from England was a major factor shifting the free labour supply curve.[24] Since the flow of convicts was determined by the transportation policy of the government in England, the supply curve for convict labour was perfectly inelastic.

The government or public sector is depicted in Figure 8.1 Apart from soldiers and a limited number of administrators, government labour was undertaken by convicts. The aggregate convict supply curve, S^*_C, defined the total convict population, q_2. The government distributed labour between sectors by retaining q_1 units of convict labour in the public sector and allocating q_1-q_2 assigned convicts to the private market. The supply curve of convicts for public labour, S_G, was shifted outwards by withholding new arrivals from assignment or by recalling assigned convicts, and was shifted inwards by assigning convicts to private employers or freeing convicts through tickets-of-leave, pardons and the expiry of their sentences.

The colonial government set an explicit maintenance wage, w_e, which was paid to all convicts. This wage was a mix of payment in kind (consisting of food, shelter and clothing) and money. An implicit convict wage, w_i, can be calculated by discounting at the appropriate interest rate the convict's output over his sentence after deducting for maintenance.[25] Contemporary accounts, together with our evidence on the quality of human capital embodied in convict workers, suggest that w_e fell well below w_i as shown in Figure 8.1.

To assess the efficiency of labour allocation, the colonial labour market is compared with a counterfactual market. This requires a number of limiting assumptions: the most important is that all labour is homogeneous, allowing free and unfree labour to be represented on the same diagram. Given our evidence that the human capital of convicts did not differ significantly from that of emigrants and free workers in England, the assumption of homogeneity is not unrealistic. More controversial is the choice of a counterfactual or alternative labour market with which to compare the actual colonial economy. According to established practice, the counterfactual market is chosen to minimise differences between the 'best' alternative and the actual labour market; we pose a counterfactual world in which all convicts are treated as free workers. In the private sector, the counterfactual supply curve, S_F, depicts free labour plus freed convicts, delivering q_3 units of labour at a market wage, w_m. The market wage for labour in the private sector is the same as that for labour in the public sector. Public sector convicts are assumed to remain, as free workers, in that sector in the alternative model. Counterfactual models more favourable to the convict system can be easily constructed. For example, we could assume the same total population, but based on a typical pre-1850 family migration flow with a larger number of young, old and female migrants. In this case the counterfactual labour supply would be quantitatively smaller and qualitatively inferior to that supplied by convicts. Or the counterfactual labour supply could be constructed on the 'likely' flow of free labour in the absence of transportation. G. Blainey has argued that rather than a population of 70,000 in 1830, in the absence of transportation under the most favourable conditions, population would not have reached 10,000.[26] The alternative model — in which all variables remain the

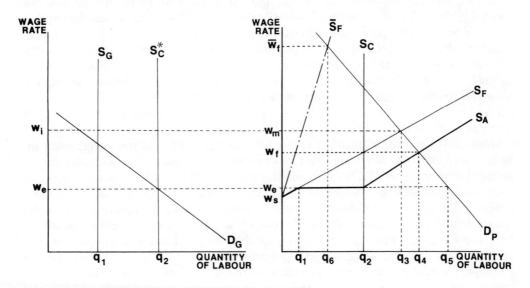

Figure 8.1:   *Public (Government)*
               Labour Market

Figure 8.2:   *Private*
               Labour Market

same except that convicts are given their freedom — means that any positive differences between the two labour markets are kept to a minimum.

Turning to the actual labour model, the supply curve for labour in the private sector in colonial New South Wales, S_A, is more complicated than that for the counterfactual market. The explicit convict maintenance wage set by the goverment meant two wage rates existed in the private sector. Convicts not allocated to public employment, q_2-q_1, were assigned to private employers at a wage, w_e, shown by the convict supply curve, S_c in Figure 8.2. Since w_e was a minimum wage, no convict labour was forthcoming below that amount. Free labour with a reservation price below w_e would have been hired in preference to convicts when private employers' labour requirements were below q_1. The operative supply curve for such free labour is w_s-q_1, but in practice it was doubtful if free workers were forthcoming at a wage below the convict minimum w_e. When the demand curve for labour fell below q_2, only assigned convicts were employed. Historically, both free and convict labour were hired by private employers in New South Wales; therefore the demand curve for labour in the private sector can be represented by D_p in Figure 8.2. Firstly, q_2 convicts were hired at the explicit maintenance wage, w_e, then q_2-q_4 free labour units were employed at the free labour wage, w_f.

The simple model highlights important growth and distributional issues within the colonial labour market. In the private market where some labour was coerced, more units of labour, q_4, were forthcoming than in an entirely free market, q_3. Since convictism allowed workers to be pushed off their preferred supply schedule, an economy with some coercion makes more labour power available, and a potentially greater output, than a free economy. Greater output in a coercive labour system may also result from forcing higher participation rates from unfree workers and controlling their location of work. While it is usually assumed that unfree workers are less productive than free labour, this assumption may not be not true if, as in New South Wales, an incentive-reward structure is part of the labour extraction process for coerced labour.[27] The distributional issues are evident in Figure 8.2 when the explicit convict wage, w_e, falls below the convict's implicit wage, w_i, transferring income from convicts to the owners of convicts, the government. More importantly, the government allowed private masters to appropriate this income differential under assignment. By failing to collect (at least until after 1825) any of the difference between the implicit wage and the maintenance wage through a tax on private employers, the government allowed income to be distributed from the state to the private employers of assigned convicts.

What do these income transfers imply for growth? Insofar as the government invested more than individual convicts did, an explicit maintenance wage created forced savings in the public sector. Not only did the government save more than convicts did; it invested in different goods. By investing in public goods, including roads, bridges and public buildings, the government created an infrastructure for the future growth of the colony. In the private sector, the forced savings of assigned convicts were appropriated by private masters. Private employers probably invested more than convicts, but certainly less than the government. The government could have charged private employers a rent on each convict equal to the difference between the free and maintenance wage, w_f-w_e, without reducing the quantity of convicts demanded, and therefore, without reducing private sector output. With the rent from private masters, the government could have purchased more investment goods. Without the transfer of income from the government to private employers the development path for the young colony would have been different, and growth probably faster.

Private versus public employment of convicts also raises the further issue of colonial development policy. There is no need to assume that homogeneous labour displays equal productivity between sectors. If the government was indifferent between public and private goods, then convicts would be assigned until the marginal productivity of convicts in public employment was equal to the marginal productivity of assigned convicts. The government was not indifferent between development paths. Certainly there was no single development strategy over the whole convict period; even within the term of each governor development policy changed. But at various times governors showed clear preference for public goods or private goods, implying that labour productivity varied between sectors. The government did not distribute labour between the public and private sectors to duplicate the economic development of a counterfactual free labour market. The detailed study of the aims of the colonial government development policy undertaken by Barrie Dyster in Chapter 9 shows that planned growth clearly involved social as well as purely economic goals. Not surprisingly, the development aims of colonial administrators often conflicted with the interests of private masters. Indeed, complaints by private employers cannot be taken as proof of inefficiences in the allocation of labour.

Figure 8.2 also indicates that the existence of convicts meant a transfer of income from free labour to employers in the private sector. In the counterfactual market economy, with convicts treated like free workers, the market wage rate, w_m, was above the free labour wage, w_f, when convicts received a maintenance wage. In the presence of coerced labour, free labour received a lower wage. The implications for growth depend on the different savings-consumption decisions of private employers, free labour and convicts.

The assignment of q_2 units of convict labour at the explicit maintenance wage led to complaints by private employers of a 'shortage' of convict labour. At the fixed wage, w_e, Figure 8.2 shows that private employers wanted to have q_5 units of coerced labour and no free labour. Two prices for homogeneous labour led to an insatiable demand for assigned convicts, although there were no labour shortages in the conventional sense. Insofar as private employers exercised political power, they could pressure the government to assign more convicts to the private sector, shifting out the supply curve, S_c. Free labour suffered: the greater the quantity of coerced labour available, the fewer the number of free workers hired and the lower the free labour wage. Not surprisingly, the use of convict labour was a major political issue fought along class lines in New South Wales.

The issues of income distribution and class become more complex with the relaxation of the homogeneous labour assumption. Figure 8.2 remains a close approximation only for subsets of labour, such as unskilled or skilled free and convict labour. Since the marginal productivity of convicts varied across skill and educational attainment, the greater a convict's marginal productivity above the explicit maintenance wage, the greater the transfer of income from convicts to the government and from the government to private employers of assigned convicts. This, in part, motivated the New South Wales government to charge private masters a rent on mechanics in the 1820s. Further, in the absence of a free market to differentiate skill through different wage rates, one explicit maintenance wage encouraged private employers to substitute skilled for unskilled assigned labour. This helps explain the persistent complaints by private employers that the assignment system denied them skilled mechanics. Such complaints reflect the desire of private employers to upgrade the skill component of their assigned servants rather than proof that assignment was inefficient. The efficiency of government assignment depends on how close government allocation approached some 'optimal' allocation, given the basket of private and public goods which the government wanted produced.

There is another crucial factor determining colonial income distribution. The Treasury in England was responsible for public expenditure not covered by local taxes and duties. The explicit wage was partly financed by Treasury grants. The more convicts assigned to private employers, the smaller the public workforce and the lower the costs of maintenance to the English taxpayer. Convict labour in the government sector was engaged totally in public works. In a free market, private underinvestment in public goods, such as roads and bridges, arises when charges for their use are impossible or prohibitively expensive to collect. Usually the state provides public goods since it has the power to collect charges for their use through taxation. Both London and the colonial administrators recognised the need for government financed public infrastructure in the early development of the new colony. However, the English government's preference for public goods was likely to be less than that of the colonial administrators in New South Wales since the benefits of public goods in Australia are directly consumed only by Australians. The British government's representative in Australia, Commissioner Bigge, valued a different basket of public and private goods than that assembled by Macquarie. The Bigge Report offered an alternative scheme for colonial development. Bigge's program had the effect of reducing the income flow from English taxpayers to the Australian colonists in terms of roads, bridges and public buildings. Rather than a test of the efficiency of the convict labour market under Macquarie, Bigge's criticism of Macquarie should be seen as the clash of two alternative development strategies.

The counterfactual labour market assumed an economy with the same amount of labour as actually existed in New South Wales, but treated convicts as free labour. An alternative counterfactual model is an economy to which no convicts were sent. Depending on how colonial adminstrators and soldiers were treated, $\bar{S}_F$ in Figure 8.2 depicts the supply of free labour, q_6, which actually migrated to Australia. Clearly, only a small quantity of labour is available, and wage rate, $\bar{w}_f$, is well above both the first counterfactual free wage, w_m, and the actual free labour wage, w_f. Since free migrants only numbered 7998 by 1830, a 'no-convict' counterfactual economy would have experienced low levels of growth, and seriously retarded development.[28] Of course, without convicts a higher level of free migration to New South Wales may have occurred. But the 'tyranny of distance' certainly would have meant much lower levels of free immigration than the transfer of labour under forced migration.

Our model of the colonial labour market yields a number of testable hypotheses concerning the economy. In a private market where some labour is coerced, more units of labour were forthcoming than in an entirely free market. Since the quality of the human capital of free British migrants and convict workers was the same, under convictism there was potentially greater output than in a free economy. Greater output depended on the ability to force coerced workers off their normal free labour supply curve, to increase their participation rate and to extract work. The success with which each of these was achieved determined the efficiency of convictism and is the major concern of Part Three of this book.

The model shows that in a private market with forced labour the wage of free workers was below that in a labour market where all workers were free. Predictably, opposition to the convict system came from free migrant labourers and ex-convicts. Ian Turner, Lelia Thomas, L.J. Hume and Max Hartwell discovered that the free workers were prominent in the agitation to end assignment and transportation.[29] Turner caught the thrust of the argument that free workers received a lower wage under convictism when he stated that 'the use of convict labour was a continuing threat to free workers as it weakened their bargaining power in the labour market.[30] The lower wage for free labour under convictism meant private masters received a wage subsidy from free workers. At least until 1825 when the government attempted to charge for assigned artisans, private masters were also subsidised by the government. The subsidy was the difference between the cost of maintaining convicts (the fixed maintenance wage) and their productivity (implicit wage). That the fixed maintenance wage was below the convicts' implicit wage also meant that private employers demanded more labour than the government would assign. The failure of the government to charge private employers a rent equal to the full economic worth of the assigned convict created a 'labour shortage', with private masters complaining that they were starved of labour. The same fixed maintenance wage across all categories of convict workers led private employers to prefer mechanics over unskilled workers, leading to the claim that they were denied artisans. While the complaints by masters over the quantity and quality of assignment reflect the government's pricing policy of convicts, these complaints are not proof of the inefficiency of convictism. The unquestioning acceptance by historians of such complaints and their assumption that such negative comments support the case that convictism was inefficient, is misplaced.

The efficiency of assignment depended on the efficacy with which the government allocated labour between the private and public sectors to further its colonial development policy. Assignment was a mechanism through which the government directed colonial development. Of course there was no one single development strategy; governments experimented with different mixes of public and private goods through the retention and assignment of convicts. Such policies frequently conflicted with the labour demands of private employers. They also conflicted with the wishes of the British government. Since part of the cost of maintaining convicts was borne by the British taxpayer, the level of public good provision (and the added cost of maintaining convicts in public employment) was a source of conflict best reflected in the Bigge Report.

Without transportation, growth in colonial New South Wales would have been much slower. The counterfactual labour market (the labour market without transportation) would have made available many fewer workers or, if we assume the same number of workers as under convictism, workers willing to work fewer hours. The greater supply of labour power under convictism created the potential for growth. Whether that potential could be realised, depended on the efficiency of the system of convict work organisation and the process of labour extraction. Historians have assumed that convictism was inefficient. We test that proposition. After evaluating convictism in terms of assignment, the work process for private and public labour and the care and treatment of convicts, Part Three of this book concludes that convictism was an efficient labour system. Below, a general test of the efficiency of convictism assesses the success of the labour market in matching convict skills to colonial jobs.

Labour market efficiency: was the allocation of labour a 'giant lottery'?

The efficiency of a labour market is judged by how well it matches the 'right' workers to the 'right' jobs. Therefore the view that assignment was a lottery is a damning criticism of the efficacy of the colonial labour market. The persistent complaints by private masters that few skilled mechanics were assigned to rural employment, and that those convict workers who were assigned were indifferently trained in their trades, lends support to the lottery thesis. The complaints by masters must be accepted cautiously. It should be remembered that private employers argued self-interest. Not only did they disparage convicts, but private masters were equally prone to complaining about the quality of free and indentured workers. Nor is their evidence free of contradiction: masters (some of whom on other occasions had complained bitterly about the convicts' work effort) frequently praised the quality and effort of assigned men. The complaints by private employers have received a full hearing from historians. In part, the grumbles of the masters have confirmed the historians' preconceived belief that convictism was inefficient. There is a second reinforcing conviction held by historians: that a partially state-administered labour market must be inferior to the free market. Ironically, even Marxist historians have argued that government intervention to control prices and wages 'stifled' the free workings of the colonial labour market.[31] Little evidence is advanced for this presumption, other than the complaints by private masters. As a first step in assessing labour relations in colonial New South Wales, the success with which convict skills were matched to Australian jobs is used to test directly the efficiency of the labour market.

The population of New South Wales was subject to a good deal of counting. The first detailed record on each convict was the indent, which was added to in meticulous detail by records on assignment, work, punishment, tickets-of-leave and pardons, marriage and death. Of course, not only convicts, but the free population, were included in some of these records. The first source of information on the whole population was the general musters, or censuses, beginning in 1791.[32] Unfortunately the quality of the musters tended to decline; free inhabitants could not be forced to attend general musters and the magistrates were inaccurate and careless in compiling the returns. In 1828 the Governor, Sir Ralph Darling, passed through the Legislative Council an Act compelling free colonists to attend the general muster, fixing a £10 fine for neglect or false statements. For the 1828 census each bench of magistrates ensured the completion of the census form and its return to the colonial secretary. A clerk, accompanied by a district constable, visited each household to complete the forms on the basis of verbal statements submitted by each householder or individual questioned. Undoubtedly there were inconsistencies and inaccuracies, but the 1828 census, where every household was visited, was certainly more accurate than today's national census.[33]

The 1828 muster provides a listing of the jobs which made up the Australian labour market. From the census, 1389 men in our sample of convicts transported to New South Wales between 1817 and 1827 were identified. Convicts in gaol and penal settlements were not included in the sample. The convicts were identified first by name, then further checked against the age, birthplace and date of arrival information on the indents. Women were excluded because they were nearly impossible to identify due to their change of name on marriage. The male convicts provide a random sample of the match between occupations in the United Kingdom and their jobs in New South Wales. The match was based on a strict definition of occupations; for example, a harnessmaker in New South Wales was treated as a different occupation than shoemaker at home, although both jobs employed similar manual skills. By matching occupations to jobs it was possible to test the efficiency of the entire labour market, not just the assignment system or the free market. Most of the convicts who arrived in 1817 or 1821 were free by servitude, pardon or tickets-of-leave by 1828 and had found jobs through the free labour market. Those convicts who arrived after 1825 were, by 1828, still mainly assigned to private masters or employed by the state in public works.

To test the efficacy of the labour market the number of convicts labouring in the same occupations in Australia as they held at home was compared to a random distribution and to a perfect match of United Kingdom skills and colonial jobs. The random distribution captures the features of a lottery, while a perfect match is the best allocation possible of the convicts' skills to New South Wales jobs. The perfect match is a computer matching of skills and job openings. Free wage markets are not as efficient as a computer in allocating workers. There are costs in using the market related to gaining information, assessing labour quality and transferring workers geographically. In the labour market workers change occupations to earn more income or better and steadier employment. Occupational shifts are not allowed in the perfect allocation, but to the extent that such shifts occur in a free market there is a movement away from the perfect match. Perhaps one of the most important opportunities available to nineteenth century migrants was the ability to seek economic advancement by changing occupations. Indeed, migrants are more occupationally mobile than native-born workers. Therefore the perfect match sets an upper bound with which to judge the labour market; the purely random allocation of workers sets the lower bound.

In Table 8.1 an index is presented to assess how close the random and actual allocation of workers corresponded to the perfect distribution. The index ranged between 1 (when the random or actual distribution coincided with the perfect) and 0 (when the random or actual distribution shared no job matches with the perfect). For the perfect distribution, a computer program took each occupation in our sample from the muster and searched for a convict with the skills to undertake the job. Most occupations had more skilled workers available to undertake the job than job openings. For example, there were 16 bakers in our sample from the census but 27 convicts who had been bakers at home. The perfect distribution would therefore have been 16. Farm workers and herdsmen were the two major exceptions: there were 479 job openings for these two occupations but only 199 convict workers with the requisite skills. In this instance the perfect distribution was determined by United Kingdom skills, that is, 199. Once the perfect distribution was constructed, the random and actual indexes were calculated. The first step was to derive the actual and random distributions, then divide these by the perfect distribution to get an index. A computer simulation program randomly allocated convict workers to each New South Wales job, providing the random distribution. For example, the random distribution did not match a single United Kingdom baker with the 16 baking jobs, so the random index in Table 8.1 is 0. However, for the 40 bookmaking jobs in the perfect distribution, the random distri-

Table 8.1: *Matching of Male Convict Skills to New South Wales Occupations 1817–28*
        (by Occupation)

Occupation	Index		Occupation	Index	
	Random	Actual		Random	Actual
Baker	0.00	0.75	Hatter	0.00	1.00
Barber	0.00	0.40	Herdsman	0.00	0.30
Blacksmith	0.00	0.67	Horsebreaker	0.00	0.00
Boatbuilder	0.00	1.00	Hutkeeper	1.00	1.00
Boatman	0.00	0.20	Ironmonger	1.00	1.00
Bookbinder	0.00	1.00	Knitter, Framework	0.00	1.00
Bookmaker	0.08	0.83	Labourer	0.19	0.32
Brassfounder	0.00	0.75	Labourer, Gang	0.24	0.41
Brazier	0.00	1.00	Limeburner	1.00	1.00
Brewer	0.00	0.00	Locksmith	0.00	1.00
Bricklayer	0.00	0.75	Mason	0.00	0.78
Brickmaker	0.10	0.30	Miller	0.00	1.00
Bruchmaker	0.00	1.00	Mineral watermaker	0.00	0.00
Butcher	0.00	0.73	Nailmaker	0.00	1.00
Buttonmaker	0.00	0.00	Painter	0.00	0.33
Cabinetmaker	0.00	1.00	Plasterer	0.00	0.80
Carpenter	0.00	0.76	Ropemaker	0.00	1.00
Carrier	0.00	0.00	Saddlemaker	0.00	1.00
Charcoalburner	1.00	1.00	Sailmaker	0.00	1.00
Clerk	0.00	0.64	Sawyer	0.00	0.60
Coachmaker	0.00	0.00	Schoolmaster	0.00	0.00
Compositor	0.00	1.00	Servant	0.13	0.27
Confectioner	0.00	0.00	Shipwright	0.00	1.00
Cooper	0.00	0.67	Silversmith	0.00	1.00
Cutlerymaker	0.00	1.00	Slater	0.00	1.00
Dresser	0.00	0.00	Stableman	0.00	0.00
Driver, Bullock	1.00	1.00	Tailor	0.00	1.00
Exciseman	1.00	1.00	Tanner	0.00	1.00
Farmworker	0.21	0.41	Telegraph signaller	1.00	1.00
Fencemaker	0.00	0.00	Upholsterer	0.00	1.00
Fisherman	0.00	0.00	Watchmaker	0.00	1.00
Gardener	0.00	0.71	Weaver	0.00	0.72
Gunsmith	0.00	0.33	Wheelwright	0.00	0.67
			Whitesmith	0.00	1.00

Source: Convict Indents.

bution chose 3 bookmakers by chance, thus the index was 3/40 or 0.08. The actual distribution counted the number of convict workers who held the same job in Australia as they had practised at home. Of the 16 baking jobs in New South Wales, 12 were held by transported bakers, yielding an index of 0.75.

Comparing the two indices in Table 8.1 the random index is near 0, indicating that allocation by luck would have resulted in few convicts being in the same occupation in New South Wales as they held at home. The actual distribution was surprisingly close to the perfect. Clearly the labour market did not operate as a lottery. For many skilled occupations in Table 8.1, including bricklayer, carpenter, mason, tailor and brazier, the actual index was 0.75 or above. To get an overall view, Table 8.2 bunches occupations

Table 8.2: *Matching of Male United Kingdom and New South Wales Occupations 1817–28 (by Skill Industry Categories)*

Skill-Industry Category	Index	
	Random	Actual
Skilled urban trades	0.03	0.70
Skill construction trades	0.01	0.59
Rural occupations	0.18	0.42
Unskilled urban labour[a]	0.21	0.32
Unskilled urban labour[b]	0.19	0.33
Domestic service	0.13	0.27
Total[c]	0.13	0.44

a. Includes labourers to quarry, road and town gangs.
b. Excludes labourers in quarry, road and town gangs.
c. Includes occupations — boatman, carrier, exciseman, schoolmaster and telegraph signaller — not assigned to a skill-industry category.
Source: Convict Indents.

into five large classes: skilled urban, skilled construction, rural occupations, unskilled urban and domestic service. Taking all five groups together, the random index at 0.13 compared to the actual index at 0.44, reinforces our conclusion that the actual labour market performed well in its allocation of convict skills to Australian jobs. The skilled urban and construction trades with an actual index of 0.70 and 0.59 respectively, illustrate how effectively the colonial administrators and the free market utilised scarce skills needed to build up the colony. There was a higher premium on the industrial and building skills than rural skills as the rural occupation index of 0.42 indicates. Nevertheless, agricultural skills were more carefully harboured than unskilled urban labour and domestic servants where the actual index was only 0.32 and 0.27 respectively. These were jobs which required little training or skill other than muscle. It was easy to substitute unskilled workers in one occupation for unskilled workers in another, different job. The actual index was significantly above the random, but compared with the perfect index, convict workers were least perfectly matched to unskilled and domestic service jobs in New South Wales.

The labour market's success in matching United Kingdom skills to Australian jobs depended on the workers' employment status. Table 8.3 shows that convicts in government service and assigned convicts were less likely to utilise their home skills in Australia than were workers who were on tickets-of-leave or free. Not surprisingly, workers with rural skills were more likely to find themselves working in similar jobs to those they held at home than convicts from an urban background. After urban convicts received their tickets-of-leave, they more successfully utilised their United Kingdom skills, bringing themselves level with the convicts from a rural background. Once the convicts were free, over 60 per cent found a job in New South Wales which used the skills they had practised at home. The further away from bondage, the better matched were home skills and colonial jobs.

Table 8.3 is not so much a measure of the efficiency of skill allocation (since there is no comparative perfect distribution), but rather a guide to the degree of job restructuring. It suggests that the needs of the public sector were met by the forced employment of many urban workers in unfamiliar jobs. Significantly, as convicts

Table 8.3: *Matching of Male United Kingdom and New South Wales Occupations 1817–27*
(by Worker's Status)
(Percentages)

Worker's status	Urban trades		Rural trades	
	Same occupation	Different occupations	Same occupations	Different occupations
Government service	34.9	65.1	45.4	54.6
Ticket-of-Leave	45.0	55.0	45.8	54.1
Free-by-Servitude	61.1	38.9	62.6	37.4

Source: Convict Indents.

gained their freedom, they chose to utilise their old skills learned at home and often practised in their own time even during their period of servitude. During the period of forced labour, Australia was fortunate in being able to assign men to jobs such as building roads and clearing land, which the state defined as important for development, but which men rejected once they gained their freedom. Of equal importance, the state chose for these jobs the men whose United Kingdom skills were least well-suited to the needs of the colony, the urban workers. Table 8.2 shows that most of the restructuring of labour skills to the needs of a rural economy were borne by the unskilled urban and the domestic service workers. The amount of retraining was significant; less than one-third of these workers found employment in jobs utilising their previous skills. From the perspective of New South Wales, 38 per cent of the 544 farm occupations in our sample from the 1828 census were filled by unskilled urban workers and general servants. Certain skilled workers, whose trades were not in great demand in New South Wales, also found employment in agricultural jobs. For example, weavers were in oversupply, with 42 per cent employed as rural labourers. In contrast, the 333 skilled urban New South Wales jobs drew 65 per cent of their workers from convicts who had engaged in similar occupations in the United Kingdom, and a further 21 per cent from other skilled occupations, leaving only 14 per cent of the colony's skilled labour force reliant on the training of unskilled workers from home. Skilled English workers were more trainable than unskilled workers, a proposition recognised by colonial administrators as much as by the labour market.

Conclusion

New South Wales had a complex system of free and forced labour markets. The public sector, in which convicts worked on government projects, acted as a vast reservoir supplying labour power to private employers through assignment. The use both of free wage workers and forced assigned convict labour meant the formation of one intertwined and mutually dependent private labour market. For the same quality of labour power there existed two wage rates, a maintenance wage for convict workers set by the government, and a competitive wage for free men dependent, in part, on the supply of convicts. From this anomaly sprang the demand by private employers for the assignment of greater numbers of (and better quality) convicts; the ability of private employers to extract rents from the convicts when their productivity differed from their maintenance wage; and the struggle within the colonial government and between the home government in London and the colonial administrators in Sydney over the best development policy for the colony.

In this chapter, the overall allocative efficiency of the labour market, including public labour, assignment and the operation of the free labour market, was tested. We found that the labour market utilised the convicts' industrial, building and agricultural skills in New South Wales to a remarkable extent. The occupations of the unskilled urban worker and domestic servant were not in great demand in the colony and these workers took the brunt of job restructuring necessary to match United Kingdom skills with Australian job requirements. The labour market was efficient, and the view that assignment was a lottery receives no empirical support. Building on the allocative efficiency of the labour market, Chapter 9 assesses the background of public labour and private assignment, Chapter 10 analyses the economics of work organisation and labour extraction for public labour, and Chapter 11 studies the operation of the largest private employer of convict labour in New South Wales, the Australian Agricultural Company. Finally, Chapter 12 evaluates the care and feeding of convicts in New South Wales within a comparative context, drawing on the experiences of free and other coerced labour. Overall, Part Three of this book finds that labour relations in New South Wales were efficient; it is the similarities that the convict system shared with other labour systems rather than the perceived differences, which stand out. If historians are to continue to present convictism as an inefficient system of labour relations for a developing colonial society, then they must begin to present empirical evidence.

NOTES

1. K.M. Dallas, 'Slavery in Australia - Convicts, Emigrants and Aborigines', *Tasmanian Historical Research Association Paper and Proceedings* 16 (1968), 63.
2. A.G.L. Shaw, *Convicts and the Colonies*, p.103.
3. *Report from the Select Committee on Transportation* (Molesworth Report), Parliamentary Paper, 1837–38, XXII, C669, 21.
4. K. Macnab and R. Ward, 'The Nature and Nurture of the First Generation of Native-Born Australians' *Historical Studies: Australia and New Zealand* 10 (1962), 292; Dallas, 'Slavery', 61.
5. D. Cubis, 'Australian Character in the Making: New South Wales, 1788–1901' *Journal of the Royal Australian Historical Society* 24 (1938), 169; Shaw, *Convict and Colonies*, p.20.
6. F. Driscoll, 'Macquarie's Administration of the Convict System', *Journal of the Royal Australian Historical Society* 27 (1941), 374.
7. K. Rowley, 'Pastoral Capitalism: Australia's Pre-Industrial Development', *Intervention* 1 (1972), 9–26.
8. M. Dunn, 'Early Australia: Wage Labour or Slave Society?' in E. Wheelwright and K. Buckley (eds.), *Essays in the Political Economy of Australian Capitalism* I, 33–46.
9. Dunn, 'Wage Labour', 45.
10. W. Nichol, 'Ideology and the Convict System in New South Wales, 1788–1820', *Historical Studies: Australia and New Zealand* 22 (1986), 1–20.
11. Nichol, 'Ideology', 9–10, 13.
12. R.W. Connell and T. Irving, *Class Structure in Australian History: Documents, Narrative and Argument*, Chapter 1–2.
13. Connell and Irving, *Class Structure*, pp.37–8.
14. J.B. Hirst, *Convict Society and Its Enemies*, p.7.
15. Hirst, *Convict Society*, p.82.
16. D. Neil, 'Free Society, Penal Colony, Slave Society, Prison?' (unpublished manuscript, 1984), 21.
17. Neil, 'Free Society', 32.
18. S.C. on Transportation, 1837–8, 31.
19. Hirst, *Convict Society*, p.21.

20. Connell and Irving, *Class Structure*, p.66.
21. S. Engerman, 'Some Considerations Relating to Property Rights to Man', *Journal of Economic History* 33 (1973), 43–4.
22. B. Klein, 'Transaction Cost Determinants of "Unfair" Contractual Arrangements', *American Economic Review* 70 (1980), 356–62.
23. The marginal revenue product is the convict's implicit wage and can be calculated as: Wage = Σ $Q_n/(l-r)^n$ where Q is yearly output net of maintenance costs, n is length of sentence and r is the interest (discount) rate. Clearly the implicit wage varies across individuals due to skill, age and sex.
24. N. Butlin, 'White Human Capital in Australia 1788–1850', *Australian National University Working Papers in Economic History* 32 (1985), 13.
25. See footnote 23.
26. G. Blainey, *The Tyranny of Distance*, p.149.
27. Engerman, 'Property Rights to Man', 46.
28. Butlin, 'White Human Capital', 13.
29. I. Turner, *In Union is Strength: A History of Trade Unions in Australia 1788–1978*, p.12; L. Thomas, *The Development of the Labour Movement in the Sydney District of New South Wales*, p.17, 20; L.J. Hume, 'Working Class Movements in Sydney and Melbourne Before the Gold Rushes' in M. Beever and F.B. Smith (eds.), *Historical Studies: Select Articles*, 39; R.M. Hartwell, *The Economic Development of Van Diemen's Land 1820–1850*, p.89.
30. Turner, *Union is Strength*, p.12. See also Hume, 'Working-Class Movements', 39.
31. Nichol, 'Ideology', 9–10.
32. M.R. Sainty and K.A. Johnson, (eds.), *Census of New South Wales: November 1828*, pp.9–20.
33. Sainty and Johnson, *Census*, pp.14–15.

Chapter Nine

Public Employment
and Assignment
to Private Masters, 1788–1821

Barrie Dyster

Introduction

It was the assignment of convicts to private masters that identified the convict system as a type of slavery, according to Sir William Molesworth and the evidence he stage-managed before the House of Commons Select Committee on Transportation in 1837. The minister responsible for prisons in 1837, Lord John Russell, Secretary of State for Home Affairs, endorsed this view. All convicts should be placed on public works to avoid 'evils ... exaggerated by the difference of the humanity, weakness, fear or caprice of different masters'.[1] By November of that year Australian colonists knew that cabinet expected to end assignment soon. The governors in New South Wales and Van Diemen's Land began to wind down the assignment system by stages.[2]

Russell became Secretary of State for Colonies at the beginning of 1839. He spoke his mind as vigorously as before:

> The servitude or slavery, which is comprehended under the word assignment, varies and must vary as slavery does, according to the temper and character of the master to whom the convict is assigned. The worst criminal may have the best master, and the most repentant may be driven into fresh offences by the oppression of which he is the victim, and the profligacy of which he is the witness.[3]

The British government stopped transporting prisoners to New South Wales in 1840. In compensation it directed twice the number to Van Diemen's Land annually as had gone there in previous years. Instead of being assigned, all newcomers in 1840 stepped ashore into public gangs. Transportation itself had not been abandoned, nor even reduced, but, in a period allegedly influenced by principles of laissez-faire, control of convicts by the private sector was judged to be at the same time cruelly arbitrary and not rigorous enough.

Yet a quarter of a century earlier, when the convict system expanded and consolidated after the Napoleonic Wars had ended in 1815, assignment had become quite explicitly the system's cornerstone. Ironically, criticism of expense and inefficiency voiced in the 1810s by Whigs and Radicals (a generation older than the Whig Russell and the Radical Molesworth) contributed to the decision that private masters should carry the cost and supervise the labour of convicts at every moment possible.

This chapter will examine the balance struck between public and private employment before 1821, the year in which both Commissioner John Thomas Bigge and Governor Lachlan Macquarie sailed from Sydney for London. More than one-fifth of the convicts sampled for this book arrived in New South Wales in the second half of Macquarie's governorship, where they experienced a regime that put many of them to public work rather than into private assignment, and that stipulated a basic wage for every prisoner. Bigge, on the other hand, who was sent by the British cabinet in 1819 to report on the Australian colonies, foreshadowed the end of the basic wage and advised that public employment should be a last resort, reserved as punishment for men and women who had committed offences in Australia itself. Bigge's recommendations guided practice in New South Wales after 1821.

Evolution 1788 — 1810

Problems of expense and of economic hardship perplexed Governor Arthur Phillip at the very outset of the colony in 1788. Phillip tried three solutions — putting everyone to work under government, leaving everyone to their own devices, and placing some people in the employ of others. Public farming and public labour held out the prospect of self-sufficiency in food and shelter, but at the cost of comprehensive supervision, and with unavoidable public outlays for seeds, livestock, clothing, tools and all other imported goods. If he left everyone to their own devices the governor sharpened the incentive to work or starve, and he reduced charges on the public purse, but it was not Britain's intention to emancipate every prisoner as soon as their foot struck Australian soil. Phillip did pardon many people before time, as encouragement to provide for themselves and others, or as reward for good behaviour, and he did decree a very brief official workday when famine was greatest so that people might develop their own vegetable gardens, but he had no mandate to convert transportation into an automatic passport to freedom.[4]

The third alternative, as servants to private masters, developed side by side with public labour and early emancipation. Phillip granted farming land to discharged non-commissioned and rank-and-file soldiers, and to some of the convicts he pardoned. To the soldiers he allotted convict labourers proportionate to rank and to size of family. It was only a matter of time before the military officers and the civil officers demanded land and labour in their turn. Superficially, assignment in New South Wales resembled the system that operated in the American colonies before 1776. In practice it was very different. Before 1776 the ship's contractor who transported prisoners across the Atlantic owned the prisoner's labour, and made his profit by hiring the prisoner for the period of sentence to an employer in America. In Australia the government retained control over the prisoner, itself deciding whether or not to assign, and whether to withdraw the convict from assignment if the servant (or, indeed, the master) misbehaved.

In the three years between Phillip's departure in 1792 and the arrival of his successor the officers ran the colony. Predictably, they extended the practice of assignment. Less predictably, they failed to amend the shortened official work day that Phillip had laid down and the consequent practice of paying convicts for any tasks done out of hours. As castaways far from any comparable settlement, soldiers and prisoners depended on each other for survival. The governor had decided that prisoners mustered at 5 a.m. could not be expected to co-operate if forced to toil in the Australian sun after 3 p.m. During famine, as we have seen, they needed to conserve their strength even more and apply their conserved strength to supplementing the scanty rations in the government storehouse. In their free time, when they were 'on their own hands', as the phrase had it, they could hire themselves for casual jobs. Officers whose concerns were still too rudimentary to afford (or house) a large permanent workforce of their own welcomed the existence of a floating labour supply that remained 'on the stores', which was to say fed and clothed by government.

The limitation on hours and the opportunity to work on their own hands, which prisoners at public labour enjoyed, could not be denied to those assigned to private masters, unless the masters were prepared to face continuous sullen resistance and concerted attempts by their servants to be returned to government. Convicts employed by government did bear one cost that assigned servants avoided, the cost of their own lodging. Before the Hyde Park Barracks was completed, as late as 1819, males under government at Sydney had to find their own accommodation in the town; some of their after-hours wages paid for this. What the man at public labour lost in disposable income, however, he gained in freedom and companionship, for assigned servants had to lodge with their masters, under conditions of the master's choosing.

A class of houseowners and landlords developed in the towns whose income derived from wages earned by prisoners employed by government; they supported this hybrid system, of course. So did local producers of food, and wholesalers and retailers of imported goods — that is to say, those officers and other free residents who owned productive land or engaged in trade — because the part-time wage earners expanded the market for consumable goods. Payment for work done after hours meant that the masters of labour — many of whom were also landlords, producers and traders — had less pressure placed on them by their assigned servants to augment the basic rations, clothing and shelter which regulations laid down, unless it were in payment for extra work done for themselves; and they had access each afternoon to the pool of workers 'on the stores', and (potentially) to any person assigned to a neighbour as well.

These practices standardised industrial relations for the masters. They held out hope to prisoners of improvement, however slight, in their standard of living. Successive governors set a rate of 10 pence for each afternoon worked, basing it on English agricultural pay scales as they understood them. Using the same yardstick the governors stipulated that men who were free were to be paid £10 a year, a fixed amount that quickly became the minimum wage in a land where the prices of imported goods far exceeded those in Britain. As the concerns of larger masters became well established their need for after hours assistance ceased being intermittent. They then came to resent the uncertainty and expense of bidding against neighbours for the services of their own assigned men. Governor King met their wishes by ordering, in October 1800, 'that if their master could give them employment for the remainder of the time — that is to say, after 3 p.m. — at the established rate, assigned servants were to do his work in preference to any other person's'.[5] Prisoners whose masters bound them permanently under this order received an annual wage of £10, the free man's minimum, equivalent to 240 afternoons on the old terms. Convicts assigned in outlying areas, or where alternative employers for their skills were scarce for other reasons, gained income from this arrangement; craftsmen whose skills were in demand probably lost; and the convicts' power to bargain undoubtedly diminished whenever a master chose to commute piece rates into the annual lump sum. From the authorities' point of view it reduced the number of prisoners wandering the roads at sundown between jobs.

It was about this time, at the turn of the century, that another aspect of the system, the ticket-of-leave, took form as well. It was the last and the least of the ways a convict could escape strict bondage. The simplest escape lay through serving out one's term of seven or fourteen years, to become 'free by servitude'; this option was obviously denied prisoners sentenced for life. An absolute pardon, conferred before the sentence expired, meant what it said. It was less common than a conditional pardon, whose 'special condition' was 'that such felon or offender shall not return within any part of [the] Kingdom of Great Britain or Ireland during the term or time which shall thus remain unexpired of his or her original sentence'.[6] The ticket-of-leave, like emancipation, allowed the convict to go 'on his own hands' completely, but he remained a convict. It thus kept each ticket holder under the scrutiny of the bench of magistrates. Misdemeanour as judged by the bench brought a ticket into jeopardy; the holder risked return to assignment or a government gang. The ticket, both before and after bestowal, was meant to be an incentive to diligence and good conduct. It introduced flexibility into the labour market at a time when assigned servants were being tied closer to their masters, and it offered ticket holders the chance of a free man's wage while denying them a free man's security. It was a neat marriage of incentive and threat.

Macquarie's decade 1810 — 21

The questions of premature freedom, and of the prisoner's wage, worried people in Britain. Both seemed to weaken transportation as a punishment and a deterrent. It was hard to object outright to the prospect of rewards as a tactic in maintaining discipline; the perennial debate throughout the decades of transportation concerned the frequency of these rewards, and the kinds of behaviour that merited a pardon or a ticket. On his installation as governor at the very beginning of 1810 Macquarie cancelled some of the conditional pardons granted by the rebel regime that had ruled the colony in 1808 and 1809. In 1811 he announced that tickets-of-leave could not be earned without an 'uninterrupted period of good conduct' of three years at least.[7] Table 9.1 shows the incidence of clemency in each year of Macquarie's term, omitting the last one, 1821.

A.G.L. Shaw has estimated that pardons issued by Macquarie differed little as a proportion of convict population from those issued by Governors Hunter (1795—1800) and King (1800—1806).[8] As the number of convicts arriving rose steeply in the second half of Macquarie's decade, and the creation of masters (through migration, or through emancipation of convicts endowed with capital and land) failed to keep pace, the number of prisoners on the stores increased. As one way of slowing the growth in public expenditure Macquarie released more of them, by pardon and ticket, to work on their own hands. Under the pressure of numbers there were times when he strayed from his own guidelines of a minimum unblemished period of servitude, and so laid himself open to criticism by anyone who was looking to find fault. If the guidelines were breached, however, to allow a convict to support a wife and children on a free man's wage, or to reward a burst of hard labour that built a bridge or road, the governor's defence lay in recognising and encouraging civic virtues that transcended the fortunate convict's individual merits.

Although convict incomes attracted less attention, once their attention was drawn observers from outside were very puzzled. In the instructions accompanying Macquarie to Sydney in 1809 Viscount Castlereagh, Secretary of State for the Colonies wrote:

It is understood that with regard to male convicts they are in general apprenticed out to the settlers for a term, the settlers engaging to find each clothing, victuals and £10 a year in money. Whether this allowance be not too great and too burdensome to the settler in all cases will require your consideration.[9]

Five months after he reached Australia Macquarie responded:

As yet no complaint has been made to me by any of the settlers respecting the high rate of wages given to such convict servants as are allowed them by government; but if it should appear on further enquiry that the wages hitherto allowed are too burthensome to the settlers, I shall frame such new regulations on that head as may appear advisable.[10]

The leading proprietors, whom he cross-examined on many matters in these early months, presumably advised him to let the matter rest.

The years that followed offered constant opportunity for 'further enquiry', and convinced Macquarie that the payment system should continue, although under stricter conditions. Regulations gazetted in 1814 admonished masters who released their servants on their own hands in the afternoon; it was a cause of disorder, he felt. The practice persisted, so in a regulation issued in December 1816 he made the £10 wage compulsory, whether the master used his convict after hours or not. Previously the amount need only be paid if the master wished the convict to be on call at all times. A wage for female convicts was also set, perhaps for the first time, at £7 a year.[11] An experienced employer, G.T. Palmer, was asked four years later: 'Which of the two modes (before or after the 1816 regulation) do you find to be the best?' He answered:

For the master I think the former was the best, as he was not obliged to employ his men in their own time, but for the Public Interest I conceive that the latter order is the best, as it prevented the men from roving about and committing crimes in the time in which they were not employed'.[12]

The minimum, now unavoidable, had also risen in real terms, although the face value, £10, seemed the same. Two standards of money circulated in the colony. Notes and coins issued in Britain, known as Sterling, were worth more than notes and coins created in Australia, known locally as 'Currency'. The exchange rate fluctuated. The pound Currency sometimes sank so low as half the value of a pound Sterling.[13] Macquarie had decided to extinguish the dual standard. The wage regulation was part of this campaign of monetary reform, carried on at the end of 1816, which culminated in the chartering of the Bank of New South Wales; the £10 male and the £7 female must be rewarded at Sterling values. Palmer said he used to pay £20 Currency, double the old minimum; at the worst rate of exchange this would equal the new minimum.[14]

Masters owning small farms, producing small surpluses, felt the revaluation hardest. They had frequently not paid a wage in the past, allowing their assigned men to do the best they could on their own time, only offering them work after hours during seasonal crises like the harvest. Landed gentlemen complained that poor farmers abused the privilege of assignment by encouraging their assigned men to hire themselves out all day for much of the year, taking a cut of the convicts' earnings — or that they resorted to sharecropping, either dividing the proceeds of the farm or allowing the servant a field of his own.[15] The 1816 regulations made these expedients even more attractive to a small master while complicating the bargain that he would have to strike with his convict servant if the practice were to continue.

The owners of large estates always had work needing to be done. They also controlled deeper reserves of cash and credit. William Cox of Richmond beside the

Hawkesbury River, to whose family 70 convicts had been assigned, estimated in 1819 that a convict cost him at least £25 and 12 shillings a year, £10 down and the rest in the official ration of meat and wheat; he gave efficient convict artisans up to £25 a year before rations.[16] John Blaxland of Newington beside the Parramatta River stated that each of his 40 convicts set him back £24, charging the rations at £14. His free shepherds earned between £15 and £25, with rations added, and he enticed free carpenters and other artisans from the nearby town with £2 a week (£104 a year), out of which they provided their own diet.[17] Blaxland presented these figures while pleading for skilled convicts. He wished to underline how much money he lost by being forced into the open market for specialised labour. Obviously he would have had to add to the bill of £24 a margin in cash or kind, as Cox did, to get the best results from the convict carpenters, millers, masons and wheelwrights he sought, but the saving would still have been significant if he paid convict artisans no larger a margin for skill than Cox did. Blaxland even thought, it appears, that saving at the most two-fifths of the outlay on a free shepherd would justify his replacement by an assigned one.

What was called 'task work' provided an alternative to payment at a flat rate. Early governors laid down schedules of pay for given quantities of timber sawn, ground ploughed, grain reaped and so on. Masters offered piece rates for other tasks at their discretion. This proved easiest to apply to prolonged undertakings. Employers with limited holdings needed many small jobs done most weeks of the year; it was too difficult to compute and administer a mixture of daily and piece rates for their permanent servants, except for bonuses at periods of intense effort and significance like the harvest.

The government under Macquarie, on the other hand, operating on a large scale through specialised gangs, concluded that permission to finish work early in the day after the fulfillment of a quota of stone quarried, bricks laid or nails forged, gained results more consistently and cheaply than did constant supervision and corporal punishment. It was a matter of good judgment to gauge an adequate measure of work that would not be botched through tiredness or resentment. In 1818 the colony's new chief engineer, Major George Druitt, increased by half the food ration allowed the sawyers at the Pennant Hills timbergetting settlement and increased proportionately the quantity of timber tasked. The sawyers considered that the augmented ration simply compensated them for the energy spent meeting the old quota. They refused to step up the pace. The chief engineer convinced the governor that this 'insolence' was 'mutiny'. He won 100 lashes for the sawyers' spokesmen. The mutiny crumbled and the new quota was imposed.[18] In the cat o' nine tails, and the chaingang, the government possessed bargaining weapons that its prisoners could not match. It is evidence of the harsh shadows thrown by lash and leg-iron, but also of awareness under Macquarie's administration that skill and stamina must not be squandered, that neither Druitt nor his specialist gangs seem to have brought on such a confrontation again.

Private employers also found, often regretfully, that convicts, like hired people, responded best to incentives. Under the compulsion, after 1816, of a revalued minimum wage many leading men hankered for the flexibility of task work, by which the industrious could be rewarded and the unsatisfactory paid nothing. Some of them did concede that much of the daily and weekly round was too piecemeal or routine to be tasked.[19] Hannibal Macarthur J.P. of Parramatta said forthrightly that the problem could only be solved by promising prisoners nothing more than food and clothing: 'That this might expose some servants to oppression is very probable: this however would soon be made known and the suffering individual could be easily relieved. If the convicts were obliged to depend on their master's liberality and sense of justice for every indulgence, it might induce them to make some exertion in order to merit his favour'.[20] Macquarie's basic wage existed presumably because the governor did not share Macarthur's confidence in the liberality of masters.

Hannibal's uncle, John Macarthur, the largest owner of land and livestock in Australia, shared his nephew's jaundice. 'My servants are not often tasked', he said in evidence given to Commissioner Bigge in 1819 or 1820, 'for they will not perform a task without continual reference to the magistrate to compel them by punishments, which I always very reluctantly do'. Despite this disparagement of his workforce, a normal wage half as much again as the minimum and the possibility of bonuses may explain why his servants built his fortunes year by year:

> The method I adopt is to feed them well, clothe them comfortably, and give sometimes extra rewards . . . I require my servants to work from sunrise to sunset, allowing them one hour for breakfast and another for dinner. Each man receives weekly seven pounds of beef or mutton, and one peck of wheat (the official ration) — In clothes, tea, sugar, tobacco and money to the value of £15 a year; unless they are unusually idle or worthless, when I confine the allowance to £10 which is the rate of wages established by government. To those who behave well, I give gratuities varying from £1 to £5 . . . [21]

Observe that money formed only part of John Macarthur's wage bill. Both free and bonded persons often had to accept some of their income in commodities.[22] Magistrates at Windsor tried to have all convicts under their jurisdiction paid in kind.[23] John Oxley, surveyor-general and substantial employer, told Commissioner Bigge that masters calculated a mark-up of between 40 per cent and 70 per cent above wholesale, 25 per cent to 35 per cent above retail, when paying in kind. Not wishing publicly to accuse himself or his peers of rapacity, he may well have underestimated the mark-up.[24] Prisoners assigned out of town, moreover, had few places except the master's store-room where whatever money they received could be spent. They had to take the prices charged on the estate. Their wages were thus effectively discounted at every stage. Masters with large establishments bought in bulk, allowing them to support more prisoners and to offer higher nominal wages to free people than could a small employer. The official rations bore less heavily, too, on owners of spreading estates. They could spare labour and land to grow the rations; a small farmer might have to find cash, particularly for the meat, and to dig into scarce reserves of saleable grain. A townsman had to buy both grain and meat at market prices.

Masters on a large scale, then, could absorb the increase imposed on them under the 1816 regulations, but as a result they became more captious about the quality of people assigned to them, more self-conscious about the return on their outlay. Employers on a small scale operated on narrower margins; when a violent flood swept down the Hawkesbury in March 1817 the devastated farmers sent over 500 convicts back to dependence on the government stores.[25]

The wave of prisoners washed back on the stores by the Hawkesbury flood met a swelling tide of freshly transported people (see Table 9.1). As many male convicts landed at Sydney Cove in five weeks in April and May 1818, for example, as had come during the whole of 1816.[26] About 500 male convicts received government rations in Sydney early in 1817; by the end of 1819 almost 2000 men were on the stores there, and

Table 9.1: *Number of Remittances Issued to Convicts, 1810–20*

Year	Absolute pardons	Conditional pardons	Tickets	Total	Convict arrivals
1810	89	32	214	335	510
1811	25	38	290	353	475
1812	77	80	73	230	324
1813	51	160	55	266	594
1814	39	146	177	362	1171
1815	13	167	157	337	1074
1816	16	167	114	297	1276
1817	11	16	202	229	1985
1818	21	312	317	650	3137
1819	25	46	366	437	2372
1820	9	201	354	564	2579
Totals	366	1365	2319	4050	15497

Sources: *Bigge Appendix, Convicts Colonial Office 201/119*; A.G.L. Shaw *Convicts and the Colonies*, Appendix, pp.364–5.

another 2000 on the stores elsewhere in the colony, out of a total male convict population approaching 9000.[27] This was the situation when John Thomas Bigge, lawyer and public servant, reached Sydney on 26 September 1819 as Commissioner of Enquiry into the twin colonies of New South Wales and Van Diemen's Land, an investigation that kept him in Australia for 17 months.

The British cabinet wanted Bigge's advice on how the colonies might better assist in solving, through strictness and economy, the perennial problem of crime in the United Kingdom, a problem intensified by the troubled period of demobilisation after the Napoleonic Wars.[28] Because his terms of reference required him to concentrate on Australia's usefulness to Britain, and how that could be improved at reduced cost, it was inevitable that the commissioner's diagnoses should differ from the governor's practice. Daily concern with local emergencies, of which the post-war influx of convicts was one, committed Macquarie to solutions whose primary test of success was their local, not their Imperial, consequences. Some policies would obviously come into question over the decade that Macquarie had ruled, and some colonists would discover and nurse grievances against the governor during that long time.

One comprehensive grievance that preoccupied Bigge broke down into three separate charges: that Macquarie withheld too many convicts from assignment and wasted their energies on public works; that the convicts he denied to the private sector included most of the skilled men; and that the few skilled men who were assigned went to the governor's favourites. Bigge had Table 9.2 drawn up to help him weigh the substance of these charges.

Excessive employment in the public sector?

The expense of feeding, clothing, supervising and (in some cases) sheltering the people employed by the government alarmed the commissioner. Bigge was the British tax-

Table 9.2: *Convict Male Arrivals and Number Retained by Government 1814–20*

Year of arrival	Total number	Total mechanics	Mechanics retained	% Total mechanics	Labourers retained	Total convicts retained	% Total
1814	819	194	122	63%	186	308	38%
1815	909	226	143	63%	203	346	38%
1816	1257	211	120	52%	142	262	21%
1817	1653	263	157	60%	243	400	24%
1818	2748	577	390	68%	531	921	34%
1819	2376	477	385	81%	865	1250	53%
1820	2003	470(a)	270(a)	70%	830	1100	55%

a. 129 farming men are included in the 470 mechanics of 1820 of whom 30 were taken by Government.

Source: Bigge Appendix, Convicts CO 201/118, Document 29; copy at Bonwick Transcript of
Evidence to Bigge Commission, Box 13, p.725, Mitchell Library.

payers' watchdog. Assignment did away with all these burdens on British taxpayers.
The majority of prisoners on the stores, moreover, were stationed in the major centres,
Sydney and Parramatta, where the 'salutary terror' of transportation was tempered, if
not sabotaged, by all the idle past-times of the town. Hopes of reform were thwarted if
too many malefactors gathered in one place; they could conspire and combine in
felony, and confirm each other in impenitence. Dispersal into assignment, Bigge
concluded, should also be dispersal into the countryside, a view pressed on him by the
landed gentry whom he interviewed at length.[29]

Macquarie regretted the expense and the congestion but what, he asked, could he
do? He believed that the colony suffered from a labour surplus. The year 1818 was very
dry, the summer crops were poor, and the Hawkesbury flooded again in 1819, sending
another 100 assigned men back on the stores. In the wake of drought and drenching rain
caterpillars attacked the pasture and fly-moths the grain. Rural demand for workers,
understandably, did not soak up the swiftly growing supply. If every convict were
assigned, many would be idle, he argued, and many would suffer hunger and neglect
because masters could not afford to support them.[30] William Cox of Richmond, a major
proprietor favoured by the governor, agreed with his patron that many small culti-
vators lacked means 'at present [1820] when the importation of convicts is far beyond
the numbers required for the labour we can successfully employ them in'.[31]

Gregory Blaxland, younger brother of John, wished to believe the opposite. 'The
labour of the prisoners may be considered the riches of the colony. Take that away and
but little will be left'.[32] Open-handed assignment of convicts boosted production, the
proceeds of which allowed settlers to house a larger workforce. For Macquarie the
Blaxlands typified the difficulties he faced. John Blaxland admitted that the brothers
avoided cultivating the soil and specialised in grazing. 'We did not persevere much in
cultivating the soil because we could not manage it with so much other business, only
by overseers and under that management we found it a losing business'.[33] This
confirmed the governor's prejudice that grazing was a pursuit for lazy masters that
created lazy servants. It also wasted space. Agriculture, on the other hand, used space
intensively, and employed more people per hectare as well. Intensive cropping, served

by market towns, held out the prospect of independence to men of little means, who might become rural or urban masters in their turn. Convicts could be taken off the stores and into assignment if estate owners like the Blaxlands changed their priorities. That, at least, was what the governor believed.

Gregory Blaxland, as every schoolchild knows, had been one of the party that crossed the Blue Mountains in 1813 in search of grazing land. Like many of his peers he asked the governor for a licence to pasture his stock beyond the coastal plains. Macquarie rejected most such petitions. He did not want to reward the graziers' neglect of farming. Concentration of settlement, moreover, simplified law enforcement. Surveillance and order would weaken if settlement sprawled, particularly if it spilled over into the Hunter valley to the northwards, at whose mouth stood the prison village of Newcastle where about 700 men toiled in isolation as punishment for offences committed in the colony.

In any case, what except meat would graziers grow if given permission to roam? The price of meat had been dropping in recent years, of which graziers complained. A glut, and low incomes, would follow expansion, Macquarie believed. If graziers took convicts off the stores to grow more meat, this would reduce demand from the commissariat which currently victualled about 30 per cent of the population; the assigned convicts might not appear elsewhere in the market, for many would feed directly from the pastures and fields of their new masters. The price of meat would fall further, and ruin its producers. Agriculturalists, on the other hand, could increase the variety and amount of goods traded by diversifying production. In particular, if the Imperial government removed the embargo on the distillation of spirits in Australia (a measure that served the interests of distillers in other parts of the empire), Australian thirsts could be slaked from local grains, canes and fruit trees, widening employment on Australian farms. Macquarie's line of argument assumed that colonial producers depended solely or mainly on a domestic market. Most sheep in New South Wales still grew coarse wool, which was hard to sell at a profit overseas. It took several generations of breeding to shift from meatbearing to a fine woolbearing carcase. Some pastoralists had begun that process, able to sustain a temporary loss of income from the flocks reserved for cross breeding, but many refused to experiment while meat prices held.[34] Roundabout voyages to London, which lengthened the gap between shearing-time and ultimate sale, and high shipping charges also deterred pastoralists. Both high freight rates and the length of the voyage came about because an act of Parliament, in the East India Company's interest, prevented ships lighter than 350 tons sailing into the Indian Ocean from Britain, which meant that arrivals in Australia were infrequent, and the ships that did arrive must then go to Asian ports for bulk cargo to fill their large holds.[35]

'The Humble Petition of the Gentlemen, Clergy, Settlers, Merchants, Landholders, etc . . . of New South Wales', sent to London in 1819, agreed with the governor about conditions in that year. The adult male population consisted 'principally of . . . Labourers for whom sufficient employment cannot be found in the present state of our agriculture'. The petitioners agreed with him also about the necessity of colonial distilleries as a stimulus to farming. They disagreed with him about Australia's potential. 'This colony should be considered principally as a pastoral country', they wrote.[36]

For Macquarie an overseas market was hypothetical, the domestic market was real. For the petitioners the overseas market beckoned. For Commissioner Bigge the overseas market was essential. Thousands of convicts waited to be assigned, thousands came each succeeding year. If they were to be dispersed into the countryside, who but graziers could take them? Small farmers lacked authority and income. The principal proprietors possessed authority already, Bigge believed, and would augment their income when they had something to sell in Great Britain. As sheep spread across the continent, growing wool rather than meat, a multitude of convicts would spread after them, their assignment relieving the British taxpayer and their dispersal tending to re-form.

In the same season that Bigge sailed from England, Parliament repealed the 350 ton minimum for vessels dispatched to the Indian Ocean. The first trading ship from Britain lighter than the old minimum weight entered Sydney Harbour in 1820. Less cargo was needed for an outward voyage; the number of ships reaching Sydney increased.[37] Less cargo was needed for a homeward voyage; the bales and barrels lying on Sydney wharves now sufficed for a paying freight straight back to England. Vessels arrived more frequently, they left more frequently; the competition, plus the speed of loading and return, brought down the costs to colonial importers and brightened the prospect of export.

The essential steps away from Macquarie's old policy of territorial containment towards Bigge's policy of territorial sprawl were taken in November and December 1820. The swift growth in population had widened demand for meat and increased the slaughter of livestock. Drought and caterpillars thinned pastures that in some cases had been exhausted by overstocking. Herds and flocks declined in numbers and strength. The commissioner convinced the governor that some of the beasts must move to fresh grasslands if the supply of meat were to grow again.[38] Permits were now issued to graze along the corridor southwest of Camden and on to the Goulburn Plains beyond. A few people had been permitted in the past five years to occupy land around Bathurst across the Blue Mountains; licences to graze there were issued freely as well. A new site for a penal station was found at Port Macquarie, further north from Newcastle, to which Newcastle's population of exiles was transferred. This opened the rich Hunter valley both to farmers (the governor's preference) and to pastoralists (the commissioner's emphasis).[39]

With the barriers gone, sheep, cattle, masters and servants staked out the new grasslands. By setting aside one of their runs for breeding fine woolled sheep while money continued to flow in from the sale of meat, stockowners gave themselves the option of shifting their weight to the boundless export sector once an over-supply of meat again depressed its price. The stage was set for converting the labour surplus into labour scarcity.

A monopoly of skill?

Macquarie used the labour surplus on a diversified program of public works. In 1819 less enthusiastically, as convicts kept coming, he began a public farm at Emu Plains, beside the Nepean River, where about 500 men cultivated enough food, it was hoped, to support themselves. Trenchant critics such as Gregory Blaxland conceded the necessity of roads, bridges and churches, but described the rest of the program as flashy windowdressing, singling out for notice the spacious battlemented government stables at Sydney (nowadays the Conservatorium of Music).[40] Bigge was in two minds about churchbuilding, and he deplored the ostentatious stables, but he also deplored Macquarie's failure to embark on a new granary at Parramatta, a new and scientifically planned gaol, a school, and a hospital. Labour and materials diverted to these untouched projects may well have cancelled out any savings that would have been made if the buildings Bigge disparaged had not been begun. Nevertheless, he echoed the complaints of major employers by blaming the scale of public works for 'the monopoly of convict labour and *skill* by the Crown'.[41]

Major Druitt, the chief engineer, spoke frankly in 1819 about the monopoly of some of the skills by the Crown. Convicts were mustered as soon as they came ashore from the transports.

> A strict examination then takes place of their previous occupations . . . I then communicate the result of this examination to his Excellency the Governor who directs me to retain as many artificers and mechanics as may be necessary for the immediate service of government; as well as the aged and crippled men; and the boys for the purpose of apprenticing them to the different trades in the lumber and dockyards.

When Bigge pressed the point: 'I conceive from the tenor of your answers that the government has considered it as an invariable rule to retain in their own service the most useful mechanics . . . ?', Druitt answered 'certainly'.[42]

The remainder of the prisoners were then distributed by the principal superintendent of convicts, William Hutchinson, 'regulated by the demands made by the magistrates and settlers'.[43] People outside the capital believed that applicants living in, or visiting, Sydney made their choice before convicts left over were assembled for districts up country. These were sent in batches to the district bench of magistrates where a further division of spoils took place. John Howe, chief constable and businessman at Windsor, was himself a beneficiary of the practice he described: '[The magistrates] have selected them for their particular wants, such as weavers, shoemakers and tanners, and if there is any choice of men, of course they take the best.' Owners of substantial estates had next pick; 'the rest obtain them by drawing lots'.[44]

No wonder masters at the end of this long chain lost patience with the people doled out to them. Most of them wanted experienced farm workers. Hutchinson estimated the requests for farm workers at four times the supply.[45] Only about one male convict in six transported to New South Wales between 1817 and 1821 stated an occupation involved with crops or animals. Country masters believed they were lumbered with London thieves, undernourished half-skilled youths and dispirited broken-down older men, left behind after the government, Sydney residents and the magistrates had commandeered the knowledgeable, the robust and the mature.[46] Gregory Blaxland, who was not a magistrate, applied for 'useful men' for the harvest at the end of 1820. 'I had two sent me, one an Irish bricklayer's labourer worn out, and the other not an able man used to trim trees in parks in England . . . On Saturday I was able to get five men. They came from the North of Ireland. I had rather they had been English labourers used to such a system of agriculture as myself, but I was probably not explicit enough in my application'.[47]

Blaxland migrated from Kent in his twenties. Why should people from other corners of the British Isles be familiar with the system of agriculture he remembered, particularly a system modified after 15 years spent in the Australian bush? Convicts who were competent and comfortable on farms in their own highly developed county in the United Kingdom might well appear foolish, stubborn or idle when pitchforked into an alien climate, landform, economy and society, where farms had to be carved out of the forest and many techniques had to be improvised. It would be a natural impulse for both master and servant to find fault with each other under these circumstances.

Some masters were perennial faultfinders, anyway. From the day they reached Australia in April 1806, the Blaxlands and each succeeding governor engaged in blazing rows about the amount of land and labour made available to the brothers. Dr Robert Townson, named by the governor among those, like the Blaxlands, 'who have always manifested an opposition to the measures and administration of Governor Macquarie' similarly disparaged the Irish convicts he received and insisted that Englishmen only be sent in future.[48] The nearby bench of magistrates at Liverpool declared Townson to be an inept and embarrassing master. He got into fights with his servants that his neighbours had to break up, undermining the authority and repute of masters in general. Yet his garden, orchard, vineyard, cattle and fine-woolled sheep were all widely admired; his Irish assistants must have been doing something right.[49] It is, after all, normal for employers to whinge about their workforce.

The issue for the Blaxlands, as for Townson, went beyond the convicts' skills to questions of control, as evidenced by John Blaxland's statement, cited earlier, about the difficulties and unprofitability of surveillance; we could manage agriculture 'only by overseers and under that management we found it a losing business'. Gregory wanted 'a body of disposable effective English farming men . . . I cannot hire such men. When they become free they get land of their own. I can only hire men to fence, fall, clear land or for any permanent jobs let by the piece, but not a body of disposable effective men ready at all times to obey my orders as every change of season or circumstances may require'.[50] A convict was preferable to a hired man in as much as he could not select the tasks he did, nor throw one master over for another. But co-operation did have to be elicited — or forced — even from a convict if profitable labour were to be extracted from him. A prisoner who needed neither instruction nor compulsion, Blaxland complained, was rarely available for assignment to him at Brush Farm.

Systematic assignment lists have not survived for these years, nor did the district benches tell the principal superintendent to whom they had allocated the men passed on to them.[51] A few sheets exist, signed by Hutchinson, that name prisoners sent beyond Sydney from recent ships. Table 9.3 has been compiled from six such lists in 1821. The lists positively identified 45 per cent of the people transported on those ships. The missing names presumably included craftsmen and labourers placed on the public works in Sydney, men assigned to workshops, houses and villas in the capital, and convicts called for personally by their future masters; these appear on the table in the column 'Already Placed'. Sixty-eight per cent of those we have classified as urban tradesmen, 53 per cent of those who were specifically 'rural', but only 46 per cent of the 'miscellaneous' had been 'Already Placed'. The residue of convicts, those appearing on Hutchinson's lists, went up-country under the custody of police constables. The column headed 'Government Gangs' referred to the various undertakings at Parramatta and the farms at Rooty Hill and Emu Plains.

The pattern presented by Table 9.3 confirms that the convicts who were left over for distribution through the benches of magistrates tended to possess a lower order of skills than those assigned to specified masters on Hutchinson's sheets and than those missing from the lists altogether. Men destined for the gangs outside Sydney were also drawn disproportionately from the occupations lumped under 'Miscellaneous'; to these were

Table 9.3: *Distribution of Males, From Six Ships Arriving in 1821*

	Specifically assigned up-country	Bench to assign	Government gangs	Already placed	Total
Urban					
Construction	1	3	-	39	43
Shoemaker	5	2	7	22	36
Weaver	4	9	6	15	34
Tailor	1	-	-	17	18
Other trades	2	16	11	51	80
Clerk	1	2	-	6	9
Rural					
Farm worker	28	16	3	53	100
Ploughman	10	5	1	12	28
Herdsman	6	2	-	9	17
Butcher	-	6	1	6	13
Gardener	1	-	-	11	12
Reaper	3	-	-	1	4
Miscellaneous					
Labourer	24	56	10	66	156
Groom, stableman	3	10	3	23	39
Sailor	1	9	5	14	29
Messenger	-	5	4	19	28
Soldier	-	6	4	5	15
Carrier	2	6	1	4	13
Bargeman	-	2	3	5	10
Other	5	17	9	20	51
Total	97	172	68	398	735

Source: Convict Guide to the State Archives of N.S.W. — Appendix M — Assignment and Distribution of Convicts from: *Adamant*, 12 Sept. 1821, pp.368–9; *Grenada* (2), 20 Sept. 1821, p.380; *Hindostan* (1), 29 Nov. 1821, pp.102–3; *John Barry* (2), 9 Nov. 1821, pp.37–8; *Minerva* I (3), 21 Dec. 1821, p.170; *Prince Regent*, 8 Feb. 1820, p.243.

added shoemakers, weavers and a few other textile tradesmen who were engaged either in making coarse cloth at the government's Parramatta Factory or in keeping the outlying gangs clad and shod. No carpenter, no mason and almost no one else from the building trades left Sydney, and only one tailor, one tanner, one ropemaker and one cooper of the trades best represented among 1821 arrivals were mentioned on Hutchinson's sheets. Among 'Miscellaneous' jobs, moreover, the classifications 'groom' and 'messenger' included stable boys and errand boys who were kept back in the town to be apprenticed, if Druitt were to be believed.

The fact that more than half the rural workers on these ships did not appear on Hutchinson's lists might well support the view that farming areas were not granted first access to the skills they wanted. Absentee landholders living in Sydney and those who could afford to visit Sydney possibly snapped up many of them; if that were the case then the well-to-do gained the advantage, and many rural workers found themselves assigned to villa lots and to the more developed estates. Others stayed with the

government. When Druitt conceded in 1819 that the government monopolised mechanics he added hastily 'but not agricultural labourers, except a few to instruct others
less skillful on the road parties. The latter description of persons is generally allotted to
the new settlers; but if a few are required for the government farms or teams, of course
they are retained'.[52] In 1820 public farming expanded, however, and the note Bigge
appended to the calculations reprinted above as Table 9.2 stated that almost one-
quarter of the arrivals he called 'farming men' went into government service that
year.

As we have seen, Governor Macquarie, William Cox J.P. and one thousand Humble
Petitioners ('Gentlemen, Clergy, Settlers, Merchants, Landholders, etc . . . ') may have
agreed that there was a surplus of labour in 1819 and 1820. This did not preclude
competition between masters over which of the convicts each of them received, nor did
it prevent conflict between the public interest, as the governor interpreted it, and the
perceived interests of some of the larger masters. Even when supply is apparently
plentiful, there need be no consensus about how demand is to be satisfied.

Artisans in 1820

Despite Bigge's own commitment to pastoral expansion, however, he showed by the
numerical survey he made of Macquarie's distribution of convicts between 1814 and
1820 (which is the basis of Table 9.2) that it was the class of people known as mechanics
who troubled him most. In August 1820 he circulated a questionnaire to each district in
the colony, from which he hoped to compile a census of skilled tradesmen.

Over half the mechanics were found in and around the main towns, Sydney and
Parramatta.[53] In answer to the questionnaire William Minchin, J.P., police superintendent, counted 517 artisans in Sydney. They professed 38 different trades. More than half
belonged to five trades only; there were 74 shoemakers, 66 carpenters, 53 sawyers, 48
stonemasons (both cutters and setters) and 44 tailors. 'The Return of Mechanics
residing within the Township of Parramatta', signed by Hannibal Macarthur, named
208 men, shoemakers, as in Sydney, being the largest trade with 34 practitioners,
followed by 20 carpenters, 17 bakers, 16 stonemasons and 15 tailers. Two days later
Macarthur submitted another 105 names from the farming districts around Parramatta.

Minchin's and Macarthur's compilations, unfortunately, defy comparison. If
Minchin were to be believed no bakers, butchers, millers, distillers, maltsters, gardeners, brickmakers or weavers (tradesmen Macarthur noted in and around Parramatta) worked anywhere in Sydney. The majority of Minchin's mechanics were in
government employ; he found only seven free and two ticketholding carpenters in the
whole of Sydney, an unlikely state of affairs in a town 30 years old, three-quarters of
whose 1084 street-front buildings (not to count their skillions and outhouses) were
weatherboard in construction.[54] Macarthur, on the other hand, named only nine men in
government employ, all in the Parramatta lumberyard, even though we know from
other schedules drawn up for Bigge that hundreds of convicts toiled on public works in
Parramatta and that many scores of them were artisans.[55] A landed proprietor like
Macarthur, living just outside a market town, would be familiar with the various
branches of the food and drink industry that were missing from the Sydney tally, but he
did not bother to make a roll-call of the government gangs, partly perhaps because of his
undisguised hostility to the governor's policy of public employment. Minchin, on the

other hand, an army officer, had become superintendent of police only four months earlier. His report simply presented totals for each trade. It was easy enough for him to secure an aggregate for those 'In Government Employ', but less congenial to tramp the streets of Sydney for the sake of a comprehensive census of trades and free tradesmen.

The returns from Sydney and Parramatta, despite the biases of the compilers, did reflect real differences between the towns. Macquarie's most ambitious structures were built in the capital. The craftsmen engaged there were, in many cases, available for private hire after 3p.m. on weekdays and 10a.m. on Saturdays. A merchant who left Sydney for England at the end of 1817 believed that only 400 of the 500 men employed by government in Sydney when he departed could find work after hours, imprecise evidence that did not specify mechanics but that did agree with Macquarie's belief in a glut of labour even at this early stage, at least in the capital.[56] This might reflect reduced employment for free workers as well. Equally anecdotal was the evidence given by G.T. Palmer of a shortage of construction workers in Parramatta three years later, in 1820; he told Bigge of the hard bargain driven by bricklayers in a public gang whom he approached one Saturday to put up a chimney.[57] Macarthur's list suggested that free bricklayers, sawyers, plasterers and painters were very scarce in his vicinity.

If the government bestowed fewer skilled building workers on Parramatta than on Sydney, nature tended to attract there food and drink processors, weavers and wheelwrights. Sydney sat on a rocky peninsula, surrounded by salt water; broken terrain and patchy soil in its neighbourhood restricting farming. Parramatta had tilled fields, pastures and orchards on every side, whose produce was trundled in carts into the town for local consumption or for dispatch down-river to Sydney. Three of the nine government convicts noticed by Hannibal Macarthur (a wheelwright, a nailer and a blacksmith) were, he wrote, 'employed at the lumberyard and have workshops in the town'. Possession of workshops indicated that they could charge high rates for commissions after hours. Of the nine wheelwrights who were free, three were apprenticed to a fourth; the only other apprentices identified in Parramatta were articled to a miller and to an agricultural machine maker.

Forty-one assigned tradesmen worked in Parramatta. All six stonemasons served the master masons who held the contract to build the Female Factory, a combination of textile factory and female prison; obviously these men had been allotted by decision of the governor himself. It is not clear in the other cases whether the assignment had been made in the capital or by the local bench of magistrates. Four of the five assigned tailors served large landholders; their skills could maintain the dignity of the master's family as well as the decency of his workforce. Shoemaking was the only trade that surpassed masonry and tailoring in the number of men assigned to the town. Three of the ten assigned shoemakers worked for large landholders whose establishments used leather for many purposes — footwear, harness and traces, saddles, machine-belting and so on. Four went to overseers of government gangs in lieu of salary. It was customary for overseers to hire out their allotted convicts (whose rations and clothing came from government) and share the income the convict earned; in Sydney as in Parramatta overseers often received shoemakers, who could, among other tasks, keep in repair the boots of the overseer's gang.[58] Two of the convict shoemakers were assigned to free men in the same trade, and the tenth was bound over to his own wife.

Those in farming areas who answered Bigge's questionnaire may have known more about their neighbours than did gentlemen in busy towns. On the south-west frontier of settlement, for instance, the district constable of Minto (between Liverpool and Campbelltown) named 17 artisans, and an anonymous correspondent in Airds (the district beyond Minto) named 56. Each reported whether the man was 'at his trade' or not.

In Minto a free shoemaker and three of the four assigned shoemakers kept their trade, as did a free wheelwright, an assigned tailor, and a 'self-taught rough carpenter' who had once been a soldier. The two other carpenters in the district had both risen to the station of landholder. Some assigned men, however, were simply and predictably 'at labour', which meant they did not ply their trades; these were a combmaker, a painter and gilder, a gunstockmaker, and all four weavers. There was no call for their skills in the neighbourhood. Constable Fletcher ended his account with a terse complaint: 'No blacksmith, no joiner, no harnessmaker, no ploughmaker'.

The more populous district of Airds was only slightly better provided with the skills whose absence in Minto Fletcher lamented. Two free and one assigned smith worked at their anvils, but a ticketholding smith did 'farm work', perhaps because it took capital he had not yet accumulated to set up a forge. A free harnessmaker and a free nailer found customers for their crafts. Free and ticket-of-leave shoemakers were able to stick to their lasts, and another cobbler, assigned to the harnessmaker, must have exercised his leatherworking skills too. Carpenters and sawyers generally found appropriate work. It was a sign of the recent occupation and rudimentary economy of the Airds district that the three brickmakers (two free and one assigned) made bricks for part of their time only (and the sole stonemason, an assigned man, did farm work), while workers in wood, leather and even iron had their hands full.

Of the men on the Airds frontier who lost their trade, some seem to have done so willingly. Two carpenters and a sawyer ran farms of their own, as did a papermaker, a glover, a tailor, a brassfounder, a ship's carpenter and a hatter. They preferred the precarious independence of smallholding to the pursuit of their trade, even if the tailor (no free tailor bothered to set up shop in Airds) and one of the carpenters supplemented his farm income by occasional craftwork. As most frontier farmers gained their title by direct grant from the governor, ownership did not necessarily imply the transfer of savings from previous financial success in their trade. It might imply the opposite. Despite the desire of the people of Minto for a blacksmith in their vicinity, at least one blacksmith petitioned for a smallholding on the ground that he could not support a wife and child at the business to which he was bred, perhaps because he could not find the funds to equip a smithy of his own.[59] Poor prospects in the towns must explain why a free clothdresser and a free filecutter turned up in Airds as farm labourers, and why all seven weavers there (whether free, ticket-of-leave or assigned) were reported at 'farm work' for someone else.

The returns of 'Tradesmen residing in the Districts of Richmond, Windsor and Pitt Town, Wilberforce and Portland Head' provided the most analytical detail of all. These districts occupied the rich floodplain of the Hawkesbury River where the outflow from its extensive catchment met navigable tidewater. By 1820, the earliest farms and riverside landing places dated back a quarter of a century, long enough for landing places to become villages and villages to become towns, long enough for farming practices to consolidate and a generation of native-born colonists to reach adulthood in the valley. Seventeen of the 248 tradesmen named on the Hawkesbury return had been born in the colony.

Nearly every one of the 17 native-born worked with wood — five sawyers, three wheelwrights, two carpenters, two shipbuilders and a boatbuilder (of the rest, two were blacksmiths, one a miller and the other a shoemaker). Timber in abundance grew close at hand. The raw material and the tools were cheap enough that an apprentice's mistakes cost the master little, except in the exacting trade of shipbuilding. These two young practitioners, John and William Griffiths, grew up in the Richmond boat yard of their emancipist father, Jonathon.[60] A developed agricultural society such as this one could afford to keep houses, barns, stores, fences, furniture, tools, carts and boats in good repair, but being a society of smallholders in the main, preferences ran to wood, a readily available material, even when there were more durable if costly alternatives.

The native-born who moved into wood working and into the upkeep of transport (blacksmiths included) had also taken advantage of a shortage of specific skills in outlying areas caused by the retention of convict builders in government gangs. Only one artisan in every nine assigned to the Hawkesbury valley professed any branch of the building trades. Yet in 1820 over one-third of all free artisans in the region earned their income by carpentry, at the sawpit or from some other aspect of construction. Free men recognised a deficiency, and filled it. By contrast, almost one-quarter of the assigned artisans and over one-third of the ticket holders made boots and shoes; there was sufficient demand in the valley for all but two of them to keep their trade while under sentence. The prevalence of convict shoemakers limited opportunities for free men; only one free mechanic in nine of those who chose to live along the Hawkesbury made shoes, and only one local youth took up the craft.

Textile and garment makers comprised the single other industrial category in the district to match the construction and the leather trades in numbers. There were as many clothworkers as leatherworkers assigned to the Hawkesbury. Yet, with the exception of those placed with the region's largest employer (as we shall see later in this chapter), not one of them plied his trade. And (again excepting employees of the same master) only one free tailor and four free but non-practising weavers lived by choice in the valley. No Australian-born tailor or weaver lived there. Finished cloth and garments, unlike leather and footwear, were imported from beyond the region, and were altered or repaired within the household.

The answers made in 1820 to Bigge's questions about mechanics showed clearly which of the craft skills transferred to Australia were in greatest demand, and which crafts fell into decay.

Favouritism in assignment?

William Cox of Richmond signed the Returns of Tradesmen submitted to Commissioner Bigge from the Hawkesbury. Without intending it he provided evidence for the third of the three grievances levelled against Macquarie's distribution of convicts — the charge of favouritism. (The other two grievances, it will be remembered, were the size of the public sector, and the government's monopoly of skill.)

Every complainant named Cox among the persons favoured. Cox's return showed 18 convict tradesmen on his own estates, and a mere four under charge of the neighbour next best endowed with convict tradesmen. One of the chief complainants, Hannibal Macarthur, if his return from Parramatta can be believed, controlled no more than four assigned mechanics himself in 1820.

Cox was the dominant magistrate on the Hawkesbury bench. The district constable's description of this bench's self-serving distribution of convicts has already been quoted. Macarthur presided over the Parramatta bench and was obviously open to similar temptations, although a greater number of substantial masters competed for the bench's patronage in his jurisdiction than in Cox's. The governor accused Macarthur and his fellow justices of using the town's many government gangs as a kind of employment exchange, dumping unsatisfactory assigned men there and dipping into gangs for talent more to the masters' liking.[61] Whether the charge was exaggerated or not, people in and close to the town certainly had the public pool to draw on after hours. Smaller gangs toiled on Hawkesbury roads and bridges, although the justices there did oversee the convict sawyers, carpenters, brickmakers, bricklayers, masons, plasterers, the quarryman, nailer, blacksmith, wheelwright and saddler, all 'in government employ', who erected St Matthew's, Windsor. The church building team had begun to form towards the close of 1817, and augmented the local supply of skilled workers, even if the project itself absorbed most of their energies.

Back in 1815 Cox had supervised construction of the highway across the Blue Mountains, and had placed the government town of Bathurst where the road ended. His dual role as public official and as contractor gave him unchallenged access to a specialised workforce which he could use after hours to haul his goods, make fences, hurdles, barns and tools for him, guard his sheep, cattle and pigs, and plough and reap his new Bathurst fields. As a reward he promised to recommend the servants for emancipation or a ticket-of-leave. Some who remained on the far side of the mountains continued to look out for his interests there. Others decided to hold their ticket or exercise their freedom near his Clarendon estate at Richmond. Richard Kippas, for example, the best fencer and hurdlemaker at the Bathurst settlement, since pardoned, appeared in 1820 on the Hawkesbury 'Return of Tradesmen' as a wheelwright working for Cox of his own free will. William Price, a currier for whom Cox obtained a ticket, undertook tanning for his benefactor in payment for various obligations, as part of a tanning, currying and shoemaking business Price ran. Assigned men sometimes received, in Bigge's words, 'what is vulgarly called Captain Cox's Liberty', a pass that allowed them to hire themselves out when he did not need them. He gained their gratitude and avoided unnecessary expense in supporting them. John Grundy, for example, appeared so thorough and honest a thrasher of Cox's wheat that he earned a pass on the understanding that he would take care of his patron's crop whenever called on.[62] This was the classic case of a master bargaining with convicts for their diligence and skill, offering them time, funds and even land so that they settled in his neighbourhood (at Richmond and at Bathurst) and stayed useful to him for the rest of their days. Business, not sentiment, governed the arrangement. Cox told Bigge that he preferred tickets-of-leave to pardons; a ticket allowed a man the illusion of liberty and the reality of property without relaxing the magistrates' control, including control over movement beyond the district in which the ticket was issued.[63]

It took more than Cox's astute management, however, to accumulate 18 assigned artisans, not yet emancipated or given a ticket by the winter of 1820. One of the few surviving letters from the governor to the superintendent of convicts, in the winter of 1817, set aside for 10 prominent masters, 36 convicts from the ship *Chapman*, their occupations unspecified, after those reserved for public works and '70 good men' for Tasmania had been subtracted from the ship's complement; but to an eleventh master,

William Cox, the superintendent should send a cook, a gardener, a shepherd, 'one shoemaker for strong work' and a house servant to wait at table.[64]

When Bigge charged Macquarie with partiality in assignment the governor answered frankly: 'Those persons who have been useful servants to the government and faithful in the discharge of their duty have surely a prior claim to men who have not been employed in public service'.[65] Cox's swift completion of the western highway, his supervision of road, bridge and church building around Richmond and Windsor and his diligence as a justice of the peace apparently qualified him for reward. The Blaxlands' refusal to engage in intensive agriculture and to co-operate in the policy of close settlement, and Macarthur's coolness towards the governor's measures, apparently qualified them for neglect.

Cox created the pattern establishment for an ambitious landholder. He commanded, by assignment, a pair of sawyers, a carpenter, a painter and glazier, two blacksmiths, a butcher, a tanner, a harnessmaker, three cobblers and a tailor. His Clarendon estate displayed one unusual feature, a full-blown textile operation. The carder, two spinners, scribbler and cloth manufacturer assigned to him all worked at their trade, unlike nearly every one of their counterparts elsewhere in the colony, side by side with three free specialists, a woolcarder, a flaxdresser and a weaver. Approximately 100,000 sheep grazed in the colony, the majority of the beasts growing coarse wool that could not be exported profitably but was adequate for the clothes and blankets that convicts and other working people used.[66] A sheepowner whose flocks multiplied under the care of convicts could have the animals' coats turned into coats for their guardians; this was his own case, Cox said, clothing the one hundred people in his service, as well as making boots and harness from the hides tanned on the Clarendon estate and hemp from the flax grown there.[67]

As far as we can tell John Blaxland was the only other rural woollen manufacturer. Assignment assisted him little. A ticket-of-leaver ran his small woollen factory, helped by the ticket holder's wife and a convict weaver who was his father (or father-in-law).[68] An abundance of sheep and weavers in New South Wales might have encouraged widespread emulation by landowners if it had not been for two fully professional ventures. One, the government's Female Factory at Parramatta, consumed between 50,000 and 60,000 pounds of wool each year; the governor supplied it with women and men to card, spin and weave, and the public gangs constituted the largest single market in Australia.[69]

The other venture, Simeon Lord's manufacturing complex at Botany, a few kilometres south of Sydney, left no records of output or employment. The complex at Botany included a tannery; an average of four tanners a year were transported to New South Wales, so that it was plausible for the owner of a rival tannery to complain that the superintendent of convicts starved him of labour when he assigned tanners to Lord and to Cox. But favouritism was unnecessary for stocking the textile mill that Lord owned.[70] About one male in 11 who arrived between 1817 and 1821 had worked in one branch or another of the textile industry, five-eighths of whom (about one man in 20) described themselves as weavers. Most of them lost their trade in New South Wales. 'Parramatta cloth', sturdier than the 'slop clothing' sent out by the British government, sufficed for convicts, but its coarseness and penal associations made it unattractive to free customers. Poorer people often chose tough Indian dungaree, while finer textiles and garments floated into port not only from India, but from England, Ireland and

China as well. The changing industrial conditions in Britain that impoverished the weavers there, and drove many into the prisons, had brought down the price of textiles so steeply that their sale in Australia as imports undermined the possibility of employment for those same prisoners after transportation.

Conclusion

It was not Cox's textile tradesmen who aroused envy in other masters, but rather the brace of assigned sawyers, the blacksmiths, the harnessmaker, the emancipist wheelwright and the five field and house servants selected from the *Chapman* in 1817. One of the dissatisfied masters, Sir John Jamison, squire of Regentville beside the Nepean, told Bigge that blacksmiths, stonemasons, quarriers, bricklayers, sawyers, house carpenters and wheelwrights were in intense demand. The governor and the superintendent allotted Jamison 59 men between the time of his arrival in Australia in 1814 and the spring of 1819 — 34 labourers, a gardener, a farmer, and four farmers' men for the fields, an old farrier and cowleech to doctor the animals, three grooms, two coachmen and a carter for the stableyard, and five others who seem to have been indoor servants. The ropemaker, sailmaker, peddler and two weavers assigned to him probably found themselves set uncongenial tasks; by contrast, the lone bricklayer, sawyer and tailor may never have been busier.[71] Jamison seemed well supplied for most purposes indoors and out, but he complained about the paucity of builders and of anyone skilled in fashioning wood and iron.

Other landowners as distant from a town as Jamison was, although less ambitious perhaps to build in stone and brick, also remarked on the unfinished state of their houses, huts and barns, the difficulty of fixing carts, ploughs and other tools. They recommended that the authorities station in every rural district a body of mechanics under an overseer, whose members could be hired out across the neighbourhood at need or on a roster system.[72] It would give rural masters some of the advantages possessed by employers in and near Sydney, Parramatta and Windsor, advantages which Macquarie deplored when manipulated by the Parramatta bench and tacitly endorsed when manipulated by the justices at Windsor.

In the governor's eyes public works fully employed skill for the general good during the influx of convicts from 1817 onwards, instead of countenancing underemployment for the convenience of masters who had done the state no service. Close settlement and a solid infrastructure provided a basis for growth; land and skilled labour would lie relatively idle and impoverished if assignment favoured the great graziers, the governor believed. There was no doubt that the scale and permanence of public works offered a mechanic continuous exercise of his skill, perhaps at a more consistent level of competence, with a wider array of tools and in company with men of his own and complementary crafts. If carpenters might never lack jobs in the colony, the necessarily piecemeal and circumscribed nature of most private projects would nevertheless threaten uneven employment for assigned stonemasons, bricklayers, plasterers, painters, brass, tin and ropeworkers, who found a niche in the government gangs and after hours in the town where the gangs were located.

On the other hand, in districts where carpenters, wrights and smiths were in short supply, practitioners of those trades under assignment or in the suggested loan-gangs might (of course, they might not) experience more variety and exercise more initiative than they would under government. The scarcity of carpenters, wrights and smiths endowed free men and ticketholders in those trades with the power of monopolists, some landowners complained, the power to get away with shoddy work at exorbitant prices; Sir John Jamison, however, drew the opposite conclusion, that their high wages provided an incentive to superior work and good behaviour.[73] Druitt and Hutchinson, the officials who presided over the system, certainly claimed that some mechanics tried to conceal their trade when mustered on arrival in Australia so that they could avoid government service and earn higher incomes under assignment (although Hutchinson added that rates of pay would decline sharply if the government gangs dwindled or disappeared and disgorged their members into the private sector).[74] Aggrieved masters believed the exact opposite, that convicts schemed to gain entry into the government gangs because of the generous rations, light labour, conviviality and town delights allegedly enjoyed there.[75]

As for experienced farming men, although masters up-country suspected that the best were spoken for before the rural benches ever saw them, they conceded that too few of them might have been transported in the first place. William Cox remembered and celebrated the able-bodied farm lads captured after the Irish uprisings who arrived in Australia at the beginning of the century, the same time as he did; indeed his overseer in those days, 'General' Joseph Holt, had been a leader of the rebellion and owned a farm in county Wicklow. Nowadays 'the English ships bring a great many boys from the manufacturing towns and London, and those from the Irish ships have a great many old men and cripples'.[76] We are unable to test Cox's comparison because our data begins in 1817, but the judgment of William Hutchinson, whose memory of colonial affairs went back further still, provides a useful corrective. In past times, he said, agriculture was primitive, with a lot of felling, clearing and burning to be accomplished before the land could be turned over with a hoe. By 1820 the leading employers owned established properties, set a wide range of tasks, and turned their soil with plough and plough team. Those Londoners who were transported 20 years ago had become skilled farm workers by now, charged good prices for their work, and showed up the latest batch of lags from London as new chums.[77] He implied that the origin of convicts had not changed, but that labour requirements in Australia had, and so had the availability of men competent under local conditions.

Whether the task was fitting together a fence, tending sheep in a rough paddock, or forming a field by removing stumps, masters agreed that emancipists and ticket of leavers did it best. Experience and higher payment ensured this. Gregory Blaxland, concerned with control and cheapness, lamented that free men insisted on being paid by the task, rather than hiring themselves out at a flat rate by the year. John Oxley, concerned with efficiency, observed that task work was completed far more quickly by people who had been in Australia longer and whose pay had been increased.[78] Between them Blaxland and Oxley represented the tension in labour management under the convict system. Blaxland sought total command over his servants' time, and lamented the lack of fit between the work experience of many newly arrived convicts and the jobs that he wished them to do for him in the Australian bush. Oxley had accepted the fact that good work must be bought, that old skills must be adapted and that new skills must be learned.

The emergence by 1820 of a body of free workers experienced under Australian conditions, some of them ex-convicts, some of them native-born, cast doubt on the competence of convicts who had recently arrived. Emancipists and native-born comprised the bulk of the free workforce before the beginning of large-scale immigration in the mid-1830s. It had thus become easier than before to distinguish the worth of free workers from that of convicts, and consequently to challenge the logic of a minimum convict wage. When the frontiers were opened at the very end of 1820, so that landholders and their livestock could spill far beyond the Sydney plain, demand strengthened in the private sector for men (though less so for women) with Australian experience, and the labour surplus began to decline. The aptness of the skills that convicts brought with them would not necessarily change, however. Woodworkers could still adapt to Australia almost instantly, textile makers could adapt hardly at all, while British or Irish farmworkers stood somewhere in between.

NOTES

1. S.M. Phillips to Undersecretary Stephen, 15 April 1837, paraphrasing Russell, *Historical Records of Australia*, Series I (hereafter *HRA*), XVIII, p.764.
2. Sir Richard Bourke to Lord Glenelg, 22 November 1837, Sir George Gipps to Glenelg, 8 October 1838, *HRA*, XIX, pp.187–8, 603–4.
3. Lord John Russell, 'Note on Transportation and Secondary Punishment', 2 January 1839, in Papers Relating to Transportation and Assignment of Convicts', p. 2, *Parliamentary Papers 1839*, XXXVIII, C582.
4. The emergence of the labour system in New South Wales is explored in T.A. Coghlan, *Labour and Industry in Australia* I, pp.48–68, A.G.L. Shaw, 'Labour', G.J. Abbott and N.B. Nairn (eds.), *Economic Growth in Australia 1788–1821*.
5. Quoted in T.A. Coghlan, *Labour and Industry* I, p.54.
6. 'Governor's Power to Remit Sentences' in W.W. Grenville to Arthur Phillip, 15 November 1790, *HRA*, I, pp.211–2.
7. Government Order, *Sydney Gazette* (hereafter *SG*), 8 June 1811.
8. A.G.L. Shaw, *Convicts and the Colonies*, p.83.
9. Castlereagh to Macquarie, 14 May 1809, *HRA*, VII, p.84.
10. Macquarie to Castlereagh, 30 April 1810, *HRA*, VII, pp.252–3.
11. *SG*, 10 September; 15 October 1814; 7 December 1816.
12. G.T. Palmer, evidence before Commissioner Bigge, 23 August 1820, *Bonwick Transcript of Evidence to Bigge Commission* (hereafter *BT*), Box 5, Mitchell Library (hereafter ML).
13. S.J. Butlin, *Foundations of the Australian Monetary System 1788–1851*, pp.74–109.
14. G.T. Palmer, *BT* 5, p.2188.
15. William Howe, evidence, 22 January 1821, *BT* 26, pp.5834–5; Sir John Jamison, evidence, 20 January 1820, *BT* 21, p.3850.
16. William Cox, evidence, 25 November 1819, *BT* 5, pp.1963, 1967; James Gordon, 'An Estimate of the Annual Expense...' 1820, *BT* 21, p.3546. A fortnight before Macquarie's regulation a Sydney employer estimated rations at £17.2.4 (probably Currency) and clothing at £5, R. Jenkins to J.T. Campbell, 28 November 1816, Archives Office of New South Wales (hereafter AONSW) *Colonial Secretary's In Letters* (hereafter CSIL) Reel 2161.
17. J. Blaxland to J.T. Bigge, 4 November 1819, *BT* 25, pp.5731–2.
18. G. Druitt, evidence 8 November 1819, *BT* I, pp.82–4, 89.
19. R. Lowe (Bringelly) to Bigge, 10 July 1820, *BT* 23, pp.4759–60; W. Cox, evidence, 1 May 1820, *BT* 22, pp.4228–30; J. Oxley, evidence, 17 November 1819, *BT* 5, pp.1913–9.
20. H. Macarthur to Bigge, 8 June 1820, *BT* 22, pp.4335–6.
21. J. Macarthur, evidence, no date, *BT* 1, pp.218, 220–1.
22. G.T. Palmer, *BT* 5, p.2187; J. Blaxland, evidence 18 August 1820, *BT* 5, pp.2122–39; James Brackenridge (soldier and shoemaker), evidence, 27 November 1820, *BT* 9, pp.4061–2; John Grundy (convict thresher), evidence, 29 November 1820, *BT* 9, pp.4091–2.
23. W. Cox, *BT* 22, pp.4226–7.

24. J. Oxley, *BT* 5, pp.1911–2.
25. Macquarie to Bathurst, 12 December 1817, *HRA* IX, p.711.
26. Macquarie to Bathurst, 16 May 1818, *HRA* IX, pp.794–7.
27. *Bigge Appendix*, Convicts, 'List of Persons in Government Employ...', ML, CO 201/118; also *BT* 21, pp.3559, 3600; T.G. Parsons, 'Public Expenditure and Labour Supply under Governor Macquarie, 1810–1821', M.A. thesis (University of Sydney, 1967), 180; Shaw, 'Labour', p.115.
28. J. Ritchie, *Punishment and Profit: The Reports of Commissioner John Bigge on the Colonies of New South Wales and Van Diemen's Land*.
29. Ritchie, *Punishment and Profit*, pp.133–5.
30. Macquarie to Bathurst, 24 March 1819, 20 July 1819, *HRA*, X, pp.88, 191–2; W.C. Wentworth, *Statistical, Historical and Political Description of the Colony of New South Wales* pp.382–3; T.G. Parsons, 'Public Expenditure', 170–8; T.G. Parsons, 'Governor Macquarie and the Assignment of Skilled Convicts in NSW', *Journal of the Royal Australian Historical Society* 58 (1972), 84–88.
31. W. Cox, *BT* 22, p.4228.
32. G. Blaxland to Bigge, 6 January 1821, *BT* 25, p.5598.
33. J. Blaxland to Bigge, 30 December 1820, *BT* 25, p.5411.
34. E.A. Beever, 'The Origin of the Wool Industry in NSW', *Business Archives and History* 5 (1965), 91–106; J.P. Fogarty, 'NSW Wool Prices in the 1820s: A Note', *Australian Economic History Review* 9 (1969), 71–77 and E.A. Beever, 'A Reply to Mr Fogarty's Note', *Australian Economic History Review* 9 (1969), 78–80.
35. M.J.E. Steven, 'The Changing Pattern of Commerce', in G.J. Abbott and N.B. Nairn (eds.), *Economic Growth*, 176–87.
36. Governor Macquarie to Earl Bathurst, 22nd March 1819, *HRA*, X, pp.55–65.
37. Steven, 'Changing Pattern', pp.182–3; J.S. Cumpston, *Shipping Arrivals and Departures, Sydney 1788–1825*, pp.120–130.
38. Bigge to Macquarie, 18 September 1820, *BT* 24, pp.5111–5120; Macquarie to Bathurst, 7 February 1821, *HRA* X, p.402.
39. *SG* 25 November, 9 December 1820; T.M. Perry, *Australia's First Frontier*, Chapter 3.
40. G. Blaxland, *BT* 25, pp.5598–5600.
41. Emphasis added. Bigge to Macquarie, 14 June 1820, *BT* 24, p.4977; also Bigge to Macquarie, 31 March, 6 June 1820, *BT* 24, pp.4962–4, 4967–72.
42. G. Druitt, evidence, 27 October 1819, *BT* I, pp.17–19.
43. G. Druitt, 27 October 1819 *BT* 1, pp.17–19; W. Hutchinson (superintendent of convicts), evidence 10, 12, November 1819, *BT* I, pp.100–123.
44. J. Howe, evidence, 15 December 1820, *BT* 2, pp.694–6.
45. *BT* I, p.114.
46. G. Best, evidence, 4 September 1820, *BT* 5, pp.2140–58; W. Cox, evidence, 25 November, no year, *BT* I, pp.189–90; Revd S. Marsden to Bigge, 31 January 1820, *BT* 21, p.3889.
47. G. Blaxland to Bigge, 7 January 1821, *BT* 25, p.5612.
48. Macquarie to Bathurst, 1 December 1817, *HRA* IX, pp.500–1.
49. Dr R. Townson, statement, April 1818, *BT* 16, pp.2167–8; extract, record book, court at Liverpool, 18 April 1818, *BT* 16, pp.2174–5; 'Robert Townson', *Australian Dictionary of Biography* (hereafter *ADB*) II, p.538.
50. G. Blaxland to Bigge, 7 January 1821, *BT* 25, pp.5613–4.
51. W. Hutchinson, *BT* I, pp.116–120.
52. G. Druitt, *BT* I, p.20.
53. The lists of mechanics submitted to Bigge in August 1820 are collected in *Bigge Appendix*, Return of Men Assigned, ML CO 201/118.
54. J. Oxley, 'A Return of the Number of Buildings in the Town of Sydney', 12 January 1821, *BT* 25, p.5654.
55. *BT* 21, pp.3559, 3600; *BT* 25, p.5399.
56. A. Riley, evidence in *Report from the Select Committee on the State of the Gaols*, P.P., 1819, VII, C579, 10.
57. *BT* 5, p.2189.
58. Macquarie to Bathurst, 31 March 1817, *HRA* IX, pp.242–3; W. Hutchinson, *BT* 1, pp.109–110; Patrick Kelly (overseer of sawyer's gang), evidence, 3 September 1820, *BT* 11, pp.4295–4302; J. Wilshire, evidence, 23 January 1821, *BT* 9, pp.3853–4.
59. William Biggs, memorial, 1 June 1818, AONSW CSIL, Reel 1066.
60. 'Jonathan Griffiths', *ADB* I, pp.485–7; B. Dyster, 'John Griffiths, Speculator', *Tasmanian Historical Research Association Papers and Proceedings* 27 (1980), 20–31.
61. Macquarie to H. Macarthur, 21 November 1820, AONSW CSIL, Reel 2166, pp.68–9, (copy at *BT* 24, pp.5270–1).

62.Bigge's enquiries into Cox's activities are in *BT* 9, pp.3984–4112 (Kippas' evidence, pp.4023, 4077, Price, pp.4094–6, Grundy, pp.4091–2); Bigge's words are from his question to J. Howe, 15 December 1820, *BT* 2, pp.706–7; Revd R. Cartwright to Bigge, 13 June 1820, *BT* 23, 4405–4410.

63.W. Cox, evidence, 25 November 1819, *BT* 5, p.2011.

64.Macquarie to Hutchinson, 1 August 1817, *BT* 16, pp.1971–2 (emphasis in original); also same to same, 1 December 1817, *BT* 16, p.2026, 18 October 1818, *BT* 17, pp.2250–1.

65.Macquarie, deposition, *BT* 11, p.4400.

66.B.H. Fletcher, *Landed Enterprise and Penal Society*, p.229.

67.W. Cox, *BT* 5, pp.1966–7.

68.J. Blaxland, evidence, 18 August 1820, *BT* 5, pp.2122–39.

69.Fletcher, *Landed Enterprise*, p.166.

70.J. Wilshire, evidence, 23 January 1821, BT 9, pp.3852–4; S. Lord to Macquarie, 18 July 1816, AONSW CSIL 4/1735, pp.87–9 Reel 2161; D.R. Hainsworth, *The Sydney Traders: Simeon Lord and his Contemporaries 1788–1821*, pp.197–203.

71.J. Jamison to Bigge, 20 January 1820, *BT* 21, p.3842; *Bigge Appendix*, Return of men assigned 1814–1819, CO 201/118.

72.R. Cartwright, *BT* 23, pp.4412–3; R. Lowe to Bigge, 10 July 1820, *BT* 23, pp.4753–4; W. Howe to Bigge, 22 January 1821, *BT* 26, pp.5832–3.

73.R. Cartwright, *BT* 23, p.4413; R. Lowe, *BT* 23, p.4754; J. Jamison, *BT* 21, p.3842.

74.G. Druitt, BT I, pp.65–6; W. Hutchinson, BT I, pp.112, 118–9.

75.R. Cartwright, *BT* 23, pp.4400–5; R. Lowe, *BT* 23, p.4752; statement by Liverpool Bench of Magistrates, SG, 25 January 1822.

76.W. Cox, *BT* 5, p.1938; also W. Cox, BT I, p.189.

77.W. Hutchinson, BT I, pp.113–5.

78.G. Blaxland, *BT* 25, p.5614; J. Oxley, *BT* 5, pp.1913–6; G. Best, evidence, 4 September 1820, *BT* 5, pp.2140–2158.

Chapter Ten

The Organisation of Public Work

Stephen Nicholas

Introduction

Men working together, not the labour of individuals working separately, accounted for much of the early economic growth and development of Australia. Gangs of men and women cut stone, worked in metal, made clothing and shoes, repaired roads, constructed bridges, carried water, unloaded ships, ploughed the fields, gathered the harvest and laboured in the commissariat store. Small scale tasks, like making nails, hinges or locks, and large construction projects, such as building the barracks or cutting a road over the Cumberland, were undertaken by gangs. But the gang system as a work organisation has received little attention from historians. Public work gangs have been depicted as brutal instruments of punishment rather than as means of organising useful work. As flogging came to form the centrepiece of work relations in the government sector, historical attention has come to be focused on the iron gangs where convicts were punished by hard labour and denied the right to work 'on their own time'.[1] In contrast, the recent historiography on assignment has emphasised the creation of a viable system of private production. Given incentives, it has been argued, the assigned servants were efficiently organised for work unlike those in government service where shirking, loafing and malingering vied with the whip as a characterisation of everyday life. In contrast to the public work gangs, the teams which ploughed and threshed on the large estates were a productive way of performing agricultural tasks. As agriculture diversified, Australian historians have pointed to the shift from gangs to unsupervised individual jobs, such as shepherding, which came to dominate the rural economy. The gang, inflexible, brutal and inefficient, stands out as a unique characteristic of public work, reflecting the state's dependence on unfree labour.

The lash and the gang were not unique to convict New South Wales; and coercion at work did not depend on unfree labour. Although they entered their contracts voluntarily, Hugh Tinker has called Indian indentured labour working on the West Indian sugar plantations a 'new system of slavery' because they were coerced at work.[2] Similarly, sailors, soldiers and bonded Melanesian workers on Australia's sugar plantations were coerced, although all freely signed labour contracts. By breaking the nexus between unfree labour and coercion, these examples of forced free labour emphasise that exploitation occurs during the work process rather than in the employment relationship. Employment contracts, whether free or coerced, deliver labour power, not labour, which is the work labour power can perform. It is not in the freedom to enter an employment relationship, but in the actual physical organisation and structuring of work, where coercion occurs. Some work structures are particularly efficient at forcing labour power to deliver more labour than they would have provided voluntarily. Departing from the current historiography, this chapter argues that the public work gang was an efficient work organisation for extracting extra labour from convicts and was not merely a device for punishment.

Australian historians have noted that the whip and the punishment gang were blunt instruments for extracting work, especially when the lash was delayed until the worker had received the judgment of the magistrates.[3] To avoid such delays assistant surveyors of the road gangs, usually military men, were appointed magistrates so that trial and punishment could be undertaken on the spot. Nevertheless, the limitations of motivating workers by physical force led to the introduction of positive incentives within the convict system. While the rewards for convicts on assignment have been scrupulously listed, historians have failed to integrate incentives in the government sector with the way public work was organised. As a result, punishments rather than rewards have been emphasised as the method for extracting work from forced labour in government service. The public sector relied on punishment because all convicts were shirkers doing the 'government stroke', just enough work to keep the flogger at bay.[4] Robert Hughes has argued that without the incentive of monetary reward, only the whip could force convicts to work.[5] According to Manning Clark, the convicts were indolent with an innate aversion to labour.[6] The result was that the convicts were terrorised into labour and their work relations were shaped by the coercion which surrounded their working days.[7] Echoing Clark, R.W. Connell and T.H. Irving depicted the convict experience in terms of terror and brute force, with assignment an adjunct to the penal system reliant on the whole state apparatus of force.[8] According to John Hirst, it was the urban convict, disorderly, unused to regular hours, regular employment or hard manual labour who was difficult to motivate. These hardened, desperate and prolifigate ruffians refused to work even for good masters, leaving little besides physical punishment to encourage work.[9]

The convicts responded to the brute force and power of the state by solidarity and protest. Russel Ward identified an 'egalitarian class solidarity', a primitive 'mateship', a comradeship and honour among thieves, which formed the worker's sole means of defence against the overwhelmingly powerful organisation of state authority.[10] In a devastating critique, Humphrey McQueen argued that it is nonsense to talk of class in the first half-century of Australian colonial society: what Australia gained from transportation was a 'deformed stratification which had itself been vomited up by the maelstrom which was delineating class in Britain.'[11] The criminal, while created by class formation, necessarily lacked class consciousness. Indeed the value system of most convicts was essentially lumpenproletariat or petty-bourgeois in character, combining hatred of authority with individual acquisitiveness. Rejecting Ward's class solidarity among the bush convicts, Alan Atkinson's study of protest identified instead a group solidarity among the urban convicts.[12] Similarly, Connell and Irving found 'very strong grounds for inferring a widespread solidarity among the convicts' in response to state power.[13] This partial solidarity never blossomed into class consciousness. The reason that class consciousness did not form, and that convict protest was so intermittent and achieved so little, was the effective repression and the sustained official terror of the convict regime.[14] Group solidarity and protest were the victims of coercion — a coercion reliant on the lash as the dominant form of physical force and the gang as the typical organisation of public work.

In contrast, we reject the notion that the labour process in colonial Australia was one of unrelenting terror and brute force. Physical punishments were inflicted on convicts in government service, but not indiscriminately, and not as the principal means of motivating workers. When the lash was used to extract work from gangs it was because pain was a cheap and efficient instrument for stimulating effort. The stereotype of road gangs as inefficient and nonproductive, driven by cruel and inhumane treatment, is at odds with the dramatic physical record — the roads, bridges and buildings — of the skill and perseverance of the convict workers.[15] Road and chain gangs were subject to physical coercion, but the use of the lash against these gangs has been overemphasised. Indeed, violence as a form of authority was not typical of government gangs or the treatment of those employed by the state.

Contemporaries used the word 'gang' as a general description encompassing all arrangements of public work, not just road and chain gangs. To confine one's attention to road gangs ignores the variations and complexities in the way convict workers were grouped together. Table 10.1 shows that the range of state jobs spawned a plethora of gangs, each taking on the name of a specific task. The gathering of men together was an economical way of completing the tasks undertaken by convicts in government service. Team organisation had important attributes related to supervising the quality of work and measuring job performance. Further, tasks were an integral part of the structure of organising gang production, and rewards were as much an incentive for hard and diligent work as physical punishment. The evidence points to convict gangs as an efficient way of organising useful work and not as institutions in the service of terror and physical force.

The theory of gangs

Colonial administrators classified gangs into 'outdoor gangs' and 'indoor gangs', dividing them roughly along unskilled and skilled lines. Using Armstrong's occupational classification 3 to identify skilled workers, Table 10.1 shows the high correlation between indoor gangs and skill. Road and bridge building and agricultural work was undertaken by outdoor gangs; here strength earned a higher premium than skill and hard work was more important than care. These gangs broke stone, dug gravel, carried stone, cleared land, harvested grain, built bridges, cut grass and carried water and consisted largely of unskilled (Armstrong category 5) labourers. While skill levels provide useful descriptions of colonial gangs, such a classification offers few insights into why teams were chosen as the organisation for structuring work. The reason lies outside the convict system and must be sought in the economics of the organisation of work.

As work organisations, gangs have two advantages: they allow metering of work effort through superior assignment, supervision and incentive attributes; and they deliver complementary labour services in the performance of a job.[16] The first motive was the economic rationale for the labour gang. Here each worker was assigned a separate, individual task, such as hoeing, weeding, shoemaking or tailoring. Assignment attributes refer to the ability of overseers and superintendents to assign workers to those individual tasks for which they are relatively well suited. Since workers are not equally suited for every task, the ability to discriminate in job assignment implies an efficiency gain. Supervision attributes involve the direct monitoring of the work

Table 10.1: *The Organisation of Public Work*

Types of gang	Labour gangs			Teams			Armstrong skill class
	Fixed	Task Variable	Jobbing	Fixed	Task Variable	Jobbing	
INDOOR							
Lumber and dock-yard workshop gangs							
Shoemaker	Y						3
Tailor	Y						3
Blacksmith						Y	3
Wheelwright						Y	3
Brassfounder						Y	3
Brickmaker				Y		Y	3
Harnessmaker			Y				3
Ropemaker				Y			3
Carpenters						Y	3
Shipwrights						Y	3
Blockmakers		Y					3
Sailmakers					Y		3
Painters		Y					3
Coopers						Y	3
Tanners					Y		3
OUTDOOR							
Skilled building gangs							
Carpenter			Y				3
Bricklayer				Y			3
Sawyer				Y			3
Plasterer	Y						3
Stonesetting	Y						3
Stonecutting				Y			
Painters			Y				3
Mason				Y			3
Agricultural gangs							
Clearing					Y		5
Ploughing					Y		4
Thrashing					Y		5
Fencing				Y			5
Hoeing		Y					5
Weeding		Y					5
Gardening		Y					
Grasscutting					Y		5
Woodcutting					Y		5
Road and mining gangs							
Road/bridge					Y		5
Quarry				Y			3
Guanomaking	Y						5
Limemaking		Y					5
Stonecutting					Y		3

Types of gang	Labour gangs			Teams			Armstrong skill class
	Fixed	Task Variable	Jobbing	Fixed	Task Variable	Jobbing	
Other Gangs							
Water Carrying				Y			5
Store							5
Carters/Bullock					Y		5
Load/Unload					Y		5
Boatman						Y	3

Sources: *Monthly Returns of the Government Working Gangs, Civil Departments and Stationary Servants*, Mitchell Library Roll 107, Series CO201/119, pp.119–208; Archives Office of New South Wales, *Assignment and Employment of Convicts 1827–1830 7/2689*; Major Evans to Secretary Goulburn, 16 June 1825; *Historical Records of Australia*, Series I, XI, pp.655–8.

process by an overseer who evaluates the productive energy expended on the job. Such monitoring prevented waste, embezzlement and incorrect handling of the product. Incentive attributes give rise to performance differences. The labour gang was an organisation of work which discouraged malingering and encouraged work intensity when a supervisor indirectly monitored work effort by assessing each individual's output. Similarly, by fixing a task in proportion to the quantity of each individual's output, the intensity of work was increased.

Teams were the second general work organisation for gangs in colonial Australia. With the assignment and supervision attributes of labour gangs, teams were an efficient form of production when two or more men produced more output working jointly than the sum of the output for each man separately after deducting the cost of organising the team. In short, teams permitted economies arising from shared labour inputs in co-operative activities. Indivisibilities in shared labour inputs are illustrated by the task of lifting logs which require the co-operation of two men in time and place. They lift and carry together and are positioned at opposite ends of the log. Labour indivisibilities mean that one man working twice as long, or two men working separately, could not perform the task of two men working together. Such indivisibilities were common in heavy manual work requiring carrying, pulling and lifting. Besides these technological nonseparabilities, the joint delivery of labour services was necessary to perform the successive stages in the production of a good or service. For example, a gang of men working together building carts internalised the costs of negotiating over the wheels, body and spokes between separate craftsmen, reducing the need to hold inventories and eliminating transport costs. When work involved joint labour inputs, the team was more efficient than labourers toiling separately.

One advantage of the gang system was its surveillance attributes, particularly important in an open prison. The assessment of work effort by an overseer involved the surveillance of the workforce at no extra cost. Of course, the guarding of a prison population does not imply the monitoring of work. From the earliest days of the colony the marines resisted doing duty as convict supervisors, refusing either to encourage the worthy or take notice of the idle.[17] Even in the late 1820s and 1830s, when, for the first time, the military was used to guard road gangs, the soldiers kept gangs at work rather than supervised work itself.[18] Gangs were economic institutions for organising work through direct monitoring by convict overseers and surveillance was an added bonus. This is not to deny the importance of the surveillance attributes of gangs. But the need to guard and watch over workers was not unique to convict gangs. Free labour gangs, like their convict counterparts, were allowed overseers to monitor unco-operative behaviour, including fighting and intimidation, and to prevent workers from leaving the workplace. Surveillance in the early Strutt and Arkwright cotton mills in England reduced child runaways trying to break their employment contracts, and most railway contractors kept overseers and private police to monitor brawling and arrest troublemakers among the navvies.[19]

On the basis of a job's labour input requirements, the economic theory of gangs divided the organisation of work into either teams or labour gangs. To test the efficacy of colonial work institutions we show that jobs were organised into the teams or labour gangs according to the labour input requirements and that the gangs in New South Wales matched the way work was arranged for the same jobs in free and other coerced labour systems.

Comparative work organisation: convicts and free labour

Indoor gangs carried a specific meaning in the colony. According to the chief engineer, Major Ovens, the dockyard and lumberyard 'assembled all the indoor tradesmen who work in shops, such as Blacksmiths, Carpenters, Sawyers, Shoemakers, Tailors'.[20] Not gangs in the popular sense, the indoor tradesmen in the carpenters' shop:

> ... made roofs, floorings, doors, frames, windows, in short most of the woodwork of the required house; the parts of the work are taken to pieces, and carried to the building they are intended for, and ultimately fixed.[21]

In his report to the colonial secretary in 1825 on the employment of indoor convict labour (see Table 10.1) Ovens described workshop-factories, where all the processes of production were carried out under one roof.[22] In an article surveying the rise of factories and factory workers in New South Wales, Walsh correctly identified the government lumberyard in Sydney as the first and the largest factory in Australia.[23] Several hundred convicts in over 40 different occupations were grouped within separate workshops or departments consisting of from 10 to 60 artisans. In addition, over 100 convict women spun and wove in the Parramatta Female Factory.

Gathering craft workers under the same roof had assignment, supervisory and incentive attributes whether in the colonial workshops of New South Wales or the factories of industrialising Britain. According to Ovens, skilled convict gangs organised into separate shops allowed overseers to 'weigh both before the receipt and issue of all the crude material in Iron, Copper or Tin in the one instance, and of the manufactured article in the other, to prevent fraud and improper waste being made of the material they work upon'.[24] Such organisation was not just born of the need to harness the labour of bonded workers. British economic historians, such as A.P. Wandsworth, J. Mann and H. Heaton have focused on the need to stop embezzlement and waste to explain the rise of factory production in England.[25] Besides controlling waste and fraud in the use of raw materials, the colonial workshop allowed the work process itself to be monitored, increasing work intensity. Labour gangs and teams gathered together men under the eye of an overseer who assessed work effort. Perhaps the best exposition of the economic rationale for factories remains Stephen Marglin's argument that the 'key to success of the factory was the substitution of capitalists' for workers' control of the production process . . . discipline and supervision could and did reduce costs without being technologically superior'.[26] Testing Marglin's theory for the woollen industry, Pat Hudson concluded that 'much early factory development occurred in order to achieve organisational economies and efficiencies and not according to technological dictates'.[27]

Of course, the provision of heat and energy, expensive machines and other costly inputs impinged on the economic decision to organise workshop production in Britain; none of these factors applied with much force in New South Wales. The gang system of work in the colony was determined largely on economic and not technical grounds. From Table 10.1, it can be seen that 'indoor gangs' engaged in both individual and team production. Tailors, shoemakers, harnessmakers, blockmakers and painters were organised into labour gangs, while the remaining skilled jobs were team activities involving the complementary input of labour services. In most cases, the team was cheaper than doing the same work with men labouring separately; it was not technically necessary. Joint team work was illustrated by wheelwright gangs which 'muster about 23 persons, and are classed as wheel, body, spoke makers and other subdivisions of the same trade, from the commencement to the final completion of the construction of carts, drays, trucks, wheelbarrows etc'.[28] Similarly, the brickmaker's gang employed 15 men and the same number of boys from the Carters' Barracks as apprentices and helpers. Bricklayers and masons worked in teams, with each craftsman having a labourer or mortarman to deliver bricks, cement and mortar. The colonial regulations fixed the joint work task of the bricklayer's gang in great detail. One bricklayer and his labourer were expected to lay one square rod of solid bricks of 1½ bricks thickness or 4500 bricks per week.[29] From the weekly returns of men employed, artisan-labourer teams were also identified in tanning, shipbuilding and repair, guano-making, and brassfounding.[30]

The workshops and factories of free workers in England were organised along the same lines as the convict workshops in Australia. During the 1820s wooden shipbuilding on the Thames depended on teams of workers hired by shipwrights, and the plaiters, boilermakers, and angle-iron-smiths continued to employ from six to eight helpers into the 1880s.[31] Before 1850, the piecemaster system — in which a craftsman headed a team of artisans and apprentices — was widespread in British engineering. In the iron trade each skilled furnaceman employed between one and four senior unskilled workers.[32] In the cutlery trade, teams were centred around a specialised striker who, manipulating the heavy double-headed hammer, made heavier articles. The coalmines were worked by gangs, called the butty, with each hewer helped by one or more labourers.[33] In the early nineteenth century the largest English brickmaking yards employed up to 34 men, but even small yards gathered together workmen to assist the moulder.[34]

Gang work was also common in free labour agriculture. 'Outside gangs' allowed efficient assignment and supervision of the work process by overseers. Unskilled individual tasks, such as hoeing, weeding and stone-gathering were performed by gang labour.[35] Although the quantity and effort of work could be regulated by the piece, direct supervision ensured the quality of the job. Labour gangs of free workers were not restricted to the period of the industrial revolution: picking grapes in the ancient world, cotton in pre-1900 America, tea in India and hops in inter-war Britain all relied on labour gangs. Team work requiring the complementary delivery of labour services was especially characteristic of the effort-intensive unskilled gangs in agriculture. Hand reaping provides a good example where one worker cut several breadth of corn until enough was cut to form a sheaf, which another worker gathered, tied and laid down ready for stooking.[36] Whether in convict New South Wales or in free labour East Anglia, barley, oats, and wheat were harvested in teams of three, where each mower had two gatherers who gathered, bound, raked and stacked the corn. Mowers were sometimes organised into larger gangs of 10, consisting of three mowers and seven helpers and reapers into gangs of six, with three reapers and three helpers. Convict teams of 20 or 30 harvesters in New South Wales were similar to the 'companies', sometimes as large as 40 men, although 20 was the average size, which worked the large fields in England.[37] The clearing gangs were organised as teams, working jointly to cut trees, stump and burn off.

In New South Wales teams of convicts built the roads and bridges, cut wood, quarried stone and constructed the public buildings. But such labour organisation was not unique to convictism. In many cases, team work was technologically necessary irrespective of the labour system. Sawyers — whether free or bond — were always assigned to work in pairs because logs could be cut only if two men were positioned at the opposite ends of the saw. The joint nature of the sawyers' work was codified into the colonial task regulation that 'the quantities of wood sawn weekly, by each pair of sawyers may be 750 feet of planking per week'.[38] Road work was also a team activity typical of free labour societies. As early as 1555 in England the surveyor of the king's highways selected days when the whole parish turned out as a gang to work on the roads, supplying free manual labour, tools, horses and carts.[39] In the ancient regime in France the levee on the roads operated each spring and autumn, and public labour by the parish was compulsory in nineteenth century Ireland and America. The most famous team workers in Victorian England were the canal and railway navvies, trained, mobile and committed excavators responsible for the provision of Britain's social overhead capital.[40] Similarly, the free and convict crews who loaded and unloaded ships, carried water, and carted goods were organised into teams since the jobs required lifting and carrying.

The size of the team or gang was determined by the technology of the job and the need to supervise work. In the limiting case, sawyer gangs in New South Wales comprised two men, but generally sawyers' shops employed 24 men, and usually two or three pairs of sawyers were allocated to bridge building. Assigning one monitor to a team of two men was clearly inefficient, so teams were combined together to save on the scarce factor in production, the overseer. The size of convict gangs displayed considerable variation around the mean. Skilled gangs of bricklayers rarely exceeded five or ten artisans and labourers; shoemakers' gangs consisted of eight persons and the blacksmith's workshop employed 45 men. The road and clearing gangs usually employed between 30 and 50 men. However, the number of supervisors per worker showed much less variation than gang size; on average, one supervisor oversaw 20 men. The large clearing and road gangs had one or two overseers or an overseer and an assistant overseer.[41]

The variations in team size reflected the flexibility and experimentation that characterised the convict system. Not all teams were engaged in joint work all the time. A gang might work as a team harvesting or ploughing one day and the next day perform individual tasks such as hoeing and weeding. There was also flexibility in the assignment of men to particular jobs. Much clearing and road building meant convicts mixed joint work with separate individual tasks. For example, a man digging a trench might be assigned to the task of helping other men lift a heavy log. The rigidity in the theoretical model is for analytical convenience, and Table 10.1 classifies gangs according to the dominant type of job involved. Unfortunately, such classification schemes do not capture the adaptability of gangs to a variety of tasks, which was perhaps their most important attribute.

Comparative work organisation: convicts and other coerced labour

Since ancient times convicts had been used to build roads, sewers and public buildings and to work in the mines and quarries.[42] At the beginning of the sixteenth century convicts were organised into teams of oarsmen on the Spanish galleys, and by the late seventeenth century Spain employed convict gangs in the dockyards and arsenals, in public works and in the mercury mines working at furnaces or bailing water.[43] By 1700, public works, including street cleaning, bridge building, port repairs, fortifications, and road and canal building were carried out by convict gangs both in Spain and in her colonial forts and garrisons of North Africa and the Caribbean. In the hulks in England convicts were mustered into gangs to land and load coal, excavate, haul timber and clean shot.[44] The English prisoners on the Bermuda and Gibraltar hulks worked in teams to build and repair the fortifications. In the Andaman Islands convict gangs felled timber for export. Perhaps the gang system closest to that in Australia operated among Indian convicts sent to Singapore. Since 1820 squads of convicts had worked on the roads, built houses and canals, and repaired the fortifications. With the erection of a permament gaol in 1860, a workyard was built containing 'shops for carpenters, blacksmiths, coopers, wheelwrights, sawyers, stonecutters and turners in wood and iron'.[45] Like the carpenters' and wheelwrights' gangs in Sydney, the carpenters' shop in Singapore 'made every necessary article required for the public building', and the wheelwrights' shop made carts and hand and wheel barrows. Inside the prison there were shops for tailors, weavers, rattan workers, coil and rope makers, and flag makers while outside the prison, workshops made brick, lime and cement.

Such convict organisation was similar to that which prevailed in other systems of coerced labour. Plantation agriculture relied on teams of slave and contract workers. In the American South, the sugar and cotton plantations used slave gangs of 30 working hands plus driver.[46] The Indian contract workers on the Caribbean sugar and cotton estates have been compared with slavery because they replaced slaves, worked under the same harsh conditions, and were organised into gangs.[47] On the Queensland sugar estates, Melanesian contract workers laboured in butty gangs cutting and loading the cane and laying portable tracks.[48] Contract labour was also employed in teams on the Queensland pastoral stations before 1860 and towards the end of the century Chinese workers were employed in gangs to work the Queensland rice fields.[49] During the nineteenth century gangs of slave or contract workers were widespread in the Far East, India, Australia and the Pacific islands, South America and the United States, harvesting tea, tobacco, coffee, cotton and sugar. Clearly, the gang was a typical work organisation across different forced labour systems and was not unique to the convict system in Australia.

Whether the workforce had voluntarily entered into their employment contracts or were unfree, the organisation of work was much the same. The nature of the job determined the best way of going about a task. The gangs in New South Wales were an efficient form of work organisation since their organisation depended on whether the job required the input of joint labour services or was individually tasked. Secondly, they were efficient in the sense that the way convicts were organised for work corresponded to the work arrangements for the same jobs in Britain and in other forced labour systems. The job, not the labour system, determined the organisation of work. To analyse convict gangs simply as a device for punishment distorts the true structure of work relations in colonial New South Wales.

Discipline, incentives and tasks

Public labour and flogging have been inexorably bound in most discussions of the convict system. Weidenhofer found that members of road gangs were flogged frequently and Hirst has emphased the institutionalisation of flogging, especially after the Bigge Report.[50] According to Hughes, the cat o' nine tails' whistle and dull crack were as much a part of the aural background to Australian life as the kookaburra's laugh.[51] Since flogging reduced, in the short term, the worker's strength and stamina and created, in the long term, a hostile workforce, why was the lash an essential element in colonial work relations? The reliance of convictism on flogging has been both exaggerated and misunderstood by Australian historians.[52] The incidence of whippings varied geographically, with repeat lashings a common feature of the places of secondary punishment, while convicts assigned up-country would have been unlikely to have seen, let alone experienced, a flogging. The Sydney convict, at least until the 1820s, was forced to watch publicly administered floggings at either the lumberyard or the barracks and, with a bench of magistrates close at hand, physical punishments were not unduly delayed. But the artisan in the lumberyard was not driven to work by repeated beatings. What the rural labourer and urban artisan shared was the ever-present fear of physical punishment. The threat of the lash, rather than actual beatings, was a powerful method of extracting work from labourers.[53]

But even the threat of physical punishment was an ambiguous tool for work extraction. Pain incentives effectively generate high levels of effort because effort varies directly with the level of anxiety, and a threat to one's physical integrity produces very high anxiety indeed.[54] Effort-intensive work such as clearing scrub and road building was particularly susceptible to being driven through fear of pain. But anxiety was inimical to care; threats of pain against skilled tailors, brickmakers and wheelwrights performing care-intensive work increased anxiety and probably reduced both the output and quality of work. Care-intensive workers were motivated largely by rewards; effort-intensive workers, by fear of pain.

The theory of gangs reveals further limitations in the use of pain incentives: since floggings were applied against individuals, careful supervision was required in order to identify the shirker. Carefulness and quality of work are attributes of skilled work which are difficult to measure; at the limit it takes one full-time skilled supervisor to monitor one skilled worker. Pain incentives applied to care-intensive workers incurred high supervision costs as well as reduced output through high levels of anxiety. Unskilled work was more easily assessed, and pain incentives were a cheap and effective way for extracting work. But the costs of supervision were related not only to the level of skill but also to the organisation of work. The input of effort and energy by an individual in team production was difficult and costly to measure; when many men were involved in carrying heavy logs and pulling stumps the effort by any one man was not easily assessed. In team production, shirkers easily escape detection even with a high level of monitoring. In the 1830s, allegedly whole teams were beaten, but the effect encouraged absconding and created a hostile workforce.[55] Such unrestricted punishment was exceptional, counterproductive to work relations and an aberration of usual work discipline. Pain incentives, then, were least effectively employed against skilled or team workers and most effectively applied to unskilled labour gangs. Given these limitations in the use of physical punishment, a structure of rewards for government servants was developed as an essential adjunct to work extraction.

Convictism was a flexible system of work, searching for the right combination of work organisation and supervision and the right mix of punishment and rewards. The economics of gang organisation explain both the use of punishment and supervision, and the use of tasks and rewards. A modified piece rate task system in New South Wales before 1819 was clear evidence of the limited ability of physical punishment to induce work, and the openness of colonial administrators to experiment with the way jobs were undertaken. Tasks were easily set for labour gangs, which hoed, weeded, cleared stones and thistles, and dug holes. The overseer monitored work effort indirectly by assessing the amount of ground hoed and weeded or the number of stones picked up or holes dug by each individual. Teams presented special problems since the amount of work performed by the whole gang could be easily assessed, but not (at least not without extremely high monitoring costs) the work effort of any individual member. Teams sent out to work without a task offered individual members of the gang both the opportunity and incentive to shirk, since there was no incentive to work diligently and no mechanism within the gang to discipline shirkers. Shirking thus became endemic and the whole gang shirked. To increase work intensity, colonial administrators tasked jobs employing convicts in government service. The task system developed early in the colony, became a formal part of the work regulations, and even with the increasing severity of convictism in the 1820s and 1830s survived as a form of work extraction.

Table 10.1 presents a typology of task work, showing the relative importance of fixed and variable tasks and jobbing. Skilled bricklayers, sawyers, quarrymen, brickmakers, tailors and shoemakers engaged in batch production were assigned fixed tasks that applied throughout the colony. Other skilled work was jobbed, with wheelwrights and brassfounders, harnessmakers and blacksmiths, and carpenters and boatmen performing their jobs as they thought best. Most of the outdoor gangs were organised as teams and assigned variable tasks. As the chief engineer explained, outdoor gangs were not easily assigned fixed tasks:

> It should be desirable to be able to fix a specified task . . . but so many reasons concur against this being done . . . The quantities of work of the outdoor parties being dependent on the weather, the varying nature of the materials . . . as well as the implements they work with render it difficult to assign a stated task . . . . A middle course, therefore, is probably recommendable for the officer in visiting each gang to determine in his own mind what the quantity of work ought to be.[56]

By itself, setting a task was not sufficient to prevent shirking. Incentives, either reward or threat of punishment, or the direct supervision of work, was required for efficient task completion. Incentives saved on the scarce supervisory factor in production, the overseer. George Druitt testified to the Bigge Commission that the overseers were the 'best conducted and most skillful in their several trades and callings' and Grace Karskens has emphasised that many of the overseers on the road gangs were highly skilled builders.[57] Since only an artisan could monitor the work of skilled craftsmen, and because such monitoring was expensive when the job involved care and quality, the use of reward incentives was likely to be more widespread in care-intensive than in effort-intensive jobs. Positive incentives were particularly applied to teamwork, with rewards shared by the whole gang. This encouraged self-policing of shirkers within the gang, since shirkers shared equally in the rewards but by withholding work effort forced the rest of the team to work harder. Also, punishment increased supervision costs when team work was involved. For these reasons a structure of short and long term rewards became an integral part of the organisation of public work.

Rewards included extra clothing and rations, indulgences (such as tea, tobacco and rum), preferred work, apprenticeship training, time to work on one's own account, special passes to Sydney, tickets-of-leave and, on occasion, additional income in money or kind. Own time working before 1819 has been seen as the most important incentive to work effort. Both skilled and unskilled workers were allowed to leave their workplace once their task was completed. After 1819 the government introduced full-day working and the incentive of leaving the workplace to work on one's own account was withdrawn. There were exceptions. At the Pennant Hills sawyard, which employed shingle-splitters and basket-weavers as well as sawyers, the convicts were allowed to earn income by hiring themselves out privately after the completion of their task, and when a tunnel to carry water to Sydney was constructed between 1827 and 1837 the indulgence of own-time working was also extended to these convicts.[58] For all convicts, leisure remained an incentive for rapid task completion. Bigge reported that task work remained the norm in many workshops in the lumberyard. While not allowed to return to barracks or their own homes after completing their assigned work, convicts ceased work once the task was completed or they slowed their workpace, ensuring the task took all day. In either case, the convicts consumed leisure. Outdoor gangs also continued to work under a task system and were motivated by leisure or material rewards. The grasscutting gangs, for example, kept any surplus grass for themselves which they sold privately once the government task was completed.[59] These rewards, while they may not have been as powerful as own time working, acted as incentives to hard work. Hirst is certainly wrong to suggest that the convicts' loss of the right to work on their own time allowed Macquarie to abolish the related indulgence of task work.[60] Nor is it correct to argue that task work was of no value without incentives. When work was supervised the setting of a task allowed the speed with which the job was being completed to be monitored, providing a measure of work effort.

Conclusion

Rewards were combined with the use of an overseer in the labour extraction process for indoor and outside gangs, creating a sophisticated system of labour management. The overseer was a foreman, directing work. Only slowly would English factory masters break down the craftworkers' resistance to foremen who were paid a wage by the capitalist to supervise the work of others. Even for semi-skilled jobs, factory owners frequently avoided direct management by subcontracting for production through a craftsman who employed a team of less skilled labourers within the capitalist's factory. The system of foremen evolved slowly in Britain, triumphing over more traditional supervisory arrangements only in the twentieth century.[61] Unfortunately, we know little about the bargaining between convict workers and government officials who set the tasks. Certainly, skilled workers with their much greater knowledge of the work process had considerable power to exaggerate the difficulty and time required to complete a job. Nor do we know what use was made of the detailed records on each gang's (and frequently each gang member's) weekly output. Not until the triumph of scientific management in the United States after 1890 and in Britain after the First World War would such detailed work records become a standard feature for free factory labour. Such records were prerequisites to defining work routines, keeping track of the output of individual workers, and determining what jobs needed to be done. The work process in colonial Australia was bureaucratic from the start: work had a fixed division of labour regulated by rules and duties subject to a hierarchy of power with written records and communications. The impact of such bureaucratic work routines on labour productivity awaits further study.

What is clear is that labour gangs and teams had assignment and incentive attributes which allowed efficiency gains by allocating workers with comparative skill advantages to those tasks which they could best perform. For example, there was a division of labour within the road and clearing gangs, with skilled quarrymen and blacksmiths working alongside unskilled labour who carried stones or shovelled bark. The assignment attributes were especially important in unskilled work when men with above average strength and endurance could be appointed to difficult tasks, and in skilled work when artisan teams could be allotted jobs. Karskens discovered that road gangs were organised according to skills; the least skilled and unskilled men, allotted the task of rough road forming, were sent to one gang, while the best masons engaged in more difficult tasks of building walls and bridges were assigned to other gangs.[62] The convergence of detailed record-keeping which allowed the capabilities and work performance of each convict to be assessed and the assignment, supervisory and incentive attributes of gangs, created a sophisticated, flexible and efficient structure for arranging production. The form of work in the colony was not unlike that in England, except for the more intense supervision and record-keeping in Australia. While there is much we do not know yet about work relations in the government sector, the traditional emphasis on punishment, malingering and the road gang as characterisations of public work is patently wrong. The organisation of public labour into gangs was an efficient way of structuring work.

NOTES

1. M. Weidenhofer, *The Convict Years: Transportation and the Penal System 1788–1868*, p.51; L. Evans and P. Nicholls, *Convicts and Colonial Society 1788–1853*, p.48.

2. H. Tinker, *A New System of Slavery: The Export of Indian Labour Overseas 1830–1920*, pp.177–235.

3. J. Hirst, *Convict Society and Its Enemies: A History of Early New South Wales*, p.64.

4. Hirst, *Convict Society*, p.73; R. Hughes, *The Fatal Shore: A History of the Transportation of Convicts to Australia 1787–1868*, p.285.

5. Hughes, *Fatal Shore*, p.285.

6. M. Clark, *A History of Australia* I, pp.243–4.

7. Clark, *History of Australia* I, pp.243–4.

8. R.W. Connell and T.H. Irving, *Class Structure in Australian History: Documents, Narrative and Argument*, p.45.

9. Hirst, *Convict Society*, pp.32, 75.

10. R. Ward, *The Australian Legend*, pp.29–30.

11. H. McQueen, 'Convicts and Rebels', *Labour History* 15 (1968), 25.

12. A. Atkinson, 'Four Patterns of Convict Protest', *Labour History* 37 (1979), 49–50.

13. Connell and Irving, *Class Structure*, p.48.

14. See Chapter 12 section I for a further discussion of whipping.

15. G. Karskens, 'Defiance, Deference and Diligence: Three Views of Convicts in New South Wales Road Gangs', *Australian Historical Archaeology* 4 (1986), 18–19.

16. For the economic theory of gangs see A. Alchian and H. Demsetz, 'Production, Information Costs, and Economic Organisation', *American Economic Review* 62 (1972), 777–95; O. Williamson, *The Economic Institutions of Capitalism*, pp.206–39.

17. E. O'Brien, *The Foundation of Australia*, p.224; Hughes, *Fatal Shore*, p.95.

18. Hirst, *Convict Society*, p.94; Karskens, 'Defiance, Defence and Diligence', 19.

19. R.S. Fitton and A.P. Wadsworth, *The Strutts and the Arkwrights 1758–1830: A Study of the Early Factory System*, p.233; S. Cohn, 'Keeping the Navvies in Line: Variations in Work Discipline Among British Railway Construction Crews' in L. Tilly and C. Tilly (eds), *Class Conflict and Collective Action*, 147.

20. Major Ovens to Secretary Goulburn, 16 June 1825, *Historical Records of Australia*, Series I (hereafter HRA), XI, p.653.

21. Sir Thomas Brisbane to Earl Bathurst, 1st May 1824, *HRA*, XI, p.254.

22. For a similar definition applied to England see M. Berg, *The Age of Manufactures, 1700–1820*, p.222.

23. G. Walsh, 'Factories and Factory Workers in New South Wales, 1788–1900', *Labour History* 21 (1971), 2.

24. Ovens to Goulburn, 16 June 1825, *HRA*, XI, p.655.

25. H. Heaton, *The Yorkshire Woollen and Worsted Industries*, pp.418–77; A.P. Wadsworth and J. Mann, *The Cotton Trade and Industrial Lancashire 1600–1780*, pp.395–444.

26. S. Marglin, 'What Do Bosses Do?', *Review of Radical Political Economics* 6 (1974), 33–50. See also D. Landes, 'What Bosses Really Do?', *Journal of Economic History* 46 (1986), 585–624.

27. P. Hudson, 'Proto-industrialisation: The Case of the West Riding Wool Textile Industry in the 18th and Early 19th Centuries', *History Workshop* 12 (1981), 46.

28. Ovens to Goulburn, 16 June 1825, *HRA*, XI, p.657.

29. Ovens to Goulburn, 16 June 1825, *HRA*, XI, p.656.

30. Ovens to Goulburn, 16 June 1825, *HRA*, XI, pp.654–9; Archives Office of New South Wales (hereafter AONSW), *Weekly Returns of Men Employed on Cowpastures*, Oct. 1822, Dec. 1823–31, 4/7028C; 2/8315.

31. S. Pollard and P. Robertson, *The British Shipbuilding Industry 1870–1914*, pp.164–5.

32. J. Jeffreys, *The Story of the Engineers 1800–1945*, p.63; K. Burgess, *The Origins of British Industrial Relations: Nineteenth Century Experience*, p.54.

33. Berg, *Age of Manufactures*, p.276; M. Flinn, *The History of the British Coal Industry*, pp.329–36.

34. R. Samuel, 'The Mineral Workers' in R. Samuel (ed.), *Miners, Quarrymen and Saltworkers*, p.25.

35. D. Morgan, 'The Place of Harvesters in Nineteenth Century Village Life', in R. Samuel (ed.), *Village Life and Labour*, p.104; E.J.T. Collins, *Sickle to Combine: A Review of Harvest Techniques*, p.8; E.J.T. Collins, 'Harvest Technology and Labour Supply in Britain 1790–1870', Ph.D. thesis (University of Nottingham, 1970).

36. Collins, *Sickle To Combine*, p.3, 241, 250.

37. F.G. Heath, *British Rural Life and Labour*, p.24; W. Hasbach, *A History of the English Agricultural Labourer*, p.200; AONSW, *Assignment and Employment of Convicts 1827–1830* 7/2689.

38. *New South Wales Superintendent of Carpenters, Parramatta, 1817–19*, Mitchell Library (hereafter ML), A2086–8; 'Ovens to Goulburn, 16 June 1825', *HRA*, XI, p.656.

39. S. and B. Webb, *English Local Government: The Story of the King's Highway*, pp.14–7.
40. D. Brooke, *The Railway Navvy*, p.15.
41. Ovens to Goulburn, 16 June 1825, HRA, XI, 265, 654–9; AONSW, *Statement of Way Convicts Were Employed at Various Government Establishments, 1824*, 4/1775, pp.164–173; *Returns Superintendent of Carpenters*, ML A2086–8.
42. T. Frank, *Rome and Italy of the Republic I*, in T. Frank (ed.), *An Economic Survey of Ancient Rome*, p.243.
43. R. Pike, *Penal Servitude in Early Modern Spain*, pp.4, 15, 53, 88–94, 108, 112–47, 356.
44. *Report on the General Treatment and Condition of Convicts on the Hulks at Woolwich*, Parliamentary Paper (hereafter P.P.), 1847, XVIII, C831, xix.
45. J.F.A. McNair, *Prisoners Their Own Warders*, pp.104–7.
46. P. David et al, *Reckoning With Slavery: A Critical Study in the Quantitative History of American Negro Slavery*, p.82.
47. Tinker, *New System of Slavery*, pp.185–8.
48. R. Schlomowitz, 'Team Work and Incentives: The Origins and Development of the Butty Gang System in Queensland's Sugar Industry, 1891–1913', *Journal of Comparative Economics* 3 (1979), 49.
49. K. Saunders, *Workers in Bondage: The Origins and Bases of Unfree Labour in Queensland, 1824–1916*, p.46.
50. Weidenhofer, *The Convict Years*, p.64; Hirst, *Convict Society*, p.61.
51. Hughes, *Fatal Shore*, p.427.
52. See Chapter 12 section 1 for a discussion of the incidence of whippings.
53. David, *Reckoning With Slavery*, p.63.
54. The argument relies on an excellent article by S. Fenoaltea, 'Slavery and Supervision in Comparative Perspective: A Model', *Journal of Economic History* 44 (1984), 635–68.
55. Hughes, *Fatal Shore*, p.432.
56. Ovens to Goulburn, 16 June 1825, HRA, XI, p.654.
57. Karskens, 'Defiance, Deference and Diligence', 22; J. Ritchie, *The Evidence of the Bigge Reports* I, p.5.
58. Hirst, *Convict Society*, p.44.
59. *Report from the Commissioner of Inquiry into the State of the Colony of New South Wales* (Bigge Report), P.P., 1822, XX, C448, 28.
60. Hirst, *Convict Society*, p.44, 67.
61. C. Littler, *The Development of the Labour Process in Capitalist Societies*; Berg, *Age of Manufactures*, S. Pollard, *The Genesis of Modern Management: A Study of the Industrial Revolution in Great Britain*.
62. Karskens, 'Definance, Deference and Diligence', 25–6.

Chapter Eleven

Convict Labour and the Australian Agricultural Company

John Perkins

Introduction

Inspired by the Bigge Report of 1823, with its emphasis upon encouraging the inflow of capital to promote rural enterprise, the Australian Agricultural Company was formed in 1824, through a combination of Act of Parliament (5 Geo IV., cap. 86) and Royal Charter, to acquire a large area of land in the colony of New South Wales. According to a German writer of the 1930s, with the entry of this enterprise into the field, 'The actual opening-up and development of Australia began'.[1] The primary and overriding objective of the Company was to employ convict labour to produce superfine or high-quality merino clothing-wool for export to Britain. As James Macarthur, one of the directors and chairman of the local or 'Colonial Committee' of the Company, observed in 1828: 'if the success of fine-woolled sheep in this colony be doubtful, the main object for which the Company was instituted is at once swept away, and with it the very existence of the Company'.[2]

At the time of its establishment conditions appeared ideal for the Company to flourish. Extraordinarily high and yet rising prices were being paid in Britain for superfine merino clothing-wool, which was entirely imported from Spain and especially from central and northern Germany.[3] Within Europe, from a combination of the climatic requirements for the production of superfine merino wool and the relatively dense and rapidly increasing population, creating an increasing demand for foodstuffs and other agricultural raw materials apart from wool, the possibilities were severely limited for expanding, or even maintaining, the area devoted to extensive sheepfarming. On the other hand, the colony of New South Wales possessed vast tracts of land and conditions apparently ideally suited for the merino. The mild winters, in particular, meant that there was no necessity for costly outlays upon housing and handfeeding stock, as was the case for a large part of the year in central Europe. According to the Company's estimate, the costs of carriage of wool from the interior of Germany were, 'in amount, equal to the costs of freight incurred by a longer voyage from New South Wales'.[4]

Early in 1826, on the recommendation of John Oxley, the Surveyor-General of New South Wales, a party consisting of Richard Dawson, the designated superintendent of the estate, the Company's surveyor, a government assistant surveyor and the secretary of the local committee of management of the Company based in Sydney explored the Port Stephens area of the central coast. Oxley may have been influenced in his recommendation of Port Stephens by the direction to locate the Company's grant with

as little interference as possible to existing landholdings.[5] The investigating party
deemed it to be ideally suited to the Company's purpose and a grant of a million acres
was immediately taken up.

The company in context

At the outset it has to be borne in mind that the Company's experience in the
employment of convict labour was in a number of respects far from typical of the
generality of pastoralist ventures in the colony at the time. In the first place, the location
at Port Stephens was then a relatively remote part of New South Wales. The overwhelming majority of convicts employed by pastoralists were on selections within far
more reasonable proximity of Sydney. Secondly, the scale of the Company's operation
was incomparably greater than that of any other venture utilising convict labour.[6] In
the mid-1830s the next five largest landholders in the colony possessed a total of
187,000 acres. The closest parallel to the Company, in terms of acreage and experience,
was the Van Diemen's Land Company, which was formed in 1825 to eventually occupy
350,000 acres in northwest Tasmania. To illustrate this point further, on the basis of the
regulations on assignment issued in May 1835, the Company was theoretically entitled
to 3128 convicts, with an additional one per 40 acres of land under cultivation.[7] On the
other hand, in 1835 a total of less than 30,000 convicts were employed outside the
public sector.[8]

Finally, the Australian Agricultural Company was the only enterprise to attempt the
systematic exploitation of convict labour as a source of profit: to attempt to develop, as
it were, a convict labour system. In fact, when in the mid-1830s the supply of convicts
was deemed inadequate for the Company's requirements, its directors endeavoured to
organise their own transportation system, through negotiations for a steady supply of
prisoners from the gaols of the city-state of Hamburg.[9]

At the same time the extant records of the Company, principally held at the Archives
of Business and Labour at the Australian National University, are extraordinarily
comprehensive and provide detailed information on the day-to-day management of the
estate that is not available for other colonial sheepfarming enterprises. Moreover, as the
activities of the Company, and in particular the extraction of labour from convicts,
were largely dissimilar only in scale from those of individual pastoralists, the records
reveal much that contributes to our understanding of the wider convict based rural
economy of New South Wales in the early nineteenth century.

The structure and discipline of the workforce

A feature of the Australian Agricultural Company's operation at Port Stephens was the
simultaneous employment, upon identical tasks, of various forms of labour. The
original nucleus of the workforce consisted of indentured servants brought out from
Europe on seven year contracts. At least during the early years of its existence, the
enterprise employed a substantial number of emancipists, persons who had served out
their sentences, and people with tickets-of-leave who had had their sentences re-
scinded for good conduct. A number of local Aborigines were also employed at various
tasks, such as crewing boats, collecting bark and acting as messengers, and there were
proposals to extend the range of occupations in which they were to be employed.[10] For

example, an experiment in growing cotton at Port Stephens in 1827 was expected to provide employment for Aborigines, presumably on the assumption that cotton was specifically a crop for 'black' labour. Finally, there were the convicts, who came to form the numerically largest category of workers.

From the beginning the physical layout of the Port Stephens settlement was designed with its convict labour force in mind. The Company's 'village' inhabited by its mainly married indentured servants, including overseers of convicts, was placed sufficiently far away from the convicts' quarters to avoid 'inconvenience and annoyance'. Not so far away, however, 'as to be beyond the hearing and control of their overseers and guards should any rioting occur'. The housing for a military guard of eight soliders under a corporal was also located so that: 'they are near enough to give assistance if required'. For the future, it was proposed in 1826 that the convicts should be accommodated in 'a barrack enclosed by a wall', while 'allowing the better conducted people to reside outside': thus utilising standards of housing provision as a source of incentive to convicts both in respect of work effort and general behaviour.[11]

A feature of the employment of convicts on the Company's estate was a duality, sometimes involving a contradiction, between the production and the punishment objectives of certain tasks. For example, a 'Chain Gang' was established for the employment of refractory convicts, who worked in irons and on the minimum government-determined rations quarrying stone for building purposes. An isolated farm on the Company's estate was utilised for what the superintendent described 'as a kind of penal place where convicts only are kept and where such as are indolent but not deserving of greater punishment are sent to labour with the axe or hoe under overseers especially appointed to superintend them'. It was to this place that most of a draft of 'boy convicts' was sent, after they were found to be 'incorrigible' and 'worth very little'. On the farm according to the superintendent, 'they must work quietly or suffer such inconveniences and privations as will compel it'.[12] This duality, of course, arose from a system possessing, at least initially, limited material incentives to enhance work effort, impose labour discipline and ensure good behaviour outside of working hours.

The lash, in multiples of 25 strokes, was the most commonly imposed form of punishment for convict misdemeanours, at least during the early years of enterprise. The first return of 'Offences, Charges and Sentences', for the three months from 30 April 1826, records nine cases involving convicts, all of whom were punished by whipping. On 23 May four convicts were each given 50 lashes for refusing to work. Five days later another was awarded the same punishment for neglect of duty. Subsequently, a convict was given 50 lashes for 'neglect of duty and false represen-tation'; yet another received the same for 'insolence and indecent language to females and refusal to work'. A convict who absented himself from his duties received 25 strokes of the lash; and finally one had a sentence of 50 lashes imposed for 'selling his trousers'.[13] As with subsequent returns, the punishment of whipping was often not connected with work related offences.

The lash had the advantage of being a dramatic and immediate form of punishment, whereby the recipient was soon in a fit condition to return to his duties and, as was intended, apply himself with more vigour. It was also obviously employed in order to encourage others to work. After a 17–year-old Irish youth was whipped for 'incorrigible idleness and absenting himself from his employment', the superintendent remarked: 'I trust it will be the means of preventing any further disagreeable measures of the same kind to others of his class'.[14] In proportion to the total labour force on the estate, however, the lash was resorted to on relatively infrequent occasions.

The superintendent himself came to doubt the efficacy of the lash. As he observed subsequently: 'working in irons for certain periods upon a reduced allowance of rations, produced incomparably better effects than the lash. So much indeed were the former dreaded, that on the conviction of offenders they have frequently petitioned me to commute them for the latter'.[15] Nonetheless, the whip was retained as a punishment, on account of its effect on the convicts assembled to watch and for its simplicity in terms of arrangement.

As with free labour in contemporary Britain, the services of organised religion were called upon on the Company's estate to inculcate respect for established authority and diligence in employment. One of the earliest requests of the superintendent was for the appointment of a resident minister of the Established Church. In the interim, prayers were read on Sundays by the superintendent himself, or by his nephew during his absences from Port Stephens, initially under the shade of a tree around which several felled trees were arranged as seats. The free people were placed on one side and the convicts on the other. Subsequently, when the prayer readings were moved to the newly-erected joiner's shop, the Catholic convicts refused to attend. Therefore, separate services were organised for them and conducted by a free tradesman of Italian descent.[16]

It had been the Company's original intention that its indentured servants brought out from Britain should essentially act as overseers of convicts, as well as occupy other positions requiring trust and the exercise of authority over others and usually conferring some social status. To the extent that this hierarchy of labour operated, the superintendent found of the indentured servants that: 'the authority which I found it necessary to give them over the convicts, who were placed in parties under them, served to increase their importance, and to make common cause with me in the advancement of the numerous objects in view'.[17] In practice, however, the system began to break down almost from the inception of the Company's activities at Port Stephens. Convicts came to be appointed to positions of authority and trust. The superintendent discovered that 'convicts make themselves valuable in particular situations to act as overseers'. The 'Constables and Floggers', who formed part of the establishment at Port Stephens, soon came to consist mostly of convicts themselves. At the early open-air prayer readings the convicts were 'attended by several constables appointed from their own body'.[18] The first schoolmaster to be appointed, a former assistant master at a Dublin school, was a convict. At the same time the 'free people' began to fraternise with the convicts, which was understandable in view of the similarity of their social origins. On the farm at Stroud, for example, the indentured servants who acted as overseers were found to have 'put themselves on a footing of equality with the convicts'.[19]

Explaining the initial lack of success

In the late 1820s the blame for the lack of success of the venture was attributed to the character and decisions of Richard Dawson, the Company's first superintendent at Port Stephens, who was dismissed in late 1828. Dawson was described by the Court of Directors on his appointment in 1824 as a 'a gentleman whose respectability, talents, and extensive agricultural as well as general experience eminently qualify him for the duties he has undertaken'.[20] Colonel Dumaresq, who visited Port Stephens during May 1826, was impressed by Dawson's achievements. He later informed the directors in London that: 'from his observation of Mr Dawson he would be disposed to place entire confidence in him — that for great activity, and competency, he thinks another such a Man could not easily be met with'.[21]

Although Dawson did in fact possess extensive agricultural experience, it had been exclusively acquired in England, and then in districts that were relatively backward agriculturally. He lacked any acquaintance with the particular climatic, pasturage and soil conditions of New South Wales. In addition, along with most of the shepherds in the Company's employ during the early years at Port Stephens, he was ignorant of the distinctive requirements of managing merinos in contrast to British breeds of sheep. These deficiencies may not have mattered all that much had Dawson been more willing to emulate colonial practices, rather than impose his own ideas in the management of the Company's sheep in Australia. In his mistaken opinion: 'There is neither mystery nor art in the management of sheep in this country, and very little, if anything, new to those who have been accustomed to sheep at home'.[22]

Contrary to the advice of the local committee of the Company, the superintendent adopted a season for lambing that exposed them to summer rains at a vulnerable age. In consequence, heavy losses were incurred. At the Company's first farm, near Stroud, he ordered sheepfolds to be erected to hold flocks overnight to manure the land for crops. This practice of infield-outfield husbandry had been widespread in England in the days when sheep were mainly kept on extensive sheepwalks in areas of poor soils. By the nineteenth century it has been largely superseded by more modern methods of farming, except in parts of the agriculturally backward southern counties of England. It may have been adaptable to conditions in colonial New South Wales, except with so delicate an animal as the merino and especially on the 'barren and . . . useless swamp' Dawson had selected for the first farm. There it entailed the sheep standing knee-deep in mud overnight before being driven to graze on a 'sterile and wretched pasture'.[23]

When a number of sheep came down with what the superintendent took to be the rot, or liver fluke — a disease then virtually unknown in Australia — he resorted to the British remedy of grazing them on what he saw as 'excellent salt marshes'. The result, with merino sheep, was heavy losses from lung disorders. On the other hand, he did little to control or eradicate 'that more than commonly troublesome disorder in this colony, the scab'. By mid-1828 there was not one sheep station on the estate that was free of the disease, in consequence of 'scabby rams being put with the ewes'. Of all the shepherds in the Company's employ, only one, a convict, refused to use infected rams. In response he was informed that he 'should obey his orders, whether right or wrong'. Told to put the infected rams to his ewes, the convict shepherd first dressed and cured them, so that his was the only flock free of the disease.[24] The local purchases of sheep by the superintendent were in many cases injudicious in terms of price and quality. Dumaresq attributed the higher than average prices paid by Dawson to 'the superior quality of the animals'. It has been stated that the grazier members of the local committee foisted upon the Company 'old and diseased sheep from their own flocks, at high prices'.[25] A rumour was current in Sydney at the time that the same graziers, on the assumption of the inevitable failure of the Company, foresaw an opportunity to repurchase the same sheep later at reduced prices.[26] There may be elements of truth in these assertions; although there is an evident contradiction between the view of the sheep being 'old and diseased' and that of an intention to repurchase them later on. Perhaps of greater relevance in explaining the injudicious purchases is Dawson's inexperience with merinos and the pressure from the Company to build up the flocks as quickly as possible. As regards the age of the sheep in question, the accusation here appears to be based upon a lack of knowledge of contemporary practices in merino breeding and does not accord with Dawson's actual procedure.

The superintendent's practice in purchasing sheep, and his intended one in respect of culling flocks, was that implemented with British mutton breeds and was quite unsuitable for merinos in New South Wales. British breeds, on account of their early maturity — a characteristic fixed by breeders with an eye to the increasingly more lucrative market for the mutton than for the wool of British sheep — were culled on the basis of age and were considered old at four to five years of age. Merino ewes, on the other hand, culled according to the degree of coarseness appearing in the fleece, were considered to deliver the best lambs from four to five years of age and, in New South Wales, so long as the wool was satisfactory, they were allowed to breed until they died, at 13 to 14 years old.[27]

Dawson's arrangements in respect of the size of flocks also appears to have been derived from British practice. As such they were relatively costly in terms of labour requirements. The sheep were divided into flocks of about 300 sheep under convict shepherds, with an indentured shepherd supervising groups of four flocks, to which a (night) watchman and hutkeeper were attached. This contrasts, for example, with the flock of 1250 sheep under the care of a single shepherd that Commander Parry came across at Yarramanbah on his journey to the Liverpool Plains in 1829. Admittedly, the relatively open country around Yarramanbah, as compared with much of the Port Stephens estate, obviated the need for a watchman, as dingos could be easily spotted. In the main, however, the superintendent's standard flock size reflected his obstinate translation of the British example to an almost totally different environment.[28]

From the very beginning the superintendent embarked upon a lavish building programme, in which deficiencies were evident in the choice of locations and in the construction of facilities. The two wharves at Port Stephens had been built at a 'very considerable expense' and yet were 'badly constructed and . . . rendered useless by their situations being ill selected'. Of the entirety of the Company's buildings, it was said that they were 'ill situated, ill contrived, badly built, and yet expense appears never to have been an object of consideration'. In all of this activity no priority seems to have been accorded the facilities required for the primary objective of the Company, the production of wool. Dawson, for example, was so busy in 1827 with the erection of a fine residence for himself, and other construction work at Port Stephens, that facilities for washing and shearing sheep were overlooked until almost the start of the shearing season and a woolpress had to be hurriedly ordered up from Sydney.[29]

The superintendent's orientation towards maximising the degree of self-sufficiency of the Company's estate proved not to be the most cost-effective arrangement. Cattle were slaughtered from the Company's herds not only to supply the beef ration allocated to employees but also to provide hides for tanning in the Company's pits, with the leather being made up into footwear and other articles. Wheat grown on the Company's land, and ground at its mill, was to meet the flour requirements of the workforce. Even the weekly allocation of tobacco was soon met from crops cultivated on the estate. Of the rations distributed to the convicts, only tea and sugar were purchased. The outlay on tea, at two ounces a week per prisoner, was inconsiderable. The issue of sugar, at one pound per week, was more substantial; and partly for this reason the superintendent evinced an early interest in the possibilities of cultivating cane on the grant. Yet the costs of self-production of supplies were such that the policy was soon abandoned after Dawson's dismissal.[30] As with the majority of holdings in the colony, a high degree of self-sufficiency was imposed by the relative absence of a market for a range of necessities and by the high cost of transportation. In the Company's case, however, it involved significant losses. For 1831 it was estimated that the 75 convicts and 14 supervisors involved in cultivating 482 acres of wheat yielded produce estimated to be worth £2048 in return for an outlay of £2816.[31] It was for this reason that Dawson's successors strove to reduce the degree of self-sufficiency insofar as developing circumstances permitted, with beneficial effects on the overall profitability of the concern.

Substantial as the inadequacies and maladministration of the superintendent were, they were far from being solely to blame for the Company's problems in the early years of its existence. John Macarthur Senior 'had no hesitation in saying that had Mr Dawson been ever so highly gifted with the ability to direct and control a large establishment, it would have been impossible for him to have succeeded in what he had undertaken.'[32] The very gradual improvement in the Company's fortunes under his successors, men of quite different characters, suggests that his methods were far from being entirely responsible for the fiasco of the early years.

What Macarthur saw as the failure of the Company by late 1828 he attributed mainly to the decisions of the directors in London. As he informed Dawson's successor in December 1829: 'the rock on which he and the Company had split was the setting out on so splendid a scale'. In particular, he castigated the latter for their action in sending out to the colony 'so large a number of persons with so much stock, before the grant had been selected, and their plans maturely considered'.[33] However, this decision, and the readiness of the directors to meet Dawson's requests for funds, were probably motivated by a stipulation of the Act of Parliament relating to the Company that required a substantial outlay of capital before land on the estate acquired at a low price could be leased or sold.[34]

Macarthur's criticism of the directors raises the question as to whether, in the conditions of the time, the corporate form of organisation, and the particular situation of the Australian Agricultural Company, were adapted to profitable sheepfarming in early nineteenth century New South Wales. Even in contemporary British industry, with concentrated production, most firms were family enterprises or partnerships where the owners were directly involved in supervising the processes of production. In the case of the Agricultural Company, the court of directors in London was ultimately responsible for directing activities scattered over a million acres of land situated at the other side of the world. Even the committee of management in Sydney, with limited powers of decision-making, was some 140 miles from Port Stephens — several days arduous journeying by road or up to a day by sea — and composed of men with substantial other interests of their own. It is perhaps little to be wondered at that, in Macarthur's words, 'the servants engaged for the Company of every class, were not at all solicitous for the Company's interests, they were only activated by an anxiety to serve themselves'.[35] In the circumstances, however, they were provided with ample opportunity to put their self-interest first.

Although it had little effect during the tenure of the superintendent, on account of the extremely limited amount of wool dispatched from the grant to Europe, the downturn of superfine wool prices from late 1825, and their failure to recover to anything like earlier heights, had a significant effect upon the Company's fortunes. The founding years of the venture coincided with radical developments in textile technology and in fashion. These resulted in a shift of demand away from superfine clothing-wool, such as that produced by the *Electoral* variety of merino from central Germany in which the Company had invested so heavily, towards combing wools, such as those produced by ordinary colonial flocks.[36] The Company, it would seem, was slow to adapt to this trend during the 1830s. Certainly, a large proportion of its clip continued to show characteristics of the *Electoral* fleece; including such deficiencies as curled and twisted wool derived from the intensive inbreeding to which the variety had been subjected. Subsequently, from 1837, it was hoped to eradicate this fault, and shift the direction of production from superfine to combing wool in line with the direction of relative prices, by means of the introduction of New Leicester blood.[37]

Reflecting the key organisational and managerial problems of the enterprise, the superintendent's departure was followed by the disbanding of the local committee and the placing of the Company's activities at Port Stephens in the sole charge of a person with the more exalted title of commissioner. The selection of a career naval officer, Sir William Edward Parry, indicates that the possession of extensive farming knowledge was subordinated to the appointee having the capacity to enforce authority (although he was the son of Dr Caleb Parry, a contemporary British authority on sheepbreeding). This particular appointment may also have arisen from another recognised reason for the Company's lack of immediate success; namely, the unsuitability of most of the original grant for the purpose of producing superfine clothing wool, or for that matter for maintaining flocks of merino sheep. Parry, from a combination of social standing and respect for his reputation as an explorer of the Arctic, was perhaps ideally suited for the essential task of negotiating the exchange of a large proportion of the Port Stephens grant for an equivalent area more adapted to merino sheepfarming.

The original grant was selected after a cursory examination, and without considering alternative areas, partly because Dawson was under some pressure to provide land for the sheep sent out from Europe and to begin to produce profits for the Company. A diversionary attraction of Port Stephens appears to have been an expectation of finding coal seams on the estate, as at nearby Newcastle. However, climatic conditions and the nature of most of the land were decidedly unfavourable for merino sheepfarming, especially for the production of fine wool. The precipitation was generally excessive for merinos to thrive. Extensive districts of the grant were 'mountainous and sterile' and large tracts along the coast were too swampy for sheep.[38]

The comparative value of convict labour

The difficulties experienced by the Company may have been partly due to an overestimation of the relative value of convict labour. It was cheap in terms of wage costs; in the final analysis because, unlike other forms of labour, the convict 'wage' was not required to reproduce that form, through being sufficient to support a family. In 1828 John Macarthur estimated the annual cost of a convict worker to be £23, or less than half the £60 paid to an emancipist and the £57 earned by an indentured servant. Another calculation, for the beginning of the 1840s, put the cost of a convict at £16, 17 shillings and 4 pence a year, as compared with £41 and 8 shillings for a 'free man', which included £25 for money wages, (and £8 and 8 shillings for 'a coolie').[39] Reflecting such relative wage costs, the Company's efforts throughout the 1830s were directed towards obtaining an increased supply of convicts and towards minimising the employment of other forms of labour. On the other hand, the productivity of convict labour on the Agricultural Company's estate was low. As Dawson later admitted, after being a fervent advocate of the employment of convicts: 'The quantity of labour extracted is exceedingly moderate, and when taken at a task [that is, on piece rates] . . . it never, in any instance, exceeded two-thirds of what would be required of similar work in England'.[40] Moreover, the superintendent's previous experience of employing agricultural labour had been in low-wage countries where productivity was well below the average for England as a whole.

The quality of much of the convict labour assigned to the Company, in terms of requisite skills and behaviour, appears to have left much to be desired. Of a party of Irish convicts assigned in April 1826, the superintendent spoke of the 'little they can do' (although that was, with one or two exceptions, 'performed with willingness and their conduct has been orderly and respectful'). On 20 May an assignment arrived that consisted 'chiefly of boys from 15 to 18 years of age'. Although some of them were 'reported to have been partially instructed in the trades of bricklayers, masons and carpenters', only two or three were 'made useful, after much trouble, in mason's work'. The rest were assigned to agricultural labour where, with few exceptions, they 'turned out to be worth very little'. The majority of a group of 11 convicts who arrived on 4 May came to be considered 'tolerable labourers' and a party of 52 from Port Macquarie contained several useful 'mechanicks'. There were several of the latter, however, whose conduct was 'of the worst description'. All in all, as the superintendent informed John Macarthur in October 1827, he desired 'something besides boys, cripples, and Manchester weavers and spinners'.[41] Such complaints, however, may have been more designed to shift the blame for managerial inadequacies than to provide an accurate assessment of the value of the labour assigned. Here it is notable that the most persistent complaint of the Company and its representatives in Australia, up to the end of transportation, was the inadequacy of the numbers of convicts assigned to its estate.

The supposedly inadequate supply of carpenters, joiners, stonemansons and other 'mechanicks' was a constant source of complaint by the Company. As Governor Darling observed in September 1826: 'The government is necessarily obliged to retain the greater number of convict mechanics, in consequence of the work it has to employ'.[42] The inadequacy of the supply of 'mechanics' on account of 'the government invariably retaining them in their own hands', remained a constant complaint by the Company. In part, however, the situation arose from the high level of demand for skilled workers and the specific skills that were required. In 1831, for example, Commissioner Parry complained about his inability to obtain a convict farrier. This was at a time when 34 per cent of the Company's establishment was employed in the 'Department of Manufactures', which consisted of a range of skilled workers such as coopers, joiners, tanners, tailors, blacksmiths, saddlers etc. Of the 133 employed in this department 106 were convicts and, although they may have included some unskilled assistants, the ratio of convicts to other workers was not significantly lower than that of other departments.[43] Perhaps it would have been impossible for any system to meet the proportionately high number of skilled workers that was demanded.

Convict labour was characterised by a relatively high turnover of workers, as men completed their sentences, or were recommended for tickets-of-leave (as a necessary inducement to good conduct) or were returned to the government for punishment on the public road gangs or to be shipped to Van Diemen's Land. The sickness rate among convicts, at least at Port Stephens, was high. This was particularly attributable to a high incidence of venereal disease contracted from sexual relations with Aboriginal women, who in turn had been infected by Europeans. At Port Stephens in the late 1820s, at any one time, between 7.5 and 10 per cent of the convicts were unable to work on account of venereal disease.[44]

The low direct cost of convict labour, towards which employers, and the Company in particular, tended to direct their attention, ignores the reltively high supervisory costs necessitated by that form of labour. This was partially overcome by the placing of convicts in positions of authority over others. Efforts were also made to shift some of the costs of policing onto the public purse.[45] However, high supervisory costs remained intrinsic to the system.

Apart from outlays required to impose labour and social discipline upon a convict workforce, in an isolated area such as Port Stephens, and with large numbers of convicts employed, provision had to be made to minimise the possibility of escape and to recapture convicts. This was particularly necessary to avoid the emergence of the phenomenon of bushranging, which was not only a threat to public safety in the area, but also likely to fan the opposition to the Company's presence in the colony, if it were to become viewed as a source of such a threat. These factors explain the fervour with which the superintendent pursued the recapture of four convicts who escaped towards the end of July 1826. Parties of soldiers and constables were immediately dispatched in pursuit and messengers were sent to Sydney and Newcastle, as well as to settlers living within a wide radius of the grant, with descriptions of the escapees. As it appeared to Dawson to be 'impossible for them to finally escape', he expressed the hope that they would be returned to the Company's establishment:

> that I may punish them by solitary confinement during the night, and working them [in] gangs on government allowance in order to guard against the emergence of others making similar attempts. Unless some means are resorted to, among so many prisoners as we may probably have here, bushranging will be a practice of frequent occurrence — and one of the most dangerous tendencies to the establishment as well as to neighbouring settlers.[46]

The cost-effectiveness of convict labour has to be considered in relation to that of other forms of labour available. In terms of overall outlays, indentured servants were clearly considered the most expensive workers. The wages of these married men had to be sufficient to meet the costs of reproducing labour, whereas in the case of convicts such costs were met by the British penal system. In addition, it was necessary to provide housing for families of a superior kind to that made available for convicts and the cost of passage from Britain had to be borne by the Company. This in turn was spread over a limited contract period of seven years, subsequently five years, with a high proportion of servants failing to serve out their indentures or declining to renew them for subsequent periods.[47] To remedy the problem of breaches of indentures, the superintendent suggested that the Company meet the cost of insuring the lives of its servants, 'to prevent them from being enticed away'.[48]

Further problems associated with the employment of indentured servants on the estate, which did not exist with convicts, arose from the families of such workers not being subject to the disciplinary means provided by the labour contract. As early as April 1826, in response to difficulties experienced with the wives of certain indentured servants, the superintendent recommended that: 'Some agreement should also be made for the services of the wife and children of every man, or they should be subject to the regulations and the authority of the principle [sic] person of the establishment'.[49]

In terms of direct wage costs, emancipists were the most expensive of workers. Opinions differed as to the quality of emancipist labour. In proportion to their numbers such workers figured less prominently on the 'Sick List' in the early years at Port Stephens, being obviously more acclimatised to the Australian environment and lacking the security of employment of indentured servants and convicts. They also tended to make the most capable shepherds on account of their familiarity with local conditions.[50]

Nevertheless, emancipists were a source of frequent complaint by the first superintendent. In August 1826 he reported that:

> Of the emancipists that have been employed here since 24th April, above 40 in number, I have little to say in their favour generally. I have found seven or eight very good men among them and such as I dare say I shall retain. As to the rest, I shall take the earliest opportunity of sending them away, as soon as I can have such a supply of convicts as will enable me to do well without them.[51]

In April of the following year the superintendent recorded that he had 'made it a principle not to employ emancipists where it can be avoided'. Being 'generally men of bad habits', they were considered to have a malign influence even upon convicts. As the Superintendent observed: 'Emancipists are sources of great annoyance where considerable numbers of convicts are employed at the same time. They have in general all the various propensities of prisoners, with the means (among convicts in particular) of doing much mischief, and no kind of separation or vigilance can prevent it'.[52] In fact the distinct impression is gained that a major deficiency of the convict labour system, from the superintendent's point of view, was that it produced a society in which emancipists increasingly preponderated.

The relatively high cost of 'free' and indentured labour in Australia was one factor motivating the expansion of labour extensive sheepfarming. John Macarthur Senior held the view that 'wherever much manual labour was employed, it must be unprofitable to the master'.[53] By the same token, low as the physical productivity of convict labour was, the high cost of alternative forms of labour was an important factor in the continuation of transportation as seemingly the only means by which capitalism could survive and prosper in the colony.

NOTES

1. W. Schaeffer, *Australiens Wirtschaft und Wirtschaftspolitik*, p. 17

2. Australian National University, *Archives of Business and Labour*, Australian Agricultural Company Deposit (hereafter *ABL*, AACo. Dep.) No. 160/89, Report of Meeting at John Macarthur's Chambers, 10 April 1824; No. 78/9/2, James Macarthur to Committee of Management, 13 Mar. 1828.

3. See J.A. Perkins, 'Rehearsal for Protectionism: Australian Wool Exports and German Agriculture, 1830–1880', *Australian Economic History Review* 25 (1985), 21.

4. ABL, AACo. Dep., No. 160/89, Report of Meeting at J. Macarthur's Chambers, Lincoln's Inn, 10 April 1824, *Australian Agricultural Company : Third Annual Report*, p.16.

5. J. Oxley to Colonial Secretary Macleay, 25. Jan. 1827, *Historical Records of Australia*, Series I, (hereafter *HRA*) XIII, p.41.

6. Govenor Bourke to Lord Glenelg, 6 Oct. 1835, *HRA* XVIII, p.131–2; J. Duxbury, 'Colonial Servitude : Indentured and Assigned Servants of the Van Diemen's Land Company', BA (Hons) thesis (Monash University, 1985).

7. S. Foster, 'Convict Assignment in the 1830s', *Push from the Bush* 15 (1983), 39–40. On the recommendation of the Governor, the Executive Council agreed to a maximum assignment of 350 convicts to the Company. Governor Bourke to Lord Glenelg, 6 Oct. 1835, *HRA*, XVIII, pp.131–34.

8. Foster, 'Convict Assignment', 35.

9. See J.A. Perkins and J. Tampke, 'The Convicts Who Never Arrived: Hamburg and the Australian Agricultural Company in the 1830s', *Push from the Bush* 19 (1985), 44–55.

10. *ABL*, AACo. Dep. No. 78/9/2, Superintendent's Report, 4 Aug. 1827.

11. *ABL*, AACo. Dep. No. 78/9/2, Superintendent's Report, 1 Aug. 1826.

12. *ABL*, AACo. Dep. No. 78/9/2, Superintendent's Report, 1 Aug. 1826.

13. *ABL*, AACo. Dep. No. 78/9/2, Superintendent's Report, 1 Aug. 1826.

14. *ABL*, AACo. Dep. No. 78/9/2, Superintendent's Report, 24 April 1826.

15. R. Dawson, *The Present State of Australia*, p. 438.

16. Dawson, *Present State*, p.38.

17. Dawson, *Present State*, p. 99. See also, *ABL*, AACo. Dep. No. 78/9/2, Superintendent's Reports, 24 April 1826, 1 Aug. 1826, 30 April 1827.

18. Dawson, *Present State*, p. 38; *ABL*, AACo. Dep. No. 78/9/2, Superintendent to Court of Directors, 30 Oct. 1827.

19. ABL, AACo. Dep. No. 78/9/3, J. Bowman to Committee of Management, 16 Nov. 1828.

20. J. Grigson, *The Australian Agricultural Company 1824–1875*, p.18.

21. *ABL*, AACo. Dep. No. 160/90, Special Court of Directors.

22. *ABL*, AACo. Dep. No. 78/9/2.

23. *ABL*, AACo. Dep. No. 78/9/2. Bowman to Local Committee, 16 Nov. 1828; John Macarthur's Report, 26 May 1828; Superintendent's Report, 24 April 1826.

24. *ABL*, AACo. Dep. No. 160/90, Court of Directors, 9 Sept. 1828; Dep. No. 78/9/2, Bowman's Report, 17 May 1828; Charles Hall's Report, 22 May 1828; Superintendent's Report, 30 April 1826; R. Dawson to James Macarthur, 31 Jan. 1828; Dep. No. 160/90, Meeting of Court of Directors, 19 Sept. 1828; Dawson, *Present State*, p. 415.

25. 'Robert Dawson' in *Australian Dictionary of Biography Vol. I: 1788–1850*, p. 30; *ABL*, AACo. Dep. No. 160/90, Special Court of Directors, 30 Nov. 1827.

26. ABL, AACo. Dep. No. 78/9/3, Minutes of Local Committee Meeting, 12 Dec. 1828.

27. ABL, AACo. Dep. No. 78/9/2, Bowman's Report, 17 May 1828; Dep. No. 160/90, Court of Directors, 19 Aug. 1828.

28. *ABL*, AACo. Dep. No. 78/9/2, Superintendent's Report, 30 April 1827; J.F. Campbell, 'The First Decade of the Australian Agricultural Company, 1824–1834', *Journal of the Royal Australian Historical Society* 9 (1923), 139.

29. *ABL*, AACo. Dep. No. 78/9/2, J. Bowman's Report, 17 May (1828), 127–30.

30. *ABL*, AACo. Dep. No. 160/91, Sir Edward Parry's Despatches, 29 July 1831.

31. *ABL*, AACo. Dep. No. 78/1/11, Parry to Court of Directors, 12 May 1931.

32. *ABL*, AACo. Dep. No. 78/9/3, Minutes of Local Committee Meeting, 12 Dec. 1828.

33. Campbell, 'Australian Agricultural Company', 125; *ABL*, AACo. Dep. No. 78/9/2, J. Bowman to J. & J. H. Macarthur, 2 Mar. 1826; Dep. No. 78/9/3, Minutes of Local Committee Meeting, 12 Dec. 1828.

34. *ABL*, AACo. Dep. No. 160/89, Court of Directors, 20 May 1825.

35. *ABL*. AACo. Dep. No. 78/9/3, Minutes of Local Committee Meeting, 12 Dec. 1828.

36. Perkins, 'Rehearsal for Protectionism', 27.

37. Grigson, 'Australian Agricultural Company', 90.

38. *ABL*, AACo. Dep. No. 78/9/3, Minutes of Local Committee Meeting, 12 Dec. 1828; G. Murray to

Darling, 19 July 1828; *HRA*, XIV, p.259; W.C. Forster, *Sir Thomas Livingston Mitchell and his World 1792–1855*, p. 159.

39.*ABL*, AACo. Dep. 78/9/2, J. Macarthur's Report, 13 Mar. 1828; NSW, *Votes and Proceedings of the Legislative Assembly*, Immigration Committee (1841) Minutes of Evidence, p.11.

40.Dawson, *Present State*, p.432.

41.*ABL*, AACo. Dep. No. 78/9/2, Superintendent's Reports, 1 April 1826, 1 Aug. 1826; Dep. 78/9/3, R. Dawson to J. Macarthur, 11 Oct. 1827.

42.Darling to Earl Bathurst, 1 Sept. 1826, *HRA*, XII, pp.515–17.

43.*ABL*, AACo. Dep. No. 78/1/11, Parry to Court of Directors, 12 May 1831.

44.*ABL*, AACo. Dep. No. 160/90, Court of Directors, 19 Sept. 1828.

45.*ABL*, AACo. Dep. No. 160/90, Court of Directors, 29 July 1831; Sir E. Parry to Colonial Secretary, 13 April 1830.

46.*ABL*, AACo. Dep. No. 78/9/2, Superintendent's Report, 1 Aug, 1826.

47.*ABL*, AACO. Dep. No. 78/9/2, Superintendent's Report, 24 April 1826.

48.*ABL*, AACo. Dep. No. 78/9/2.

49.*ABL*, AACo. Dep. No. 78/9/2.

50.*ABL*, AACo. Dep. No. 78/9/2, Superintendent's Report, 30 April 1827; J. Bowman to Local Committee, 16 Nov. 1828.

51.*ABL*, AACo. Dep. No. 78/9/2, Superintendent's Report, 1 Aug. 1826.

52.*ABL*, AACo. Dep. No. 78/9/2, Superintendents' Report, 1 Aug. 1826, 30 April 1827; 4. Aug. 1827.

53.*ABL*, AACo. Dep. No. 78/9/3, Minutes of Local Committee Meeting, 12 Dec, 1828.

Chapter Twelve

The Care and Feeding of Convicts

Stephen Nicholas

Introduction

Questions concerning the care of convicts, except for the detailed recounting of
corporal punishment, have been largely neglected by Australian historians. John
Hirst's *The Convict System and Its Enemies* is a notable exception, but even Hirst fails to
consider the quality of housing, the nutritional content of the standard ration and the
access to medical care provided for convict workers. At best, there are only scattered
references in the historiography to mortality and morbidity, the frequency of suicides
and the quality of the convicts' environment. The material condition of the convicts is
rarely compared with that of ex-convicts or of free settlers. A peculiar insularity in
Australian historiography treats the nineteenth century convict experience as unique;
and comparisons with the condition of free labour in England, slaves in the United
States or bonded Indians in the Caribbean are largely neglected. This chapter on the
care and feeding of convicts provides a comparative analysis of the convicts' physical
punishment, diet, hours of work, housing and medical care. It represents a first attempt
to evaluate the material and non-material needs of the convict workers, outlining a
methodology and area for future research. However, the conclusions are neither
speculative nor tentative, since only errors of exceptional magnitude could revise the
thrust of our main conclusions: that the convicts received good treatment, nutritious
food, decent housing, adequate medical services and reasonable hours of work relative
both to other forced and free workers.

The frequency of flogging

The lash, or the threat of the lash, was a daily feature of the working lives of many of
Australia's convict settlers. But New South Wales was not the only society in which
workers faced physical punishment. The whip was also a common feature in English
society. Indeed the lash in Australia was wielded 'in accordance with the prevailing
English code and was really an extension of a habitual attitude'.[1] Throughout the
nineteenth century the whip remained in use in England as a legal form of punishment
and its use against trivial offences was so widespread that the frequency of whipping
was impossible to determine.[2] In Chapter 9 we showed that the incidence of flogging
depended on whether work was organised into teams or labour gangs and the degree to
which effort or care was required for task completion. Further, the lash was only one
device for eliciting work, and physical punishment was balanced against rewards as a

means of motivating workers. Here we show that the traditional picture of the indiscriminate use of the lash creating a society terrorised by corporal punishment is not borne out by the evidence on flogging itself.[3] The statistics on beatings suggest that the lash was used judiciously in colonial Australia.

Hirst, in presenting perhaps the best balanced view of beatings, selected 1835 for his study when 7103 floggings were administered to the 27,340 convicts to assess physical punishment in Australia. He noted the wide range of 'convict crimes', including insolence, absconding, drunkenness and neglect of work, which could earn a beating and the fact that nearly one-quarter of all convicts could have received a whipping. But 1835 witnessed the highest rate of floggings since Governor Gipps started to collect statistics in 1830 and, as Hirst acknowledges, the calculation that one-quarter of the convicts were whipped certainly overestimated physical punishment since it neglected repeat beatings. There can be no doubt that incorrigibles received a disproportionate share of the lashes.[4] In our assessment of the probability of whipping, no adjustment was made for repeat beatings. We assumed that beatings were independent random events occurring with equal probability for all workers. We further assumed that convicts served, on average, five years of their sentences. While the rules on the granting of tickets-of-leave were subject to many changes, generally a convict was eligible for a ticket after four years of a seven year sentence, and six years of a fourteen year sentence. On this basis, Table 12.1 shows the probability of an 'average' convict receiving a flogging. The probability of being beaten every year was only 0.001 and roughly two-thirds of all convicts received one or no floggings during their sentences. The official statistics on corporal punishment give no support to the popular version of convictism as a society where workers were demoralised physically and psychologically by repeated subjection to the whip.

This simple calculation sustains the argument put forward by Eris O'Brien that the lash was no more widespread in convict Australia than in the English army or navy.[5] Compared with whippings in the convict system, drunkenness, absence without leave, and violence towards officers earned the death sentence in the army. All other military crimes, including a wide range of trivial misdemeanours, were punishable by flogging. Sentences of 25 to 500 lashes were 'relatively common', and as late as 1825 one soldier was sentenced to 1900 lashes, and actually received 1200 of them.[6] The practice was thought necessary to intimidate and control the rank and file who had no possessions of which they could be deprived, a similiar justification to that applied to convicts in New South Wales.[7] Like the convict, the soldier received his punishment on the parade

Table 12.1: *Probability of Flogging for the Average Convict Serving a Five Year Sentence*[a]

No. of Beatings	Probability
5	0.001
4	0.015
3	0.088
2	0.264
1	0.396
None	0.237

a. Based on the assumption that one-quarter of the convicts were flogged each year.

ground in front of the whole regiment. The navy also relied on the lash. Before 1871, flogging was common for 'all sorts of offences serious and trivial alike, often indiscriminately given and sometimes with a brutality amounting to sadism'.[8]

In early nineteenth century English prisons, official violence could be employed for even more minor offences. An ugly look, a quick reply or impatient manner earned a prisoner a visit to the governor or his deputy, and idleness, refusing labour or back chat were common offences for which one could suffer a public flogging.[9] On the hulks prisoners were flogged with a cat o' nine tails, and overseers and chief officers whipped prisoners with a birch in disregard of the regulations requiring the superintendent be informed before physical punishments were administered.[10] American slaves suffered mild or severe whipping as a primary punishment, followed by (in increasing order of severity) deprivation of various privileges, confinement, sale, branding and death.[11] Bennet Barrow, a Louisiana planter, kept a diary of the whippings on his estate. Eighty per cent of the 66 men on the Barrow plantation and 70 per cent of the females (including seven who were pregnant) were lashed at least once during the 23 months covered by the diary.[12] Convicts in New South Wales certainly fared better than Barrow's slaves and better than the Spanish galley convicts, whipped while at the oars, and retained in the galleys after the completion of their sentences.[13]

Convicts were not the only forced labour in Australia to suffer the lash. Kay Saunders found that floggings and assaults on Melanesian bonded labour were common occurrences on the plantations and pastoral stations.[14] In *A New System of Slavery*, Hugh Tinker reported that the bonded labour system employing Indians 'provided almost nothing for the workers by way of incentives and succeeded in keeping them hard at work by a system of penalties and punishment'.[15] The Indian bonded workers were disciplined through deferred payments, stoppages in wages, cuts in food rations and the lash.[16] Beatings occurred as a routine element in plantation discipline right into the twentieth century.[17] The work crimes of Indian contract workers, including absenteeism, refusing or neglecting to carry out orders, drunkenness and using threatening or abusive language corresponded to those of convict workers. Like the convicts, bonded Indian workers were required to be taken to the magistrates court for punishment, but this was frequently ignored with punishment being meted out by private masters on the spot.[18]

Some free labourers were disciplined in much the same way as Australian convicts. With the abolition of slavery in the Dutch West Indies in 1863, ostensibly free labour was subject to the penal sanction of public work if they failed to sign or fulfil their labour contracts. As late as 1915 fines and imprisonment with forced labour and brutal treatment by overseers remained part of the labour system.[19] In the Netherlands East Indies, 42 to 52 days' compulsory service on public works ended only in the 1880s. In Haiti the abolition of slavery in 1793 was followed by compulsory plantation labour where disobedience, laziness and insolence were penal offences, punished by whippings and fetters.[20] In nineteenth century England, where a high percentage of the workforce in the new cotton factories was made up of children, work was motivated largely by punishment. Sidney Pollard found that 'unsatisfactory work was punished by corporal punishment, by fines and by dismissal' with factory masters placing an overwhelming reliance on punishment as a means of enforcing factory discipline.[21] Clearly, positive incentives were hard to devise in a system which drove children to labour in mills for 12 to 14 hours a day.

One last form of work discipline, common to both coerced and free labour systems, was extramural discipline. Perhaps the best known discipline outside the workplace was the use of religion as a cultural monitor. Dissenters, like the Strutts or the Gregs, built chapels, Anglican employers built churches, and Quakers, like the Darbys, joined with their staff in regular religious meetings.[22] The railway contractors realised that time spent in church was time not spent drinking or fighting, so Samuel Peto, the Victorian railway builder, appointed one scripture reader to 900 navvies.[23] While the encouragement of religious observances by workers was commonplace, few firms went to the length of the Taff Vale Railroad which promised promotion to those who attended Sunday and other Holy Day services (when not required on duty).[24] In New South Wales, the mustering of convicts for Sunday service was aimed as much at creating a sober workforce as at saving souls. According to A. Grocott, the rigid enforcement of compulsory religious service turned the convicts' mood of indifference and cynicism towards religion to one of hatred and opposition; the churches failed to win the hearts and the minds of the convict settlers.[25] Forced attendance at religious service, which meant that the convicts were not getting drunk, marked the limits of the reforming power of religion in creating a well-behaved workforce in Australia.

The figures on whippings do not confirm New South Wales as a society uncommonly terrorised by beatings and physical violence. Almost 66 per cent of the convicts received only one beating or no beating at all during their sentences. Elsewhere in the world, other 'coerced' workers (sailors, soldiers, kanakas and indentured Indians) and unfree American blacks and Spanish galley slaves were punished by the lash, with many of these coerced workers receiving more brutal treatment than Australia's convicts. Even free workers in Britain were whipped as a means of work discipline. Most Australian historians have overemphasised beatings as a peculiar feature of colonial society, presenting an exaggerated picture of a brutal and terrorised society. Even those historians who have provided a more balanced view of whipping depict physical punishment and rewards as simple alternatives. But as we showed in Chapter 9, the use of the lash was more complex, for its use as a means of labour extraction depended on how work was organised and whether care or effort was the most important requirement for the completion of the job. Only for some workers was the lash (or the threat of the lash) a powerful incentive to hard work. The whip was not administered indiscriminately; rather, it was used judiciously, regulated by the organisation of work and the nature of the job. The data on beatings provides no support for the popular picture of a brutal and terrorised society in which convicts were demoralised physically and psychologically by the whip.

Diet, calories and nutrition

Australian historians have shown surprisingly little interest in the content, nutrition and energy of the convicts' standard ration. The food supply, particularly the calories and level of nutrition, determines the capacity of men to work, that is, it is a determinant of the level of labour productivity. Table 12.2 calculates the convicts' weekly and daily calorie intake and compares the ration with that of other forced labour. The convict rations in Table 12.2 consist of the minimum food allowances, and exclude supplementary rations for heavy work and food indulgences. According to Hirst, convicts indulged with rum, sugar, tea and tobacco, had a higher per capita consump-

Table 12.2: *Weekly Rations and Calories of Convict, Coerced and Unfree Labour*[a]

Food	1 Convict 1819 (lb)	2 Convict 1820 (lb)	3 English gaol 1813 (lb)	4 British army 1813–57 (lb)	5 Indian bonded (lb)	6 Civilian Nazi Germany (lb)	7 Eastern POWs Nazi Germany (lb)	8 American slave (lb)
Meat	10½	7	1	5¼	7	1	1	4
Pork		(or 4)						
Flour	10½	7						
Sugar	1½	1			7			
Rice	1				2			
Maize		3			1¾			
Tea		¼						
Salt		½			⅛			
Fats						½		
Potatoes			7				¼	
Bread			9½	7		11½	11½	
Oatmeal			2			6	5¾	
Corn								2

		Meat	Pork						
Weekly calories	34,419	27,433	22,344	19,040	22,250	26,507	14,509	13,152	28,392
Daily calories	4,903	3,919	3,192	2,720	3,178	3,787	2,073	1,879	4,056

a. Calories were calculated from A.A. Paul and D.A.T. Southgate, *McCane and Widdowson's The Composition of Foods* (4th edition, M.R.C. Special Report No. 297 H.M.S.O. London, 1987) using a computer program provided by Dr Ann Walker, Food Sciences, University of Reading.

Sources: 1.   *Report from the Commission of Inquiry into the State of the Colony of New South Wales (Bigge Report)*, Parliamentary Paper, 1822, XX C448, 63.

          2.   *Statement on Way Convicts Were Employed in Various Government Establishments*, 1824, AONSW 4/1775.

          3.   P. Priestley, *Victorian Prison Lives: English Prison Biography*, p.150.

          4.   E.Spiers, *The Army and Society 1815–1914*, p.58; A.R. Shelley, *The Victorian Army at Home*, pp.64–4.

          5.   K. Saunders, *Workers in Bondage: The Origins and Bases of Unfree Labour in Queensland 1824–1916*, p.82.

          6. & 7.   E. Homze, *Foreign Labour in Nazi Germany*, p.272.

          8.   P.A. David, *Reckoning With Slavery*, p.261–5. The basic pork and corn ration delivered 2808 calories per day, but was supplemented with milk, butter, wheat, potatoes and meat.

tion of these goods than free workers in England.[26] The convicts' energy intake from the standard ration varied between 3192 and 4903 calories per day, averaging 4005 calories, which compared favourably with that of the Indian bonded labourers, and American slaves. The upper bound meat diet of 4903 calories was biased downward by selecting mutton rather than beef as the meat ration and by selecting the poorest quality cut of mutton. Beef had a higher caloric content than mutton and its inclusion in the rations would have significantly increased the upper bound estimates of the rations weekly and daily calories. Even the lower bound estimates of the convicts' calorie intake was much more substantial than that for prisoners in English gaols and soldiers in the British army. On the hulks at Woolwich, a very large proportion of the convicts were affected with spongy gums and other symptoms of scurvy, reflecting a seriously deficient diet.[27] This did not occur in New South Wales. The ration was more favourable than Table 12.2 implies since the convicts' working week was about 25 per cent less than that of American slaves and at least 6 per cent shorter than that of bonded Indians. On this basis convicts were better fed than other forced workers.

The quality of the calorie content of the convicts' diet depended on the energy requirements of the work undertaken. Making a similar calculation for American slaves, Richard Sutch argued that an adult male weighing 65 kg and doing light activity, rest and sleeping required 1.4 calories per minute.[28] For the remaining 112 hours of light activity, rest and sleep per week (after working an average 56 hours) a convict required 9408 calories. Given an average 28,381 calories per week, this left 18,973 calories for work or 5.4 calories per minute. Table 12.3 displays Sutch's grading system of energy expenditure for men. On this basis, convicts would have been able to maintain continuous moderate grade work for the entire week or some combination of heavy and light work on the government ration. Heavy tasks included dragging logs, felling trees and digging ditches, while moderate work involved mowing with a scythe, hoeing and clearing brush and scrub. So long as heavy labour by road and iron gangs was mixed with light work, or a period of rest given, then the convict ration was adequate for the work requirements. Since all workers received the standard ration, artisans and workers involved in light work received generous food allowances. Extra rations, consisting of more meat and bread, were also provided for gangs engaged in heavy labour to enable them to work better.[29]

It is perhaps not surprising that the convicts' ration compared favourably with other nineteenth century coerced labour. However, it is staggering to realise how well the diet of the convicts compared with the calorie intake of free workers today. Table 12.4 shows the convict ration offered more calories than the 1979 recommended dietary intake for 18 to 35 year old Australian males established by the Nutrition Committee of the National Health and Medical Research Council. It also delivered more energy than the 1979 United Kingdom Department of Health and Social Security diet for very active (18–34 year old) young men, considerably more than the average working class diet in 1900, and more than modern day Scottish coal miners, forestry workers and English army cadets engaged in high levels of activity.

Table 12.3: *Grading System of Energy Expenditure for Men*

Grade of work	Calories per minute (for averge adult of 65kg)
Light	2.0–4.9
Moderate	5.0–7.4
Heavy	7.5–9.9
Very Heavy	10.0–12.4

Source: P.A. David, *Reckoning With Slavery*, p.267.

Table 12.4: *Energy and Nutrient Requirements*

	Convicts	1 1979 Australian National Health men 18–35	2 1979 UK Department of Health and Social Security men 18–34 very active	3 English working class 1887–1900	4 Scottish coal miners	5 Forestry worker cadet	6 English army
Calories	3919	2762	3350	2077	3660	3670	3490
Thiamin (mg)	3.5	1.3	1.3				
Riboflavin (mg)	1.6	1.6	0.5				
Calciuum (mg)	410.8	500.0	479.5				
Iron (mg)	34.7	10.0	13.0				
Protein (g)	88	84	56				
Protein (%)	16.3	-	12.5				
Fat (%)	35.2	-	27.7				
Carbohy (%)	48.6	-	59.8				

Sources: 1. *Dietary Allowances for Use in Australia* Nutrition Committee of the National Health and Medical Research Council.
2. Department Health and Social Security *Recommended Daily Accounts of Food Energy and Nutrients for Groups of People in the United Kingdom* (London, H.M.S.O. 1979).
3. D.J. Oddy, 'Working Class Diets in Late Nineteenth-Century Britain', *Economic History Review* 23 (1970), 314–25.
4. P. David, *Reckoning with Slavery*, p.266.
5. David, *Reckoning with Slavery*, p.266.
6. David, *Reckoning with Slavery*, p.266.

How nutritional was the convict diet? Table 12.4 shows that the daily supply of nutrients in the convict ration was greater than those recommended by the United Kingdom Health Department today, except for calcium. The daily nutrients were greater or equivalent to the amounts recommended for Australian men by the National Health and Medical Research Council. The nutritional quality of average working class diets in England at the end of the nineteenth century was significantly poorer than that of the convicts in New South Wales — and free English workers at the end of the century had a much higher dietary standard than did those of the 1820s. English family budget surveys show that working class families consumed less than 1½ lb of meat per week in the generation before 1914.[30] According to James Kay's 1832 report on the urban factory workers during the industrial revolution, little or no fresh meat was consumed.[31] Kay described the daily life of a Manchester cotton operative: 'he rose at 5 a.m., worked at the mill until 7 p.m. or later consuming tea or coffee with a little bread for breakfast, boiled potatoes, with melted lard and sometimes a few pieces of fried fat bacon at dinner and after he returned home at night, tea and bread sometimes mingled with spirits'.[32] William Cobbett, Edwin Chadwick and Sir Robert Peel all argued that the prisoners on the 1843 gaol diet (Table 12.2) were better fed than free labourers; yet the gaol diet delivered only two-thirds the nutritional value of the average convict ration in Australia.[33]

There are important caveats in our estimate of the convicts' diet. These are provisional estimates of calorie intake and nutrition and considerably more research needs to be done on the basic ration and food indulgences. There was undoubtedly a good deal of regional and seasonal variation which the 'average' ration disguised. These figures apply to the period after 1817, and take no account of the severe food deficiencies in the first years of settlement. Overall, the standard convict ration was substantial, with a very high nutritional content. This is true whether compared to modern dietary standards or to the rations of other forced workers. The convict diet was significantly better than that of free English workers in the early nineteenth century. Importantly, relative to the tasks convicts were required to perform, the standard ration delivered sufficient energy to ensure a high level of labour productivity.

Hours of work

The convicts in New South Wales generally laboured 5½ days per week to perform an average 56 hours of work. After 1819, convicts worked from sunrise to sunset during the summer, and from 8 a.m. until sunset in winter. In the summer, two hours were allowed for dinner, but this was shortened to one hour during the winter. The hours of light determined the work day, and artisans inside workshops laboured the same hours as outside gangs. It can be seen from Table 12.5 that convicts worked fewer hours than most other coerced, contract and free workers. A six-day working week was the standard for bonded Indians and Spanish and American slaves as well as free labourers in Britain. In part, the relatively favourable hours of the convicts sprang from a fixed working week of 5½ days. However, even if the convicts had worked a six-day week, their average weekly hours would have been about 60, still less than most free labourers in England at the time, and most coerced and contract workers.

While the convicts had more regular and shorter hours of work than many workers in England, coercion meant the loss of the freedom to choose the structuring of one's own pattern of labour. The irregular work habits of English artisans and domestic workers have been depicted as subject to the casual rhythms of a pre-market economy, where community and custom accounted for the marked leisure preference of workers.[34] Artisans often did no work on Monday, and little on Tuesday, but for the rest of the week they toiled late into the night by the light of candles to complete the piece work necessary to earn a customary wage. Convicts were denied not only the right to impose their own order on work time, but the framework of community and mutuality which made up the context of workplace relations at home.

However, this picture of convict and free worker is in need of revision. From the 1750s, free workers experienced many of the same constraints on work time and work structure as convicts. It has usually been argued that the imposition of labour discipline in England coincided with the growth of factories. Recently, Maxine Berg has situated the 'disciplining' of labour in the pre-industrial household in response to changing forms of production to meet the rise of new consumption patterns.[35] Placing the roots of work discipline in the pre-factory period suggests that the leisure preference and informal work patterns of pre-industrial British workers have been overemphasised.

Table 12.5: *Hours of Work and Length of Work Week for Comparative Labour Systems*

Category of worker	Hours of work (average over year)	Work week
Convict		
Pre-1819	48	5½
Post-1819	56	5½
English hulks[a]	57	6
Coerced		
Soviet[b]	76–84	7
Spain[c]	62–88	6
Slaves[d]	70–75	6
Contract		
Queensland sugar[e]	60	6
Caribbean[f]	72	6
Free English[g]		
Factory children	72–84	6
Agricultural labour	57	6
Home workers	48–90	
Nailmakers	78	6
Metal	84	6–7
Iron	78	6
Tailors	72	6
Miners	42–48	6
Cotton mills	72–90	6
Indoor skilled (harness makers, coopers, weavers, shoemakers)	78	6
Outdoor skilled (brickmaker, painter, carpenters, painter, shipwrights)	57	6
Royal dockyards	63	6

Sources: a. Reports of J.H. Capper, July 1816–Jan. 1817; July 1839–Feb. 1844, ML.Q365/G.
     b. D.J. Dallin and B. Nicolaevsky, *Forced Labour in Soviet Russia*, pp.10–11.
     c. R. Pike, *Penal Servitude in Early Modern Spain*, p.85.
     d. P. David, *Reckoning With Slavery*, p.267.
     e. K. Saunders, *Workers in Bondage: The Origins and Bases of Unfree Labour in Queensland 1824–1916*, p.73.
     f. H. Tinker, *A New System of Slavery: The Export of Indian Labour Overseas 1830–1920*, p.190.
     g. J. Rule, *The Labouring Classes in Early Industrial England 1750–1850*, pp.132–5; J. Rule, *The Experience of Labour in Eighteenth Century Industry*, pp.38–62; M.D. George, *England in Transition: Life and Work in the Eighteenth Century*, p.138.

Artisans worked longer and harder and with much more regularity and discipline than previously thought. Transported to Australia, these workers would not have found it difficult to adjust to the fixed work days and working week under convictism.

The work discipline of the household was extended and magnified in the factory. Adult operatives and older children who had laboured up to 16 hours per day in the cotton mills would easily have adjusted to convict work patterns and shorter hours. In the early industrial revolution factories, discipline was enforced through punctuality, constant attendance and fixed hours. One of the early factory masters, Josiah Wedgwood, laid down precise times that a bell should be rung (at 5.45a.m. or a quarter of an hour before the men could see to work and again when the workers could no longer see) to signal the beginning and end of the work day.[36] In the early Strutt factories and in the Crowley ironworks labourers were fined for being late or absent from work without leave as well as for idleness, looking out of the window, telling lies, being saucy, making noise and 'misconduct outside working hours'.[37] Such rules would find an echo, and a more severe punishment, in the convict system in Australia. Disciplined to stable work patterns at home, transported workers, whether artisan, urban factory hand or agricultural labourer, had workplace experiences which eased adjustment to the highly structured regime of labour under convictism. There is little evidence to support Hirst's suggestion that urban convicts were unused to regular hours and regular employment.[38] While many urban convicts undoubtedly experienced a painful process of job restructuring in Australia, they would have found the rules and regulations and the regular fixed work day and week of the convict system not unlike that of the factory and workshop at home. The greatest difference was that most convicts found themselves working fewer hours in colonial New South Wales than they had as free men and women in England.

Housing

Before 1819, all convicts lodged privately, were summoned to work by a bell (not unlike Josiah Wedgwood's pottery workers) and allowed to work on their own account after 3 p.m. and all day Saturday to earn rent money to pay for their accommodation. For some publicly employed convicts the indulgence of living in private houses continued until the end of convictism. Using private accommodation for convicts was not uncommon; the prisoners at Singapore lived privately for 30 years before a permanent barracks was constructed.[39] After 1819, many New South Wales convicts in government service were housed in barracks. This is not surprising. Barracks are the standard form of housing for workforces of unmarried men and women without dependents, and until recently barrack accommodation was commonly provided for army and navy personnel, gangs of grape pickers in California and shearers in Australia.[40] Barracks are cheap to build, with a low unit cost per person. For a convict population they have the additional advantage of providing greater security. When the migrant inflow was composed of families, then barracks were not a housing option except for temporary hostel accommodation. Free migrants and slave families were lodged in relatively high cost separate houses, an expense which Australia largely avoided.

The stone and brick barracks at Hyde Park, Parramatta, Windsor and Liverpool provided a high standard of accommodation with lofty ceilings and good ventilation, although the stockades and houses on wheels used to house rural road gangs were of much poorer quality. In the barracks at Hyde Park, hammocks were slung for 70 men in the large rooms and 30 in the small ones, providing each convict with 14 square feet of sleeping space.[41] Living space at Hyde Park totalled about 170,000 cubic feet in the 12 main rooms (the six small rooms were 35 x 19 feet and the six large rooms were 65 x 19 feet) or 425 cubic feet of living space per convict for the designed capacity of 400 convicts, but only 270 cubic feet for the more usual complement of 630 convicts.[42] The persistent problem of overcrowding meant each man had between 211 and 253 cubic feet of space (when the dormitory measuring 80 x 17 feet where newly arrived convicts were housed is included). The Carters' Barracks, for apprentices, and the barracks at Parramatta and Windsor, provided similar sleeping space, 14 square feet with a three foot passage between the two rows of hammocks.[43] The new Female Factory was built to hold 300 women, but after 1827 always contained more than 300 inmates living in crowded conditions.[44] At Emu Plains, the convicts were housed in 'substantially built' cottages, containing between two and ten men with mattresses on wooden trellises for beds.[45] The worst housing was reserved for the road and iron gangs. These convicts were lodged in 'prisoners boxes', which were either fixed for many months or years within a stockade. Alternatively, they lived in similar houses mounted on wheels which were designed to move forward with the progress of work. Up to 24 convicts were housed in each box, which did 'not afford more than 18 inches in width for each individual to lie down in'.[46]

Even the poorest barrack accommodation for convicts in New South Wales compared favourably with the huts of mud and turf for which the railway contractors charged navvies a shilling per week rent in Devon. They were no worse than the wooden barracks accommodating 25 men, each paying a shilling's rent, which housed Peto's railroad navvies.[47] The barracks for soldiers during the Napoleonic period were hastily erected, extremely small, with cramped and poorly ventilated sleeping quarters; 60 per cent had no washing facilities. Each solder was entitled to 450 cubic feet of space, but this was rarely attained due to overcrowding and most men were lucky to get 300 or even 250 cubic feet.[48] For seamen, the normal space between the suspending points of the hammock was 17–18 inches, so that when the men were extended in their beds their bodies were in constant touch. One warship slung 130 men in a space of 54 x 6 feet providing only 2½ square feet or 38 cubic feet (using the generous assumption of 15 foot ceilings) of sleeping space per man.[49] Generally, ships were 'grossly crowded' and the men 'starved for decent air' living in an atmosphere of ever-present dampness.[50] On the Woolwich hulks, the prisoners were divided into classes or areas of deckspace, which allowed each man between 70 and 124 cubic feet of space, or just one-half that provided convicts in the Hyde Park Barracks.[51] The quality of the hulks varied, some were rotting, others were in need of a dockyard refit, while some were in a good state of repair, but all were poorly ventilated, unsupplied with water and equipped with unsanitary water closets.[52]

Forced labour has been traditionally housed in barrack conditions.[53] In Nazi Germany, Russian POWs who worked in German industry were housed in closed barracks and closely guarded, and non-Eastern POWs were quartered in a subcamp of the Stalag, containing between 20 men in rural and over 1000 men in urban areas, usually within walking distance of work.[54] On the Queensland sugar estates some Pacific Islanders constructed their own huts from cane sheaves on swampy poorly-drained land, while others lived in wooden barracks holding up to 60 men provided by the masters.[55] The huts, with one large wicker bed upon which all workers slept, were repeatedly criticised by physicians and government officials as unhealthy, crowded and poorly ventilated. On one estate, five men inhabited a hut measuring only 11½ square feet.[56] Indian indentured labour on the Caribbean sugar plantations were frequently quartered in the old slave houses.[57] However, the standard accommodation for indentured

Indians was a line of 30 or 40 rooms, with another line 'back to back', with up to six men per room.[58] As late as 1870 in Mauritius up to 30 coolies were packed into one room, and in Malaya up to 18 bonded workers lived in a room 21 x 14 feet described by a Commission of Enquiry as 'squalid hovels constructed of mud'.[59] On the American slave plantations, house sizes and family sizes varied greatly, but the typical slave log cabin was 15 feet square, with 6.25 persons per cabin providing 36 square feet of living space per person.[60] Assuming three-quarters of the space was used for sleeping, slaves had 215 cubic feet, which was near the lower limit enjoyed by the convicts lodged at Hyde Park. There were 'comfortable' slave quarters, but especially on small shareholdings, many slave cabins had decaying logs, open floors, leaking roofs and crowded rooms.[61] After analysing slave housing, Sutch concluded that slaves were housed at a level commensurate with absolute necessity; the convicts were housed better.[62]

During the industrial revolution, factory towns and villages were built by the mill owners. In a few cases, industrial revolution workers were housed in barrack conditions. Thomas Boulton put his workers on the top floor of the wing of the first block at Solo and at Paisley, 35 families were housed in one building near the mill.[63] As late as 1900, quarrymen working in the large Welsh quarries lived in company barracks.[64] The quality of employer-provided housing in early nineteenth century England varied from 'good stone cottages' to 1000 apprentices living in one row of 18 cottages.[65]

The quality of the convicts' accommodation in New South Wales compared well with Engels' description of the poorer housing in mid-Victorian London, where 'scarcely a whole window pane can be found, the walls are crumbling, door posts and window frames loose and broken doors of old boards nailed together . . . here live the poorest of the poor, the worst paid workers . . . the majority of Irish or of Irish extraction'.[66] In industrialising northern Britain, over 60 per cent of the houses in Nottingham and Leeds were back-to-back, preventing ventilation and the penetration of light except through the front window. The smaller two room back-to-backs in Sheffield and Manchester had only 144 cubic feet, although the average back-to-back had 300 cubic feet, accommodating three or four people.[67] These houses, outlawed in Sheffield in 1864 and Manchester in 1884, were much superior to the cellar dwellings in Manchester (where 20,000 people found accommodation in 1833) or Liverpool (where an average of three to four persons were crowded into 8000 cellars).[68] The typical cellar was 15 square feet, although cellars of 10 square feet were not unusual, providing only 30 cubic feet of living space per occupant.[69] As late as 1842, 22 per cent of Manchester's population lived in cellars, paying one shilling or one shilling and six pence rent for damp inferior housing.

In the decade before 1850, the tenements (houses subdivided into separately occupied floors or rooms) in the London parishes of Westminister and St George housed one-half of all workingmen and their families in a single room.[70] The average tenement room was only 20 square feet, and in St Giles one 30 square foot room 'accommodated' eight people, providing about 25 cubic feet per person. Of course, some of England's working class lived in better housing, but for a large section of the labouring classes the accommodation described above was typical working class housing. Overall, the barracks in New South Wales offered high quality housing, free of damp and well ventilated, and while sometimes crowded, gave each convict more space than the one room tenements and cellars of Britain's great urban cities.

Medical care

The routine medical inspection of convicts began before embarkation in England and continued with more or less regularity throughout their period of detention. Before boarding the transports all prisoners were obliged to have a medical certificate and each convict ship had a medical attendant. A medical officer examined the state of health of each convict before disembarkation at Sydney.[71] From the first days of the colony tents were set aside as a hospital, and a hospital was one of Sydney's first public buildings.[72] A brick hospital was built in 1796 at Parramatta and under Macquarie, new hospitals were started at Sydney and Parramatta. Medical care was free to all convicts until 1831 when the Secretary for State, George Murray, instructed Governor Darling to implement Bigge's recommendation that private masters should pay for the medical costs of their assigned men.[73] While convicts in public service were not affected, the legislation reduced the incentives of private employers to bring their servants to the hospital. The supply of medical care increased throughout the 1820s and 1830s, as the ratio of qualified medical practioners rose from 0.38 per thousand of the population in 1820 to 1.40 in 1841.[74] This was combined with a relatively low rate of morbidity in the colony; the 1812 Committee on Transportation was told that there was not a more healthy country than New South Wales and the editor of the Sydney Gazette recommended that English doctors not emigrate for 'there is not sickness enough in the colony to provide them a genteel living'.[75] Medical statistics are patchy for New South Wales, but infant mortality, a good guide to the healthiness of the population, ranged between 4 per cent and 10 per cent in 1840, and even in the first difficult years of settlement before 1800 infant deaths only reached 20 per cent.[76] By comparison, English infant mortality was 30 per cent in 1839, reaching nearly 54 per cent in the great industrial towns.[77]

In England general hospitals were founded in most of the large cities in the eighteenth century, while specialist hospitals, for maternity, fever, children and women, waited until the nineteenth century before being established. The quality of surgical and medical treatment was certainly no worse, and overall perhaps marginally better, in the colony than in England. Hospitals were not 'gateways to death'; the in-patient mortality rate at Hobart hospital was about 8 per cent in 1821–31 which compares favourably with Woodward's findings that mortality rarely exceeded 10 per cent in the large voluntary hospital in Britain during the same period.[78] Admission to hospital was strictly controlled in Britain. A patient obtained a letter from a governor (who held his post because of the contributions he made to the hospital) and deposited a certain sum of money to cover funeral expenses, before being admitted to a bed.[79] This greatly restricted access to hospitals, forcing most of the working class sick to rely on the workhouse infirmary after 1834. The standard of medical care in the workhouse was inferior to that provided in the voluntary hospitals, with unsanitary and overcrowded wards, once a week visits by the doctor and nursing care by untrained workhouse inmates.[80] As late as 1910 Sidney and Beatrice Webb reported that 'a majority of the rural district authorities and not a few urban authorities have no hospital accommodation, even for the most infectious diseases'.[81]

The convicts received a higher standard of medical attention than the prisoners on the hulks. An 1847 Select Committee report on the hulks at Woolwich found the hospital ship *Unite* had an 'utter disregard and neglect of the ordinary means of cleanliness' with the 'great majority of patients infested with vermin'.[82] There was no clean linen, bedding or towels, and the hospital hulks were ineffectively ventilated, forcing the ill prisoners to exist in an 'unwholesome, and almost insupportable, stench prevailing between decks'. The commissioners found a want of method, arrangement and regularity in the execution of the medical duties by the surgeon.[83]

The convicts' medical care also compared favourably with the treatment received by indentured Pacific islanders, Indians and American slaves. The convicts escaped the epidemics and fevers which swept the ranks of the Indian bonded workers in Jamaica and Mauritius.[84] The stone and brick hospitals in New South Wales contrasted favourably both with the 'filthy holes' that the British Guiana Commission called the Caribbean plantation hospitals and the primitive plantation hospitals in Queensland which were without even the minimum requirements of bedding, blankets, clothes and nourishing foods.[85] As late as 1900 mortality rates in Malaya were 8 per cent of the coolie population and in the Straits Settlements 11.6 per cent of the indentured workforce.[86]

One comparative measure of medical care is the treatment of malingering. According to Sutch, the Barrow plantation slaves pretending to be sick were punished by gaol or the whip and bonded Indians working on the Guiana plantations were placed in stocks.[87] In New South Wales, only 3.5 per cent of the convicts were punished by the benches for feigning sickness in 1833, although Bill Nichol argued that this figure understated 'malingering' which was widespread.[88] Nichol's account of malingering suggests that masters treated convicts as though they were sick, sending them to the nearest hospital (which might be 60 or 100 miles away) even when they thought the worker was feigning illness.[89]

A second comparative measure of medical care is the infant mortality rate. A child mortality of 20 per cent among American slaves and 60 per cent stillborn births among indentured Indian women compared with between 4 per cent and 10 per cent mortality among the offspring of convicts and ex-convicts suggests a much superior standard of health and medical care in New South Wales.[90] Convict New South Wales had a death rate half that of Britain, suggesting a healthier environment.[91] Infant mortality rates, with a higher urban-rural variance than death rates at other ages, provide an excellent proxy for the quality of nineteenth century urban life. The infant mortality of 54 per cent in Britain's great towns implied an urban infant death rate 1.73 times the average for the whole country (while the death rate over all ages in towns was only 1.39 times the average).[92]

The great cities of London, Liverpool, Manchester, Glasgow and Dublin displayed all the problems related to industrialisation and rapid urbanisation. As early as 1805, Charles Hall, a medical practitioner, declared the manufacturing towns 'rickety, squalid, dwarfed, distorted objects responsible for spreading disease and sickness', a view confirmed by successive select committees, royal commissions and poor law reports on the state of Britain's cities.[93] The 1840 Select Committee on Health of Towns reported that Leeds' working class streets were 'deficient in sewerage, unrepaired, full of holes with deep channels formed by rain', and the dwellings 'sometimes rendered untenantible by the overflowing of sewers and other offensive drains, with ash-holes ... never emptied ... and the refuse accumulated in cellars, piled against the walls or thrown into the streets' and Chadwick's poor law commissioners found working class houses in the Bethnal Green and Whitechapel areas of London were in the most miserable condition, surrounded by vast collections of filth and putrifying matter, without gutters or sewerage.[94] The speculative builders maximised space by building the houses close together, separated only by narrow streets and intersected by closed courts and alleys where filth was permitted to accumulate. In the industrialising cities these slums were typical of the workers' urban environment, with unpaved roads, unlit streets, open and festering sewers (where they existed) and water supplied by one communal standpipe in the street. The 1844 Select Committee on Large Towns pointed to the lack of building codes and regulation, insufficient drainage, deficient water supplies, over-crowded and poorly ventilated buildings and pollution by offensive manufacturing processes as sources of disease for urban dwellers.[95]

The urban environment of Sydney, even including the Rocks with its irregular accumulation of crowded houses, narrow lanes and streets, shared nothing in common with the fetid lanes, alleys and passages of Britain's great towns. As early as 1810, building was regulated in New South Wales, and Bigge described the outcome as wide streets, with each house separated from the footpath by a large front garden.[96] John Silter, a framework knitter from Nottingham, wrote to his wife in 1819 that even the poorer houses were neat with every house having a garden.[97] In a social survey of Sydney in 1858, the economist, W.S. Jevons, described the large number of brick and weatherboard cottages which provided small, but not unenviable abodes.[98] There was undoubtedly overcrowding, and some houses needed repairs, but Jevons was surveying a housing stock which was successfully coping with a very large immigrant inflow. According to Governor Darling, the quality and good ventilation of the dwellings, combined with the low incidence of disease, the salubrity of the climate, the quality and quantity of the food, and the exercise and frequent bathing by the population, explained the low incidence of disease in the colony.[99] Bryan Gandevia thought that the classical infectious and epidemic diseases of England did not survive the long sea voyage and even if they did arrive the population was too small to facilitate their spread or ensure their continued survival.[100] When typhoid fever did reach Sydney in 1838 it was brought from England by ships which were immediately quarantined.[101] Overall the convicts were provided with a better standard of medical care than they could have expected as free workers in Britain; they were healthy; and they lived in a climate and an environment conducive to the maintenance of that good health.

Other material benefits

Convicts were issued a clothing allowance consisting, in winter, of a coarse woollen jacket, waistcoat of yellow or grey cloth, a pair of duck trousers, a pair of worsted stockings, a pair of shoes, two cotton or linen shirts, a neckhandkerchief and one woollen cap or hat. Every six months each convict received a woollen jacket or frock, trousers, a pair of shoes and a linen shirt. For those in barracks, summer clothing included a canvas smock, one linen or cotton shirt, two pairs of trousers, one pair of shoes and one cap.[102] Those convicts performing arduous forms of labour, such as quarrymen, carters and bullock drivers, received a new pair of shoes every three months.

This clothing allowance compared favourably with that of many bonded Indians in Jamaica, who worked in a state of near nudity. Tinker found that hardly any of them were decently dressed.[103] In Mauritius a royal commission painted a picture of Indian labour dressed in 'shabby, old cast-off regimental coats and jackets, and other clothing made out of gunny-bags, with a greasy handkerchief upon their heads'.[104] The Melanesians labouring in Queensland found the masters negligent in supplying the necessary quantity of clothes, and many Islanders worked in ragged, dirty and vermin-infested clothes for months on end.[105] Convicts were about as well clothed as American slaves who received two or three pairs of pants and shirts a year.[106]

Compared with many free households in England and Ireland, the convicts were better dressed. The story of ragged pre-famine Irish migrant workers passing through Liverpool has been told many times. In the southern and eastern English counties agricultural labourers' budgets often recorded no expenditure at all on clothing, and what clothing a household had was begged, received from charity or bought excep-tional from harvest earnings.[107] Naturally, English workers in full-time employment, and in better paid jobs, had several changes of good quality clothes each year.

One final proxy for living conditions in forced labour systems was the suicide rate. Suicides were common among indentured Indians in Fiji, reaching 831 per million (or one in every 900) in 1910.[108] Quarrels over women (due to their shortage) and the coolie's monotonous and unattractive life were the official reasons for the high rates of suicide. In the prisons at home, the authorities took precautions against suicide. The upper galleries in all 60 prisons in England and Wales were netted with wire to prevent prisoners jumping to their deaths, and P. Priestley recounted examples of hangings, of prisoners' cutting their own throats and of prisoners poisoning themselves in Britain's Victorian gaols.[109] The Select Committee on the Treatment and Condition on the Woolwich Hulks took evidence on attempted suicides.[110]

In contrast, in New South Wales, the incidence of suicide among the convicts was low.[111] Despair and disillusionment leading to suicide has been traced at some length by Robert Hughes in his study of the penal outstation of Norfolk Island.[112] Hughes reported that a group of convicts would choose two men by drawing straws: one to die, the other to kill him. The other convicts stood by as witnesses. Since capital offences could not be tried on Norfolk Island, all the witnesses, and the murderer, were sent to trial at Sydney, gaining release from Norfolk Island. Such complicated group murder-suicides described by Hughes were not widespread; the planning, lottery and execution of such 'suicide' pacts strain the imagination. That they occurred at all is remarkable; that they were common is doubtful.

Conclusion

The convicts were not well treated for humanitarian or reformist reasons. The convict workers were seen as a productive asset, and their care and feeding reflected the value which employers and the government placed upon them as human and physical capital. They were not mistreated, starved or denied medical care, nor were they overworked and driven to suicide. Physical punishment was an institutionalised and formalised part of the labour system, but the lash was not used indiscriminately. The use of the whip for extracting labour depended on the organisation of work and the skill required to perform the task. The evidence on flogging suggested that 63 per cent of the New South Wales convicts were lashed once or not at all during their sentences, challenging the traditional picture of a society terrorised by physical violence.

Convictism must be understood in a comparative context alongside other coercive labour systems. Whether compared with slaves in the United States, bonded Indians in Mauritius or Fiji, or Pacific island indentured servants in Queensland, the convicts' worklife and daily lives were benign. Compared with free workers in Britain, the convicts were well fed and clothed, and provided with a high standard of medical care and housing. The convicts generally worked fewer hours than British labourers. Remarkably, the convict ration reached current Australian and British minimum recommended daily levels of calories and nutrients. Much more research needs to be done on the care and feeding of convicts, including the collection of more quantitative data, the refinement of the data to include regional variations, and the inclusion of new variables such as comparative 'wage' rates. Nevertheless, the broad picture is clear: the convicts received fair treatment, good rations, adequate housing, comprehensive medical care and a reasonable work day and week.

NOTES

1. L. Thomas, *The Development of the Labour Movement in the Sydney District of New South Wales*, p.3.
2. J. Tobias, *Crime and Industrial Society in the 19th Century*, pp.202–3; D. Philips, *Crime and Authority in Victorian England*, pp.172–3.
3. See Chapter 10 pp.152–4 for a brief survey of the historiography on corporal punishment.
4. J. Hirst, *Convict Society and Its Enemies*, p.58.
5. E. O'Brien, *The Foundation of Australia*, p.264.
6. E. Spiers, *The Army and Society 1815–1914*, pp.62–3.
7. A.R. Skelley, *The Victorian Army at Home*, p.148.
8. M. Lewis, *The Navy in Transition 1814–1864: A Social History*, p.169; M. Lewis, *A Social History of the Navy 1793–1815*, p.100.
9. P. Priestly, *Victorian Prison Lives: English Prison Biography*, pp.197–203.
10. *Report on the General Treatment and Condition of Convicts in the Hulks at Woolwich*, Parliamentary Paper (hereafter P.P.), 1847 XVIII, C831, xviii.
11. R. Fogel and S. Engerman, *Time on the Cross: The Economics of American Negro Slavery*, p.145.
12. P. David et al, *Reckoning with Slavery: A Critical Study in the Quantitative History of American Negro Slavery*, p.65.
13. R. Pike, *Penal Servitude in Early Modern Spain*, p.14.
14. Saunders, *Workers in Bondage: The Origins and Bases of Unfree Labour in Queensland 1824–1916*, pp.76–7.
15. H. Tinker, *A New System of Slavery: The Export of Indian Labour Overseas 1830–1920*, p.178.
16. Tinker, *New System of Slavery*, pp.285–8; W. Kloosterboer, *Involuntary Labour Since the Abolition of Slavery*, p.9.
17. Tinker, *New System of Slavery*, p.195, 227.
18. Kloosterboer, *Involuntary Labour*, pp.12–3.
19. Kloosterboer, *Involuntary Labour*, pp.32–8.
20. Kloosterboer, *Involuntary Labour*, pp.41–2, 155–9.
21. S. Pollard, *The Gensesis of Modern Management: A Study of the Industrial Revolution in Great Britain*, pp.185–6.
22. Pollard, *Modern Management*, p.212.
23. S. Cohn, 'Keeping the Navvies in Line: Variations in Work Discipline Among British Railway Construction Crews' in L. Tilly and C. Tilly (eds.), *Class Conflict and Collective Action*, 156–7.
24. M. Molloy, 'The Realisation of Labour Power in Early New South Wales', BA (Hons.) thesis (University of New South Wales, 1984), 131.
25. A. Grocott, *Convicts, Clergymen and Churches: Attitudes of Convicts and Ex-convicts Towards the Churches and Clergy in New South Wales from 1788 to 1851*, p.281.
26. Hirst, *Convict Society*, p.39.
27. *Report on Hulks at Woolwich*, 1847, xvi.

28.David, *Reckoning with Slavery*, pp.265–8.
29.F. Driscoll, 'Macquarie's Administration of the Convict System', *Journal of the Royal Australian Historical Society* 27 (1941), 405.
30.D.J. Oddy, 'A Nutritional Analysis of Historical Evidence: The Working Class Diet, 1880–1914', in D. Oddy and D. Miller (eds.), *The Making of the Modern British Diet*, p.221.
31.J. Burnett, *Plenty and Want: A Social History of Diet in England from 1815 to the Present Day*, p.44.
32.Burnett, *Plenty and Want*, p.44.
33.Tobias, *Crime and Industrial Society*, pp.206–7.
34.E.P. Thompson, *The Making of the English Working Class*, pp.400–18.
35.M. Berg, *The Age of Manufactures 1700–1820*, pp.172–5.
36.N. McKendrick, 'Josiah Wedgwood and Factory Discipline', *Historical Journal* 4 (1961), 41.
37.R.S. Fitton and A.P. Wadsworth, *The Strutts and Artkwrights 1750–1830*, pp.234–5; M. Flinn, *Men of Iron: The Crowleys in the Early Iron Industry*, p.240.
38.Hirst, *Convict Society*, p.32.
39.J.F.A. McNair, *Prisoners Their Own Warders*, p.77.
40.L.E. Howard, *Labour in Agriculture*, p.300; M. Reisler, *By the Sweat of Their Brow: Mexican Immigrant Labour in the United States 1900–1940*, p.84.
41.*Report from the Commissioner of Inquiry into the State of the Colony of New South Wales (Bigge Report)*, P.P., 1822, XX, C448, 22.
42.*Bigge Report*, 1822, 21; J.S. Kerr, *Design for Convicts: An Account of Design for Convict Establishments in the Australian Colonies During the Transportation Era*, pp.40–1.
43.*Bigge Report*, 1822, p.22.
44.A. Salt, *These Outcast Women: The Parramatta Female Factory 1821–1848*, pp.51–2, 127.
45.*Bigge Report*, 1822, 25.
46.M. Weidenhofer, *The Convict Years: Transportation and the Penal System 1788–1868*, p.64; A.G.L. Shaw, *Convicts and the Colonies*, p.215; S. Ingham, 'A Footnote to Transportation to New South Wales: James Ingham 1824–1828', *Historical Studies: Australia and New Zealand* 12 (1967), 531.
47.M. Molloy, 'The Realisation of Labour Power', 130; J.H. Clapham, *An Economic History of Modern Britain* I, p.410.
48.Spiers, *Army and Society*, pp.55–6.
49.Lewis, *Navy in Transition*, p.252.
50.Lewis, *Navy in Transition*, p.241.
51.*Report on Hulks at Woolwich*, 1847, Appendix, 485.
52.*Report on Hulks at Woolwich*, 1847, xxiii.
53.D.J. Dallin and B.I. Nicolaevsky, *Forced Labour in Soviet Russia*, p.12.
54.E. Homze, *Foreign Labour in Nazi Germany*, pp.47, 78.
55.Saunders, *Workers in Bondage*, pp.79–80.
56.Saunders, *Workers in Bondage*, p.80.
57.Tinker, *New System of Slavery*, p.177.
58.Tinker, *New System of Slavery*, p.207.
59.Tinker, *New System of Slavery*, pp.207–8.
60.David, *Reckoning With Slavery*, pp.293–5.
61.David, *Reckoning With Slavery*, p.294.
62.David, *Reckoning With Slavery*, p.298.
63.Pollard, *Modern Management*, p.200.
64.R.M. Jones, *The North Wales Quarrymen 1874–1922*, p.21.
65.J. Rule, *The Labouring Classes in Early Industrial England, 1750–1850*, pp.99–100.
66.F.I. Engels, *The Condition of the Working Class in England*, pp.60–1.
67.J. Burnett, *A Social History of Housing, 1815–1870*, p.75.
68.Rule, *Labouring Classes*, p.97.
69.Burnett, *History of Housing*, p.60; *Report from the Select Committee on the Health of Towns*, P.P., 1840, C384, XI, xi.
70.Burnett, *History of Housing*, p.66.
71.C. Bateson, *The Convict Ships 1787–1868*, p.60; B. Gandevia, 'Occupation and Disease in Australia Since 1788', *Bulletin of the Post-Graduate Committee in Medicine* November (1971), 160–1.
72.J.F. Watson, *The History of the Sydney Hospital 1811–1911*, pp.2–4.
73.W. Nichol, '"Malingering" and Convict Protest', *Labour History* 47 (1984), 21.
74.W. Nichol, 'The Medical Profession in New South Wales, 1788–1850', *Australian Economic History Review* 24 (1984), 124.
75.Nichol, 'Medical Profession', 116, 124.
76.B. Gandevia, *Tears Often Shed: Child Health and Welfare in Australia From 1788*, pp.20–35.
77.M.C. Buer, *Health, Wealth and Population in the Early Days of the Industrial Revolution*, pp.28–35.

78. W.G. Rimmer, *Portrait of a Hospital, The Royal Hobart*, p.37; J. Woodward, *To Do The Sick No Harm: A Study of the British Voluntary Hospital System to 1875*, p.144.
79. J. Woodward, *Sick No Harm*, pp.38–9; C. Dainton, *The Story of England's Hospitals*, pp.102–3; B. Abel-Smith, *The Hospitals 1800–1948*, p.15.
80. Dainton, *England's Hospitals*, pp.111–2.
81. S. and B. Webb, *English Poor Law History Part II The Last Hundred Years* II, pp.756–7.
82. *Report on Hulks at Woolwich*, 1847, xv.
83. *Report on Hulks at Woolwich*, 1847, xvi.
84. Tinker, *New System of Slavery*, pp.197–8.
85. Tinker, *New System of Slavery*, p.199; Saunders, *Workers in Bondage*, p.88.
86. Tinker, *New System of Slavery*, pp.199–200.
87. David, *Reckoning With Slavery*, pp.282–3; Tinker, *New System of Slavery*, p.200.
88. Nichol, 'Malingering', 23.
89. Nichol, 'Malingering', 23–7.
90. David, *Reckoning With Slavery*, pp.283–92; Gandevia, *Tears*, pp.20–1.
91. Rimmer, *Portrait*, p.30.
92. Buer, *Health*, pp.28–35.
93. Rule, *Labouring Classes*, p.75.
94. *Health of Towns*, 1840, XI, C384, xi; *Report from the Poor Law Commissioners on an Inquiry into the Sanitary Condition of the Labouring Population* (Chadwick Inquiry), P.P., 1842, XXVII, (H.L.).
95. *Report of the Commissioners on the State of Large Towns and Populous Districts*, P.P., 1844, XVII, C572, x-xv.
96. *Bigge Report*, 1822, 42.
97. A. Colon, 'Mine is a Sad Yet True Story: Convict Narratives, 1818–1850', *Journal of the Royal Australian Historical Society* 55 (1969), 53.
98. W.S. Jevons, *A Social Survey of Australia's Cities 1858*, frame 6–13, Mitchell Library, MLB864.
99. Governor Darling to Under Secretary Twiss, 12th Feb. 1830, Historical Records of Australia, Series I (hereafter *HRA*), XV, p.374.
100. B. Gandevia, *Tears Often Shed*, p.36.
101. A.W. Greig, 'Letters from Australian Pioneers', *The Victorian Historical Magazine* 12 (1927), 47.
102. *Bigge Report*, 1822, p.61; Major Ovens to Secretary Goulbourn, 16th June 1825, *HRA* XI, p.659.p.659.
103. Tinker, *New System of Slavery*, p.212.
104. Tinker, *New System of Slavery*, p.212.
105. Saunders, *Workers in Bondage*, pp.76–7.
106. David, *Reckoning With Slavery*, pp.298–9.
107. Rule, *Labouring Classes*, p.68.
108. Tinker, *New System of Slavery*, pp.190–200, 337.
109. Priestley, *Victorian Prison Lives*, pp. 100–4.
110. *Report on Hulks at Woolwich*, 1847, 602.
111. Weidenhofer, *Convict Years*, p.67.
112. R. Hughes, *The Fatal Shore*, pp.467–8.

Chapter Thirteen

A New Past

Stephen Nicholas

How did Australian historians get it so wrong? In place of a cross section of the British and Irish working classes they saw a criminal class; rather than an inflow of literate and fit young men and women with useful skills they emphasised an uneducated, vice-ridden mass of unskilled labourers; instead of an efficient labour market they identified the allocation of convict labour as a 'giant lottery'. This traditional interpretation of the convict workers distorts our past, leaving the convict settlers without positive achievements and without a culture. Even the convicts' most obvious physical accomplishments — the roads and buildings — stand merely as symbols of endurance to a harsh and brutal system of forced labour, where work was extracted by the lash from a physically and psychologically demoralised workforce.

The convicts' only achievement was survival. There was no massive resistance to convictism and no class solidarity against a repressive regime. Convict insurrections, such as Castle Hill in 1804 and Norfolk Island in 1834, were the exception. Historians, sympathetic to the plight of convicts, have uncovered mainly passive protest to the system whose basic parameters were widely accepted by the transportees. Perhaps the convicts' most widespread form of protest was malingering, hardly the stuff of which heroes are made. Indeed, malingering confirms the convicts as lazy shirkers, crafty, scheming criminals intent on avoiding hard work. Small wonder that mateship (honour among thieves), hatred of authority and individual acquisitiveness marked for most historians the meagre cultural baggage that the convicts brought with them to Australia. These singularly unattractive values were the convicts' only contribution to the formation of Australian culture.

Such an interpretation does much violence to the understanding of Australia's white past. It has bequeathed to a generation of Australians a popular image of convict society as brutal, unproductive and sterile; and of convicts as unskilled professional criminals. Except for some buildings and roads, and folklore, the convicts appear to have left Australia with little besides a record of wasted lives. The truth is very different.

The transportion of convicts to Australia was part of a much larger system of forced global migration. Not only did the British transport Indian and Burmese criminals to penal colonies in Asia, but the Spanish, French and Russians sent their convicts to North Africa, the New World, the Pacific and Asiatic Russia. The flow of convicts to New South Wales formed one element in forced global migration which included the trading in black slaves and the contracting for bonded Indians and Pacific Islanders. These forced labour flows were complementary to the international movement of free

Europeans in the nineteenth century. Transportation was not unique to Australia; the convicts are best seen as Australia's first migrants.

As immigrants they possessed a unique age-sex distribution, concentrated in the most productive age groups. The young and old-age dependents were left at home. This contrasted with the movement of free immigrants to New South Wales, and the alternative source of labour for the colony, the free transatlantic emigrants, who moved in family units, with their children. One result of Australia's dependence on convict immigrants was a high participation rate by the convicts in the work force, and an exceptional rate of over 65 per cent of the population which were members of the male workforce. Never again in Australia's history would the proportions be so favourable to economic development.

The convicts transported to New South Wales were representative of the British and Irish working classes. This meant that they brought a cross-section of useful skills, many immediately suited to the needs of a growing colony. Convicts were better educated than the working population left at home, and their size and physical fitness suggests that they were as productive as free workers in Britain and Ireland. The female convicts shared these traits; they were not mainly prostitutes, but ordinary working class women possessing skills which required no adapting to the Australian environment.

An elite group of English labour aristocrats were among the British working class transported to Australia. They brought the values of their class — independence, respectability and status — and as members of the early Australian trade unions, benefit societies and mechanics institutes left their mark on the institutions and culture of the young colony. While the values of respectability and mutuality might have been claimed by the elite workers exclusively for themselves, they were common values, widely shared by other members of the working class transported to Australia. Our early culture was forged in the furnace of the Australian environment using values brought from Britain by ordinary working class men and women. The experience of servitude did not destroy the values of free workers in an industrialising society: the cultural baggage of freedom survived transportation.

The convicts' skills were recognised and valued by colonial administrators and the labour market. Most skilled convict workers found themselves employed in the same jobs in Australia as they had held at home prior to conviction. Of course, not all skills suited Australian requirements. Many workers suffered the painful process of job restructuring. But the retraining was not arbitrary; it involved urban unskilled labourers who would have experienced the same adjustments to the needs of a rural economy had they arrived in Australia as free migrants. The Australian labour market did not operate as a 'giant lottery'. It identified those convicts with useful skills and put them to work at their usual trades; it retrained those whose skills were not suited to Australia's needs.

The organisation of public work into workshops and gangs was efficient. Positive incentive and rewards, more than punishments and lashings, characterised convict work conditions. The good treatment of the convicts extended to the nutritional and caloric content of their standard ration, the quality of their housing, their hours of labour and the provision of free medical care. The convicts were a valuable human asset; recognised as such, they received good treatment by the government and private employers.

The growth performance of colonial Australia was highly correlated with the quality and quantity of its convict and ex-convict workforce. Noel Butlin's preliminary estimates of current price domestic product and, after 1828, real product suggest rapid growth before 1840.[1] This is consistent with our evidence of a workforce with a significant investment in human capital. It is hard to believe that an inefficient labour system, resting on the twin pillars of coercion and professional criminals, could have promoted such rapid growth.

Like all revisionist history, our new view of the convict system reinterprets the past by asking new and different questions, collecting new data sets and employing new methodologies. Here is the explanation of why traditional historians have been misled in analysing our convict past. They asked the wrong questions and neglected the data on the convicts' occupations, literacy and height, which offered them the means to assess the comments of contemporaries on the workings of the convict system. We have sought to provide an assessment of how the convict system in New South Wales actually worked. Of course, our new view is a captive of our economic questions, quantitative data and statistical techniques in the same way that the old historiography is shaped by the framework and data employed by these older historians.

Like all history, our study owes much to the work of other historians, including those we criticise. It forms part of an on-going re-evaluation of our past. Clearly, our reinterpretation of convictism is not 'definitive'; as much as anything it sets a research agenda, points to neglected areas and opens up new avenues for future study. Many of our arguments will be revised by younger historians, asking different questions and employing new techniques. All we ask is that our interpretation be judged on its own terms, the standards of quantitative history.

The arguments presented in the preceding pages are controversial. Many will be criticised. Some, it is hoped, will be sustained by more detailed empirical investigation. But the book will have served its purpose if it unshackles Australia's 'founding fathers and mothers' — the transported convicts — from a history which ignores their human capital, and implicitly discounts their contribution to our economic and social development.

NOTES

1. N. Butlin, 'Contours of the Australian Economy 1788–1866', *Australian Economic History Review* 26 (1986), 96–100.

Statistical Appendix

CONVICTS TRANSPORTED
TO NEW SOUTH WALES
1817–40

Kris Corcoran and Stephen Nicholas

(based upon analysis of the indents of 19,711 convicts
who arrived in New South Wales in
1817, 1818, 1820, 1821, 1825, 1827, 1830, 1833
1835, 1837, 1839, 1840)

Ships arriving in 1817-18, 1820-21, 1825, 1827, 1830, 1833, 1835, 1837, 1839 and 1840 were sampled and data on 19,711 convicts were computerised. The 18 tables in the Statistical Appendix provide a description of the most important data in the sample.

Except for data on literacy before 1827, all the variables on the convicts' human capital were available for the 1817-40 period. However, in 1825 only ships from Ireland were surveyed. The number of Welsh convicts, less than 200, were too few to warrant separate inclusion in the tables.

While there were missing data, the absent information, on age, birthplace, occupation or crime was randomly spread throughout the indents. For this reason the tables contain less than the full complement of 19,711 observations. For example, the absence of birthplace affects Tables A1 (hence the unknown category), A4, A5, A6, A8 and A10; missing occupational data affect Tables A11–A16; and missing age data affect Tables A2 and A3. The amount of missing data is, however, remarkably low, and the sample provides the most extensive data set yet collected on the characteristics of those convicts who contributed to the make-up of the Australian workforce.

Conventions

The figure 0 in the tables indicates that data were available for that variable, but that no convict possessed that particular characteristic.

The symbol + appears in a table when all data were unavailable.

Table of Contents

TABLE A1:   COUNTRY OF BIRTH AND SEX

Country	Male No. (%)	Female No. (%)	Total No. (%)
England	11030 (93.6)	760 (6.4)	11790 (100.0)
Ireland	5005 (79.9)	1259 (20.1)	6264 (100.0)
Scotland	434 (82.5)	92 (17.5)	526 (100.0)
Foreign	320 (95.2)	16 (4.8)	336 (100.0)
Welsh/Unknown	711 (89.4)	84 (10.6)	795 (100.0)
Total	17500 (88.8)	2211 (11.2)	19711 (100.0)

TABLE A2:   AGE AND SEX BY COUNTRY OF TRIAL

Age group	England Male No. (%)	England Female No. (%)	England All No. (%)	Ireland Male No. (%)	Ireland Female No. (%)	Ireland All No. (%)
16	541 (4.9)	11 (1.5)	552 (4.7)	322 (6.4)	23 (1.8)	345 (5.5)
16-20	3054 (27.8)	209 (27.5)	3263 (27.8)	1189 (23.8)	273 (21.7)	1462 (23.3)
21-25	3499 (31.9)	194 (25.5)	3693 (31.5)	1368 (27.3)	384 (30.5)	1752 (28.0)
26-30	1685 (15.3)	150 (19.7)	1835 (15.6)	977 (19.5)	286 (22.7)	1263 (20.2)
31-35	825 (7.5)	66 (8.7)	891 (7.6)	406 (8.1)	93 (7.4)	499 (8.0)
36+	1378 (12.6)	130 (17.1)	1508 (12.8)	743 (14.9)	200 (15.9)	943 (15.0)
Total	10982 (100.0)	760 (100.0)	11742 (100.0)	5005 (100.0)	1259 (100.0)	6264 (100.0)

TABLE A2:   AGE AND SEX BY COUNTRY OF TRIAL (Continued)

Scotland			Foreign			Total		
Male	Female	All	Male	Female	All	Male	Female	All
No.	No.	No.	No.	No.	No.	No.	No.	No.
(%)	(%)	(%)	(%)	(%)	(%)	(%)	(%)	(%)
38	1	39	3	0	3	904	35	939
(8.8)	(1.1)	(7.4)	(0.9)	(0.0)	(1.0)	(5.4)	(1.6)	(5.0)
129	19	148	48	1	49	4420	502	4922
(29.7)	(20.7)	(28.1)	(15.0)	(6.2)	(14.6)	(26.4)	(23.6)	(26.1)
119	31	150	102	4	106	5088	613	5701
(27.4)	(33.7)	(28.5)	(31.9)	(25.0)	(31.5)	(30.4)	(28.8)	(30.2)
58	12	70	61	4	65	2781	452	3233
(13.4)	(13.0)	(13.3)	(19.1)	(25.0)	(19.3)	(16.6)	(21.3)	(17.1)
33	12	45	32	3	35	1296	174	1470
(7.6)	(13.0)	(8.6)	(10.0)	(18.8)	(10.4)	(7.7)	(8.2)	(7.8)
57	17	74	74	4	78	2352	351	2603
(13.1)	(18.5)	(14.1)	(23.1)	(25.0)	(23.2)	(13.5)	(16.5)	(13.8)
434	92	526	320	16	336	16741	2127	18868
(100.0)	(100.0)	(100.0)	(100.0)	(100.0)	(100.0)	(100.0)	(100.0)	(100.0)

TABLE A3:   AGE AND SEX BY YEAR OF ARRIVAL

	16			Age in Years 16-20			21-25		
Year	Male No. (%)	Female No. (%)	All No. (%)	Male No. (%)	Female No. (%)	All No. (%)	Male No. (%)	Female No. (%)	All No. (%)
1817	32 (3.1)	0 (0.0)	32 (3.1)	265 (25.6)	0 (0.0)	265 (25.6)	320 (30.9)	0 (0.0)	320 (30.9)
1818	9 (3.0)	0 (0.0)	9 (3.0)	31 (10.3)	0 (0.0)	31 (10.3)	94 (31.3)	0 (0.0)	94 (31.3)
1820	213 (7.3)	0 (0.0)	213 (7.3)	824 (28.2)	0 (0.0)	824 (28.2)	773 (26.4)	0 (0.0)	773 (26.4)
1821	26 (2.5)	0 (0.0)	26 (2.5)	345 (32.6)	0 (0.0)	345 (32.6)	283 (26.7)	0 (0.0)	283 (26.7)
1825	12 (2.2)	1 (1.5)	13 (2.2)	136 (25.2)	13 (20.0)	149 (24.6)	129 (23.9)	23 (35.4)	152 (25.1)
1827	4 (1.0)	5 (2.1)	9 (1.4)	135 (33.2)	54 (23.2)	189 (29.6)	138 (34.0)	71 (30.5)	209 (32.7)
1830	104 (3.8)	4 (0.9)	108 (3.4)	880 (32.5)	104 (23.5)	984 (31.2)	806 (29.7)	114 (25.7)	920 (29.2)
1833	22 (4.3)	0 (0.0)	22 (4.3)	167 (32.6)	0 (0.0)	167 (32.6)	156 (30.4)	0 (0.0)	156 (30.4)
1835	96 (6.8)	0 (0.0)	96 (6.8)	412 (29.3)	0 (0.0)	412 (29.3)	415 (29.5)	0 (0.0)	415 (29.5)
1837	160 (5.5)	5 (0.9)	165 (4.8)	684 (23.4)	127 (23.8)	811 (23.4)	977 (33.4)	144 (26.9)	1121 (32.4)
1839	100 (6.3)	8 (1.1)	108 (4.7)	320 (20.2)	185 (25.3)	505 (21.9)	533 (33.7)	222 (30.4)	755 (32.6)
1840	158 (7.7)	5 (2.6)	163 (7.3)	371 (18.1)	56 (29.3)	427 (19.0)	664 (32.3)	54 (28.3)	718 (32.0)
Total	936 (5.4)	28 (1.3)	964 (4.9)	4570 (26.2)	539 (24.5)	5109 (26.0)	5288 (30.3)	628 (28.6)	5916 (30.1)

TABLE A4 : URBAN OR RURAL BIRTHPLACE AND SEX BY COUNTRY OF TRIAL

Location	England			Ireland			Scotland			Total		
	Male No. (%)	Female No. (%)	All No. (%)	Male No. (%)	Female No. (%)	All No. (%)	Male No. (%)	Female No. (%)	All No. (%)	Male No. (%)	Female No. (%)	All No. (%)
Urban	5094 (48.2)	360 (48.7)	5454 (48.2)	1490 (34.0)	379 (32.4)	1869 (33.6)	295 (70.6)	63 (70.0)	358 (70.5)	6879 (44.8)	802 (40.1)	7681 (44.2)
Rural	5471 (51.8)	379 (51.3)	5850 (51.8)	2896 (66.0)	792 (67.6)	3688 (66.4)	123 (29.4)	27 (30.0)	150 (29.5)	8490 (55.2)	1198 (59.9)	9688 (55.8)
Total	10565 (100.0)	739 (100.0)	11304 (100.0)	4386 (100.0)	1171 (100.0)	5557 (100.0)	418 (100.0)	90 (100.0)	508 (100.0)	15369 (100.0)	2000 (100.0)	17369 (100.0)

TABLE A3: AGE AND SEX BY YEAR OF ARRIVAL (Continued)

	26-30			31-35			36+			Total	
Male No. (%)	Female No. (%)	All No. (%)	Male No. (%)	Female No. (%)	All No. (%)	Male No. (%)	Female No. (%)	All No. (%)	Male No. (%)	Female No. (%)	All No. (%)
168 (16.2)	0 (0.0)	168 (16.2)	86 (8.3)	0 (0.0)	86 (8.3)	164 (15.9)	0 (0.0)	164 (15.9)	1035 (100.0)	0 (0.0)	1035 (100.0)
63 (21.0)	0 (0.0)	63 (21.0)	41 (13.7)	0 (0.0)	41 (13.7)	62 (20.7)	0 (0.0)	62 (20.7)	300 (100.0)	0 (0.0)	300 (100.0)
478 (16.4)	0 (0.0)	478 (16.4)	220 (7.5)	0 (0.0)	220 (7.5)	414 (14.2)	0 (0.0)	414 (14.2)	2922 (100.0)	0 (0.0)	2922 (100.0)
177 (16.7)	0 (0.0)	177 (16.7)	75 (7.1)	0 (0.0)	75 (7.1)	153 (14.4)	0 (0.0)	153 (14.4)	1059 (100.0)	0 (0.0)	1059 (100.0)
114 (21.1)	13 (20.0)	127 (21.0)	55 (10.2)	6 (9.2)	61 (10.1)	94 (17.4)	9 (13.9)	103 (17.0)	540 (100.0)	65 (100.0)	605 (100.0)
59 (14.5)	51 (21.9)	110 (17.2)	23 (5.7)	17 (7.3)	40 (6.3)	47 (11.6)	35 (15.0)	82 (12.8)	406 (100.0)	233 (100.0)	639 (100.0)
438 (16.2)	106 (24.0)	544 (17.2)	193 (7.1)	40 (9.0)	233 (7.4)	291 (10.7)	75 (16.9)	366 (11.6)	2712 (100.0)	443 (100.0)	3155 (100.0)
75 (14.6)	0 (0.0)	75 (14.6)	43 (8.4)	0 (0.0)	43 (8.4)	50 (9.7)	0 (0.0)	50 (9.7)	513 (100.0)	0 (0.0)	513 (100.0)
231 (16.4)	0 (0.0)	231 (16.4)	86 (6.1)	0 (0.0)	86 (6.1)	168 (11.9)	0 (0.0)	168 (11.9)	1408 (100.0)	0 (0.0)	1408 (100.0)
497 (17.0)	121 (22.6)	618 (17.9)	248 (8.5)	36 (6.7)	284 (8.2)	358 (12.2)	102 (19.1)	460 (13.3)	2924 (100.0)	535 (100.0)	3459 (100.0)
284 (18.0)	141 (19.3)	425 (18.4)	129 (8.2)	58 (7.9)	187 (8.1)	214 (13.6)	117 (16.0)	331 (14.3)	1580 (100.0)	731 (100.0)	2311 (100.0)
363 (17.7)	34 (17.8)	397 (17.7)	185 (9.0)	17 (8.9)	202 (9.0)	312 (15.2)	25 (13.1)	337 (15.0)	2053 (100.0)	191 (100.0)	2244 (100.0)
2947 (16.9)	466 (21.2)	3413 (17.4)	1384 (7.9)	174 (7.9)	1558 (7.9)	2327 (13.3)	363 (16.5)	2690 (13.7)	17452 (100.0)	2198 (100.0)	19650 (100.0)

TABLE A5:   URBAN OR RURAL BIRTHPLACE AND SEX BY YEAR OF ARRIVAL

Year	Urban Male No. (%)	Urban Female No. (%)	Urban All No. (%)	Rural Male No. (%)	Rural Female No. (%)	Rural All No. (%)	Total Urban No. (%)	Total Rural No. (%)	All No. (%)
1817	632 (63.9)	0 (0.0)	632 (63.9)	357 (36.1)	0 (0.0)	357 (36.1)	632 (63.9)	357 (36.1)	989 (100.0)
1818	204 (72.6)	0 (0.0)	204 (72.6)	77 (27.4)	0 (0.0)	77 (27.4)	204 (72.6)	77 (27.4)	281 (100.0)
1820	1688 (63.2)	0 (0.0)	1688 (63.2)	983 (36.8)	0 (0.0)	983 (36.8)	1688 (63.2)	983 (36.8)	2671 (100.0)
1821	565 (55.4)	0 (0.0)	565 (55.4)	455 (44.6)	0 (0.0)	455 (44.6)	565 (55.4)	455 (44.6)	1020 (100.0)
1825	+ (0.0)	+ (0.0)	+ (0.0)	+ (0.0)	+ (0.0)	+ (0.0)	+ (0.0)	+ (0.0)	+ (0.0)
1827	183 (45.8)	88 (38.3)	271 (43.0)	217 (54.2)	142 (61.7)	359 (57.0)	271 (43.0)	359 (57.0)	630 (100.0)
1830	1071 (40.1)	138 (31.2)	1209 (38.8)	1600 (59.9)	305 (68.9)	1905 (61.2)	1209 (38.8)	1905 (61.2)	3114 (100.0)
1833	176 (35.0)	0 (0.0)	176 (35.0)	327 (65.0)	0 (0.0)	327 (65.0)	176 (35.0)	327 (65.0)	503 (100.0)
1835	438 (31.7)	0 (0.0)	438 (31.7)	945 (68.3)	0 (0.0)	945 (68.3)	438 (31.7)	945 (68.3)	1383 (100.0)
1837	1118 (40.4)	242 (46.8)	1360 (41.4)	1649 (59.6)	275 (53.2)	1924 (58.6)	1360 (41.4)	1924 (58.6)	3284 (100.0)
1839	602 (39.5)	314 (43.8)	916 (40.8)	923 (60.5)	403 (56.2)	1326 (59.2)	916 (40.8)	1326 (59.2)	2242 (100.0)
1840	560 (28.7)	88 (46.3)	648 (30.3)	1390 (71.3)	102 (53.7)	1492 (69.7)	648 (30.3)	1492 (69.7)	2140 (100.0)
Total	7237 (44.8)	870 (41.5)	8107 (44.4)	8923 (55.2)	1227 (58.5)	10150 (55.6)	8107 (44.4)	10150 (55.6)	18257 (100.0)

TABLE A6: URBAN OR RURAL BIRTHPLACE AND RELIGION BY COUNTRY OF TRIAL

Religion	England Urban No. (%)	England Rural No. (%)	England All No. (%)	Ireland Urban No.. (%)	Ireland Rural No. (%)	Ireland All No. (%)
Protestant	2708 (87.3)	4252 (91.0)	6960 (89.5)	236 (17.4)	461 (14.9)	697 (15.7)
Roman Catholic	348 (11.2)	380 (8.2)	728 (9.4)	1117 (82.5)	2634 (85.1)	3751 (84.3)
Other	46 (1.5)	39 (0.8)	85 (1.1)	1 (0.1)	1 (0.0)	2 (0.0)
Total	3102 (100.0)	4671 (100.0)	7773 (100.0)	1354 (100.0)	3096 (100.0)	4450 (100.0)

TABLE A6: URBAN OR RURAL BIRTHPLACE AND RELIGION BY COUNTRY OF TRIAL (Continued)

	Scotland				Total			Irish Resident in England		
	Urban No. (%)	Rural No. (%)	All No. (%)	Urban No. (%)	Rural No. (%)	All No. (%)	Urban No. (%)	Rural No. (%)	All No. (%)
	252 (94.4)	108 (84.3)	360 (91.1)	3196 (67.7)	4821 (61.1)	8017 (63.5)	29 (22.0)	41 (14.3)	70 (16.6)
	11 (4.1)	19 (14.8)	30 (7.6)	1476 (31.2)	3033 (38.4)	4509 (35.7)	105 (78.0)	247 (85.7)	352 (83.4)
	4 (1.5)	1 (0.8)	5 (1.3)	51 (1.1)	41 (0.5)	92 (0.8)	0 (0.0)	0 (0.0)	0 (0.0)
	267 (100.0)	128 (100.0)	395 (100.0)	4723 (100.0)	7895 (100.0)	12618 (100.0)	134 (100.0)	288 (100.0)	422 (100.0)

TABLE A7:   LITERACY AND SEX BY COUNTRY OF TRIAL

Literacy	England			Ireland		
	Male No. (%)	Female No. (%)	Total No. (%)	Male No. (%)	Female No. (%)	Total No. (%)
Neither read nor write	1858 (26.3)	130 (17.2)	1988 (25.4)	1092 (33.0)	631 (53.3)	1723 (38.4)
Read	1589 (22.5)	359 (47.4)	1948 (24.9)	709 (21.5)	421 (35.6)	1130 (25.2)
Read and write	3614 (51.2)	268 (35.4)	3882 (49.7)	1503 (45.5)	131 (11.1)	1634 (36.4)
Total	7061 (100.0)	757 (100.0)	7818 (100.0)	3304 (100.0)	1183 (100.0)	4487 (100.0)

TABLE A8:   URBAN OR RURAL BIRTHPLACE AND LITERACY
BY COUNTRY OF TRIAL

Literacy	England			Ireland		
	Urban No. (%)	Rural No. (%)	Total No. (%)	Urban No. (%)	Rural No. (%)	Total No. (%)
Neither read nor write	649 (21.0)	1321 (28.3)	1970 (25.4)	442 (32.7)	1266 (40.9)	1708 (38.4)
Read	709 (22.9)	1230 (26.4)	1939 (25.0)	332 (24.6)	789 (25.5)	1121 (25.2)
Read and write	1737 (56.1)	2115 (45.3)	3852 (49.6)	577 (42.7)	1040 (33.6)	1617 (36.4)
Total	3095 (100.0)	4666 (100.0)	7761 (100.0)	1451 (100.0)	3095 (100.0)	4446 (100.0)

TABLE A7: LITERACY AND SEX BY COUNTRY OF TRIAL (Continued)

	Scotland			Foreign			All		
	Male No. (%)	Female No. (%)	Total No. (%)	Male No. (%)	Female No. (%)	Total No. (%)	Male No. (%)	Female No. (%)	Total No. (%)
	36 (11.5)	7 (7.6)	43 (10.6)	173 (54.0)	6 (37.5)	179 (53.3)	3159 (28.7)	774 (37.8)	3933 (30.1)
	60 (19.0)	45 (48.9)	105 (25.8)	28 (8.8)	6 (37.5)	34 (10.1)	2386 (21.7)	831 (40.6)	3217 (24.7)
	219 (69.5)	40 (43.5)	259 (63.6)	119 (37.2)	4 (25.0)	123 (36.6)	5455 (49.6)	443 (21.6)	5898 (45.2)
	315 (100.0)	92 (100.0)	407 (100.0)	320 (100.0)	16 (100.0)	336 (100.0)	11000 (100.0)	2048 (100.0)	13048 (100.0)

TABLE A8: URBAN OR RURAL BIRTHPLACE AND LITERACY
BY COUNTRY OF TRIAL (Continued)

	Scotland			All		
	Urban No. (%)	Rural No. (%)	Total No. (%)	Urban No. (%)	Rural No. (%)	Total No. (%)
	26 (9.7)	16 (12.5)	42 (10.6)	1117 (23.7)	2603 (33.0)	3720 (29.5)
	78 (29.2)	25 (19.5)	103 (26.1)	1119 (23.7)	2044 (25.9)	3163 (25.1)
	163 (61.1)	87 (68.0)	250 (63.3)	2477 (52.6)	3242 (41.1)	5719 (45.4)
	267 (100.0)	128 (100.0)	395 (100.0)	4713 (100.0)	7889 (100.0)	12602 (100.0)

Statistical Appendix

ENGLAND

	Literacy											
	Neither Read nor Write			Read			Read and Write			Total		
Year	Male No. (%)	Female No. (%)	Total No. (%)	Male No. (%)	Female No. (%)	Total No. (%)	Male No. (%)	Female No. (%)	Total No. (%)	Male No. (%)	Female No. (%)	Total No. (%)
1827	53 (16.9)	10 (14.3)	63 (16.4)	97 (30.9)	39 (55.7)	136 (35.4)	164 (52.2)	21 (30.0)	185 (48.2)	314 (100.0)	70 (100.0)	384 (100.0)
1830	433 (23.5)	28 (22.2)	461 (23.4)	468 (25.4)	56 (44.5)	524 (26.5)	946 (51.2)	42 (33.3)	988 (50.1)	1847 (100.0)	126 (100.0)	1973 (100.0)
1833	85 (29.6)	0 (0.0)	85 (29.6)	68 (23.7)	0 (0.0)	68 (23.7)	134 (46.7)	0 (0.0)	134 (46.7)	287 (100.0)	0 (0.0)	287 (100.0)
1835	249 (28.6)	0 (0.0)	249 (28.6)	197 (22.7)	0 (0.0)	197 (22.7)	423 (48.7)	0 (0.0)	423 (48.7)	869 (100.0)	0 (0.0)	869 (100.0)
1837	521 (27.9)	38 (16.8)	559 (26.7)	382 (20.4)	101 (44.7)	483 (23.1)	965 (51.7)	87 (38.5)	1052 (50.2)	1868 (100.0)	226 (100.0)	2094 (100.0)
1839	273 (27.7)	26 (15.4)	299 (25.9)	196 (19.9)	77 (45.6)	273 (23.6)	517 (52.4)	66 (39.0)	583 (50.5)	986 (100.0)	169 (100.0)	1155 (100.0)
1840	244 (27.4)	28 (16.9)	272 (25.8)	181 (20.3)	86 (51.8)	267 (25.3)	465 (52.3)	52 (31.3)	517 (48.9)	890 (100.0)	166 (100.0)	1056 (100.0)
Total	1858 (26.3)	130 (17.2)	1988 (25.4)	1589 (22.5)	359 (47.4)	1948 (24.9)	3614 (51.2)	268 (35.4)	3882 (49.7)	7061 (100.0)	757 (100.0)	7818 (100.0)

IRELAND

Year	Male No. (%)	Female No. (%)	Total No. (%)	Male No. (%)	Female No. (%)	Total No. (%)	Male No. (%)	Female No. (%)	Total No. (%)	Male No. (%)	Female No. (%)	Total No. (%)
1827	28 (37.8)	75 (48.4)	103 (44.9)	11 (14.9)	56 (36.1)	67 (29.3)	35 (47.3)	24 (15.5)	59 (25.8)	74 (100.0)	155 (100.0)	229 (100.0)
1830	199 (29.4)	143 (45.7)	342 (34.5)	125 (18.4)	132 (42.2)	257 (25.9)	354 (52.2)	38 (12.1)	392 (39.6)	678 (100.0)	313 (100.0)	991 (100.0)
1833	55 (28.8)	0 (0.0)	55 (28.8)	56 (29.3)	0 (0.0)	56 (29.3)	80 (41.9)	0 (0.0)	80 (41.9)	191 (100.0)	0 (0.0)	191 (100.0)
1835	126 (30.0)	0 (0.0)	126 (30.0)	99 (23.6)	0 (0.0)	99 (23.6)	195 (46.4)	0 (0.0)	195 (46.4)	420 (100.0)	0 (0.0)	420 (100.0)
1837	274 (37.3)	165 (54.8)	439 (42.4)	162 (22.1)	108 (35.9)	270 (26.1)	298 (40.6)	28 (9.3)	326 (31.5)	734 (100.0)	301 (100.0)	1035 (100.0)
1839	111 (30.3)	248 (59.9)	359 (46.0)	67 (18.3)	125 (30.2)	192 (24.6)	188 (51.4)	41 (9.9)	229 (29.4)	366 (100.0)	414 (100.0)	780 (100.0)
1840	299 (35.5)	0 (0.0)	299 (35.5)	189 (22.5)	0 (0.0)	189 (22.5)	353 (42.0)	0 (0.0)	353 (42.0)	841 (100.0)	0 (0.0)	841 (100.0)
Total	1092 (33.0)	631 (53.3)	1723 (38.4)	709 (21.5)	421 (35.6)	1130 (25.2)	1503 (45.5)	131 (11.1)	1634 (36.4)	3304 (100.0)	1183 (100.0)	4487 (100.0)

TABLE A9: LITERACY AND SEX BY COUNTRY OF TRIAL AND YEAR OF ARRIVAL (Continued)

SCOTLAND

Year	Neither Read nor Write			Read			Read and Write			Total		
	Male No. (%)	Female No. (%)	Total No. (%)	Male No. (%)	Female No. (%)	Total No. (%)	Male No. (%)	Female No. (%)	Total No. (%)	Male No. (%)	Female No. (%)	Total No. (%)
1827	0 (0.0)	0 (0.0)	0 (0.0)	0 (0.0)	0 (0.0)	0 (0.0)	5 (100.0)	0 (0.0)	5 (100.0)	5 (100.0)	0 (0.0)	5 (100.0)
1830	5 (7.7)	0 (0.0)	5 (7.7)	10 (15.4)	0 (0.0)	10 (15.4)	50 (76.9)	0 (0.0)	50 (76.9)	65 (100.0)	0 (0.0)	65 (100.0)
1833	0 (0.0)	0 (0.0)	0 (0.0)	0 (0.0)	0 (0.0)	0 (0.0)	3 (100.0)	0 (0.0)	3 (100.0)	3 (100.0)	0 (0.0)	3 (100.0)
1835	7 (16.3)	0 (0.0)	7 (16.3)	9 (20.9)	0 (0.0)	9 (20.9)	27 (62.8)	0 (0.0)	27 (62.8)	43 (100.0)	0 (0.0)	43 (100.0)
1837	10 (13.9)	0 (0.0)	10 (13.9)	20 (27.8)	0 (0.0)	20 (27.8)	42 (58.3)	0 (0.0)	42 (58.3)	72 (100.0)	0 (0.0)	72 (100.0)
1839	10 (12.5)	7 (8.7)	17 (10.6)	12 (15.0)	38 (46.9)	50 (31.0)	58 (72.5)	36 (44.4)	94 (58.4)	80 (100.0)	81 (100.0)	161 (100.0)
1840	4 (8.5)	0 (0.0)	4 (6.9)	9 (19.2)	7 (63.6)	16 (27.6)	34 (72.3)	4 (36.4)	38 (65.5)	47 (100.0)	11 (100.0)	58 (100.0)
Total	36 (11.4)	7 (7.6)	43 (10.6)	60 (19.0)	45 (48.9)	105 (25.8)	219 (69.6)	40 (43.5)	259 (63.6)	315 (100.0)	92 (100.0)	407 (100.0)

ALL

Year	Neither Read nor Write			Read			Read and Write			Total		
	Male No. (%)	Female No. (%)	Total No. (%)	Male No. (%)	Female No. (%)	Total No. (%)	Male No. (%)	Female No. (%)	Total No. (%)	Male No. (%)	Female No. (%)	Total No. (%)
1827	81 (20.6)	85 (37.8)	166 (26.9)	108 (27.5)	95 (42.2)	203 (32.8)	204 (51.9)	45 (20.0)	249 (40.3)	393 (100.0)	225 (100.0)	618 (100.0)
1830	637 (24.6)	171 (39.0)	808 (26.7)	603 (23.3)	188 (42.8)	791 (26.1)	1350 (52.1)	80 (18.2)	1430 (47.2)	2590 (100.0)	439 (100.0)	3029 (100.0)
1833	140 (29.1)	0 (0.0)	140 (29.1)	124 (25.8)	0 (0.0)	124 (25.8)	217 (45.1)	0 (0.0)	217 (45.1)	481 (100.0)	0 (0.0)	481 (100.0)
1835	382 (28.7)	0 (0.0)	382 (28.7)	305 (22.9)	0 (0.0)	305 (22.9)	645 (48.4)	0 (0.0)	645 (48.4)	1332 (100.0)	0 (0.0)	1332 (100.0)
1837	805 (30.1)	203 (38.5)	1008 (31.5)	564 (21.1)	209 (39.7)	773 (24.1)	1305 (48.8)	115 (21.8)	1420 (44.4)	2674 (100.0)	527 (100.0)	3201 (100.0)
1839	394 (27.5)	281 (42.3)	675 (32.2)	275 (19.2)	240 (36.1)	515 (24.6)	763 (53.3)	143 (21.6)	906 (43.2)	1432 (100.0)	664 (100.0)	2096 (100.0)
1840	547 (30.8)	28 (15.8)	575 (29.4)	379 (21.3)	93 (52.6)	472 (24.1)	852 (47.9)	56 (31.6)	908 (46.5)	1778 (100.0)	177 (100.0)	1955 (100.0)
Total	2986 (28.0)	768 (37.8)	3754 (29.5)	2358 (22.1)	825 (40.6)	3183 (25.0)	5336 (49.9)	439 (21.6)	5775 (45.5)	10680 (100.0)	2032 (100.0)	12712 (100.0)

TABLE A10: URBAN OR RURAL BIRTHPLACE AND LITERACY BY
YEAR OF ARRIVAL

	Literacy											
	Neither Read nor Write			Read			Read and Write			Total		
Year	Urban No. (%)	Rural No. (%)	Total No. (%)	Urban No. (%)	Rural No. (%)	Total No. (%)	Urban No. (%)	Rural No. (%)	Total No. (%)	Urban No. (%)	Rural No. (%)	Total No. (%)
1827	59 (21.7)	110 (30.6)	169 (26.8)	79 (29.0)	129 (35.9)	208 (33.0)	134 (49.3)	120 (33.5)	254 (40.2)	272 (100.0)	359 (100.0)	631 (100.0)
1830	228 (18.4)	603 (31.4)	831 (26.3)	292 (23.6)	533 (27.7)	825 (26.1)	717 (58.0)	787 (40.9)	1504 (47.6)	1237 (100.0)	1923 (100.0)	3160 (100.0)
1833	44 (25.0)	96 (29.4)	140 (27.9)	43 (24.4)	86 (26.4)	129 (25.7)	89 (50.6)	144 (44.2)	233 (46.4)	176 (100.0)	326 (100.0)	502 (100.0)
1835	106 (24.3)	290 (30.7)	396 (28.7)	97 (22.2)	223 (23.6)	320 (23.1)	234 (53.5)	432 (45.7)	666 (48.2)	437 (100.0)	945 (100.0)	1382 (100.0)
1837	354 (26.0)	666 (34.6)	1020 (31.0)	313 (23.0)	483 (25.0)	796 (24.2)	693 (51.0)	778 (40.4)	1471 (44.8)	1360 (100.0)	1927 (100.0)	3287 (100.0)
1839	227 (24.9)	463 (35.0)	690 (30.9)	266 (29.2)	316 (23.9)	582 (26.0)	419 (45.9)	543 (41.1)	962 (43.1)	912 (100.0)	1322 (100.0)	2234 (100.0)
1840	151 (23.4)	473 (31.7)	624 (29.2)	142 (22.0)	374 (25.1)	516 (24.1)	353 (54.6)	645 (43.2)	998 (46.7)	646 (100.0)	1492 (100.0)	2138 (100.0)
Total	1169 (23.2)	2701 (32.6)	3870 (29.0)	1232 (24.4)	2144 (25.8)	3376 (25.3)	2639 (52.4)	3449 (41.6)	6088 (45.7)	5040 (100.0)	8294 (100.0)	13334 (100.0)

TABLE A11: ARMSTRONG SKILL CLASSIFICATION
BY SEX AND COUNTRY OF TRIAL

	England			Ireland		
Skill	Male No. (%)	Female No. (%)	Total No. (%)	Male No. (%)	Female No. (%)	Total No. (%)
1	35 (0.3)	0 (0.0)	35 (0.3)	10 (0.2)	0 (0.0)	10 (0.2)
2	336 (3.1)	0 (0.0)	336 (2.9)	132 (2.6)	0 (0.0)	132 (2.1)
3	5004 (45.6)	289 (38.0)	5293 (45.0)	1706 (34.1)	274 (21.8)	1980 (31.6)
4	2893 (26.3)	322 (42.4)	3215 (27.4)	1068 (21.3)	664 (52.7)	1732 (27.6)
5	2714 (24.7)	149 (19.6)	2863 (24.4)	2089 (41.8)	321 (25.5)	2410 (38.5)
Total	10982 (100.0)	760 (100.0)	11742 (100.0)	5005 (100.0)	1259 (100.0)	6264 (100.0)

TABLE A12: ARMSTRONG SKILL CLASSIFICATION BY URBAN OR RURAL BIRTHPLACE AND COUNTRY OF TRIAL

Skill	England Urban No. (%)	Rural No. (%)	Total No. (%)	Ireland Urban No. (%)	Rural No. (%)	Total No. (%)	Scotland Urban No. (%)	Rural No. (%)	Total No. (%)	All Urban No. (%)	Rural No. (%)	Total No. (%)
1	18 (0.3)	13 (0.2)	31 (0.2)	5 (0.3)	3 (0.1)	8 (0.1)	0 (0.0)	0 (0.0)	0 (0.0)	23 (0.3)	16 (0.2)	39 (0.2)
2	172 (3.1)	145 (2.5)	317 (2.8)	60 (3.2)	71 (1.9)	131 (2.4)	8 (2.2)	3 (2.0)	11 (2.2)	240 (3.1)	219 (2.2)	459 (2.7)
3	2898 (52.9)	2196 (37.4)	5094 (44.9)	631 (33.8)	783 (21.2)	1414 (25.5)	180 (50.3)	58 (38.7)	238 (46.9)	3709 (48.1)	3037 (31.3)	6746 (38.7)
4	1236 (22.5)	1907 (32.5)	3143 (27.7)	449 (24.0)	1196 (32.4)	1645 (29.6)	80 (22.4)	64 (42.7)	144 (28.3)	1765 (22.9)	3167 (32.6)	4932 (28.3)
5	1159 (21.2)	1608 (27.4)	2767 (24.4)	723 (38.7)	1635 (44.4)	2358 (42.4)	90 (25.1)	25 (16.6)	115 (22.6)	1972 (25.6)	3268 (33.7)	5240 (31.1)
Total	5483 (100.0)	5869 (100.0)	11352 (100.0)	1868 (100.0)	3688 (100.0)	5556 (100.0)	358 (100.0)	150 (100.0)	508 (100.0)	7709 (100.0)	9707 (100.0)	17416 (100.0)

TABLE A11: ARMSTRONG SKILL CLASSIFICATION
BY SEX AND COUNTRY OF TRIAL (Continued)

Scotland Male No. (%)	Female No. (%)	Total No. (%)	Foreign Male No. (%)	Female No. (%)	Total No. (%)	All Male No. (%)	Female No. (%)	Total No. (%)
0 (0.0)	0 (0.0)	0 (0.0)	4 (1.2)	0 (0.0)	4 (1.2)	49 (0.3)	0 (0.0)	49 (0.2)
11 (2.5)	0 (0.0)	11 (2.1)	44 (13.8)	0 (0.0)	44 (13.1)	523 (3.1)	0 (0.0)	523 (2.8)
221 (50.9)	27 (29.4)	248 (47.2)	163 (50.9)	8 (50.0)	171 (50.9)	7094 (42.4)	598 (28.1)	7692 (40.8)
105 (24.2)	43 (46.7)	148 (28.1)	72 (22.5)	6 (37.5)	78 (23.2)	4138 (24.7)	1035 (48.7)	5173 (27.4)
97 (22.4)	22 (23.9)	119 (22.6)	37 (11.6)	2 (12.5)	39 (11.6)	4937 (29.5)	494 (23.2)	5431 (28.8)
434 (100.0)	92 (100.0)	526 (100.0)	320 (100.0)	16 (100.0)	336 (100.0)	16741 (100.0)	2127 (100.0)	18868 (100.0)

TABLE A13: ARMSTRONG SKILL CLASSIFICATION
BY COUNTRY OF TRIAL, SEX AND YEAR OF ARRIVAL

ENGLAND

Year	Skill 1 Male No. (%)	Skill 1 Female No. (%)	Skill 1 Total No. (%)	Skill 2 Male No. (%)	Skill 2 Female No. (%)	Skill 2 Total No. (%)	Skill 3 Male No. (%)	Skill 3 Female No. (%)	Skill 3 Total No. (%)
1817	4 (0.4)	0 (0.0)	4 (0.4)	68 (7.3)	0 (0.0)	68 (7.3)	488 (52.4)	0 (0.0)	488 (52.4)
1818	0 (0.0)	0 (0.0)	0 (0.0)	12 (4.3)	0 (0.0)	12 (4.3)	151 (54.3)	0 (0.0)	151 (54.3)
1820	9 (0.4)	0 (0.0)	9 (0.4)	56 (2.8)	0 (0.0)	56 (2.8)	1008 (50.5)	0 (0.0)	1008 (50.5)
1821	3 (0.5)	0 (0.0)	3 (0.5)	83 (12.3)	0 (0.0)	83 (12.3)	300 (44.6)	0 (0.0)	300 (44.6)
1825	0 (0.0)	0 (0.0)	0 (0.0)	0 (0.0)	0 (0.0)	0 (0.0)	0 (0.0)	0 (0.0)	0 (0.0)
1827	0 (0.0)	0 (0.0)	0 (0.0)	5 (1.6)	0 (0.0)	5 (1.3)	141 (44.9)	22 (31.4)	163 (42.4)
1830	6 (0.3)	0 (0.0)	6 (0.3)	30 (1.6)	0 (0.0)	30 (1.5)	835 (45.2)	56 (44.5)	891 (45.1)
1833	1 (0.4)	0 (0.0)	1 (0.4)	7 (2.4)	0 (0.0)	7 (2.4)	142 (49.3)	0 (0.0)	142 (49.3)
1835	3 (0.3)	0 (0.0)	3 (0.3)	24 (2.8)	0 (0.0)	24 (2.8)	436 (49.9)	0 (0.0)	436 (49.9)
1837	6 (0.3)	0 (0.0)	6 (0.3)	21 (1.2)	0 (0.0)	21 (1.0)	721 (38.0)	91 (39.9)	812 (38.2)
1839	1 (0.1)	0 (0.0)	1 (0.1)	20 (2.0)	0 (0.0)	20 (1.7)	453 (45.6)	58 (34.1)	511 (43.9)
1840	2 (0.2)	0 (0.0)	2 (0.2)	10 (1.1)	0 (0.0)	10 (1.0)	329 (37.0)	62 (37.3)	391 (37.0)
Total	35 (0.3)	0 (0.0)	35 (0.3)	336 (3.1)	0 (0.0)	336 (2.9)	5004 (45.6)	289 (38.0)	5293 (45.1)

IRELAND

Year	Skill 1 Male No. (%)	Skill 1 Female No. (%)	Skill 1 Total No. (%)	Skill 2 Male No. (%)	Skill 2 Female No. (%)	Skill 2 Total No. (%)	Skill 3 Male No. (%)	Skill 3 Female No. (%)	Skill 3 Total No. (%)
1817	0 (0.0)	0 (0.0)	0 (0.0)	2 (3.2)	0 (0.0)	2 (3.2)	15 (24.2)	0 (0.0)	15 (24.2)
1818	0 (0.0)	0 (0.0)	0 (0.0)	0 (0.0)	0 (0.0)	0 (0.0)	0 (0.0)	0 (0.0)	0 (0.0)
1820	1 (0.1)	0 (0.0)	1 (0.1)	32 (4.4)	0 (0.0)	32 (4.4)	197 (27.2)	0 (0.0)	197 (27.2)
1821	0 (0.0)	0 (0.0)	0 (0.0)	22 (6.5)	0 (0.0)	22 (6.5)	97 (28.5)	0 (0.0)	97 (28.5)
1825	0 (0.0)	0 (0.0)	0 (0.0)	0 (0.0)	0 (0.0)	0 (0.0)	540 (100.0)	0 (0.0)	540 (89.3)
1827	0 (0.0)	0 (0.0)0	0 (0.0)	2 (2.7)	0 (0.0)	2 (0.9)	20 (27.0)	21 (13.6)	41 (17.9)
1830	2 (0.3)	0 (0.0)	2 (0.2)	15 (2.2)	0 (0.0)	15 (1.5)	223 (32.9)	96 (30.6)	319 (32.2)
1833	2 (1.0)	0 (0.0)	2 (1.0)	3 (1.6)	0 (0.0)	3 (1.6)	58 (30.2)	0 (0.0)	58 (30.2)
1835	2 (0.5)	0 (0.0)	2 (0.5)	24 (5.7)	0 (0.0)	24 (5.7)	130 (31.0)	0 (0.0)	130 (31.0)
1837	0 (0.0)	0 (0.0)	0 (0.0)	10 (1.3)	0 (0.0)	10 (1.0)	158 (20.9)	67 (22.0)	225 (21.2)
1839	0 (0.0)	0 (0.0)	0 (0.0)	6 (1.6)	0 (0.0)	6 (0.8)	106 (28.3)	90 (21.4)	196 (24.6)
1840	3 (0.4)	0 (0.0)	3 (0.4)	16 (1.9)	0 (0.0)	16 (1.9)	162 (19.2)	0 (0.0)	162 (19.2)
Total	10 (0.2)	0 (0.0)	10 (0.2)	132 (2.7)	0 (0.0)	132 (2.1)	1706 (34.1)	274 (21.8)	1980 (31.6)

TABLE A13: ARMSTRONG SKILL CLASSIFICATION
BY COUNTRY OF TRIAL, SEX AND YEAR OF ARRIVAL (Continued)

ENGLAND

Skill 4			Skill 5			Total		
Male No. (%)	Female No. (%)	Total No. (%)	Male No. (%)	Female No. (%)	Total No. (%)	Male No. (%)	Female No. (%)	Total No. (%)
226 (24.3)	0 (0.0)	226 (24.3)	145 (15.6)	0 (0.0)	145 (15.6)	931 (100.0)	0 (0.0)	931 (100.0)
45 (16.2)	0 (0.0)	45 (16.2)	70 (25.2)	0 (0.0)	70 (25.2)	278 (100.0)	0 (0.0)	278 (100.0)
489 (24.5)	0 (0.0)	489 (24.5)	436 (21.8)	0 (0.0)	436 (21.8)	1998 (100.0)	0 (0.0)	1998 (100.0)
141 (20.9)	0 (0.0)	141 (20.9)	146 (21.7)	0 (0.0)	146 (21.7)	673 (100.0)	0 (0.0)	673 (100.0)
0 (0.0)	0 (0.0)	0 (0.0)	0 (0.0)	0 (0.0)	0 (0.0)	0 (0.0)	0 (0.0)	0 (0.0)
139 (44.3)	48 (68.6)	187 (48.7)	29 (9.2)	0 (0.0)	29 (7.6)	314 (100.0)	70 (100.0)	384 (100.0)
775 (42.0)	29 (23.0)	804 (40.8)	201 (10.9)	41 (32.5)	242 (12.3)	1847 (100.0)	126 (100.0)	1973 (100.0)
107 (37.1)	0 (0.0)	107 (37.1)	31 (10.8)	0 (0.0)	31 (10.8)	288 (100.0)	0 (0.0)	288 (100.0)
338 (38.7)	0 (0.0)	338 (38.7)	73 (8.3)	0 (0.0)	73 (8.3)	874 (100.0)	0 (0.0)	874 (100.0)
300 (15.8)	108 (47.4)	408 (19.2)	848 (44.7)	29 (12.7)	877 (41.3)	1896 (100.0)	228 (100.0)	2124 (100.0)
146 (14.7)	68 (40.0)	214 (18.4)	373 (37.6)	44 (25.9)	417 (35.9)	993 (100.0)	170 (100.0)	1163 (100.0)
187 (21.0)	69 (41.6)	256 (24.2)	362 (40.7)	35 (21.1)	397 (37.6)	890 (100.0)	166 (100.0)	1056 (100.0)
2893 (26.3)	322 (42.4)	3215 (27.4)	2714 (24.7)	149 (19.6)	2863 (24.3)	10982 (100.0)	760 (100.0)	11742 (100.0)

IRELAND

Skill 4			Skill 5			Total		
Male No. (%)	Female No. (%)	Total No. (%)	Male No. (%)	Female No. (%)	Total No. (%)	Male No. (%)	Female No. (%)	Total No. (%)
13 (21.0)	0 (0.0)	13 (21.0)	32 (51.6)	0 (0.0)	32 (51.6)	62 (100.0)	0 (0.0)	62 (100.0)
0 (0.0)	0 (0.0)	0 (0.0)	0 (0.0)	0 (0.0)	0 (0.0)	0 (0.0)	0 (0.0)	0 (0.0)
117 (16.1)	0 (0.0)	117 (16.1)	379 (52.2)	0 (0.0)	379 (52.2)	726 (100.0)	0 (0.0)	726 (100.0)
50 (14.7)	0 (0.0)	50 (14.7)	171 (50.3)	0 (0.0)	171 (50.3)	340 (100.0)	0 (0.0)	340 (100.0)
0 (0.0)	65 (100.0)	65 (10.8)	0 (0.0)	0 (0.0)	0 (0.0)	540 (100.0)	65 (100.0)	605 (100.0)
44 (59.5)	129 (83.2)	173 (75.5)	8 (10.8)	5 (3.2)	13 (5.7)	74 (100.0)	155 (100.0)	229 (100.0)
260 (38.3)	84 (26.7)	344 (34.7)	178 (26.3)	134 (42.7)	312 (31.4)	678 (100.0)	314 (100.0)	992 (100.0)
87 (45.3)	0 (0.0)	87 (45.3)	42 (21.9)	0 (0.0)	42 (21.9)	192 (100.0)	0 (0.0)	192 (100.0)
224 (53.3)	0 (0.0)	224 (53.3)	40 (9.5)	0 (0.0)	40 (9.5)	420 (100.0)	0 (0.0)	420 (100.0)
104 (13.8)	182 (59.9)	286 (27.0)	483 (64.0)	55 (18.1)	538 (50.8)	755 (100.0)	304 (100.0)	1059 (100.0)
39 (10.4)	204 (48.5)	243 (30.5)	224 (59.7)	127 (30.2)	351 (44.1)	375 (100.0)	421 (100.0)	796 (100.0)
130 (15.4)	0 (0.0)	130 (15.4)	532 (63.1)	0 (0.0)	532 (63.1)	843 (100.0)	0 (0.0)	843 (100.0)
1068 (21.3)	664 (52.7)	1732 (27.6)	2089 (41.7)	321 (25.5)	2410 (38.5)	5005 (100.0)	1259 (100.0)	6264 (100.0)

Statistical Appendix

TABLE A13: ARMSTRONG SKILL CLASSIFICATION
BY COUNTRY OF TRIAL, SEX AND YEAR OF ARRIVAL (Continued)

ALL

Year	Skill 1			Skill 2			Skill 3		
	Male No. (%)	Female No. (%)	Total No. (%)	Male No. (%)	Female No. (%)	Total No. (%)	Male No. (%)	Female No. (%)	Total No. (%)
1817	4 (0.4)	0 (0.0)	4 (0.4)	70 (6.8)	0 (0.0)	70 (6.8)	529 (51.1)	0 (0.0)	529 (51.1)
1818	0 (0.0)	0 (0.0)	0 (0.0)	13 (4.3)	0 (0.0)	13 (4.3)	164 (54.7)	0 (0.0)	164 (54.7)
1820	10 (0.3)	0 (0.0)	10 (0.3)	93 (3.2)	0 (0.0)	93 (3.2)	1300 (44.5)	0 (0.0)	1300 (44.5)
1821	3 (0.3)	0 (0.0)	3 (0.3)	107 (10.1)	0 (0.0)	107 (10.1)	423 (39.9)	0 (0.0)	423 (39.9)
1825	0 (0.0)	0 (0.0)	0 (0.0)	0 (0.0)	0 (0.0)	0 (0.0)	540 (100.0)	65 (100.0)	605 (100.0)
1827	0 (0.0)	0 (0.0)	0 (0.0)	8 (2.0)	0 (0.0)	8 (1.2)	170 (41.9)	45 (19.3)	215 (33.7)
1830	9 (0.3)	0 (0.0)	9 (0.3)	48 (1.8)	0 (0.0)	48 (1.5)	1160 (42.8)	152 (34.3)	1312 (41.6)
1833	3 (0.6)	0 (0.0)	3 (0.6)	12 (2.3)	0 (0.0)	12 (2.3)	215 (41.9)	0 (0.0)	215 (41.9)
1835	7 (0.5)	0 (0.0)	7 (0.5)	56 (3.9)	0 (0.0)	56 (3.9)	618 (43.9)	0 (0.0)	618 (43.9)
1837	6 (0.2)	0 (0.0)	6 (0.2)	34 (1.2)	0 (0.0)	34 (1.0)	1024 (35.0)	162 (30.0)	1186 (34.2)
1839	2 (0.1)	0 (0.0)	2 (0.1)	27 (1.7)	0 (0.0)	27 (1.2)	670 (42.4)	182 (24.6)	852 (36.7)
1840	6 (0.3)	0 (0.0)	6 (0.3)	65 (3.2)	0 (0.0)	65 (2.9)	622 (30.3)	66 (34.5)	688 (30.7)
Total	50 (100.0)	0 (0.0)	50 (0.3)	533 (3.0)	0 (0.0)	533 (2.7)	7435 (42.6)	672 (30.4)	8107 (41.2)

TABLE A14: ARMSTRONG SKILL CLASSIFICATION
BY URBAN OR RURAL BIRTHPLACE BY YEAR OF ARRIVAL

Year	Skill 1			Skill 2			Skill 3		
	Urban No. (%)	Rural No. (%)	Total No. (%)	Urban No. (%)	Rural No. (%)	Total No. (%)	Urban No. (%)	Rural No. (%)	Total No. (%)
1817	4 (0.6)	0 (0.0)	4 (0.4)	31 (4.9)	38 (10.6)	69 (7.0)	371 (58.4)	131 (36.7)	502 (50.6)
1818	0 (0.0)	0 (0.0)	0 (0.0)	8 (3.9)	4 (5.2)	12 (4.3)	123 (59.7)	31 (40.3)	154 (54.4)
1820	6 (0.4)	2 (0.2)	8 (0.3)	61 (3.6)	24 (2.4)	85 (3.2)	891 (52.5)	292 (29.6)	1183 (44.0)
1821	2 (0.4)	0 (0.0)	2 (0.2)	47 (8.3)	56 (12.3)	103 (10.0)	274 (48.2)	132 (28.9)	406 (39.6)
1825	0 (0.0)	0 (0.0)	0 (0.0)	0 (0.0)	0 (0.0)	0 (0.0)	0 (0.0)	0 (0.0)	0 (0.0)
1827	0 (0.0)	0 (0.0)	0 (0.0)	3 (1.1)	4 (1.1)	7 (1.1)	125 (45.9)	86 (24.0)	211 (33.4)
1830	6 (0.5)	3 (0.1)	9 (0.3)	31 (2.5)	17 (0.9)	48 (1.5)	692 (55.9)	628 (32.6)	1320 (41.7)
1833	2 (1.1)	1 (0.3)	3 (0.6)	3 (1.7)	7 (2.1)	10 (2.0)	92 (52.3)	122 (37.3)	214 (42.5)
1835	2 (0.5)	4 (0.4)	6 (0.4)	23 (5.2)	32 (3.4)	55 (4.0)	233 (52.8)	374 (39.5)	607 (43.8)
1837	1 (0.1)	4 (0.2)	5 (0.1)	17 (1.2)	16 (0.8)	33 (1.0)	540 (39.6)	574 (30.0)	1114 (33.9)
1839	2 (0.2)	0 (0.0)	2 (0.1)	12 (1.3)	12 (0.9)	24 (1.1)	373 (40.7)	443 (33.4)	816 (36.3)
1840	0 (0.0)	4 (0.3)	4 (0.2)	12 (1.8)	17 (1.1)	29 (1.3)	217 (33.5)	435 (29.2)	652 (30.5)
Total	25 (0.3)	18 (0.2)	43 (0.2)	248 (3.0)	227 (2.2)	475 (2.6)	3931 (48.2)	3248 (31.9)	7179 (39.2)

TABLE A13: ARMSTRONG SKILL CLASSIFICATION
BY COUNTRY OF TRIAL, SEX AND YEAR OF ARRIVAL (Continued)

ALL

Skill 4			Skill 5			Total		
Male No. (%)	Female No. (%)	Total No. (%)	Male No. (%)	Female No. (%)	Total No. (%)	Male No. (%)	Female No. (%)	Total No. (%)
249 (24.0)	0 (0.0)	249 (24.0)	183 (17.7)	0 (0.0)	183 (17.7)	1035 (100.0)	0 (0.0)	1035 (100.0)
47 (15.7)	0 (0.0)	47 (15.7)	76 (25.3)	0 (0.0)	76 (25.3)	300 (100.0)	0 (0.0)	300 (100.0)
658 (22.5)	0 (0.0)	658 (22.5)	861 (29.5)	0 (0.0)	861 (29.5)	2922 (100.0)	0 (0.0)	2922 (100.0)
198 (18.7)	0 (0.0)	198 (18.7)	328 (31.0)	0 (0.0)	328 (31.0)	1059 (100.0)	0 (0.0)	1059 (100.0)
0 (0.0)	0 (0.0)	0 (0.0)	0 (0.0)	0 (0.0)	0 (0.0)	540 (100.0)	65 (100.0)	605 (100.0)
189 (46.5)	183 (78.5)	372 (58.2)	39 (9.6)	5 (2.2)	44 (6.9)	406 (100.0)	233 (100.0)	639 (100.0)
1099 (40.5)	114 (25.7)	1213 (38.4)	396 (14.6)	177 (40.0)	573 (18.2)	2712 (100.0)	443 (100.0)	3155 (100.0)
207 (40.4)	0 (0.0)	207 (40.4)	76 (14.8)	0 (0.0)	76 (14.8)	513 (100.0)	0 (0.0)	513 (100.0)
598 (42.5)	0 (0.0)	598 (42.5)	129 (9.2)	0 (0.0)	129 (9.2)	1408 (100.0)	0 (0.0)	1408 (100.0)
460 (15.7)	294 (54.4)	754 (21.8)	1400 (47.9)	84 (15.6)	1484 (42.8)	2924 (100.0)	540 (100.0)	3464 (100.0)
214 (13.6)	346 (46.8)	560 (24.1)	667 (42.2)	211 (28.6)	878 (37.9)	1580 (100.0)	739 (100.0)	2319 (100.0)
369 (17.9)	79 (41.4)	448 (19.9)	991 (48.3)	46 (24.1)	1037 (46.2)	2053 (100.0)	191 (100.0)	2244 (100.0)
4288 (24.6)	1016 (46.0)	5304 (27.0)	5146 (29.5)	523 (23.6)	5669 (28.8)	17452 (100.0)	2211 (100.0)	19663 (100.0)

TABLE A14: ARMSTRONG SKILL CLASSIFICATION
BY URBAN OR RURAL BIRTHPLACE BY YEAR OF ARRIVAL (Continued)

Skill 4			Skill 5			Total		
Urban No. (%)	Rural No. (%)	Total No. (%)	Urban No. (%)	Rural No. (%)	Total No. (%)	Urban No. (%)	Rural No. (%)	Total No. (%)
142 (22.4)	96 (26.9)	238 (24.0)	87 (13.7)	92 (25.8)	179 (18.0)	635 (100.0)	357 (100.0)	992 (100.0)
36 (17.5)	9 (11.7)	45 (15.9)	39 (18.9)	33 (42.9)	72 (25.4)	206 (100.0)	77 (100.0)	283 (100.0)
359 (21.1)	262 (26.5)	621 (23.1)	381 (22.4)	408 (41.3)	789 (29.4)	1698 (100.0)	988 (100.0)	2686 (100.0)
115 (20.2)	77 (16.9)	192 (18.8)	130 (22.9)	191 (41.9)	321 (31.4)	568 (100.0)	456 (100.0)	1024 (100.0)
0 (0.0)	0 (0.0)	0 (0.0)	0 (0.0)	0 (0.0)	0 (0.0)	0 (0.0)	0 (0.0)	0 (0.0)
118 (43.4)	251 (69.9)	369 (58.5)	26 (9.6)	18 (5.0)	44 (7.0)	272 (100.0)	359 (100.0)	631 (100.0)
312 (25.2)	904 (47.0)	1216 (38.5)	197 (15.9)	373 (19.4)	570 (18.0)	1238 (100.0)	1925 (100.0)	3163 (100.0)
48 (27.3)	154 (47.1)	202 (40.2)	31 (17.6)	43 (13.2)	74 (14.7)	176 (100.0)	327 (100.0)	503 (100.0)
102 (23.1)	490 (51.8)	592 (42.7)	81 (18.4)	46 (4.9)	127 (9.1)	441 (100.0)	946 (100.0)	1387 (100.0)
303 (22.2)	407 (21.1)	710 (21.6)	501 (36.8)	926 (48.1)	1427 (43.4)	1362 (100.0)	1927 (100.0)	3289 (100.0)
212 (23.2)	332 (25.0)	544 (24.3)	317 (34.6)	539 (40.7)	856 (38.2)	916 (100.0)	1326 (100.0)	2242 (100.0)
119 (18.4)	311 (20.8)	430 (20.1)	300 (46.3)	725 (48.6)	1025 (47.9)	648 (100.0)	1492 (100.0)	2140 (100.0)
1866 (22.9)	3293 (32.3)	5159 (28.1)	2090 (25.6)	3394 (33.4)	5484 (29.9)	8160 (100.0)	10180 (100.0)	18340 (100.0)

220

TABLE A15: NICHOLAS-SHERGOLD SKILL CLASSIFICATION BY SEX AND COUNTRY OF TRIAL

Skill	England Male No. (%)	England Female No. (%)	England Total No. (%)	Ireland Male No. (%)	Ireland Female No. (%)	Ireland Total No. (%)
1	2408 (22.4)	67 (8.9)	2475 (21.5)	1777 (40.2)	126 (10.8)	1093 (34.1)
2	543 (5.1)	28 (3.7)	571 (5.0)	265 (6.0)	106 (9.1)	371 (6.6)
3	928 (8.7)	0 (0.0)	928 (8.1)	205 (4.6)	0 (0.0)	205 (3.7)
4	4425 (41.2)	65 (8.7)	4490 (39.1)	1136 (25.7)	68 (5.8)	1204 (21.6)
5	802 (7.5)	1 (0.1)	803 (7.0)	283 (6.4)	2 (0.2)	285 (5.1)
6	302 (2.8)	0 (0.0)	302 (2.6)	96 (2.2)	0 (0.0)	96 (1.7)
7	455 (4.2)	0 (0.0)	455 (4.0)	192 (4.4)	0 (0.0)	192 (3.4)
8	177 (1.6)	0 (0.0)	177 (1.5)	77 (1.7)	0 (0.0)	77 (1.4)
9	694 (6.5)	593 (78.6)	1287 (11.2)	388 (8.8)	862 (74.1)	1250 (22.4)
Total	10734 (100.0)	754 (100.0)	11488 (100.0)	4419 (100.0)	1164 (100.0)	5583 (100.0)

TABLE A16: NICHOLAS-SHERGOLD SKILL CLASSIFICATION BY SEX AND YEAR OF ARRIVAL

Year	Skill 1 Male No. (%)	Female No. (%)	Total No. (%)	Skill 2 Male No. (%)	Female No. (%)	Total No. (%)	Skill 3 Male No. (%)	Female No. (%)	Total No. (%)	Skill 4 Male No. (%)	Female No. (%)	Total No. (%)	Skill 5 Male No. (%)	Female No. (%)	Total No. (%)
1817	176 (17.4)	0 (0.0)	176 (17.4)	38 (3.7)	0 (0.0)	38 (3.7)	83 (8.2)	0 (0.0)	83 (8.2)	406 (40.0)	0 (0.0)	406 (40.0)	117 (11.5)	0 (0.0)	117 (11.5)
1818	74 (25.2)	0 (0.0)	74 (25.2)	5 (1.7)	0 (0.0)	5 (1.7)	28 (9.5)	0 (0.0)	28 (9.5)	121 (41.1)	0 (0.0)	121 (41.1)	13 (4.4)	0 (0.0)	13 (4.4)
1820	762 (27.9)	0 (0.0)	762 (27.9)	174 (6.4)	0 (0.0)	174 (6.4)	174 (6.4)	0 (0.0)	174 (6.4)	1052 (38.5)	0 (0.0)	1052 (38.5)	100 (3.6)	0 (0.0)	100 (3.6)
1821	293 (27.9)	0 (0.0)	293 (27.9)	7 (0.7)	0 (0.0)	7 (0.7)	69 (6.6)	0 (0.0)	69 (6.6)	370 (35.3)	0 (0.0)	370 (35.3)	122 (11.6)	0 (0.0)	122 (11.6)
1825	0 (0.0)	0 (0.0)	0 (0.0)	0 (0.0)	0 (0.0)	0 (0.0)	0 (0.0)	0 (0.0)	0 (0.0)	0 (0.0)	0 (0.0)	0 (0.0)	0 (0.0)	0 (0.0)	0 (0.0)
1827	32 (7.9)	1 (0.4)	33 (5.2)	107 (26.5)	17 (7.3)	124 (19.5)	38 (9.4)	0 (0.0)	38 (5.9)	158 (39.1)	20 (8.6)	178 (27.9)	16 (4.0)	0 (0.0)	16 (2.5)
1830	298 (11.0)	165 (37.6)	463 (14.7)	30 (1.1)	60 (13.7)	90 (2.9)	217 (8.0)	0 (0.0)	217 (6.9)	1130 (41.7)	42 (9.6)	1172 (37.2)	594 (21.9)	2 (0.4)	596 (18.9)
1833	57 (11.2)	0 (0.0)	57 (11.2)	9 (1.8)	0 (0.0)	9 (1.8)	43 (8.5)	0 (0.0)	43 (8.5)	200 (39.4)	0 (0.0)	200 (39.4)	30 (5.9)	0 (0.0)	30 (5.9)
1835	72 (5.1)	0 (0.0)	72 (5.1)	327 (23.3)	0 (0.0)	327 (23.3)	124 (8.8)	0 (0.0)	124 (8.8)	561 (40.0)	0 (0.0)	561 (40.0)	45 (3.2)	0 (0.0)	45 (3.2)
1837	1256 (43.9)	10 (1.9)	1266 (37.5)	3 (0.1)	19 (3.7)	22 (0.6)	192 (6.7)	0 (0.0)	192 (5.7)	879 (30.7)	33 (6.4)	912 (27.0)	51 (1.8)	1 (0.2)	52 (1.5)
1839	611 (39.1)	21 (2.9)	632 (27.6)	4 (0.3)	40 (5.5)	44 (1.9)	119 (7.6)	0 (0.0)	119 (5.2)	604 (38.7)	36 (4.9)	640 (28.0)	23 (1.5)	0 (0.0)	23 (1.0)
1840	854 (41.6)	0 (0.0)	854 (38.1)	154 (7.5)	5 (2.6)	159 (7.1)	129 (6.3)	0 (0.0)	129 (5.7)	616 (30.0)	9 (4.7)	625 (27.9)	62 (3.0)	0 (0.0)	62 (2.8)
Total	4485 (27.0)	197 (9.4)	4682 (25.0)	858 (5.2)	141 (6.7)	999 (5.3)	1216 (7.3)	0 (0.0)	1216 (6.5)	6097 (36.8)	140 (6.6)	6237 (33.4)	1173 (7.1)	3 (0.1)	1176 (6.3)

221

TABLE A15: NICHOLAS-SHERGOLD SKILL CLASSIFICATION BY SEX AND COUNTRY OF TRIAL (Continued)

	Scotland			Foreign			All		
	Male No. (%)	Female No. (%)	Total No. (%)	Male No. (%)	Female No. (%)	Total No. (%)	Male No. (%)	Female No. (%)	Total No. (%)
	70 (16.5)	1 (1.1)	71 (13.7)	34 (10.6)	0 (0.0)	34 (10.1)	4289 (27.0)	194 (9.6)	4483 (25.0)
	17 (4.0)	5 (5.4)	22 (4.3)	5 (1.6)	0 (0.0)	5 (1.5)	830 (5.2)	139 (6.9)	969 (5.4)
	28 (6.6)	0 (0.0)	28 (5.4)	24 (7.5)	0 (0.0)	24 (7.1)	1185 (7.5)	0 (0.0)	1185 (6.6)
	211 (49.6)	5 (5.4)	216 (41.7)	81 (25.3)	0 (0.0)	81 (24.1)	5853 (36.8)	138 (6.8)	5991 (33.4)
	22 (5.2)	0 (0.0)	22 (4.3)	35 (10.9)	0 (0.0)	35 (10.4)	1142 (7.2)	3 (0.1)	1145 (6.4)
	15 (3.5)	0 (0.0)	15 (2.9)	7 (2.2)	0 (0.0)	7 (2.1)	420 (2.6)	0 (0.0)	420 (2.3)
	31 (7.3)	0 (0.0)	31 (6.1)	52 (16.2)	0 (0.0)	52 (15.5)	730 (4.6)	0 (0.0)	730 (4.1)
	10 (2.4)	0 (0.0)	10 (1.9)	22 (6.9)	0 (0.0)	22 (6.6)	286 (1.8)	0 (0.0)	286 (1.6)
	21 (4.9)	81 (88.1)	102 (19.7)	60 (18.8)	16 (100.0)	76 (22.6)	1163 (7.3)	1552 (76.6)	2715 (15.2)
	425 (100.0)	92 (100.0)	517 (100.0)	320 (100.0)	16 (100.0)	336 (100.0)	15898 (100.0)	2026 (100.0)	17924 (100.0)

TABLE A16: NICHOLAS-SHERGOLD SKILL CLASSIFICATION BY SEX AND YEAR OF ARRIVAL (Continued)

Year	Skill 6			Skill 7			Skill 8			Skill 9			Total		
	Male No. (%)	Female No. (%)	Total No. (%)	Male No. (%)	Female No. (%)	Total No. (%)	Male No. (%)	Female No. (%)	Total No. (%)	Male No. (%)	Female No. (%)	Total No. (%)	Male No. (%)	Female No. (%)	Total No. (%)
1817	22 (2.2)	0 (0.0)	22 (2.2)	80 (7.9)	0 (0.0)	80 (7.9)	19 (1.9)	0 (0.0)	19 (1.9)	73 (7.2)	0 (2.0)	73 (7.2)	1014 (100.0)	0 (0.0)	1014 (100.0)
1818	8 (2.7)	0 (0.0)	8 (2.7)	24 (8.2)	0 (0.0)	24 (8.2)	4 (1.4)	0 (0.0)	4 (1.4)	17 (5.8)	0 (0.0)	17 (5.8)	294 (100.0)	0 (0.0)	294 (100.0)
1820	68 (2.5)	0 (0.0)	68 (2.5)	144 (5.2)	0 (0.0)	144 (5.2)	65 (2.4)	0 (0.0)	65 (2.4)	194 (7.1)	0 (0.0)	194 (7.1)	2733 (100.0)	0 (0.0)	2733 (100.0)
1821	29 (2.8)	0 (0.0)	29 (2.8)	52 (4.9)	0 (0.0)	52 (4.9)	15 (1.4)	0 (0.0)	15 (1.4)	92 (8.8)	0 (0.0)	92 (8.8)	1049 (100.0)	0 (0.0)	1049 (100.0)
1825	0 (0.0)	0 (0.0)	0 (0.0)	0 (0.0)	0 (0.0)	0 (0.0)	0 (0.0)	0 (0.0)	0 (0.0)	0 (0.0)	0 (0.0)	0 (0.0)	0 (0.0)	0 (0.0)	0 (0.0)
1827	14 (3.5)	0 (0.0)	14 (2.2)	10 (2.5)	0 (0.0)	10 (1.6)	3 (0.7)	0 (0.0)	3 (0.5)	26 (6.4)	195 (83.7)	221 (34.7)	404 (100.0)	233 (100.0)	637 (100.0)
1830	95 (3.5)	0 (0.0)	95 (3.0)	119 (4.4)	0 (0.0)	119 (3.8)	41 (1.5)	0 (0.0)	41 (1.3)	187 (6.9)	170 (38.7)	357 (11.3)	2711 (100.0)	439 (100.0)	3150 (100.0)
1833	17 (3.4)	0 (0.0)	17 (3.4)	24 (4.7)	0 (0.0)	24 (4.7)	17 (3.4)	0 (0.0)	17 (3.4)	110 (21.7)	0 (0.0)	110 (21.7)	507 (100.0)	0 (0.0)	507 (100.0)
1835	56 (4.0)	0 (0.0)	56 (4.0)	98 (7.0)	0 (0.0)	98 (7.0)	27 (1.9)	0 (0.0)	27 (1.9)	94 (6.7)	0 (0.0)	94 (6.7)	1404 (100.0)	0 (0.0)	1404 (100.0)
1837	60 (2.1)	0 (0.0)	60 (1.8)	155 (5.4)	0 (0.0)	155 (4.6)	37 (1.3)	0 (0.0)	37 (1.1)	229 (8.0)	455 (87.8)	684 (20.2)	2862 (100.0)	518 (100.0)	3380 (100.0)
1839	27 (1.7)	0 (0.0)	27 (1.2)	69 (4.4)	0 (0.0)	69 (3.0)	16 (1.0)	0 (0.0)	16 (0.7)	89 (5.7)	630 (86.7)	719 (31.4)	1562 (100.0)	727 (100.0)	2289 (100.0)
1840	39 (1.9)	0 (0.0)	39 (1.7)	60 (2.9)	0 (0.0)	60 (2.7)	39 (1.9)	0 (0.0)	39 (1.7)	100 (4.9)	177 (92.7)	277 (12.3)	2053 (100.0)	191 (100.0)	2244 (100.0)
Total	435 (2.6)	0 (0.0)	435 (2.3)	835 (5.0)	0 (0.0)	835 (4.5)	283 (1.7)	0 (0.0)	283 (1.5)	1211 (7.3)	1627 (77.2)	2838 (15.2)	16593 (100.0)	2108 (100.0)	18701 (100.0)

TABLE A17: ARMSTRONG SKILL CLASSIFICATIONS

Skill 1:- Accountant, Actuary, Architect, Broker, Journalist, Landed proprietor, Lawyer, Navy officer, Officer, Physician, Shipmaster, Surveyor.

Skill 2:- Artist, Auctioneer, Bookseller, Druggist, Excise man, Farmer, Greengrocer, Grocer, Haberdasher, Ironmonger, Law clerk, Livestock dealer, Manufacturer, Merchant, Milk seller, Optician, Pawnbroker, Pilot, Poulterer, Publican, Salesman, Schoolmaster, Shopkeeper, Teacher, Tobacconist, Veterinary surgeon, Wine dealer, Wool stapler.

Skill 3:- Anchorsmith, Bailiff, Baker, Barber, Bellowsmaker, Blackingmaker, Blacksmith, Blindmaker, Boat builder, Boilermaker, Boneworker, Bookbinder, Bootmaker, Boxmaker, Brass dresser, Brass founder, Brass moulder, Bricklayer, Brushmaker, Bucklemaker, Building operator, Butcher, Buttonmaker, Cabinetmaker, Canalman, Caneworker, Carpenter, Carpet manufacturer, Carpet weaver, Cereal dealer, Chainmaker, Cheesemonger, Chemist, Clerk, Clothier, Clothmaker, Clothshearer, Coachmaker, Coalminer, Colourman, Combmaker, Compositer, Confectioner, Cook, Cooper, Copper manufacturer, Copper plater, Coppersmith, Cornmiller, Cotton cutter, Cotton dresser, Cotton piecer, Cotton spinner, Cotton weaver, Currier, Cutlerymaker, Domestic implement maker, Draper, Dresser, Dressmaker, Driver, Dry salter, Embroiderer, Engine driver, Engineer, Engine maker, Engraver, Farm Bailiff, Farrier, Filemaker, Fishmonger, Furniture maker, Game keeper, Games equipment maker, Gasfitter, Gilder, Glassblower, Glassmaker, Glass-setter, Glazier, Glover, Gluemaker, Goldbeater, Goldsmith, Gunsmith, Hatter, Housekeeper, Housemaid, Hurdlemaker, Instrument maker, Iron founder, Iron goods manufacturer, Iron moulder, Iron refiner, Iron roller, Iron stamper, Jeweller, Knacker/castrator,Knitter, Lace manufacturer, Lace weaver, Lampmaker, Lapidary, Leather goods, Linen weaver, Locksmith, Machinery maker, Map maker, Mason, Matmaker, Metal goods maker, Milliner, Millwright, Miner, Mineral water maker, Mould maker, Musical instrument maker, Musician, Nailmaker, Nautical instrument maker, Nurse, Nurseryman, Optical goods maker, Ornament maker, Overseer, Painter, Paint maker, Paperhanger, Paper maker, Paper stainer, Pattern maker, Pencil maker, Performer, Pewterer, Piecer, Pipemaker, Plasterer, Plumber, Policeman, Polisher, Potter, Press maker, Printer, Quarrier, Quilldresser, Reedmaker, Ribbon weaver, Rope spinner, Saddlemaker, Sailmaker, Sailor, Sawmaker, Sawyer, Screw maker, Seaman, Ship steward, Shipwright, Shopman, Silkspinner, Silk weaver, Silversmith, Skinner, Slater, Slopseller, Smith, Smith apprentice, Snuffermaker, Soapmaker, Soldier, Spinner, Spinplater, Spirit dealer, Sportsman, Spring maker, Stable keeper, Steel pen maker, Stocking maker, Stone cutter, Sweep, Swordmaker, Tailor, Tallow chandler, Tanner, Tape weaver, Tendermaker, Textile equipment maker, Thatcher, Tobacco maker, Toolmaker, Toymaker, Trunkmaker, Type founder, Umbrella maker, Upholsterer, Valet, Viceman, Waiter, Warehouseman, Watchmaker, Water motion man, Weaver, Weighing machine maker, Wellsinker, Wheelwright, Whitesmith, Wire frame maker, Wire maker, Wood carver, Wood dealer, Woodman, Wood turner, Wool sorter, Wool spinner.

Skill 4:- Bar attendant, Bargeman, Boatman, Brazier, Brewer, Brickmaker, Butler, Calender, Cardmaker, Carrier, Chambermaid, Coachman, Corkcutter, Cotton carder, Cotton dyer, Cotton manufacturer, Cow keeper, Dairy hand, Dairy producer, Distiller, Drover, Dyer, Farm labourer, Farm servant, Fence maker, Fireman, Fisherman, Fishing equipment maker, Fitter, Flagger, Gardener, General servant, Governess, Groom, Gunpowder maker, Herdsman, Horse breaker, Lamp lighter, Laundress, Laundry maid, Lime burner, Maltster, Marine,

Needlemaker, Net maker, Nursemaid, Pavior, Ploughman, Reaper, Rigger, Riveter, Ropemaker, Seamstress, Shearer, Silkdresser, Silkdyer, Silk manufacturer, Stableman, Sugar Refiner, Vermin destroyer, Wool carder, Wool dresser.

Skill 5:- All work, Cleaner, Drifter, Factory apprentice, Factory labourer, Gypsy, Grave digger, Hawker, Jabber, Kitchen hand, Labourer, Messenger, Newsboy, Porter, Road labourer, Shoeboy, Slave, Tarboy, Tollman.

The skill breakdown in this table is based on, Armstrong W.A, "The Use of information about occupation" in Wrigley, E.A. (ed.), Nineteenth Century Society: Essays in the Use of Quantitative Methods for the Study of Social Data, Cambridge, C.U.P., 1972.

TABLE A18: NICHOLAS-SHERGOLD SKILL CLASSIFICATIONS

Skill 1:- (Urban unskilled). All work, Cleaner, Drifter, Factory apprentice, Factory labourer, Gypsy, Grave digger, Hawker, Labourer, Newsboy, Porter, Road labourer, Shoeboy, Sweep, Tarboy, Vermin destroyer.

Skill 2:- (Rural unskilled). Dairy hand, Farm labourer, Farm servant, Limeburner, Slave.

Skill 3:- (Construction, skilled or semi-skilled). Bricklayer, Brickmaker, Building operator, Carpenter, Glazier, Mason, Painter, Paperhanger, Plasterer, Plumber, Sawyer, Slater, Stone cutter, Thatcher.

Skill 4:- (Manufacturing or transport, skilled or semi-skilled). Anchorsmith, Baker, Barber, Bargeman, Bellowsmaker, Blackingmaker, Blacksmith, Blindmaker, Boatbuilder, Boatman, Boilermaker, Boneworker, Bookbinder, Bootmaker, Boxmaker, Brassdresser, Brassfounder, Brassmoulder, Brazier, Brewer, Brushmaker, Bucklemaker, Butcher, Buttonmaker, Cabinetmaker, Calender, Canalman, Caneworker, Cardmaker, Carpet manufacturer, Carpet weaver, Carrier, Chainmaker, Chemist, Clothmaker, Clothshearer, Coachmaker, Coalminer, Colorman, Combmaker, Compositor, Confectioner, Cooper, Copper manufacturer, Copperplater, Coppersmith, Corkcutter, Corn miller, Cotton carder, Cotton cutter, Cotton dresser, Cotton dyer, Cotton manufacturer, Cotton piecer, Cotton spinner, Cotton weaver, Currier, Cutlerymaker, Distiller, Dresser, Dressmaker, Driver, Dry salter, Dyer, Embroiderer, Engine driver, Engineer, Engine maker, Engraver, Filemaker, Fireman, Fishing equipment maker, Fitter, Flagger, Furniture maker, Games equipment maker, Gas fitter, Gilder, Glassblower, Glassmaker, Glass setter, Glover, Gluemaker, Goldbeater, Goldsmith, Gunpowder maker, Gunsmith, Hatter, Instrument maker, Iron founder, Irongoods maker, Iron moulder, Iron refiner, Iron roller, Iron stamper, Jabber, Jeweller, Knitter, Lace manufacturer, Lace weaver, Lamplighter, Lamp maker, Lapidary, Leather goods maker, Linen weaver, Locksmith, Machinery maker, Maltster, Manufacturer, Map maker, Matmaker, Messenger, Metal goods manufactuer, Milliner, Millwright, Miner, Mineral water maker, Mouldmaker, Musical instrument maker, Nailmaker, Nautical instrument maker, Needlemaker,

Netmaker, Optical goods maker, Optician, Ornament maker, Overseer, Paint maker, Papermaker, Paperstainer, Patternmaker, Pavior, Pencil maker, Pewterer, Piecer, Pilot, Pipemaker, Polisher, Potter, Pressmaker, Printer, Quarrier, Quilldresser, Reedmaker, Ribbonweaver, Rigger, Riveter, Ropemaker, Ropespinner, Saddlemaker, Sailmaker, Sawmaker, Screwmaker, Seamstress, Shipmaster, Shipsteward, Shipwright, Silkdresser, Silkdyer, Silk manufacturer, Silkspinner, Silkweaver, Silversmith, Skinner, Smith, Smith apprentice, Snuffermaker, Soapmaker, Spinner, Spinplater, Springmaker, Stablekeeper, Stableman, Steel pen maker, Stockingmaker, Sugar refiner, Swordmaker, Tailor, Tanner, Tapeweaver, Tendermaker, Textile equipment maker, Tobacco maker, Tollman, Toolmaker, Toymaker, Trunkmaker, Umbrella maker, Upholsterer, Viceman, Warehouseman, Watchmaker, Water motion man, Weaver, Weighing machine maker, Wellsinker, Wheelwright, Whitesmith, Wire frame maker, Wood carver, Wood turner, Wool carder, Wool dresser, Wool sorter, Wool spinner, Wool stapler.

Skill 5:- Cowkeeper, Dairy producer, Drover, Farm bailiff, Farmer, Farrier, Fencemaker, Fisherman, Gamekeeper, Gardener, Herdsman, Horsebreaker, Hurdlemaker, Knacker/castrator, Landed proprietor, Nurseryman, Ploughman, Reaper, Shearer, Woodman.

Skill 6:- Bookseller, Cereal dealer, Cheesemonger, Clothier, Draper, Druggist, Fishmonger, Greengrocer, Grocer, Haberdasher, Ironmonger, Livestock dealer, Milkseller, Pawnbroker, Poulterer, Publican, Salesman, Shopkeeper, Shopman, Slopseller, Spirit dealer, Tallow chandler, Tobacconist, Wine dealer, Wood dealer.

Skill 7:- Exciseman, Marine, Navy officer, Officer, Sailor, Seaman, Soldier.

Skill 8:- Accountant, Actuary, Architect, Artist, Auctioneer, Bailiff, Broker, Clerk, Journalist, Law clerk, Lawyer, Medical student, Mercant, Musician, Performer, Physician, Policeman, Schoolmaster, Sportsman, Student, Surveyor, Teacher, Veterinary surgeon.

Skill 9:- Bar attendant, Butler, Chambermaid, Coachman, Cook, General servant, Governess, Groom, Housekeeper, Housemaid, Kitchenhand, Laundress, Laundrymaid, Nurse, Nursemaid, Valet, Waiter.

The skill breakdown in this table is based upon an alternative and more detailed distribution of occupations. It seeks to separate urban from rural skills; to separate construction workers from manufacturing and transport workers; and to distinguish professionals, dealers, military personnel and domestic servants.

BIBLIOGRAPHY

Primary Sources

Annual Report of the Registrar General: Births, Deaths and Marriages in England (Eyre and Spottiswoode, London, 1838–42).

Australian Agricultural Company: Third Annual Report (London, 1927).

Australian National University, *Archives of Business and Labour* Australian Agricultural Company Deposit, Nos. 78/9/2; 78/9/3; 78/1/11; 160/89; 160/90; 160/91.

Australian Dictionary of Biography I and II (Australian National University, Canberra, 1963).

Bigge Appendix. Return of Men Assigned 1814–1819, Mitchell Library (hereafter ML) C0 201/118; Convicts, 'List of Persons in Government Employ . . . ' ML CO 201/118.

Bonwick Transcript of Evidence to Bigge Commission ML BT5.

Colonial Secretary's In Letters Archives Office of NSW (hereafter AONSW) Reel 2161, 1066.

Colquhoun, P., *A Treatise on the Police of the Metropolis: Containing A Detail of the Various Crimes and Misdemeanors by Which Public and Private Property and Security Are, At Present, Injured and Endangered: And Suggesting Remedies for Their Prevention* (J. Mawman, London, 1805).

Confidential Reports of Police Magistrates to the Governor, ML A1267–12, A1267–13.

Dawson, R., *The Present State of Australia: A Description of the Country, Its Advantages and Prospects, With Reference to Emigration and a Particular Account of the Manners, Customs and Conditions of its Aboriginal Inhabitants* (Smith, Elder, London, 1830).

Department of Immigration and Ethnic Affairs, *Statistics Monthly*, October (Government Printing Office, Canberra, 1987).

Great Britain 1841 Census, , Parliamentary Papers (hereafter P.P.), 1841, II, C52 [Irish University Press Reprint Series (hereafter IUP), *Population*, 3].

Great Britain, Foreign Office, Historical Section, 'Eastern Siberia', *Handbook* No. 55 (H.M. Stationery Office, London, 1890).

Grigson, J., *The Australian Agricultural Company 1824–1875* (Sydney, 1907).

Historical Records of Australia, Series 1 — Governors Despatches to and from England 1–26, J.F. Watson (ed.), (The Library Committee of the Commonwealth Parliament, Melbourne, 1914–25).

Historical Statistics of the United States: Colonial Times to 1970 (U.S. Department of Commerce, Washington, 1975).

Jevons, W.S., *A Social Survey of Australia's Cities 1858* MLB 864.

King, C.A., *A Warning Voice from a Penitent Convict: The Life, Hardships and Dreadful Sufferings of Charles Adolphius King* (Reprinted Swansea Printers, Victoria, 1956).

Mayhew, H., *London Labour and the London Poor: A Cyclopaedia of the Condition and Earnings of Those That Will Work, Those That Cannot Work, And Those That Will Not Work* (Cass, London, 1967).

Morgan, J., *Life and Adventures of William Buckley: Thirty-two Years A Wandering Amongst the Aborigines* (A. McDougall, Hobart, 1852).

Marjoribanks, A., *Travel in New South Wales* (Smith, Elder, London, 1847).

Morton, J.C., *Handbook of Farm Labour* (Cassell, Petter and Galpin, London, 1868).

New South Wales Superintendent of Carpenters, Parramatta 1817–19 ML A2086–8.

Minutes of Evidence Taken Before the Select Committee on Transportation, P.P. 1837, XIX, C518 [IUP, CP *Transportation*, 2].

Reports of J.H. Capper, Two reports of J.H. Capper Esq., Superintendent of Ships and Vessels employed for the confinement of offencers under sentence of transportation . . . 29th July 1839 — 29th February 1844, (London HMSO 1840–44) ML Q365/G.

Report from the Select Committee on Convict Establishments, P.P., 1810, IV, C348 [IUP, CP *Transportation*, 1].

Report from the Select Committee on Transportation, P.P., 1812, II, C306 [IUP, CP *Transportation*, 1].

Report from the Select Committee on the State of the Gaols, P.P. 1819, VII, C579. [IUP, CP *Prisons*, 1].

Report from the Commissioner of Inquiry into the State of the Colony of New South Wales (Bigge Report) P.P., 1822, XX, C448 [IUP, Australia, 1].

Report from the Select Committee on Secondary Punishments, P.P., 1831, VII, C276 [IUP, CP Transportation, 1].

Report from the Select Committee on Secondary Punishments, P.P., 1831–32, VII, C547 [IUP, CP Transportation, 1].

Report from the Select Committee on Gaols and Houses of Correction, P.P., 1835, XI, C438 [IUP, CP Prisons, 3].

Report from the Select Committee on Transportation (Molesworth Report), P.P., 1837–38, XXII, C669 [IUP, CP Transportation, 3].

Papers Relating to Transportation and Assignment of Convicts, P.P., 1839, XXXVIII, C582, [IUP, CP Transportation, 6].

Report from the Select Committee on the Health of Towns, P.P., 1840, XI, C384 [IUP, Health, 2].

Report of the Commissioners Appointed to Take the Census of Ireland For The Year 1841, P.P., 1843, XXIV, C504 [IUP, Population, 2].

Report from the Poor Law Commissioners on an Inquiry into the Sanitary Condition of the Labouring Population (Chadwick Inquiry), P.P., 1842, XXVII, (H.L.), [IUP, Health, 3].

Report of the Commissioners on the State of Large Towns and Populous Districts P.P., 1844, XVII, C572, [IUP, Health, 5].

Report on the General Treatment and Condition of Convicts in the Hulks at Woolwich P.P., 1847, XVIII, C831 [IUP, CP Prisons, 12].

Report of the Indian Jails Committee, P.P., 1919–20, I, Cmd1303.

Report of the Committee on Overseas Settlement, P.P., 1922, XII, Cmd1804.

Statement of Way Convicts Were Employed at Various Government Establishments, 1824, AONSW 4/1775.

Statistical Abstract of the United States 1979 (U.S. Department of Commerce, Washington, 1980).

Statistical Abstract of the United States 1981 (U.S. Department of Commerce, Washington, 1982).

Sydney Gazette ML NA108.

Sydney Mechanics School of Arts, Third Annual Report for the Year 1835, ML 374.9/S.

Votes and Proceedings of the Legislative Assembly (NSW), Immigration Committee (1841).

Weekly Returns of Men Employed on Cowpastures, Oct. 1822, Dec. 1823–31, AONSW 4/7028C; 2/8315.

Wentworth, W.C., Statistical, Historical and Political Description of the Colony of New South Wales and Its Dependent Settlements in Van Diemen's Land (Sydney, 1819), ML 991/W.

White, C., Convict Life in New South Wales and Van Diemen's Land (C & G.S. White, Bathurst, 1889).

Secondary Sources

Abel-Smith, B., The Hospitals 1800–1948 (Heinemann, London, 1964).

Alchian, A. and Demsetz, H., 'Production, Information Costs and Economic Organisation', American Economic Review 62 (1972), 777–95.

Alford, K., Production or Reproduction? An Economic History of Women in Australia, 1788–1850 (Oxford University Press, Melbourne, 1984).

Anderson, C.A. and Bowman, M.J. (eds.), Education and Economic Development (Aldine, Chicago, 1965).

Armstrong, T., Russian Settlement in the North (Cambridge University Press, Cambridge, 1965).

Armstrong, W.A., 'The Use of Information About Occupation', in E.A. Wrigley (ed.), Nineteenth-Century Society: Essays in the Use of Quantitative Methods for the Study of Social Data (Cambridge University Press, Cambridge, 1972), 191–310.

Ashton, T.S., The Industrial Revolution 1760–1830 (Oxford University Press, London, 1948).

Atkinson, A. and Aveling, M., Australians 1838 (Fairfax, Syme and Weldon Assoc., Sydney, 1987).

Atkinson, A., 'Four Patterns of Convict Protest', Labour History 37 (1979), 28–51.

Baines, D.E., 'The Labour Supply and the Labour Market 1860–1914', in R. Floud and D. McCloskey (eds.), The Economic History of Britain Since 1700 II, (Cambridge University Press, Cambridge, 1981), 144–74.

Barnard, M., Macquarie's World (Melbourne University Press, Melbourne, 1947).

Bateson, C., The Convict Ships 1787–1868 (Brown, Son and Ferguson, Glasgow, 1959).

Beattie, J.M., 'The Criminality of Women in Eighteenth-Century England', Journal of Social History 8 (1975), 80–116.

Becke, L. (ed.), Old Convict Days (Penguin, Ringwood, 1975).

Beever, E.A., 'The Origin of the Wool Industry in N.S.W.', Business Archives and History 5 (1965), 91–106.

Beever, E.A., 'A Reply to Mr. Fogarty's Note', Australian Economic History Review 9 (1969), 78–80.

Belbenoit, R., Hell on Trial (Jarrods, London, no date).

Berg, M., The Age of Manufactures 1700–1820 (Fontana, London, 1985).

Blainey, G., The Tyranny of Distance (Sun Books, Melbourne, 1967).

Blair, S., 'The Felonry and the Free? Divisions in Colonial Society in the Penal Era', Labour History 45 (1983), 1–16.

Blaug, M., *An Introduction to Economics of Education* (Allen Lane, London, 1970).

Bourdet-Pleville, M., *Justice in Chains: From the Galleys to Devil's Island* (Robert Hale, London, 1960).

Bouvier, L., Macisco, J. and Zarate, A., 'Towards a Framework for the Analysis of Differential Migration: The Case of Education' in A.H. Richmond and D. Kabat (eds.), *Internal Migration: The New World and the Third World* (Sage Publications, California, 1976), 24–36.

Bradford, E., *Gibraltar: The History of a Fortress* (Hart and Davis, London, 1971).

Braverman, H., *Labor and Monopoly Capital: The Degradation of Work in the Twentieth Century* (Monthly Review Press, N.Y., 1974).

Brooke, D., *The Railway Navvy* (David and Charles, Newton Abbot, 1983).

Buer, M.C., *Health, Wealth and Population in the Early Days of the Industrial Revolution* (Routledge and Kegan Paul, London, 1969).

Burgess, K., *The Origins of British Industrial Relations: The Nineteenth Century Experience* (Croom Helm, London, 1975).

Burnett, J., *Plenty and Want: A Social History of Diet in England from 1815 to the Present Day* (Thomas Nelson, London, 1966).

Burnett, J., *A Social History of Housing 1815–1870* (David and Charles, Newton Abbot, 1978).

Butlin, N., 'White Human Capital in Australia 1788–1850' *Australian National University Working Paper in Economic History* 32 (1985), 1–37.

Butlin, N., 'Contours of the Australian Economy 1788–1860', *Australian Economic History Review* 26 (1986), 96–125.

Butlin, S.J., *Foundations of the Australian Monetary System 1788–1851* (Sydney University Press, Sydney, 1968).

Campbell, J.F., 'The First Decade of the Australian Agricultural Company, 1824–1834', *Journal of the Royal Australian Historical Society* 9 (1923), 113–60.

Chapman, S.D., (ed.), *The History of Working-Class Housing: A Symposium* (David and Charles, Newton Abbot, 1971).

Christian, J.L., 'Denmark's Interest in Burma and the Nicobar Islands (1620–1883)', *Journal of the Burma Research Society* 29 (1962), 215–32.

Clapham, J.H., *An Economic History of Modern Britian* I (Cambridge University Press, Cambridge, 1926).

Clark, C.M.H., *A History of Australia* I, *From the Earliest Times to the Age of Macquarie* (Melbourne University Press, Melbourne, 1962).

Clark, C.M.H., *A History of Australia* II, *New South Wales and Van Diemen's Land 1822–1838* (Melbourne University Press, Melbourne, 1968).

Clark, C.M.H., 'The Origins of the Convicts Transported to Eastern Australia, 1787–1852', *Historical Studies, Australia and New Zealand* 7 (1956), 121–35, 314–27.

Clawson, D., *Bureaucracy and the Labor Process: The Transformation of U.S. Industry, 1860–1920* (Monthly Review Press, N.Y., 1980).

Coghlan, T.A., *Labour and Industry in Australia* I (Oxford University Press, London, 1969).

Cohn, S., 'Keeping the Navvies in Line: Variations in Work Discipline Amongst British Railway Construction Crews' in L. Tilly and C. Tilly (eds.), *Class Conflict and Collective Action* (Sage, Beverly Hills, 1981), 143–66.

Cole, G.D.H., *Workshop Organisation* (Hutchinson, London, 1973).

Collins, E.J.T., *Sickle to Combine: A Review of Harvest Techniques* (University of Reading, Museum of English Rural Life, Reading, 1969).

Collins, E.J.T., *Harvest Technology and Labour Supply in Britain 1790– 1870* Ph.D. thesis, (University of Nottingham, 1970).

Colon, A., 'Mine is a Sad Yet True Story, Convict Narratives, 1818–1850', *Journal of the Royal Australian Historical Society* 55 (1969), 43–82.

Connell, R.W. and Irving, T.H., *Class Structure in Australian History: Documents, Narrative and Argument* (Longman Cheshire, Melbourne, 1980).

Corris, P., *Passage, Port and Plantation: A History of Soloman Islands Labour Migration, 1870–1914* (Melbourne University Press, Melbourne, 1973).

Crossick, G., 'The Labour Aristocracy and Its Values: A Study of Mid- Victorian Kentish London', *Victorian Studies* 19 (1976), 301–28.

Crossick, G., *An Artisan Elite in Victorian Society: Kentish London 1840–1880* (Croom Helm, London, 1978).

Cubis, D., 'Australian Character in the Making: New South Wales, 1788– 1901', *Journal of the Royal Australian Historical Society* 24 (1938), 165–85.

Cumpston, J.S., *Shipping Arrivals and Departures, Sydney 1788–1825* (Roebuck Society, Canberra, 1977).

Dainton, C., *The Story of England's Hospitals* (Museum Press, London, 1961).

Dallas, K.M., 'Slavery in Australia — Convicts, Emigrants and Aborigines', *The Tasmanian Historical Research Association Papers and Proceedings* 16 (1968), 61–76.

Dallas, K.M., *Trading Posts or Penal Colonies* (Fullers Bookshop, Hobart, 1969).

Dallin, D.J., and Nicolaevsky, B.I., *Forced Labour in Soviet Russia* (Yale University Press, New Haven, 1947).

David, P.A. et al, *Reckoning With Slavery: A Critical Study in the Quantitative History of American Negro Slavery* (Oxford University Press, N.Y., 1976).

Dixson, M., *The Real Matilda, Women and Identity in Australia 1788-1975* (Penguin, Melbourne, 1976).

Dobb, M., *Studies in the Development of Capitalism* (Routledge and Kegan Paul, London, 1946).

Driscoll, F., 'Macquarie's Administration of the Convict System', *Journal of the Royal Australian Historical Society* 27 (1941), 373–433.

Dunlop, O.J., *The Farm Labourers* (Fisher Unwin, London, 1913).

Dunn, M., 'Early Australia: Wage Labour or Slave Society?' in E. Wheelwright and K. Buckley (eds.), *Essays in the Political Economy of Australian Capitalism* I (Australian and New Zealand Book Co., Sydney, 1975), 33–46.

Duxbury, J., 'Colonial Servitude: Indentured and Assigned Servants of the Van Diemen's Land Company', BA (Hons) thesis, (Monash University, 1985).

Dyster, B., 'John Griffiths, Speculator', *Tasmanian Historical Research Association Papers and Proceedings* 27 (1980), 20–31.

Eisenstein, Z., 'Constructing a Theory of Capitalist Patriarchy and Socialist Feminism', *The Insurgent Sociologist* 7 (1977), 2–18.

Elbaum, B. and Wilkinson, F., 'Industrial Relations and Uneven Development: A Comparative Study of the American and British Steel Industries', *Cambridge Journal of Political Economy* 3 (1979), 275–303.

Ellis, F., *The Banana Export Activity in Central America 1947-1976* Ph.D. thesis, (University of Sussex, 1978).

Eltis, D., 'Free and Coerced Transatlantic Migrations: Some Comparisons', *American Historical Review* 88 (1983), 251–80.

Engels, F.I., *The Condition of the Working Class in England* (Granada edn., London, 1982).

Engerman, S., 'Some Considerations Relating to Property Rights to Man', *Journal of Economic History* 33 (1973), 43–65.

Engerman, S., 'Contract Labor, Sugar and Technology in the Nineteenth Century', *Journal of Economic History* 43 (1983), 635–659.

Engerman, S., 'Servants to Slaves to Servants: Contract Labor and European Expansion' in E. van den Boogaart and P.C. Emmer, (eds.), *Comparative Studies in Overseas History* (forthcoming).

Erickson, C., *Emigration from Europe 1815-1914: Select Documents* (A. and C. Black, London, 1976).

Erickson, C., 'Emigration from the British Isles to the U.S.A. in 1831', *Population Studies* 35 (1981), 175–97.

Evans, L. and Nicholls, P., *Convicts and Colonial Society 1788-1853* (Cassell, Stanmore, 1976).

Evans, R., 'The Military Draft as a Slave System: An Economic View', *Social Science Quarterley* 50 (1969), 535–543.

Evans, R., 'Some Notes on Coerced Labour', *Journal of Economic History* 30 (1970), 861–66.

Eveleth, P.B. and Tanner, J.M., *Worldwide Variations in Human Growth* (Cambridge University Press, Cambridge, 1976).

Fenoaltea, S., 'Slavery and Supervision in Comparative Perspective: A Model', *Journal of Economic History* 44 (1984), 635–68.

Ferenczi, I. and Willcox, W.F., *International Migrations* I and II (Gordon and Breach, N.Y., 1969).

Findlay, R., 'Slavery, Incentives and Manumission: A Theoretical Model', *Journal of Political Economy* 83 (1975), 923–33.

Fitton, R.S. and Wadsworth, A.P., *The Strutts and the Arkwrights 1758-1830: A Study of the Early Factory System* (Manchester University Press, Manchester, 1958).

Fletcher, B.H., *Landed Enterprise and Penal Society* (Sydney University Press, Sydney, 1976).

Flinn, M.W., *Men of Iron: The Crowleys in the Early Iron Industry*, (University of Edinburgh Press, Edinburgh, 1962).

Flinn, M.W., *The History of the British Coal Industry* (Clarendon Press, Oxford, 1984).

Floud, R., 'A Tall Story? The Standard of Living Debate', *History Today* 33 (1983), 36–40.

Floud, R., 'Measuring European Inequality: The Use of Height Data', (mimeo, Conference of the Social Science History Association, 1986), 1–32.

Floud, R. and Wachter, K.W., 'Poverty and Physical Stature: Evidence on the Standard of Living of London Boys 1770-1870', *Social Science History* 6 (1982), 422–52.

Fogarty, J.P., 'N.S.W. Wool Prices in the 1820: A Note', *Australian Economic History Review* 9 (1969), 71–77.

Fogel, R.W. and Engerman, S.L., *Time on the Cross: The Economics of American Negro Slavery* (Wildwood House, London, 1974).

Forsyth, W.D., *Governor Arthur's Convict System: Van Diemen's Land 1824-36* (Sydney University Press, Sydney, 2nd edn., 1970).

Foster, W.C., *Sir Thomas Livingston Mitchell and His World 1792–1855* (Institution of Surveyors, N.S.W. Sydney, 1985).

Foster, J., *Class Struggle and the Industrial Revolution: Early Industrial Capitalism in Three English Towns* (Weidenfeld and Nicholson, London, 1974).

Foster, S., 'Convict Assignment New South Wales in the 1830s', *Push From the Bush* 15 (1983), 35–80.

Frank, T., *Rome and Italy of the Republic* I, in T. Frank (ed.), *An Economy Survey of Ancient Rome* (Johns Hopkins Press, N.Y., 1959).

Galenson, D., *White Servitude in Colonial America* (Cambridge University Press, Cambridge, 1981).

Galenson, D., 'The Rise and Fall of Indentured Servitude in the Americas: An Economic Analysis' *Journal of Economic History* 44, (1984), 1–28.

Galloway, R., *Annals of Coal Mining and the Coal Trade* (David and Charles, Newton Abbot, 1971).

Gandevia, B., 'Medical History in Its Australian Environment' *Medical Journal of Australia*, 18 (1967), 941–6.

Gandevia, B., 'Occupation and Disease in Australia Since 1788' *Bulletin of the Post Graduate Committee in Medicine* Nov. (1971), (Australian Medical Publishing Co., Sydney, 1971).

Gandevia, B., *Tears Often Shed: Child Health and Welfare in Australia From 1788* (Pergamon Press, Sydney, 1978).

Gandevia, B., 'The Height and Physical Characteristics of Convicts Transports to Australia, c.1820–1850', *Australasian Association for the History and Philosophy of Science-Proceedings* 7 (1975), 2–8.

Gandevia, B., 'Some Physical Characteristics, Including Pock Marks, Tattoos and Disabilities, of Convict Boys Transported to Australia from Britain c.1840', *Australian Paediatric Journal* 12 (1976), 6–12.

Gandevia, B., 'A Comparison of the Height of Boys Transported to Australia from England, Scotland and Ireland, C.1840, with Later British and Australian Developments', *Australian Paediatric Journal* 13 (1977), 91–6.

Gatrell, V.A.C. and Hadden, T.B., 'Criminal Statistics and Their Interpretation', in E.A. Wrigley (ed.), *Nineteenth Century Society: Essays in the Use of Quantitative Methods for the Study of Social Data* (Cambridge University Press, Cambridge, 1972), 336–96.

George, M.D., *England in Transition: Life and Work in the Eighteenth Century* (Penguin, Harmondsworth, 1962).

Gould, S.J., *The Mismeasure of Man* (W.W. Norton and Co., New York, 1981).

Gras, N.S.B., *Industrial Evolution* (A.M. Kelly, N.Y., 1969).

Graves, A., 'The Nature and Origin of Pacific Island Labour Migration to Queensland, 1864–1906', in P. Richardson and S. Marks (eds.), *International Labour Migration: Historical Perspectives* (M. Temple Smith, Middlesex, 1984), 112–139.

Gray, R.Q., *The Labour Aristocracy in Victorian Edinburgh* (Clarendon Press, Oxford, 1976).

Greig, A.W., 'Letters from Australian Pioneers', *The Victorian Historical Magazine* 12 (1927), 21–108.

Griffith, G., *In An Unknown Land: An Account of Convicts and Colonists in New Caledonia* (Hutchinson, London, 1901).

Griffiths, P., *The History of the Indian Tea Industry* (Weidenfeld and Nicholson, London, 1967).

Grocott, A.M., *Convicts, Clergymen and Churches: Attitudes of Convicts and Ex-Convicts Towards the Churches and Clergy in New South Wales from 1788 to 1851* (Sydney University Press, Sydney, 1980).

Gutman, H.G., *Slavery and the Numbers Games* (University of Illinois Press, Urbana, 1975).

Hainsworth, D.R., *The Sydney Traders: Simeon Lord and His Contemporaries 1788–1821* (Cassell, Melbourne, 1972).

Hartwell, R.M., *The Economic Development of Van Diemen's Land 1820–1850* (Melbourne University Press, Melbourne, 1954).

Hasbach, W., *A History of the English Agricultural Labourer* (Frank Cass, London, 1966).

Heath, F.G., *British Rural Life and Labour* (P.S. King, London, 1911).

Heaton, H., *The Yorkshire Woollen and Worsted Industries* (Clarendon Press, Oxford, 2nd edn., 1965).

Hills, G., *Rock of Contention. A History of Gilbraltar* (Robert Hale and Company, London, 1974).

Hirst, J.B., *Convict Society and Its Enemies: A History of Early New South Wales* (George Allen and Unwin, Sydney, 1983).

Hobsbawm, E., 'The Labour Aristocracy in Nineteenth Century Britain', in E. Hobsbawm (ed.), *Labouring Men* (Weidenfeld and Nicholson, London, 1968), 272–315.

Homze, E., *Foreign Labour in Nazi Germany* (Princeton University Press, Princeton, 1967).

Hooson, D.J., *A New Soviet Heartland?* (Van Nostrand, Princeton, 1964).

Horne, D., *The Australian People* (Angus and Robertson, Sydney, 1972).

Howard, L.E., *Labour in Agriculture* (Oxford University Press, Oxford, 1935).

Hudson, P., 'Proto-industrialisation: The Case of the West Riding Wool Textile Industry in the 18th and Early 19th Centuries', *History Workshop* 12 (1981), 34–61.

Hughes, R., *The Fatal Shore: A History of the Transportation of Convicts to Australia, 1787–1868* (Collins Harvill, London, 1987).

Hume, L.J., 'Working Class Movements in Sydney and Melbourne Before the Gold Rushes' in M. Beever and F.B. Smith (eds.), *Historical Studies: Select Articles* (Melbourne University Press, Melbourne, 1967), 30–50.

Ingham, S., 'A Footnote to Transportation to New South Wales: James Ingham 1824–1848', *Historical Journal* 12 (1967), 522–40.

Jackson, J.A., *The Irish in Britain* (Routledge and Kegan Paul, London, 1963).

Jeffreys, J., *The Story of the Engineers 1800–1945* (Lawrence and Wishart, London, 1946).

Jenkins, D., *The West Riding Wool Textile Industry 1770–1835* (Pasold Research Fund, Wiltshire, 1975).

John, A.M., 'The Demography of Slavery in Nineteenth-Century Trinidad', unpublished Ph.D. thesis, (Princeton University, 1984).

Johnson, A.C., *Roman Egypt*, II, in T. Frank (ed.), *An Economic Survey of Ancient Rome* (Johns Hopkins Press, Baltimore, 1936).

Johnston, V., 'Local Prisons Diets, 1835–1878', in D. Oddy and D. Miller (eds.), *Diet and Health in Modern Britain* (Croom Helm, London, 1985), 207–230.

Jones, A.H.M., 'Slavery in the Ancient World', *Economic History Review* 9 (1956), 185–199.

Jones, D., *Crime, Protest, Community and Police in Nineteenth-Century Britain* (Routledge and Kegan Paul, London, 1982).

Jones, R.M., *The North Wales Quarrymen: 1874–1922* (University of Wales Press, Cardiff, 1981).

Karskens, G., 'Defiance, Deference and Diligence: Three Views of Convicts in New South Wales Road Gangs' *Australian Historical Archaeology* 4 (1986), 17–28.

Kenyon, E.R., *Gibraltar Under Moor, Spaniard and Briton* (Methuen, London, 1938).

Kerr, J.S., *Design For Convicts: An Account of Design for Convict Establishments in the Australian Colonies During the Transportation Era* (Library of Australian History in Association with The National Trust of Australia (NSW), Sydney, 1984).

Kingston, B., *The World Moves Slowly* (Cassell, Sydney, 1977).

Kingston, B., *My Wife, My Daughter and Poor Mary Ann* (Thomas Nelson (Aust.), Melbourne, 1977).

Kirchner, J.A., *Sugar and Seasonal Labour Migration* (University of Chicago Press, Chicago, 1980).

Kitteringham, J., 'County Workgirls in Nineteenth Century England', in Raphael Samuel (ed.), *Village Life and Labour* (Routledge and Kegan Paul, London, 1975), 73–138.

Klein, B., 'Transaction Cost Determinants of "Unfair" Contractual Arrangements', *American Economic Review* 70 (1980), 356–62.

Klein, H.S., *The Middle Passage: Comparative Studies in the Atlantic Slave Trade* (Princeton University Press, Princeton, 1978).

Klein, H.S. and Engerman, S.L., 'A Note on Mortality in the French Slave Trade in the Eighteenth Century' in H.A. Gemery and J.S. Hogendorn (eds.), *The Uncommon Market: Essays in the Economic History of the Atlantic Slave Trade* (Academic Press, N.Y., 1979), 261–72.

Kloosterboer, W., *Involuntary Labour Since the Abolition of Slavery* (E.J. Brill, Leiden Netherlands, 1960).

Kloss, C.B., *In The Andamans and Nicobars* (John Murray, London, 1903).

Landes, D., 'What Do Bosses Really Do?', *Journal of Economic History* 46 (1986), 585–623.

Lewis, M., *A Social History of the Navy 1793–1815* (George Allen and Unwin, London, 1960).

Lewis, M., *The Navy In Transition 1814–1864: A Social History* (Hodder and Stoughton, London, 1965).

Littler, C., *The Development of the Labour Process in Capitalist Societies* (Heinemann, London, 1982).

McConville, S., *A History of English Prison Administration* I, *1750–1877* (Routledge and Kegan Paul, London, 1981).

McKendrick, N., 'Josiah Wedgwood and Factory Discipline', *Historical Journal* 4 (1961), 30–55.

McKendrick, N., 'Home Demand and Economic Growth: A New View of the Role of Women and Children in the Industrial Revolution' in N. McKendrick (ed.), *Historical Perspectives: Studies in English Thought and Society*, (Europa Publication, London, 1974), 152–210.

McNair, J.F.A., *Prisoners Their Own Warders* (Archibald Constable, London, 1899).

McQueen, H., 'Convicts and Rebels', *Labour History* 15 (1968), 3–30.

McQueen, H., *A New Britannia: An Argument Concerning the Social Origins of Australian Radicalism and Nationalism* (Penguin, Harmondsworth, 1970).

Mackaness, G., 'T. Watling' in G. Mackaness, *Letters From An Exile at Botany Bay* (Review Publications, Dubbo, 1979).

Macnab, K. and Ward, R., 'The Nature and Nurture of the First Generation of Native-Born Australians', *Historical Studies: Australia and New Zealand* 10 (1962), 289–308.

Madgwick, R.B., *Immigration into Eastern Australia 1788–1851* (Longmans, London, 1937).

Mantoux, P., *The Industrial Revolution in the 18th Century* (Jonathan Cape, London, 1961).

Marglin, S., 'What Do Bosses Do? — The Origins and Functions of Hierarchy in Capitalist Production', Part I, *Review of Radical Political Economics* 6 (1974), 60–112.

Melling, J., 'Non-Commissioned Officers: British Employers and Their Supervisory Workers, 1880–1920', *Social History* 5 (1980), 183–221.

Mills, L.A., *British Malaya 1824–67* (Oxford University Press, Kuala Lumpur, 1966).

Mokyr, J., *Why Ireland Starved: A Quantitative and Analytical History of the Irish Economy, 1800–1850* (George Allen and Unwin, London, 1983).

Mokyr, J. and O'Grada, C., 'Emigration and Poverty in Pre-famine Ireland', *Explorations in Economic History* 19 (1982), 360–84.

Mokyr, J. and O'Grada, C., 'New Developments in Irish Population History, 1700–1850', *Economic History Review* 37 (1984), 473–88.

Molloy, M., 'The Realisation of Labour Power in Early New South Wales: The Convict Labour Supply and Work Organisation in the Macquarie Years', unpublished BA (Hon) thesis, (University of New South Wales, 1984).

Moorehouse, H.F., 'The Marxist Theory of Labour Aristocracy', *Social History* 3 (1978), 61–82.

Morgan, D., 'The Place of Harvesters in Nineteenth Century Village Life', in R. Samuel (ed.), *Village Life and Labour* (Routledge and Kegan Paul, London, 1975), 27–72.

Morgan, D., *Harvesters and Harvesting 1840–1900* (Croom Helm, London, 1982).

Neil, D., 'Free Society, Penal Colony, Slave Society, Prison?', (Unpublished manuscript, 1984), 1–65.

Newby, H., *The Deferential Worker: A Study of Farm Workers in East Anglia* (Allen Lane, London, 1977).

Nichol, W., '"Malingering" and Convict Protest', *Labour History* 47 (1984), 18–27.

Nichol, W., 'The Medical Profession in New South Wales, 1788–1850', *Australian Economic History Review* 24 (1984), 115–31.

Nichol, W., 'Medicine and the Labour Movement in New South Wales, 1788–1850', *Labour History* 49 (1985), 19–37.

Nichol, W., 'Ideology and the Convict System in New South Wales, 1788–1820', *Historical Studies: Australia and New Zealand* 22 (1986), 1–20.

Nichol, W., 'Brothels, Slaughter Houses and Prisons: An Account of Hospital Conditions in New South Wales: 1788–1820', *Push from the Bush* 22 (1986), 6–29.

Nicholas, S. and Shergold, P., 'The Height of British Male Convict Children Transported to Australia, 1825–1840 Part I and Part II', *Australian Paediatric Journal* 18 (1982), 1–11.

Nicholas, S. and Shergold, P., 'Human Capital and the Pre-Famine Irish Emigration to England', *Explorations in Economic History* 24 (1987), 158–77.

Nicholas, S. and Shergold, P., 'Intercounty Labour Mobility During the Industrial Revolution: Evidence from Australian Transportation Records', *Oxford Economic Papers* 39 (1987), 624–40.

Nicholas, S. and Shergold, P., 'Internal Migration in England, 1818–1839', *Journal of Historical Geography* 13 (1987), 155–68.

Nicholas, S. and Shergold, P., 'Irish Intercounty Mobility Before 1840', *Irish Economic and Social History* forthcoming 14 (1987).

Nicholas, S. and Shergold, P., 'Convicts in Australia' in *Bicentennial History of Australia, Historical Atlas* (Fairfax, Syme and Weldon Assoc., Sydney, 1987).

Nicholas, S. and Shergold, P. in J. Jupp (ed.), *Bicentennial Encylopaedia of the Australian People* (forthcoming, 1988).

Obolensky-Ossinky, V.V., 'Emigration From and Immigration Into Russia', in I. Ferenczi and W.F. Willcox, *International Migrations* II (Gordon and Breach, N.Y., 1969), 521–80.

O'Brien, E., *The Foundation of Australia: 1786–1800: A Study in English Criminal Practice and Penal Colonisation in the 18th Century* (Greenwood, Conn., 1970).

Oddy, D.J., 'A Nutritional Analysis of Historical Evidence: The Working Class Diet, 1880–1914', in D. Oddy and D. Miller (eds.), *The Making of the Modern British Diet* (Croom Helm, London, 1976), 214–31.

Oddy, D.J., 'Working Class Diets in Late Nineteenth Century Britain', *Economic History Review* 23 (1970), 314–25.

O'Farrell, P., *The Irish in Australia* (New South Wales University Press, Sydney, 1987).

Oxley, D., 'Who Were the Female Convicts?', *Journal of the Australian Population Association* 4 (1987), 56–71.

Parsons, T.G., 'Governor Macquarie and the Assignment of Skilled Convicts in New South Wales', *Journal of the Royal Australian Historical Society* 58 (1972), 84–8.

Parsons, T.G., 'Public Expenditure and Labour Supply Under Governor Macquarie 1810–1821', M.A. thesis (University of Sydney, 1967).

Payne, H.S., 'A Statistical Study of Female Convicts in Tasmania, 1843–53', *Tasmanian Historical Research Association Papers and Proceedings* 9 (1961), 56–59.

Penglase, B.M., 'An Enquiry into Literacy in Early Nineteenth-Century New South Wales', *Push From the Bush* 16 (1983), 39–60.

Perkins, J.A., 'Rehearsal for Protectionism: Australian Wool Exports and German Agriculture 1830–1880', *Australian Economic History Review* 25 (1985), 20–38.

Perkins, J.A. and Tampke, J., 'The Convicts Who Never Arrived: Hamburg and the Australian Agricultural Company', *Push From the Bush* 19 (1985), 44–55.

Perkins, R., 'Push and Pull Politics: Prostitution, Prejudice and Punishment', *Arena* 74 (1986), 90–103.

Perrott, M., *A Tolerable Good Success: Economic Opportunities for Women in New South Wales 1788–1830* (Hale and Iremonger, Sydney, 1983).

Perry, T.M., *Australia's First Frontier: The Spread of Settlement in New South Wales 1788–1829* (Melbourne University Press, Melbourne, 1963).

Philips, D., *Crime and Authority in Victorian England: The Black Country 1835–1860* (Croom Helm, London, 1977).

Pike, R., *Penal Servitude in Early Modern Spain* (University of Wisconsin Press, Madison, 1983).

Pinchbeck, I., *Women Workers and the Industrial Revolution 1750–1850* (Cass, London, 1930).

Pollard, S. and Robertson, P., *The British Shipbuilding Industry 1870–1914* (Harvard University Press, Cambridge Mass., 1979).

Pollard, S., *The Genesis of Modern Management: A Study of the Industrial Revolution in Great Britain* (Penguin, London, 1968).

Pollard, S., 'Labour in Great Britain', in P. Mathias and M.M. Postan (eds.), *The Cambridge Economic History of Europe. The Industrial Economies: Capital, Labour and Enterprise* (Part I, VII, Cambridge University Press, Cambridge, 1978), 97–179.

Pope, D., 'Assisted Immigration and Federal-State Relations, 1901–30', *Australian Journal of Politics and History* 28 (1982), 21–31.

Postgate, R.W., *The Builders' History* (Pelican, London, 1923).

Postma, J., 'Mortality in the Dutch Slave Trade, 1675–1795' in H.A. Gemery and J.S. Hogendorn (eds.), *The Uncommon Market: Essays in the Economic History of the Atlantic Slave Trade* (Academic Press, N.Y., 1979), 239–260.

Prest, J., *The Industrial Revolution in Coventry* (Oxford University Press, Oxford, 1960).

Price, Richard, *Masters Unions and Men: Work Control in Building and the Rise of Labour* (Cambridge University Press, N.Y., 1980).

Priestley, P., *Victorian Prison Lives: English Prison Biography* (Methuen, London, 1985).

Rajendra, N., 'Transmarine Convicts in the Straits Settlements', *Asian Profile* 11 (1983), 509–17.

Ravenstein, E.G., 'The Laws of Migration', Part I, 48 (1885), *Journal of the Royal Statistical Society* 48 (1885), 162–227.

Reisler, M., *By the Sweat of Their Brow: Mexican Immigrant Labor in the United States, 1900–1940* (Greenwood Press, Conn., 1976).

Renaudot, F., *L'histoire des Francais en Algerie, 1830–1962* (Robert Laffont, Paris, 1979).

Rimmer, W.G., 'Hobart' in P. Statham (ed.), *The Origins of Australia's Capital Cities* (Oxford Univerisity Press, Sydney, 1988).

Rimmer, W.G., *Portrait of a Hospital, The Royal Hobart* (Royal Hobart Hospital, Hobart, 1981).

Ritchie, J., *Punishment and Profit: The Reports of Commissioner John Bigge on the Colonies of New South Wales and Van Diemen's Land* (Heinemann, Melbourne, 1970).

Ritchie, J. (ed.), *The Evidence of the Bigge Reports* I *Oral Evidence* (Heinemann, Melbourne, 1971).

Ritchie, J., 'Towards Ending An Unclean Thing: The Molesworth Committee and the Abolition of Transportation to N.S.W. 1837–40', *Historical Studies: Australia and New Zealand* 17 (1976), 144–64.

Robinson, P., *The Hatch and Brood of Time: A Study of the First Generation Native-Born White Australians 1788–1828* (Oxford University Press, Melbourne, 1985).

Robson, L.L., *The Convict Settlers of Australia: An Enquiry Into the Origin and Character of the Convicts Transported to New South Wales and Van Diemen's Land 1787–1852*, (Melbourne University Press, Carlton, 1965).

Robson, L.L., 'The Origins of the Women Convicts Sent to Australia, 1787– 1852', *Historical Studies: Australia and New Zealand* 11 (1963), 43–53.

Rodway, S., *Guiana: British, Dutch and French* (T. Fisher Unwin, London, 1913).

Rosenfeld, E., 'Verschickung freiwillig auswandernder Insassen der Gefängnisse von Mecklenburg nach Brasilien in der Jahren 1824 und 1825', *Zeitschrift fär die gesamte Strafrechtswissenschaft* XXIV (1903/4), 412–25.

Rowley, K., 'Pastoral Capitalism: Australia's Pre-Industrial Development', *Intervention* 1 (1972), 9–26.

Rude, G., *Protest and Punishment, The Story of the Social and Political Protesters Transported to Australia 1788–1968* (Oxford University Press, Melbourne, 1978).

Rude, G., *Criminal and Victim: Crime and Society in Early Nineteenth Century England* (Oxford University Press, Oxford, 1985).

Rule, J., *The Experience of Labour in Eighteenth Century Industry* (Croom Helm, London, 1981).

Rule, J., *The Labouring Classes in Early Industrial England, 1750–1850* (Longman, London, 1986).

Saha, P., *Emigration of Indian Labour, 1834–1900* (People's Publishing House, Delhi, 1970).

Sainty, M.R. and Johnson, K.A. (eds.), *Census of New South Wales: November 1828* (Library of Australian History, Sydney, 1980).

Salt, A., *These Outcast Women: The Parramatta Female Factory 1821–1848* (Hale and Iremonger, Sydney, 1984).

Samuel, R., 'Mineral Workers' in R. Samuel (ed.), *Miners, Quarrymen and Saltworkers* (Routledge and Kegan Paul, London, 1977), 1–97.

Sandhu, K.S, *Indians in Malaya: Some Aspects of Their Immigration and Settlement, 1786–1957* (Cambridge University Press, London, 1969).

Sandhu, K.S., 'Tamil and Other Indian Convicts in the Straits Settlements, A.D. 1700–1873', in *Proceedings of the First International Conference Seminar of Tamil Studies*, 216–39.

Saunders, K., *Workers in Bondage: The Origins and Bases of Unfree Labour in Queensland 1824–1916* (University of Queensland Press, St. Lucia, 1982).

Schaeffer, W., *Australiens Wirtschaft und Wirtschaftspolitik* (Hannover, 1931).

Schedvin, M.B. and Schedvin, C.B., 'The Nomadic Tribes of Urban Britain: A Prelude to Botany Bay', *Historical Studies: Australia and New Zealand* 18 (1978), 254–76.

Schluss, D.F., *Methods of Industrial Remuneration* (Williams and Nargate, London, 1892).

Schlomowitz, R., 'Team Work and Incentives: The Origins and Development of the Butty Gang System in Queensland's Sugar Industry, 1891–1913', *Journal of Comparative Economics* 3 (1979), 41–55.

Schlomowitz, R., 'Melanesian Labor and the Development of the Queensland Sugar Industry, 1863–1906', in P. Uselding, (ed.), *Research in Economic History* 7 (1982), 327–361.

Schofield, R.S., 'Dimensions of Illiteracy, 1750–1850', *Explorations in Economic History* 10 (1973), 437–54.

Schroder, F., 'Die Deportatin Mecklenburgischer Strafgefangener nach Brasilien 1824/14', *Deutschtum im Ausland* CII (1929), 497–8.

Secretariat to the Committee to Advise on Australia's Immigration Policies, *Understanding Immigration* (Australian Government Printing Service, Canberra, 1987).

Sein, D.M., *The Administration of Burma* (Oxford University Press, London, 1973).

Shaw, A.G.L., *Convicts and the Colonies: A Study of Penal Transportation from Great Britain and Ireland to Australia and Other Parts of the British Empire* (Faber, London, 1966).

Shaw, A.G.L., 'Labour' in G.J. Abbott and N.B. Nairn (eds.), *Economic Growth in Australia 1788–1821* (Melbourne University Press, Melbourne, 1969), 105–18.

Sherington, G., *Australia's Immigrants 1788–1978* (George Allen and Unwin, Sydney, 1980).

Siddique, C. and Shotam, N., *Singapore's Little India: Past, Present and Future* (Institute of South East Asians Studies, Pasir Panjang, 1982).

Simmington, M., 'Australia's Political and Economic Relations with New Caledonia 1873–1945', Ph.D. thesis, (University of New South Wales, 1978).

Skelley, A.R., *The Victorian Army at Home* (Croom Helm, London, 1977).

Smith, A.E., *Colonists in Bondage: White Servitude and Convict Labor in America 1607–1776* (University of North Carolina Press, Chapel Hill, 1947).

Sokoloff, K.L. and Villafloe, G.C., 'The Early Achievement of Modern Stature in America', *Social Science History* 6 (1982), 453–81.

Spiers, E., *The Army and Society 1815–1914* (Longman, London, 1980).

Stedman-Jones, G., 'Class Struggle and the Industrial Revolution' *New Left Review* 90 (1975), 35–69.

Steven, M.J.E., 'The Changing Pattern of Commerce', in G.J. Abbott and N.B. Nairn (eds.), *Economic Growth in Australia, 1788–1821* (Melbourne University Press, Melbourne, 1969), 176–87.

Stewart, J.D., *Gibraltar the Keystone* (John Murray, London, 1967).

Strobe, H., *The Story of Bermuda* (Jarrods, London, 1935).

Sturma, M., 'Eye of the Beholder: The Stereotype of Women Convicts, 1788–1852', *Labour History* 34 (1978), 3–10.

Sturma, M., *Vice in a Vicious Society: Crime and Convicts in Mid-Nineteenth Century New South Wales* (University of Queensland Press, St. Lucia, 1983).

Summers, A., *Damned Whores and God's Police: The Colonization of Women in Australia* (Penguin, Victoria, 1976).

Swift, R., 'Anti-Catholicism and Irish Disturbances: Public Order in Mid-Victorian Wolverhampton' *Midland History* 9 (1984), 87–108.

Thomas, L., *The Development of the Labour Movement in the Sydney District of New South Wales* (Society for Study of Labour History, Canberra, 1962).

Thomis, M.I. and Grimmett, J., *Women in Protest 1800–1850* (Croom Helm, London, 1982).

Thompson, E.P., *The Making of the English Working Class* (Vintage Book, New York, 1963).

Thompson, V. and Adloff, R., *The French Pacific Islands, French Polynesia and New Caledonia* (California University Press, Berkeley, 1971).

Tinker, H., *A New System of Slavery: The Export of Indian Labour Overseas, 1830–1920* (Oxford University Press, London, 1974).

Tobias, J.J., *Crime and Industrial Society in the 19th Century* (Penguin, London, 1967).

Tobias, J.J., *Crime and Police in England 1700–1900* (Gill and Macmillan, Dublin, 1979).

Toutain, J., *The Economic Life of the Ancient World* (Kegan Paul and Co., London, 1930).

Townsend, N., 'A "Mere Lottery": The Convict System in New South Wales Through the Eyes of the Molesworth Committee', *Push From the Bush* 21 (1985), 58–86.

Trudgill, E., 'Prostitution and Paterfamilias', in H.J. Dyos and M. Wolff (eds.), *The Victorian City: Images and Realities* II, (Routledge and Kegan Paul, London, 1973), 693–706.

Tucker, T., *Bermuda Yesterday and Today, 1503–1973* (Robert Hale, London, 1975).

Turnbull, C.M., 'Convicts in the Straits Settlements, 1826–1867' *Journal of the Malaysian Branch of the Royal Asiatic Society* 43 (1970), 87–103.

Turnbull, C.M., *A History of Singapore 1819–1975* (Oxford University Press, Kuala Lumpur, 1977).

Turner, I., *In Union is Strength: A History of Trade Unions in Australia 1788–1974* (Nelson, Melbourne, 1978).

U.S. Federal Works Agency, *Migratory Workers of the South West* (Greenwood Press, Westport, 1941).

Vaidya, S., *Islands of the Marigold Sun* (Robert Hale, London, 1960).

Wadsworth, A.P. and Mann, J., *The Cotton Trade and Industrial Lancashire 1600–1780* (Manchester University Press, Manchester, 1931).

Walsh, G., 'Factories and Factory Workers in New South Wales, 1788–1900', *Labour History* 21 (1971), 1–16.

Ward, R., *The Australian Legend* (Oxford University Press, Melbourne, 1978).

Watson, J.F., *The History of the Sydney Hospital, From 1811–1911* (University of New South Wales Press, Sydney, 1964).

Webb, R.K., 'Working Class Readers in Early Victorian England', *English Historical Review* 65 (1950), 333–51.

Webb, S. and Webb, B., *English Local Government: The Story of the King's Highway* (Frank Cass, London, 1963).

Webb, S. and Webb, B., *English Local Government: English Poor Law History* Part I, *The Old Poor Law* (Frank Cass, London, 1963).

Webb, S. and Webb, B., *English Poor Law History* Part II *The Last Hundred Years* II (Archon Books, N.Y., 1963).

Weber, A.F., *The Growth of Cities in the Nineteenth Century* (Greenwood Press, N.Y., 1969).

Weidenhofer, M., *The Convict Years: Transportation and the Penal System 1788–1868* (Landsdowne Press, Melbourne, 1973).

Wickizer, V.D., *Coffee, Tea and Cocoa* (Stanford University Press, Stanford, 1951).

Wienderlich, F., *Farm Labour in Germany 1810–1945* (Princeton University Press, Princeton, 1961).

Wilkinson, H.C., *Bermuda From Sail to Steam: The History of the Island From 1784 to 1901* II (Oxford University Press, London, 1973).

Williams, E., *Capitalism and Slavery* (Deutsch, London, 1964).

Williams, J., 'Irish Female Convicts and Tasmania', *Labour History* 44 (1983), 1–17.

Williamson, J.G., 'The Structure of Pay in Britain, 1710–1911', in P. Uselding (ed.), *Research in Economic History* 7 (1982), 1–54.

Williamson, O., *The Economic Institutions of Capitalism* (Free Press, New York, 1985).

Willock, R., 'Account of Life in the Convict Hulks' (3 Parts), *Bermuda Historical Quarterly* 8 (1951).

Willock, R., *Bulwark of Empire: Bermuda's Fortified Naval Base, 1860–1920* (Author, Princeton, 1962).

Wood, G.A., 'Convicts', *The Royal Australian Historical Society Journal and Proceedings* 8 (1922), 177–208.

Woodward, J., *To Do the Sick No Harm: A Study of the British Voluntary Hospital System to 1875* (Routledge and Kegan Paul, London, 1974).

INDEX

References to the Statistical Appendix are indicated by the letter A. Tables in the Appendix are referred to by their numbers, e.g. A4, A14.

Scotland
  convicts born in, 3, 44-6, 54, 69, 75, 81, A1
  convicts tried in, 44-7, 54-5, 89-91, 93, A2, A4, A6-A9, A11-A12, A15
  dependent population, 50
  free emigrants, 49, 51
  free labour, 185-6, 191, 193
  labour elite, 100, 102
Scott, *Rev.* T.H., 20-21, 25
Select Committees
  Health of Towns (1840), 193
  Large Towns (1844), 194
  Prisons (House of Lords, 1835), 19, 21
  Secondary Punishments (1831), 18, 20, 22
  Secondary Punishments (1832), 18-19, 22
  Treatment and Condition on the Woolwich Hulks (1847), 192-3, 195
  Transportation (1812), 15, 17, 192
  Transportation (Molesworth Committee, 1837-8), **15-24**, 86, 111, 113, 127
selection of convicts for transportation, 14, 47-9, 58, 77
sentences
  & labour market, 112-13
  & offences, 14, 29, 33, 88
  regional differences, 90-91
  & selection for transportation, 14
  statistical data, 4, 44
  & treatment in Australia, 19-21, 130
  see also remittances
serfs, 112
servants, domestic, *see* domestic servants
sex ratio of convicts, **51-3**
  & age, 47, 200
  & birthplace, 51
  & economic development, 8, 10, 52-3, 59-60
  & education, 10, 75-6, 82, A7, A9
  cf emigrants, 51-2, 59-60
  cf English prison population, 74
  Irish, 46, 51
  & marital status, 48
  & mobility, 56-7
  & occupational skills, 70, A15-A16
  & population growth, 17, 52-3
  statistical data & analysis, 3-4, 44, 85, A1-A5, A7, A9, A11, A15-A16
Shaw, A.G.L., 4-5, 10, 43, 62, 85-6, 88, 95, 111, 130
sheep grazing, 136-7, 139, 146, 167, 171-4, 177
  see also pastoral capitalism
Shergold, Peter R., ix
  see also Nicholas-Shergold skill classification
Sherrington, Geoffrey, 59
shipboard conditions, 9, 17, 46-8, 59
Siam, 36
Siberia, 29-30, 36-37
sickness, *see* health
Silter, John, 194
Singapore, *see* Straits Settlements
size, *see* height of convicts
skill classifications, 69-72, 123
  Armstrong, 69-72, 91, 103, 123, 154-6, A11-A14, A17

Nicholas-Shergold, 69, 71-2, A15-A16, A18
skilled labour, *see* labour aristocracy; occupational skills
slavery
  abolition, 28, 34-5, 182
  conditions, 12, 180, 182-5, 187-91, 193, 195-6
  cf contract labour, 37, 152
  cf convictism, 4, 7, 11-12, 31-2, 37-8, 59, 81, **111-13**, 127, 199
  mortality, 47-8
  work organisation, 59, 111, 152, 160
  see also American slaves
Smith, Adam, 43
soldiers, *see* military personnel
Southgate, D.A.T., 184
Spain
  conscripts, height of, 82
  convicts, 7, 34, 36, 160, 182-3, 187-8, 199
  wool, 167
Spearman's rank coefficient, 73-4
Spiers, E., 184
Sri Lanka (Ceylon), 30, 32-4
standard of living, 78, 100, 102, 111-13, 129, 180, 184-7
statistics, *see* convicts, statistical data & analysis
Stedman Jones, G., 102
Stephen, John, 25
Straits Settlements, 7, 29-30, 32-3, 36-7, 160, 189, 191, 193
strikes, 99
Stroud (NSW), 170-71
Strutt factories, 157, 183, 189
subsidised migration, *see* assisted migration
sugar production, 28-9, 35, 152, 160, 173, 188, 190
suicide, 180, 195
Sumatra, 30, 32
supervision of convicts
  Australian Agricultural Co., 169-70, 176-7
  by private masters, 127, 139
  costs, 15-16, 18, 128, 132, 134, 139, 161
  & expansion of settlement, 136, 147
  gangs, 154, 156-7, 159, 161-4
  in England, 182
  labour elite, 101-2
  on transports, 17
Sutch, Richard, 185, 191, 193
Swedish migrants, 49-51
Sydney Mechanics School of Arts, 10, 99, 107

Tanner, J.M., 78
Tasmania, *see* Van Diemen's Land
taxes, 116, 118
teams, *see* labour gangs
Temple, R.C., 34
Thailand (Siam), 36
theft
  commonest offence, 4, 7
  female convicts, 4, 7, 88, **89-91**, 95
  work-related, 7, 63-5, 67, 82, 89
Thomas, Lelia, 98-9, 129
Thompson, E.P., 100

wool, *see* sheep grazing
work organisation
    Australian Agricultural Co., **168-70**
    convicts cf contract labour, 152, 157, **160-61**
    convicts cf free labour, 11, **157-60**
    convicts cf slaves, 59, 111, 152, 160
    efficiency, 11, 60, 113, 119
    labour elite, 101, 107
    public work, 11, 125, **152-66**, 200
    & punishment, 183, 195
    rural labour, 158-9
    work-related theft, 7, 63-5, 67, 82, 89
work relations, 125, 129, 132, 161-2, 199
workforce, *see* labour market
working class
    attitudes to transportation, 21
    convicts as cross-section, 63, 71, 73-6, 82, 98, 105
    cf criminal class, 4, 7-8, 69, **85-91**, 92, 94-6, 98,
        199-200
    education, 9, 76
    female convicts, 10, 86-7, 92
    health, 192
    height, 79-81
    housing in Britain, 12, 190-91, 193-4
    Irish, 7, 69, 75, 82
    labour elite in, 99-100, 103, 105
    nutrition, 186
    physical fitness, 9
    skills, 9
    see also rural labour; urban workers

Yarramanbah (NSW), 172
year of arrival, 130, 134-5, A3, A5-A10, A14,